Offenders or Citizens?

Offenders or Citizens?

Readings in rehabilitation

Edited by Philip Priestley and Maurice Vanstone

WILLAN
PUBLISHING

Published by

Willan Publishing
Culmcott House
Mill Street, Uffculme
Cullompton, Devon
EX15 3AT, UK
Tel: +44(0)1884 840337
Fax: +44(0)1884 840251
e-mail: info@willanpublishing.co.uk
website: www.willanpublishing.co.uk

Published simultaneously in the USA and Canada by

Willan Publishing
c/o ISBS, 920 NE 58th Ave, Suite 300,
Portland, Oregon 97213-3786, USA
Tel: +001(0)503 287 3093
Fax: +001(0)503 280 8832
e-mail: info@isbs.com
website: www.isbs.com

First published 2010

ISBN 978-1-84392-529-3 paperback
     978-1-84392-530-9 hardback

British Library Cataloguing-in-Publication Data

A catalogue record for this book is available from the British Library

FSC
Mixed Sources
Product group from well-managed
forests and other controlled sources

Cert no. SGS-COC-2482
www.fsc.org
© 1996 Forest Stewardship Council

Project managed by Deer Park Productions, Tavistock, Devon
Typeset by GCS, Leighton Buzzard, Bedfordshire, LU7 1AR
Printed by TJ International, Padstow, Cornwall

Contents

Acknowledgements

We are grateful to the following for permission to reproduce copyright material:

Branden Publishing Co. for an extract from *On Crimes and Punishments*. Second Edition by Cesare Beccaria, edited by Adolph Caso. Boston: Branden Books, ISBN 978-0828318006, copyright © 1983, Branden Books; University of Pittsburgh Press for an extract from *The Positive School of Criminology: Three Lectures by Enrico Ferri* edited by Stanley E. Grupp, copyright © 1968. Reprinted by permission of the University of Pittsburgh Press; American Society of Criminology for extracts from 'The Radicals and the Rehabilitative Ideal 1890–1930' by Philip Jenkins, *Criminology*, Vol. 20, Issue 3–4, 1982, pp. 347–372; 'Justice, Sanctioning, and the Justice Model' by Gray Cavender, *Criminology*, Vol. 22, Issue 2, 1984, pp. 203–213; 'The New Penology: notes on the emerging strategy of corrections and its implications' by Malcolm Feeley and Jonathan Simon, *Criminology*, Vol. 30, Issue 4, 1992, pp. 449–474; and 'An exploratory study of exiting from criminal careers' by Thomas Meisenhelder, *Criminology*, Vol. 15, Issue 3, 1977, pp. 319–334 © 2009 American Society of Criminology. Granted with permission of the authors and American Society of Criminology; The National Association of Probation Officers for extracts from 'The Value of the Probation System as Applied to Women', by Mrs Cary, 1913, *The National Association of Probation Officers*, 3 by A. Celnick and W. McWilliams, pp. 15–14; 'Social Clubs for Probationers; their Needs and Objects', by Mrs Cary, 1915, *The National Association of Probation Officers*, 6, pp. 102–103; 'Probation Work among Children' by H. Chinn, 1916, *National Association of Probation Officers*, 7, pp. 123–125; 'The Problem of the Difficult Case' by C. Rankin, 1921, *National Association of Probation Officers*, 16, pp. 321–323; 'The Spiritual Factor in Probation Work' by F. Poulton, 1925, *National Association of Probation Officers*, 23, pp. 546–547; and *A Handbook of Probation* by L. Le Mesurier, 1935, *National Association of Probation Officers*, pp. 124–129 copyright © NAPO; Harvard Law Review for an extract from 'Principles of a Rational Penal Code' by Sheldon Glueck, *Harvard Law Review*, 41, pp. 453–482 copyright © Harvard Law Review Association, 1928, permission conveyed through Copyright Clearance Center; Victor Serge Foundation for an extract from *Men in Prison* by Victor Serge, Writers and Readers Publishing Co-operative, originally published 1930,

Essay Collection and Other Short Pieces by C. S. Lewis copyright © C. S. Lewis Pte Ltd 2000. Extract reprinted by permission; Sony/ATV Music Publishing LLC for the lyrics 'In the Ghetto', words and music by Scott Davis. Copyright © 1969 Sony/ATV Music Publishing LLC, R & H Music Company. All rights administered by Sony/ATV Music Publishing LLC. All rights reserved. Used by permission; Farrar, Straus, and Giroux, LLC for an extract from *Struggle for Justice: A Report on Crime and Punishment in America* prepared for The American Friends Service Committee. copyright © 1971 by Hill and Wang. Reprinted by permission of Hill and Wang, a division of Farrar, Straus, and Giroux, LLC; Columbia University Press for an extract from *Task Centred Casework* by W. J. Reid and L. Epstein copyright © 1972 Columbia University Press; The Home Office for extracts and a table from 'Social Work in Prison. An experiment in the use of extended contact with offenders', Home Office Research Studies 22. London: HMSO, pp. 13–14; 1974, http://www.homeoffice.gov.uk/rds/pdfs05/hors22.pdf; 'Social Work in the Environment. A Study of One Aspect of Probation Practice', HORS 21. London: HMSO, pp. 91–92, http://www.homeoffice.gov.uk/rds/pdfs05/hors21.pdf; and 'The effectiveness of sentencing: a review of the literature', Brody, S. R. (1976) Home Office Research Study No 35. London: HMSO, http://www.homeoffice.gov.uk/rds/pdfs05/hors35.pdf. Crown Copyright material is reproduced with permission under the terms of the Click-Use License; Taylor and Francis Books for extracts from 'New Careers: power sharing in social work' by Philip Priestley in *Towards a New Social Work* edited by H. Jones. Routledge and Kegan Paul, 1975; *Rehabilitation and Deviance* by Philip Bean, Routledge and Kegan Paul, 1976; and *The Politics of Redress: Crime, Punishment, and Penal Abolition* by W. de Haan, Unwin Hyman, 1989. Copyright © 1975, 1976, 1989, Taylor and Francis Books; Professor Ronald Blackburn for an extract from *Still not working? A look at recent outcomes in offender rehabilitation* by Ronald Blackburn (1980) University of Aberdeen. Paper presented at the Scottish Branch of the British Psychological Society Conference on 'Deviance', University of Stirling, pp. 9–14, copyright © Professor R. Blackburn; Blackwell Publishing for extracts from *Limits to Pain* by Nils Christie 1982, published by Martin Robertson; and 'Beyond the Prison Paradigm: From Provoking Violence to Preventing It by Creating "Anti-Prisons" (Residential Colleges and Therapeutic Communities)' by J. Gilligan and B. Lee from *Annals of the New York Academy of Sciences* Vol. 1036, December 2004, pp. 300–324, copyright © 1982, 2004, Wiley-Blackwell. Reproduced with permission of Blackwell Publishing Ltd; Sage Publications for extracts from 'Reasoning and rehabilitation', by Robert R. Ross, Elizabeth A. Fabiano and Crystal D. Ewles, *International Journal of Offender Therapy and Comparative Criminology*, Vol. 32, 1, 1988, pp. 29–35; 'A Re-Examination of Correctional Alternatives' by Kevin N. Wright, *International Journal of Offender Therapy and Comparative Criminology*, Vol. 24, 2, 1980, pp. 179–192; 'Evidence-Based Corrections: Identifying What Works' by Doris Layton MacKenzie, *Crime & Delinquency* Vol. 46, 4, 2000, pp. 457–471; 'American Social Work, Corrections and Restorative Justice: An Appraisal' by Edward J. Gumz, *International Journal of Offender Therapy and Comparative Criminology*, Vol. 48, 4, 2004, pp. 449–460; and 'The kindness of prisoners: strengths-based resettlement in theory and in action' by Ros Burnett and Shadd Maruna, *Criminology & Criminal Justice*, Vol.

Probation, Vol. 68, 2, 2004 pp. 797–810; and 'What Works in Prisoner Re-entry? Reviewing and Questioning the Evidence', by Joan Petersilia, *Federal Probation*, Vol. 68, 2, 2004, pp. 4–8, http://www.uscourts.gov copyright © 2004, Federal Probation. Reprinted with permission; National Association of Drug Court Professionals for extracts including 'Keeping the Fidelity of the Drug Court Model' from *Painting the Current Picture: A National Report Card on Drug Courts and Other Problem-Solving Court Programs in the United States* May 2005. Vol. I, No. 2 by C. West Huddleston, III., Judge Karen Freeman-Wilson, D. B. Marlowe and A. Roussell copyright © National Drug Court Institute; Center for Court Innovation, for an extract from *Best Practice. Principles of Problem-Solving Justice* by Robert V. Wolf, 2007, copyright © Center for Court Innovation, http://www.courtinnovation.org; and Youth at Risk for an extract from *Too Much to Ask? The Leaps and Bounds Story* by Rod Morgan, in reference to 'Ballet Hoo', a project designed by the charity Youth at Risk (UK), Arts Council England and Solomon White Publications, copyright © 2009, Youth at Risk.

In some instances we have been unable to trace the owners of copyright material and we would appreciate any information that would enable us to do so.

General introduction

When remedies for crime are becoming more rather than less punitive, the time is right for a properly focused debate about how best to help people who offend to seek non-criminal means of resolving their problems. Because of the exploitation of crime in the media and the sometimes desperate political responses to perceived crises in law and order, it is becoming more and more difficult to have a rational debate about the future of legal and penal policy, and in particular, how best to respond to crime in a way which affords the best chance of lessening future harm to individuals and communities. The focus of this book is on what as editors we believe affords that best chance, namely rehabilitation. In keeping that focus inevitably the book pays attention to the principal means of assisting the rehabilitation of people who have offended, namely supervision and intervention (mostly, although not always in the community) by agencies such as probation. In a sense, we are joining other commentators like Ward and Maruna (2007) in the call for the re-establishment of a concept currently lost in the fog of punitive rhetoric but with a long, and we would argue, distinguished history.

Our definition of rehabilitation is guided firstly by the distinction Forsyth (1987) makes between the concepts of rehabilitation and reform, the latter being the attempt to change an individual's behaviour or moral values while the former is concerned with the restoration of the individual's reputation and status as a citizen; and secondly, by Celnick and McWilliams' (1991) assertion that rehabilitation should be premised on help involving the aspirations of the individual rather than an agenda set by others. As McWilliams and Pease (1990: 15) make clear, '[the] attempt to help the offender return to and remain as a full member of society, with the status and obligations which that membership confers, is rehabilitation'. Each of these definitions fit neatly with Rotman's (1986: 1026) argument that humanistic rehabilitation rather than trying to change people 'through subtly imposed paradigms' offers individuals the chance to change the direction of their lives in dialogues which encourage self-awareness, new insights and a new trajectory towards a 'genuine sense of social responsibility'.[1]

Moreover, we should make clear at the outset that we are concerned to concentrate debate mainly on rehabilitation in its practical applications and not merely on abstract formulations. Of course, practical application cannot occur within a theoretical and moral vacuum, and this Reader includes a wide range of extracts which embed the practice of rehabilitation in an ontological and philosophical framework. However, central to the rationale for this book is the belief that the history and future of rehabilitation has most meaning when viewed in practical terms, viz. how can society offer individuals the best chance of living a crime-free life?

Thus, when we consider the history of rehabilitation we are drawn to examples of the courts utilising ways of providing a *second chance*, some of them as Vanstone (2007) has pointed out relating to the Anglo-Saxon king Athelstane's form of binding over; the Pilgrim Fathers' use of something akin to probation in the seventeenth century; the practice of the concept of benefit of clergy which exempted some ecclesiastics from trial in secular courts; the use of recognisance in sixteenth-century England by justices of the peace to prevent violence; the London 'City Custom of Apprentices' whereby the partially private court of the Chamberlain of London dealt with the delinquent behaviour of apprentices; the bailing of people appearing before the courts in Massachusetts by John Augustus; and the development of recognisance by Matthew Davenport Hill and Edward Cox in the United Kingdom. These are all examples of what might be termed precursors to modern-day community penalties, but the roots of reform and correction lie in the institutional soil of pre-sixteenth-century monasteries (Raynor and Robinson, 2005); and the first secular example of the use of the institution in the United Kingdom to achieve moral correction was the sixteenth-century Bridewell for the undeserving poor of London. The significant period for the development of correction in the penal system has been specified as from the late-eighteenth century to the mid-nineteenth century (Foucault 1977; Ignatieff 1978), and for the discovery of the individual as an object of interest which paved the way for (among other initiatives) rehabilitation in the community, a relatively short period at the end of the nineteenth century and beginning of the twentieth century. The notion of rehabilitation emerged from Christian-inspired moral correction and was transformed into a state-sponsored project focused on changing the individual who had offended. That history of attempts to reform individuals whether in institutions or the community has been retold many times, and it is not the purpose of this book to rehearse them yet again. Rather it is to make available to the reader a wide range of examples of how significant players in that history have engaged with the theory and practice of rehabilitation in order to provide a foundation for a more rational debate than has hitherto been possible.

Current debate is either polarised (for example, psychology versus sociology, punitiveness versus 'do-gooding'), or partial (for example, how best to change the psychological make-up of people or how to change their environment), or based on polemics as opposed to evidence. Moreover, often it is based on limited knowledge of history, and so bandwagons are rolled out repeatedly and the wheel is reinvented. Much of the literature is segmented and the pieces enclosed in particular and distinct disciplines with the result that, while sharing the same concern with crime and its aftermath, social workers, sociologists, psychologists, police and lawyers often engage in their *own world* discourses. This is a generalisation, of course, but to the degree to which it does happen important work from one field can be relatively ignored in another. (For example, Bottoms and McWilliams' seminal paper on the 'Non-Treatment Paradigm' appeared in the *British Journal of Social Work* (1979) so is very familiar to probation officers but maybe less so to psychologists and others.) Also, some writings on rehabilitation are based on evidence, some on ideology, some on faith and some on a mixture of all three.

This Reader attempts to stimulate and furnish a debate about how, at the beginning of the twenty-first century, society can offer effective rehabilitation opportunities to those who offend – about ways to do this rather than *whether* it should take place. Within Rotman's (1986) humanistic model of rehabilitation probation officers should be committed to helping those who offend for reasons of morality as well as efficacy. Only if this applies equally to the criminal justice and penal systems is there any chance of countering the punitive obsession and the mania for imprisonment which have been in the ascendancy in the US and the UK during the past ten years or more, and which, as Bryan Stevenson[2] has recently argued, have led to changes in American society in particular that 'no civilised society should want to replicate'. Moreover, the best chance of this occurring emanates from an acceptance, by those with the power, of Rotman's model premised as it is on the notion that people labelled 'offenders' have rights and in particular a right to the opportunity of rehabilitation.

It should be remembered that this is *a* Reader on the subject of rehabilitation and not *the* Reader, and accordingly the extracts are neither definitive nor all-inclusive. No doubt, different editors would have produced a different list and might see glaring omissions in ours: they are *our* choices and, therefore, inevitably subjective. They reflect our range of knowledge, our interests, our experience and our biases, but they are informed by the purposes implied above. Moreover, the reader should not assume that length of entry equates with importance: each one brings something of significance to the debate we aim to stimulate. With that aim in mind we have included positions and arguments that represent more than one side of a debate about rehabilitation and emanate from the realms of philosophy, psychology, sociology and anthropology, social work and law. Moreover, while many extracts represent the thinking of significant theorists and philosophers, we have been determined to ensure that the voice of some practitioners is heard so that some sense of the micro world of rehabilitation is revealed; and here and there, we have included some words by those who are the focus of all this rehabilitative effort, their scarcity here and in the literature generally a telling illustration of exclusion. All this fits with our aim of bringing together a diverse range of contributions within a single criminological text, and in particular including work that might be relatively obscure, neglected and less accessible to students.

The entries themselves are organised in three time periods, namely, (1) the historical roots and early forms of rehabilitation that led us to contemporary thinking; (2) modern trends and forms; and (3) the future – can rehabilitation be rehabilitated? The extracts in Part One provide a historical overview of how criminologists and practitioners have explored the purposes of criminal justice and engaged with the competing philosophies of punishment and rehabilitation. They will throw light on (among other things) the nature of criminal justice, the purpose of punishment, the function of prison and the meaning of rehabilitation, and in so doing may present the basis of a debate about historically grounded values associated with a plural and non-punitive response to crime.

The readings in Part Two deal with developments during the latter part of the twentieth century, an era characterised by enormous expansions of the prison population in the United States, and England and Wales, and ending with the virtual extinction of probation as a rehabilitative service. Not that all was doom and gloom, however, during these years: we report a variety of proposals, initiatives and experiments that sought to reinvent a creative response to criminal behaviour in the face of criticisms about the morality and effectiveness of 'treatment' approaches. They include ideas that were put forward to recast probation as a court social work service, ditching compulsion and emphasising contractual relationships. There were also innovations in working methods, e.g. targeted group-work for women, probation intake and sex offending; community service; day centres; the New Careers movement; task-centred casework; Heimlerian counselling; and the advent of cognitive behavioural methods as part of the 'what works' phenomenon. Many of these projects made efforts to measure their own effectiveness in terms of reduced risk or reconvictions.

Part Three asks large questions about the possible revival of rehabilitation as part of a plural response to crime. It focuses on the future of probation in particular as its primary vehicle, operating within a structural framework of community justice and pursuing broadly restorative aims. The extracts are used specifically to map a way forward for policy and practice which includes an emphasis on harm reduction, community protection, personal responsibility, choice and consent, self-change, citizenship and education. In general, the extracts here illustrate things that do work – or that might work – and provide a sketch of how they might be delivered by a reflexive, learning-organisation – one that respects the people it works with as 'citizens' rather than 'offenders'. (In our own contributions to the book we endeavour to show our respect too by avoiding the use of that label. In the past, we have ourselves been guilty of this verbal offence, but have since turned over a new leaf.) Inevitably, there is some overlap in titles and content, in particular, between Parts Two and Three where some extracts refer to and even quote others in the collection. In addition to this general introduction, intended to outline the terms of the overall debate, we will, as editors, provide introductions to each time-based section, setting the selections in context and underlining why they are important and what aspects of rehabilitation they explore, and a conclusion which summarises the themes of the debate.

Notes

1. It must be remembered, however, that not everyone is readily amenable for rehabilitation. See the introduction to Part Three and the Gilligan and Lee extract for further discussion on this point.
2. American human rights lawyer writing in the *Guardian*, 10 December 2008.

Part One

The historical roots and early forms of rehabilitation

Introduction

Marking a specific starting point for the history of rehabilitation is unrealistic because the notion of reform or 'going straight' has permeated philosophical and religious thinking about punishment from early times: indeed, even in the eighteenth century when jails were local, usually private with no state oversight and few regulations there were attempts to reform Houses of Correction to ensure that prisoners were put to work and that the purposes of reform and punishment could be established (McConville 1998). Moreover, the history of rehabilitation in thought and action is a vast subject, impossible to fully represent in a Reader inevitably constrained by space; as we indicated in the introduction to this book, we do not intend to repeat coverage of the subject that students and practitioners can find easily elsewhere. (There are many very useful expositions of the history of rehabilitation, for example, Hudson 1996 and more recently Raynor and Robinson 2005.) What we attempt to do in this section is to include what we judge to be critical (and simply interesting) contributions both to theory and practice, particularly as far as they relate to distinctive themes and developments relevant to state intervention designed to bring about change in people who have offended, and as far as they are likely to stimulate current debate. Inevitably, this ties us to the history of both prison and probation: however whilst we will focus on prison, it has been closely aligned with punishment, and given that we are looking beyond punishment to more community-based means of changing people and protecting society from the harm caused by crime, our emphasis here is on the latter.

The entries are listed chronologically, not because we believe in a simple, linear process of the humanising of criminal justice (Pratt 2002), but because doing so demonstrates not only how thinking about, and practice of, rehabilitation have developed but also how they have been contradictory, contentious and repetitious. Predictably, perhaps, we begin with Beccaria. Commonly, he is accorded a prominent place in the history of criminology, but it is less known that the attribution of this status is the subject of some controversy (Newman and Marongui 1990): they challenge the orthodox view of Beccaria's contribution to criminological thinking generally and they make a strong case. Nevertheless, we have included what we judge to be his relevant thinking on rehabilitation because he provides an important signpost for the direction that the battle between religion and science would take

5

as theorists and philosophers struggled with the moral problem of punishment. In particular, the extracts are included because of their close link to twenty-first-century policy concerns; they highlight the importance of science (what in modern parlance might be described as evidence), the relevance of a focus on positives (the current strengths-based approach) and the use of rewards as a means of encouraging change (motivation). Religiously inspired morality is an important element of Beccaria's approach to punishment, and it might be described as more dominant than any scientific thinking. This is true also of utilitarian approaches: nevertheless, Bentham (who Newman and Marongui argue is more worthy of the status in the criminological pantheon usually offered to Beccaria) is a more than appropriate starting point for the student interested in the interplay between religion and science. The stimulation of moral and Christian self-contemplation for the prisoner is central to Bentham's thinking about how the criminal mind can be purified, but his thinking about the framework within which this might take place is essentially scientific. Here, we have included two letters, the first describing the physical design of the Panopticon, and the second about how it would be applied to punishment and reformation. The significance of the Panopticon lies in its promulgation firstly of the prevention of communication and constant supervision in order to create an ideal setting for contemplation and reflection, and secondly labour as a punishment and deterrent. Of course, it never materialised but it has a significant place in the theory (shared and put into practice by the prison architect William Blackburn) that space and stone could fashion human personality and that the architecture of prisons could induce self-regulation and eliminate contamination (Evans 1982; McGowen 1998). Ultimately, the typical Victorian prison, symbolised best in the opening of Pentonville in 1842, was based on the American penitentiary, but as these extracts show, science was assuming a growing significance in thinking about how to turn people away from crime.

Contemplative or self-reflective thinking about sin, the cornerstone of those eighteenth-century theories of rehabilitation, was closely aligned to the idea of a second chance which in the early part of the nineteenth century became enshrined in the concept of recognisance. That history has been told many times (Bochel 1976; King 1969; McWilliams 1983; Vanstone 2007) and will not be repeated here; however, it is an essential element in the story of rehabilitation, and its early proponents are represented in the extracts. Matthew Davenport Hill and Edward Cox[1] are key figures in the development of the use of recognisance in the United Kingdom. In 1841 Hill built on the system of recognisance used by the Warwickshire magistrates by introducing the keeping of a register and follow-up inquiries, and Cox combined the use of recognisance with the employment of a special inquiry officer. The extracts used give a detailed account of the rationale for the use of what Hill describes as an experiment and provide practical illustrations of its implementation; in addition, they provide the reader with a clear insight into the essential roots of what was to become probation.

However, the development of probation as a core component of rehabilitation would not have been possible without the practical application of the principles and theories underpinning recognisance, and this came from pioneers like John Augustus in America and Thomas Holmes in the United Kingdom. Both the extracts included here illustrate how early practice was focused on the problems associated with drink and temperance and how the personal commitment of the practitioner was underpinned by religious zeal and moral certainty but also by a basic humanity and concern for the unfortunate. Both exemplify a strand of rehabilitative effort that has woven its way through to the twenty-first century, namely the importance of the relationship and its cornerstones, empathy, concreteness and genuineness (Truax and Carkhuff 1967). In addition though, both Augustus and Holmes (and we can only surmise that they were typical) convey implicit and sometimes explicit assumptions about the degree to which the people they were trying to help were responsible for their fate. A reading of their work suggests that they believed in what May (1991) describes as *soft determinism* – they had limited rationality and limited responsibility, but only up to a point. Holmes in particular – as one of his extracts shows – believed that rehabilitation was a community responsibility and that the environment was an important cause of crime, but the accounts of practice reveal an expectation that the person to be saved had a responsibility to take the chance being offered. It is this conflict between determinism and freewill that permeates several of the other extracts.

William Tallack[2] is important because he encouraged the idea of probation in the United Kingdom in the 1880s by disseminating information about the American system of probation. The extract from his book *Penological and Preventative Principles* positively describes the mechanics of adult probation in Massachusetts which he argued should be adopted in the United Kingdom. Interestingly, the extract exposes a complicated mixture of Christian-based attitudes towards people who offend and a range of contradictory theories drawn from classical and neo-classical criminology. So, he opposed what he saw as the indulgence of prisoners in American prisons; he advocated punishment tempered by realistic humanitarianism (the doctrine of less eligibility); he abhorred socialist philanthropy yet theorised about poverty as a cause of crime; and believed that the physical and psychological defects caused by poverty were passed on genetically but that prisoners were morally responsible citizens who deserved the opportunity to reform.

A less equivocal position was taken by Ferri, who as Garland (1985) has argued, firmly rejected the notion of freewill and held a conclusive belief in the determinist position. As a consequence he was a strong advocate of a *scientific approach* to eliminating crime – what he described as the 'gangrenous plague of crime' – which eschewed guilt and responsibility. For him, the appropriate focus was on the reasons an individual committed a crime and the treatment of that individual. But the extract from his lecture to students at the University of Naples is interesting also because of the trenchant criticism of punishment as a way of responding to crime. We can be critical of his contribution to the development of positivism, but his attitude towards punishment has a very modern resonance; his critique of the blind worship of punishment would make useful reading for politicians (on both sides of the Atlantic) responsible for the neo-punitive putsch of recent years. Similarly, Darrow takes a determinist position which almost seems to absolve the person committing a crime of any responsibility at all. Darrow's piece is all the more remarkable because it was an address to prisoners, and while it might be easy to dismiss his total determinism it should be of interest to the modern reader because of what it offers to a debate about rehabilitation and punishment. In some senses, it is a remarkably modern treatise: it argues against the use of prison; it humanises and dignifies the prisoner; it challenges the difference between the non-offending and offending populations by highlighting white-collar crime and labelling; it argues against the efficacy of deterrence; and it locates the key to rehabilitation in the improvement of socio-economic conditions. It should be read, however, alongside Jenkins' salutary piece which provides a succinct critique of Darrow's positivism and puts into sharp relief the paradoxical nature of his faith in the 'massive discretionary powers' of the scientists.

Perhaps, it is Saleilles who steered the most effective course through the conflict between freewill and total determinism and pointed to the compromise inherent in most rehabilitative effort in the near hundred years since his book *The Individualization of Punishment*. He accepted what liberal-minded people might consider a truism today, that life chances are not the same for everyone and that, therefore, individual freedom and responsibility might vary from one person to another depending on factors such as a person's state of health, pathology or mental disorder. For him the decision about how to respond to a person's offending rests on what is discovered about the degree of moral freedom involved in the decision to commit a crime, and the right to opportunities of rehabilitation rests on the knowledge gained from scientific inquiry.

In effect, this compromise position combined with the growing dominance of science over religion facilitated the professionalisation (and in some senses the institutionalisation) of rehabilitation. At the core of this professionalisation was the body of knowledge provided by psychiatry (Rose 1985, 1996). During the final quarter of the nineteenth century and the first quarter of the twentieth psychological perspectives on deviance and abnormality triumphed over environmental arguments about their causes and solutions. Experts acknowledged the significance of the environment but when they theorised about crime and applied those theories to practice invariably they focused on changing the personality and behaviour of the individual. Psychology acquired its status through its ability to provide a relevant, coherent discourse which could be applied to the problems posed by deviant behaviour, and in the field of rehabilitation aspects of this discourse emerged in the shape and form of casework. Casework itself was crucial to the professionalisation of rehabilitative work because it provided the flexibility necessary to embrace the variety of *folk theories* (Vanstone 2007) which would inform that work through most of the twentieth century. As the writings of practitioners (Holmes, Chinn, Rankin, Poulton, Golding and Parkinson)[3] included here show, its lineage stretches over a sixty-year period.

Holmes's work is full of references to psychology, and although he acknowledges the social and legal dimensions of the problem of crime in general he gives weight to the psychology of deviant behaviour. However, his first extract is important because it demonstrates the importance of personal commitment to the individual in the attempt to rehabilitate, and like the other contributions from practitioners it reminds us of the significance of vocation in early work. Probably, Chinn was probation's definer of casework and he describes the elements of probation work with children and in particular how inquiries into the character of the child were undertaken, and how after the probation order was made, (in an interestingly modern way), he negotiates a collaborative relationship with the parents. Rankin ruminates on the sociological causes and illustrates the practice and theory of probation by describing problem cases with proposed solutions gathered from officers around the country: two cases are included here. Casework-oriented insights permeate both, but Poulton's extract reminds us that the spiritual element of efforts to rehabilitate survived well into the twentieth century. Some thirty years later, as can be seen in the Golding extract, psychotherapy was firmly entrenched in the writings of some probation officers. However, Golding is not only interesting because of his vivid description of the influence of psycho-analysis[4] but because he prefigures a modern concern with effectiveness. The final account in this group of practitioners by Parkinson further exemplifies discourse around the theoretical paradigm drawn from the psychoanalysis. Moreover, he provides a very clear example of the idiosyncratic development of ad hoc personal theory in practice situations.

Of course, glossy representations of practice do not ensure professional status. Another important aspect of the story of the professionalisation of rehabilitative work is the creation of theoretical and practical blueprints combined with a framework of values. Leeson provided the first in 1914 which included a checklist for social inquiry with all the features of professional diagnosis and a call for a professional identity. The short extract here gives some practical illustrations of the practice requirements of such an identity. Over the next fifty years numerous writers contributed to the refinement of the casework model, and we have chosen what we believe to be among the most significant on both sides of the Atlantic: Le Mesurier who edited the first definitive handbook for probation in the United Kingdom; Glueck who produced a book of essays in honour of Herbert Parsons designed to show that probation required theory and practice from psychology, mental hygiene, social casework and adult education; Weiss who in the same volume posited probation work firmly within Mary Richmond's social casework model; Gordon who was more explicitly critical of the deleterious effects of prison but delineated a clear set of principles upon which rehabilitative effort should be based; Schmideberg who articulated a psychotherapeutic theory for work with probationers; and Biestek who outlined arguably the most influential set of values on which the casework relationship should be founded.

Also in Part One we have included extracts related to themes that will be given a much more substantial airing in Part Two: first, innovative work which has always been a feature of practice in agencies like probation; and second the critical assault on the casework model incorporating as it did the treatment paradigm. The main point to note about the kind of innovation described by Mrs Cary (with her very early, simple groupwork approach to working with girls) and Bissell, Freeguard and McCullough (with their more theoretically informed groupwork) is that it was essentially dependent on the creativity, energy and motivation of individual practitioners and often happened despite and not because of agency support. The extract from Victor Serge's *Men in Prison* may be viewed as a very early attack on the casework/treatment model or certainly on the insidiously negative consequences of humanitarianism detailed by C. S. Lewis in Part Two. As Priestley's extract vividly illustrates it was a humanitarianism underpinned by a disciplinary agenda within prisons which was driven by religion. However, it was Hunt's treatise on the unconscious desire for discipline, authority and control in young people on probation or in Borstal which created the fertile ground required by later critics of casework and treatment.

Notes

1. Hill practised as a lawyer in the Warwickshire Magistrates' Courts and later in 1841 became a Recorder in Birmingham. Edward Cox was both the Recorder of Portsmouth and Chairman of the Second Court of the Middlesex Sessions from 1870 to his death in 1879.
2. William Tallack was secretary of the Howard Association from 1866 to 1901.
3. The first a Police Court Missionary, the rest probation officers.
4. In all probability the work of many probation officers had a practical focus at this time, but psychoanalytical theory was very much the professional creed of probation and figured prominently in training courses (Vanstone 2007).

1. Science, rewards and education

Cesare Beccaria

Of the Sciences Would you prevent crimes? Let liberty be attended with knowledge. As knowledge extends, the disadvantages which attend it diminish, and the advantages increase. A daring impostor, who is always a man of some genius, is adored by the ignorant populace, and despised by men of understanding. Knowledge facilitates the comparison of objects, by showing them in different points of view. When the clouds of ignorance are dispelled by the radiance of knowledge, authority trembles, but the force of the laws remains immovable. Men of enlightened understanding must necessarily approve those useful conventions, which are the foundation of public safety; they compare, with the highest satisfaction, the inconsiderable portion of liberty of which they are deprived, with the sum total sacrificed by others for their security; observing that they have only given up the pernicious liberty of injuring their fellow creatures, they bless the throne, and the laws upon which it is established.

It is false that the sciences have always been prejudicial to mankind. When they were so, the evil was inevitable. The multiplication of the human species on the face of the earth introduced war, the rudiments of arts, and the first laws, which were temporary compacts arising from necessity, and perishing with it. This was the first philosophy, and its few elements were just, as indolence and want of sagacity, in the early inhabitants of the world, preserved them from error.

[...]

The second may be found in the difficult and terrible passage from error to truth, from darkness to light. The violent shock between a mass of errors, useful to the few and powerful, and the truths so important to the many and the weak, with the fermentation of passions, excited on that occasion, were productive of infinite evils to unhappy mortals. In the study of history, whose principal periods, after certain intervals, much resemble each other, we frequently find, in the necessary passage from the obscurity of ignorance to the light of philosophy, and from tyranny to liberty, its natural consequence, one generation sacrificed to the happiness of the next. But when this flame is extinguished, and the world delivered from its evils, after a very slow progress, sits down with monarchs on the throne, and is worshipped in the assemblies of nations. Shall we then believe, that light diffused among the people is more destructive than darkness, and that the knowledge of the relations of things can ever be fatal to mankind?

Ignorance may indeed be less fatal than a small degree of knowledge, because this adds, to the evils of ignorance, the inevitable errors of a confined view of things on this side the bounds of truth; but a man of enlightened understanding, appointed guardian of the laws, is the greatest blessing that a sovereign can bestow on a nation. Such a man is accustomed to behold truth, and not to fear it; unacquainted with the greatest part of those imaginary and insatiable necessities, which so often put virtue to the proof, and accustomed to contemplate mankind from the most elevated point of view, he considers the nation as his family, and his fellow citizens as brothers; the distance between the great and the vulgar appears to him the less, as the number of mankind he has in view is greater.

The philosopher has necessities and interests unknown to the vulgar, and the chief of these is not to belie in public the principles he taught in obscurity, and the habit of loving virtue for its own sake.

[...]

Of Rewards Yet another method of preventing crimes is, to reward virtue. Upon this subject the laws of all nations are silent. If the rewards, proposed by academies for the discovery of useful truths, have increased our knowledge, and multiplied good books, is it not probable, that rewards, distributed by the beneficent hand of a sovereign, would also multiply virtuous actions? The coin of honour is inexhaustible, and is abundantly fruitful in the hands of a prince who distributes it wisely.

Of Education Finally, the most certain method of preventing crimes is, to perfect the system of education. But this is an object too vast, and exceeds my plan; an object, if I may venture to declare it, which is so intimately connected with the nature of government, that it will always remain a barren spot, cultivated only by a few wise men.

A great man, who is persecuted by that world he hath enlightened, and to whom we are indebted for many important truths, hath most amply detailed the principal maxims of useful education. This chiefly consists in presenting to the mind a small number of select objects; in substituting the originals for the copies, both of physical and moral phenomena; in leading the pupil to virtue by the easy road of sentiment, and in withholding him from evil by the infallible power of necessary inconveniences, rather than by command, which only obtains a counterfeit and momentary obedience.

From: C. Beccaria (1992) An Essay on Crimes and Punishments. *Second Edition. Boston: International Pocket Library, pp. 92–97 (Originally published by F. Newberry 1775).*

2. The Panopticon

Jeremy Bentham

Letter II. Plan for a Penitentiary Inspection-House

Before you look at the plan, take in words the general idea of it.

The building is circular.

The apartments of the prisoners occupy the circumference. You *may* call them, if you please, the *cells*.

These *cells* are divided from one another, and the prisoners by that means excluded from all means of communication with each other, by *partitions* in the form of *radii* issuing from the circumference towards the centre, and extending as many feet as shall be thought necessary to form the largest dimension of the cell.

The apartment of the inspector occupies the centre; you may call it if you please the *inspector's lodge*.

It will be convenient in most, if not all cases, to have a vacant *space* or *area* all round, between such centre and such circumference. You may call it if you please the *intermediate* or *annular* area.

About the width of a cell may be sufficient for a *passage* from the outside of the building to the lodge.

Each cell has in the outward circumference, a *window*, large enough, not only to light the cell, but, through the cell, to afford light enough to the correspondent part of the lodge.

The inner circumference of the cell is formed by an iron *grating*, so light so as not to screen any part of the cell from the inspector's view.

Of this grating, a part sufficiently large opens, in form of a *door*, to admit the prisoner at his first entrance; and to give admission at any time to the inspector or any of his attendants.

To cut off from each prisoner the view of every other, the partitions are carried on a few feet beyond the grating into the intermediate area: such projecting parts I call the *protracted partitions*.

It is conceived, that the light, coming in this manner through the cells, and so across the intermediate area, will be sufficient for the inspector's lodge. But, for this purpose, both the windows in the cells, and those corresponding to them in the lodge, should be as large as the strength of the building, and what will be deemed a necessary attention to economy, will permit.

To the windows of the lodge there are *blinds*, as high up as the eyes of the prisoners in their cells can, by any means they can employ, be made to reach.

To prevent *thorough light*, whereby, notwithstanding the blinds, the prisoners would see from the cells whether or no any person was in the lodge, that apartment is divided into quarters, by *partitions* formed by two diameters to the circle, crossing each other at right angles. For these partitions the thinnest materials might serve; and they might be made removable at pleasure; their height, sufficient to prevent the prisoners seeing over them from the cells. Doors to these partitions, if left open at any time, might produce the thorough light. To prevent this, divide each partition into two, at any part required, setting down the one-half at such distance from the other as shall be equal to the aperture of the door.

These windows of the inspector's lodge open into the intermediate area, in the form of *doors*, in as many places as shall be deemed necessary to admit of his communicating readily with any of the cells.

Small *lamps*, in the outside of each window of the lodge, backed by a reflector, to throw light into the corresponding cells, would extend to the night the security of the day.

To save troublesome exertion of the voice that might otherwise be necessary, and to prevent one prisoner from knowing that the inspector was occupied by another prisoner at a distance, a small *tin tube* might reach from each cell to the inspector's lodge, passing across the area, and so in at the side of the corresponding window of the lodge. By means of this implement, the slightest whisper of the one might be heard by the other, especially if he had proper notice to apply his ear to the tube.

With regard to *instruction*, in cases where it cannot be duly given without the instructor's being close to the work, or without setting his hand to it by way of example before the learner's face, the instructor must indeed here as elsewhere, shift his station as often as there is occasion to visit different workmen; unless he calls the workmen to him, which in some of the instances to which this sort of building is applicable, such as that of imprisoned felons, could not so well be. But in all cases where directions, given verbally and at a distance, are sufficient, these tubes will be found of use. They will save, on the one hand, the exertion of voice it would require, on the part of the instructor, to communicate instruction to the workmen without quitting his central station in the lodge; and, on the other, the confusion which would ensue if different instructors or persons in the lodge were calling to the cells at the same time. And, in cases of hospitals, the quiet that may be insured by this little contrivance, trifling as it may seem at first sight, affords an additional advantage.

A *bell*, appropriated exclusively to the purposes of *alarm*, hangs in a *belfry* with which the building is crowned, communicating by a rope with the inspector's lodge.

The most economical, and perhaps the most convenient, way of *warming* the cells and area, would be by flues surrounding it, upon the principle of hot-houses. A total want of every means of producing artificial heat might, in such weather as we sometimes have in England, be fatal to the lives of the prisoners; at any rate, it would often times be altogether incompatible with their working at any sedentary employment. The flues, however, and the fire-places belonging to them, instead of being on the outside, as in hot-houses, should be in the inside. By this means, there would be less waste of heat, and the current of air that would rush in on all sides through the cells, to supply the draught made by the fires, would answer so far the purpose of ventilation. But of this more under the head of hospitals.

[…]

Letter VIII. uses – Penitentiary-houses – Reformation

In my last, I endeavoured to state the advantages which a receptacle, upon the plan of the proposed building, seemed to promise in its application to places of *confinement*, considered merely in that view. Give me leave now to consider it as applicable to the joint purposes of *punishment*, *reformation*, and *pecuniary economy*.

That in regard to persons of description of those to whom punishments of the nature in question are destined, solitude is in its nature subservient to the purpose of reformation, seems to be as little disputed, as its tendency to operate in addition to the mass of sufferance. But that upon this plan that purpose would be effected, at least as completely as it could be on any other, you cannot but see at first glance, or rather you must have observed already. In the conditions of *our* prisoners (for so I call them for shortness sake) you may see the student's paradox, *nunquam minus solus quam cum solus*, realized in a new way; to the keeper, a *multitude*, though not a *crowd*; to themselves, they are *solitary* and *sequestered* individuals.

What is more, you will see this purpose answered more completely by this plan, than it could possibly be on any other. What degree of solitary it was proposed to reduce them to in the once-intended penitentiary-houses, need not be considered. But for one purpose, in buildings of any mode of construction that could then and there have been in view, it would be necessary, according to the express regulations of that plan, that the law of solitude should be dispensed with; I mean, so often as the prisoners were to receive the benefits of attendance on Divine service. But in my brother's circular penitentiary-houses, they might receive these benefits, in every circumstance, without stirring from their cells. No thronging nor jostling in the way between the scene of work and the scene destined to devotion; no quarrelings, nor confederating, nor plotting to escape; nor yet any whips or fetters to prevent it.

From: J. Bentham, (1823) 'Panopticon: or, The Inspection House', in P. Rock (ed.) (1994) History of Criminology. *Aldershot: Dartmouth.*

3. Working in the Police Court

John Augustus

I put my hand to the plough in 1841, in the Police Court, the scene of my earliest efforts to reform the drunkard, which acts on my part were wholly voluntary and have been so to the present time, and equally voluntary have those acted who have aided me to prosecute effectually the work I began.

I cannot better describe my mode of action in the Police Court than by introducing an every-day scene there. It was at this time that the great Washingtonian Temperance reform was exciting the attention of the public mind, and when a general interest pervaded the hearts of the philanthropic, to liberate the wretched inebriate from the prison of his own destructive vice, and to loose the bonds which held him captive, by removing from him the pernicious influences by which he had been surrounded, and by causing him to feel that he was still a man.

In the month of August, 1841, I was in court one morning, when the door communicating with the lock-room was opened and an officer entered, followed by a ragged and wretched looking man, who took his seat upon the bench allotted to prisoners. I imagined from the man's appearance, dint his offence was that of yielding to his appetite for intoxicating drinks, and in a few moments I found that my suspicions were correct, for the clerk read the complaint, in which the man was charged with being a common drunkard. The case was clearly made out, but before sentence had been passed, I conversed with him for a few moments, and found that he was not yet past all hope of reformation, although his appearance and his looks precluded a belief in the minds of others that he would ever become a *man* again. He told me that if he could be saved from the House of Correction, he never again would taste intoxicating liquors; there was such an earnestness in that tone, and a look expressive of firm resolve, that I determined to aid him; I bailed him, by permission of the Court. He was ordered to appear for sentence in *three* weeks from that time. He signed the pledge and became a sober man; at the expiration of this period of probation, I accompanied him into the court room; his whole appearance was changed and no one, not even the scrutinizing officers, could have believed that he was the same person who less than a month before, had stood trembling on the prisoner's stand. – The Judge expressed himself much pleased with the account we gave of the man, and instead of the usual penalty, – imprisonment in the House of

Correction, – he fined him one *cent* and costs, amounting in all to $3,76, which was immediately paid. The man continued industrious and sober, and without doubt has been by this treatment, saved from a drunkard's grave.

[...]

In 1842 I continued to attend the court and to bail as many as I could attend to, those whom I believed might be benefited by such acts on my part; but here I found my efforts materially cramped, and in some measure limited, for my business affairs of course, claimed a share of my attention, as I was at that time engaged in the boot-making business, in Franklin Avenue, near the court house. I generally went into court about half past nine in the morning, thinking to return to my shop in a short time, but very frequently found it impossible to leave the court room till twelve or one o'clock, as I waited to bail some unfortunate person; this course broke in upon my business engagements at my shop, and the delay which caused the evil arose in most cases, from the opposition of the officers of the court to my mode of operation, and in some cases when I left the court room for a few moments, the unhappy object whose welfare was my aim, would be examined, and sentenced before my return. I resolved not to be frustrated in this manner, and thus sacrificed much valuable time.

I continued on in this way for some time, and found that occasions rapidly multiplied where I was called upon to bail the prisoner, and to counsel and aid the wretched. It soon became generally known in the city that I was saving drunkards from the House of Correction, and daily calls upon my attention were increased; my business at my shop suffered sadly by neglect. In August, 1842, I found that I had bailed thirty persons.

Scarcely an hour in the day elapsed, but some one would call at my house or my shop and tell their tale of sorrow; one had a husband who had been arrested by the police, another a wife who had been dragged to the watch house; she had perhaps, been taken out of bed at midnight and hurried away with her babe and family.

[...] Similar cases were constantly occurring. I would carefully note their names and residences; then go to court and watch perhaps for hours, til some one whose name I had entered, was brought in from the lock-up, and would then make an effort to save him.

From: John Augustus (1852) A Report of the Labors of John Augustus, for the Last Ten Years, in Aid of the Unfortunate: Containing a Description of his Method of Operation: Striking Incidents, and Observation upon the Improvement of some of Our City Institutions, with a View to the Benefit of the Prisoner and Society. *Boston: Wright & Hasty, Printers. Reprinted as* John Augustus, First Probation Officer *by the National Probation Association in 1939, pp. 4–8.*

4. Recognizance

Matthew Davenport Hill

Charge of October, 1848

[…]

It was probably known to most of them, that for a period of seven years, beginning early in the year 1841, he had thus acted with regard to juvenile offenders: – that when there was ground for believing that the individual was not wholly corrupt – when there was reasonable hope of reformation – and when there could be found persons to act as guardians kind enough to take charge of the young convict (which at first sight would appear to present a great difficulty, but which in practice furnished little impediment to the plan), he had felt himself justified in at once handing over the young offender to their care, in the belief that there would be better hope of amendment under such guardians than in the gaol of the county. And he was happy to say that the intelligent officer at the head of the police, informed him that a much greater number so disposed of were withdrawn from evil courses than of those who, having no such advantages, had been consigned to prison.

'We take (said the Recorder) as much care as we can not to be imposed upon, either by too sanguine a hope of amendment, or from imperfect information as to the results actually obtained. At unexpected periods a confidential officer visits the guardian, makes inquiries, and registers the facts of which he is thus informed, in an account which has been regularly kept from the beginning.' The results he would now submit to them. The number of young offenders so disposed of was 166; of these the conduct of 71 was good. Of the greater number of that 71 the good conduct had been of such long standing that he was warranted in assuming their reformation to be complete and assured. The conduct of 40 was doubtful. That was said partly because it had not been quite consistent, and partly because some of the lads had passed out of sight, and therefore could not be spoken of with certainty. Of 53 the conduct had been bad, and two were dead.

Sequel to Charge of September 1854

[…]

To return, however, to the magistrates of the Warwickshire Sessions, in whose court I practised. Their kindness and good sense, let me hasten to say, led them to discard this illusory treatment in the few instances in which opportunity was favourable. Sometimes they ventured, when the prosecutor came before them and humanely consented to receive back his dishonest young servant or apprentice, to consign the youth immediately to his care. On these occasions I have narrowly watched the countenances of the prisoner and his friends, including the prosecutor – his best friend – to enable me to form a conjecture as to whether the experiment was likely to be successful; and the conclusions which I drew from the imperfect evidence at my command were favourable to the plan. But it was tried under many disadvantages. It frequently happened that the evidence of the prosecutor not being required, he remained at home, and in such case his assent could not be obtained. Again, the magistrates had no means of forming an estimate of the prosecutor's respectability but from his appearance; and, if that were against him, they felt, and rightly felt, bound not to entrust the prisoner to his care. But the most serious defect of the plan was that they had no sure means of learning the results of their clemency; except that, in case of failure, it sometimes happened that the prisoner came again before them, but not always, as he might have chosen a field for the exercise of his calling in a district out of their jurisdiction. Being, however, much impressed with the value, or what, with all its drawbacks, I considered to be the value, of this mode of disposing of juvenile prisoners, I determined, when I was appointed Recorder of Birmingham, to try the experiment myself, under circumstances more favourable than those under which the County Magistrates acted; because at Birmingham the master or the parent was at hand, even if not in court; because inquiry could readily be made as to their character; and, above all, because by keeping a register, the failure and success of the plan, in each instance, could be recorded. Aided by the Chief Superintendent of Police, I have had inquiries made, from time to time, as to the conduct of the prisoner; and the result of these inquiries being reduced to writing, I am possessed of all the means necessary for accurately testing the value of such a measure.

[…]

Sir, when considering the hope of reformation which the plan I have adopted holds out, we must never forget that it is in truth but a rude expedient, labouring under one enormous defect. The young person is sent back into the same position exactly as that which he occupied when he fell. He is open to the same temptations, it is difficult to keep him aloof from the same companions; and thus, while he is too often exposed to the scorn and reproach of persons whose ill opinion he most dreads, he has the far greater misfortune of being open to the seductions of those whom his former errors have armed with a pernicious influence over his actions. It, however, has one redeeming feature, which is worthy of the most attentive consideration – the young offender is received into the bosom of a family! And the head of that family is moved to this act of Christian benevolence, by feelings which give no slight guarantee that he will faithfully execute his trust.

From: M. D. Hill (1857) Suggestions for the Repression of Crime Contained in Charges Delivered to the Grand Juries of Birmingham Supported by Additional Facts and Arguments: Together with Articles from Reviews and Newspapers Controverting or Advocating the Conclusions of the Author. *London: John. W. Parker & Son, pp. 117–18 and pp. 350–2*

5. Recognizance and the suspension of judgment

Edward W. Cox

Mitigation of Punishment

[…]

But there is yet an alternative which, having employed it to a considerable extent, I can very confidently recommend. Even a short imprisonment is a severe punishment to one who has not been a habitual criminal and who has never experienced the loss of personal liberty. It is not the pain he endures within the prison walls; the greater penalty by far is the loss of his position socially, the blight upon his home, the difficulty of obtaining employment and the jeers of his fellows. If this ruin of character can be avoided, many cases present themselves to the considerate Judge in which it will appear to him desirable so to do.

Recognizances to come up for judgment when called upon provide this desirable alternative. Practice has proved to me the excellence of this substitute for punishment and with growing experience I am more and more inclined to its adoption. It is, in my view of it, infinitely to be preferred to the short imprisonment so decidedly condemned by the prison authorities. It gives to the criminal who has made only a first step in crime a chance of redemption under the most favourable circumstances. He goes from the court without the stamp of penal discipline upon him – with a public recognition that he is not utterly lost – that the Judge had hope of a good future for him – that he was not yet registered as a convict – that he had been the subject of mercy after all the facts connected with his fault had been taken into account. These are considerations in themselves calculated to induce, if anything can, reformation. All the sermons in the world would not preach to the guilty man at the bar the short lesson that comes from the lips of the Judge and is burned into his memory: 'You have been rightfully found guilty of this offence. I have inquired into your history and I am glad to learn that hitherto you have borne a good character and so far as is known this is your first lapse into crime. In the anxious hope that it will also be your last offence, that you will strive by future good conduct to regain the good character you have lost, it is not my intention to inflict upon you any punishment. If some friend will become bound for you to bring you up for judgment when called on, you shall leave that dock a free man. So long as you conduct yourself properly you will hear nothing more of this, and I trust that in time your fault will be forgotten by others as it is forgiven by me. But if you offend again against the law in any manner, you will be brought up on this conviction and then severely punished for what you have now done. Go home now and by your good conduct show your gratitude for the mercy that has been extended to you.'

The suspension only of the judgment, the knowledge that if he offends he may yet be punished – the hold which his bail thus has upon him, to a great extent guarantee that if there is in him an inclination to redeem himself he will return to a life of honesty.

And experience has simply confirmed this anticipation. I am aware that I have been blamed for having more largely used this power than has been the practice with Judges. But the results are the best justification. No exact account has been taken of the number of convicts so treated during the last twelve years, but it must be considerable. It is a remarkable fact that of all the many cases so dealt with, in two instances only has it been found necessary to require the offender to come up for judgment under these recognizances.

On the other hand I have received repeated assurances of the good effect of the course so adopted. Years afterwards letters have come expressing the profoundest gratitude to me for having been the means of saving the writers from ruin. One instance is so remarkable that the reader will perhaps excuse a reference to it in illustration of the argument.

Two young men, brothers, had landed from an American ship. While rambling about London they had spent their money and wanting more to pay their lodgings had been tempted to take some article from a shop. They pleaded guilty and in pursuance of a practice I have observed where no account of the convict can be given by others, I invited them to tell me who and what they were and their inducements to crime. They had come from New York, where they had friends, and but for this offence, which they appeared bitterly to lament, they were to have sailed on the return voyage in a few days. Having caused inquiry to be made as to the truth of this, I resolved to discharge them on their own recognizances, on a promise that they would at once go back to their ship and return with her to America; telling them that if they remained in England for a week they should be at once arrested and brought up for punishment. They expressed the utmost gratitude at the unexpected mercy shown to them and left the dock. Two years afterwards I received a letter from New York in which the writers reminded me of this act of grace to them – stated that they thought I might be pleased to learn that it had not been thrown away – that they had got into respectable situations and were doing well and that they owed their salvation to me.

From: E. W. Cox (1877) The Principles of Punishment as Applied in the Administration of the Criminal Law by Judges and Magistrates. *London: Law Times Office, pp. 163-6*

6. Adult probation

William Tallack

In reference to present human dealings with offenders against the laws and rights of the community, it is a primary matter of justice that these shall be restrained and discouraged from continuing in crime, by means of a merciful severity, and by a gradual cumulation of penalties certain, but not too heavy. On the other hand, the general circumstances and antecedents of the offender are, in fairness to him, deserving of practical consideration; as, for example, whether he has been driven to crime by powerful hereditary impulses and passions, in combination with ignorance, privation, and neglect, especially parental and social neglect. If the Law has also permitted such persons to be subjected to excessive temptations, as, for example, from a disproportionate abundance of licensed facilities for drunkenness or other vice, the law-makers and the community are themselves partially responsible for the effects thus produced. The writer, in visiting an English prison, was struck with the remark of a veteran warder who spoke of the heartless inconsiderateness of a large section of the public towards the more unfortunate class of offenders. He said, 'People are apt to exclaim, on seeing, for instance, a lad in jail, "The young rascal! he has wickedness imprinted on his face; it is a good thing to punish him sharply," "Well, perhaps so," the warder would remark, in reply to such an observation; "but let us remember that the lad (like many of his class) is the son of parents, both of whom were thieves and drunkards; both of whom deserted him; that he had no home; no early training in virtue; that he usually found a bed under arches, or on doorsteps, in holes and corners of the city, until the police-cell, or the work-house, or the prison received him into comparative luxury, though accompanied by restraints hateful to his wild habits." ' For such an one, justice demands a prolonged training to self-supporting industry, if possible, at some expense to his parents, if otherwise, at the cost of the State, which also has, in some measure probably, neglected him or his progenitors.

Again, as to the pauper; he, too, may have fought the battle of life against a heavy over-weight of disadvantage, from miserable parentage, hereditary incapacity or disease, or both – and in a wretched home, perhaps a 'hell upon earth,' with a bad example on the part of those around him, as to intemperance and vice. If having the offer of labour, he refuses it, then it is just to let him suffer, either punishment, or sharp privation. But he should be enabled to procure, somewhere and somehow, an opportunity of at least escaping starvation. The English Poor Law, by its offer of admission to the workhouse, secures this; though sometimes by granting it without first affording sufficient inducements to thrift and self-help. The Dutch and German Agricultural 'Colonies,' and the Bremen work-house, for furnishing occupations at low wages, afford interesting modes of operation, though on a very limited scale. Count Rumford's plan of compulsory industry, for mendicants and paupers in Bavaria, was also a decidedly successful and instructive experiment, illustrating the needful combination of merciful justice with beneficent deterrence for the idle or thriftless.

[…]

How much of the vice and crime of Glasgow, Edinburgh, and other crowded cities arises, almost by sheer irresistible necessity, from the shocking crowding of whole families into *single rooms*, or houses of a *single room* – the sole scene of birth, wedlock and death, feeding, living, and sleeping. Yet near some of these cities, thousands of fair acres are permanently kept waste, for the enjoyment of a few sportsmen. Is not this a grave injustice towards men and towards God? When will Scotland, in particular, rouse herself and deliver her poorest population from such terrible evils of criminal over-crowding and cruelly locked land?

The severity of penalty and the rigour of discipline should be everywhere qualified by just consideration; and also by the fact that honour is due to all men, by reason of the intrinsic worth of each soul gifted with a capacity for immortal life, and endless moral development.

[…]

Massachusetts adult 'probation'

There are two descriptions of conditional liberty, or probation, applicable alike to juveniles or adults; and both of which are had recourse to, in Massachusetts, for each of the two classes. There is, firstly, Conditional Liberation, *after* undergoing a sentence of detention in a prison or reformatory. This is no novelty, having long ago been adopted in Bavaria, Great Britain, and elsewhere. And secondly, there is Conditional Liberty, not necessarily accompanied by any detention at all. It is to be remembered that the *principle* of conditional liberty (as distinguished from conditional liberation) had long been practically recognised in England under the forms of BAIL, or personal RECOGNISANCES; and in the 'BINDING OVER' of certain quarrelsome or offensive persons to 'keep the peace' towards their fellow-subjects, for a given period, as an alternative to imprisonment.

The law of Massachusetts, in 1880, instituted as a special CLASS, 'PROBATION OFFICERS' for ADULTS, to be appointed by the respective Municipalities. It was then enacted, in regard to each of such functionaries, as follows: 'He shall, in the execution of his official duties, have the powers of Police officers, and may be a member of the police force of his city or town.' 'Such Probation Officer shall carefully inquire into the character and offence of every person arrested for crime, for the purpose of ascertaining whether the accused may reasonably be expected to reform without punishment; and shall keep a full record of the result of his investigation. The Officer, if then satisfied that the best interests of the public and of the accused would be subserved by placing him upon Probation, shall recommend the same to the Court trying the case; and the Court may permit the accused to be placed upon Probation, upon such terms as it may deem best, having regard to his reformation.' When the Probation Officer considers it advisable for any person placed on probation to be sent out of the State, the local authorities may make the necessary appropriation for the purpose, to be expended by him, under the direction of the superintendent of police. 'The Probation Officer shall, as far as practicable, visit the offenders placed on probation by the Court at his suggestion, and render such assistance and encouragement as will tend to prevent their again offending. Any person placed upon probation, upon his recommendation, may be re-arrested by him, upon approval of the superintendent of police, without further warrant, and again brought before the Court; and the Court may thereupon proceed to sentence, or may make any other lawful disposition of the case. It shall be the special duty of every Probation Officer to inform the Court, as far as possible, whether a person on trial has previously been convicted of any crime.' The above are the principal clauses of the Massachusetts Law of 1880, permitting the experiment of Adult Probation, and which at once went into operation. It may be observed that it is *permissive* in its nature, and entrusts large powers of discrimination and decision, both to the Courts and to the Probation and Police Officers. Such must necessarily be the case, from the very nature of probation.

From: W. Tallack, (1984) Penological and Preventative Principles. *New York and London: Garland Publishing, Inc. (original publication 1889 London: Wertheimer, Lea & Co.), pp. 39–41 and pp. 303-4.*

7. The blind worship of punishment

Enrico Ferri

Lecture III [Remedies]

[…]

It is a noble mission to oppose the ferocious penalties of the Middle Ages. But it is still nobler to forestall crime. The classic school of criminology directed its attention merely to penalties, to repressive measures after crime had been committed, with all its terrible moral and material consequences. For in the classic school, the remedies against criminality have not the social aim of improving human life, but merely the illusory mission of retributive justice, meeting a moral delinquency by a corresponding punishment in the shape of legal sentences. This is the spirit which is still pervading criminal legislation, although there is a sort of eclectic compromise between the old and the new. The classic school of criminology has substituted for the old absolutist conceptions of justice the eclectic theory that absolute justice has the right to punish, but a right modified by the interests of civilized life in present society. This is the point discussed in Italy in the celebrated controversy between Pasquale Stanislao Mancini and Terencio Mamiani,[1] in 1847. This is in substance the theory followed by the classic criminologists who revised the penal code, which public opinion considers incapable of protecting society against the dangers of crime. And we have but to look about us in the realities of contemporaneous life in order to see that the criminal code is far from being a remedy against crime, that it remedies nothing, because either premeditation or passion in the person of the criminal deprive the criminal law of all prohibitory power. The deceptive faith in the efficacy of criminal law still lives in the public mind, because every normal man feels that the thought of imprisonment would stand in his way, if he contemplated tomorrow committing a theft, a rape, or a murder. He feels the bridle of the social sense. And the criminal code lends more strength to it and holds him back from criminal actions. But even if the criminal code did not exist, he would not commit a crime, so long as his physical and social environment would not urge him in that direction. The criminal code serves only to isolate temporarily from social intercourse those who are not considered worthy of it. And this punishment prevents the criminal for a while from repeating his criminal deed. But it is evident that the punishment is not imposed until after the deed has been done. It is a remedy directed against effects, but it does not touch the causes, the roots, of the evil.

We may say that in social life penalties have the same relation to crime that medicine has to disease. After a disease has developed in an organism, we have recourse to a physician. But he cannot do anything else but to reach the effects in some single individual. On the other hand, if the individual and the collectivity had obeyed the rules of preventive hygiene, the disease would have been avoided 90 times in 100, and would have appeared only in extreme and exceptional cases, where a wound or an organic condition break through the laws of health. Lack of providence on the part of man, which is due to insufficient expression of the forces of the intellect and pervades so large a part of human life, is certainly to blame for the fact that mankind chooses to use belated remedies rather than to observe the laws of health, which demand a greater methodical control of one's actions and more foresight, because the remedy must be applied before the disease becomes apparent. I say occasionally that human society acts in the matter of criminality with the same lack of forethought that most people do in the matter of tooth-ache. How many individuals do not suffer from toothache, especially in the great cities? And yet any one convinced of the miraculous power of hygiene could easily clean his teeth every day and prevent the microbes of tooth rot from thriving, thereby saving his teeth from harm and pain. But it is tedious to do this every day. It implies a control of one's self. It cannot be done without the scientific conviction that induces men to acquire this habit. Most people say: 'Oh well, if that tooth rots, I'll bear the pain.' But when the night comes in which they cannot sleep for tooth-ache, they will swear at themselves for not having taken precautions and will run to the dentist, who in most cases cannot help them any more.

The legislator should apply the rules of social hygiene in order to reach the roots of criminality. But this would require that he should bring his mind and will to bear daily on a legislative reform of individual and social life, in the field of economics and morals as well as in that of administration, politics, and intelligence. Instead of that, the legislators permit the microbes of criminality to develop their pathogenic powers in society. When crimes become manifest, the legislator knows no other remedy but imprisonment in order to punish an evil which he should have prevented. Unfortunately this scientific conviction is not yet rooted and potent in the minds of the legislators of most of the civilized countries, because they represent on an average the backward scientific convictions of one or two previous generations. The legislator who sits in parliament today was the university student of thirty years ago. With a few very rare exceptions he is supplied only with knowledge of outgrown scientific research. It is a historical law that the work of the legislator is always behind the science of his time. But nevertheless the scientist has the urgent duty to spread the conviction that hygiene is worth as much on the field of civilization as it is in medicine for the public health.

This is the fundamental conviction at which the positive school arrives: That which has happened in medicine will happen in criminology. The great value of practical hygiene, especially of social hygiene, which is greater than that of individual hygiene, has been recognized after the marvelous scientific discoveries concerning the origin and primitive causes of the most dangerous diseases. So long as Pasteur and his disciples had not given to the world their discovery of the pathogenic microbes of all infectious diseases, such as typhoid fever, cholera, diphtheria, tuberculosis, etc., more or less absurd remedies were demanded of the science of medicine. I remember, for instance, that I was compelled in my youth, during an epidemic of cholera, to stay in a closed room, in which fumigation was carried on with substances irritating the bronchial tubes and lungs without killing the cholera microbes, as was proved later on. It was not until the real causes of those infectious diseases were discovered, that efficient remedies could be employed against them. An aqueduct given to a center of population like Naples is a better protection against cholera than drugs, even after the disease has taken root in the midst of the people of Naples. This is the modern lesson which we wish to teach in the field of criminology, a field which will always retain its repressive functions as an exceptional and ultimate refuge, because we do not believe that we shall succeed in eliminating all forms of criminality. Hence, if a crime manifests itself, repression may be employed as one of the remedies of criminology, but it should be the very last, not the exclusively dominating one, as it is today.

It is this blind worship of punishment which is to blame for the spectacle which we witness in every modern country, the spectacle that the legislators neglect the rules of social hygiene and wake up with a start when some form of crime becomes acute, and that they know of no better remedy than an intensification of punishment meted out by the penal code. If one year of imprisonment is not enough, we'll make it ten years, and if an aggravation of the ordinary penalty is not enough, we'll pass a law of exception. It is always the blind trust in punishment which remains the only remedy of the public conscience and which always works to the detriment of morality and material welfare, because it does not save the society of honest people and strikes without curing those who have fallen a prey to guilt and crime.

The positive school of criminology, then, aside from the greater value attributed to daily and systematic measures of social hygiene for the prevention of criminality, comes to radically different conclusions also in the matter of repressive justice. The classic school has for a cardinal remedy against crime a preference for one kind of punishment, namely imprisonment, and gives fixed and prescribed doses of this remedy. It is the logical conclusion of retributive justice that it travels by way of an illusory purification from moral guilt to the legal responsibility of the criminal and thence on to a corresponding dose of punishment, which has been previously prescribed and fixed.

We, on the other hand, hold that even the surviving form of repression, which will be inevitable in spite of the application of the rules of social prevention, should be widely different, on account of the different conception which we have of crime and of penal justice.

In the majority of cases, composed of minor crimes committed by people belonging to the most numerous and least dangerous class of occasional or passionate criminals, the only form of civil repression will be *the compensation of the victim for his loss*. According to us, this should be the only form of penalty imposed in the majority of minor crimes committed by people who are not dangerous. In the present practice of justice the compensation of the victim for his loss has become a laughing stock, because this victim is systematically forgotten. The whole attention of the classic school has been concentrated on the juridical entity of the crime. The victim of the crime has been forgotten, although this victim deserves philanthropic sympathy more than the criminal who has done the harm. It is true, every judge adds to the sentence the formula that the criminal is responsible for the injury and the costs to another authority. But the process of law puts off this compensation to an indefinite time, and if the victim succeeds a few years after the passing of the sentence in getting any action on the matter, the criminal has in the meantime had a thousand legal subterfuges to get away with his spoils. And thus the law itself becomes the breeding ground of personal revenge, for Filangieri says aptly that an innocent man grasps the dagger of the murderer, when the sword of justice does not defend him.

Let us say at this point that the rigid application of compensation for damages should never be displaced by imprisonment, because this would be equivalent to sanctioning a real class distinction. For the rich can laugh at damages, while the proletarian would have to make good a sentence of 1000 lire by 100 days in prison, and in the meantime the innocent family that tearfully waits for him outside would be plunged into desperate straits. Compensation for damages should never take place in any other way than by means of the labor of the prisoner to an extent satisfactory to the family of the injured. It has been attempted to place this in an eclectic way on our law books, but this proposition remains a dead letter and is not applied in Italy, because a stroke of legislator's pen is not enough to change the fate of an entire nation.

These practical and efficient measures would be taken in the case of lesser criminals. For the graver crimes committed by atavistic or congenital criminals, or by persons inclining toward crime from acquired habit or mental alienation, the positive school of criminology reserves segregation for an indefinite time, for it is absurd to fix the time beforehand in the case of a dangerous degenerate who has committed a grave crime.

[...]

This radical reform of principles carries with it a radical transformation of details. Given an indeterminate segregation, there should be organs of guardianship for persons so secluded, for instance permanent committees for the periodical revision of sentences. In the future, the criminal judge will always secure ample evidence to prove whether a defendant is really guilty, for this is the fundamental point. If it is certain that he has committed the crime, he should either be excluded from social intercourse or sentenced to make good the damage, provided the criminal is not dangerous and the crime not grave. It is absurd to sentence a man to five or six days imprisonment for some insignificant misdemeanor. You lower him in the eyes of the public, subject him to surveillance by the police, and send him to prison from whence he will go out more corrupted than he was on entering it. It is absurd to impose segregation in prison for small errors. Compensation for injuries is enough. For the segregation of the graver criminals, the management must be as scientific as it is now in insane asylums. It is absurd to place an old pensioned soldier or a hardened bureaucrat at the head of a penal institution. It is enough to visit one of those compulsory human beehives and to see how a military discipline carries a brutal hypocrisy into it. The management of such institutions must be scientific, and the care of their inmates must be scientific, since a grave crime is always a manifestation of the pathological condition of the individual. In America there are already institutions, such as the Elmira Reformatory, where the application of the methods of the positive school of criminology has been solemnly promised. The director of the institution is a psychologist, a physician.[2] When a criminal under age is brought in, he is studied from the point of view of physiology and psychology. The treatment serves to regenerate the plants who, being young, may still be straightened up.

[...]

Bentham narrates that the postal service in England, in the eighteenth century, was in the hands of stage drivers, but this service was not connected with the carrying of passengers, as became the custom later. And then it was impossible to get the drivers to arrive on time, because they stopped too often at the inns. Fines were imposed, imprisonment was resorted to, yet the drivers arrived late. The penalties did not accomplish any results so long as the causes remained. Then the idea was conceived to carry passengers on the postal stages, and that stopped the drivers from being late, because whenever they made a halt, the passengers, who had an interest in arriving on time, called the drivers and did not give them much time to linger. This is an illustration of a substitute for punishment.

[...]

Since we have made the great discovery that malaria, which weighs upon so many parts in Italy, is dependent for its transmission on a certain mosquito, we have acquired the control of malarial therapeutics and are enabled to protect individuals and families effectively against malaria. But aside from this function of protecting people, there must be a social prevention, and since those malarial insects can live only in swampy districts, it is necessary to bring to those unreclaimed lands the blessing of the hoe and plow, in order to remove the cause and do away with the effects. The same problem confronts us in criminology. In the society of the future we shall undertake this work of social hygiene, and thereby we shall remove the epidemic forms of criminality. And nine-tenths of the crimes will then disappear, so that nothing will remain of them but exceptional cases. There will remain, for instance, such cases as that of the bricklayer which I mentioned, because there may always be accidents, no matter what may be the form of social organization, and nervous disorders may thus appear in certain individuals. But you can see that these would be exceptional cases of criminality, which will be easily cured under the direction of science, that will be the supreme and beneficent manager of institutes for the segregation of those who will be unfit for social intercourse. The problem of criminality will thus be solved as far as possible, because the gradual transformation of society will eliminate the swamps in which the miasma of crime may form and breed.

[...]

Labor is the sole perennial energy of mankind which leads to social perfection. But if you have 100,000 persons in a city like Naples who do not enjoy the certainty and discipline of employment at methodical and common labor, you need not wonder that the uncertainty of daily life, an illfed stomach, and an anemic brain, result in the atrophy of all moral sentiment, and that the evil plant of the Camorra spreads out over everything. The processes in the law courts may attract the fleeting attention of public opinion, of legislation, of government, to the disease from which this portion of the social organism is suffering, but mere repression will not accomplish anything lasting.

The teaching of science tells us plainly that in such a case of endemic criminality social remedies must be applied to social evils. Unless the remedy of social reforms accompanies the development and protection of labor; unless justice is assured to every member of the collectivity, the courage of this or that citizen is spent in vain, and the evil plant will continue to thrive in the jungle.

Taught by the masterly and inflexible logic of facts, we come to the adoption of the scientific method in criminal research and conclude that a simple and uniform remedy like punishment is not adequate to cure such a natural and social phenomenon as crime, which has it own natural and social causes. The measures for the preservation of society against criminality must be manifold, complex and varied, and must be the outcome of persevering and systematic work on the part of legislators and citizens on the solid foundation of a systematic collective economy.

From: E. Ferri (1972) 'The Positive School of Criminology', in Stanley E. Grupp (ed.), Theories of Punishment. *Bloomington, IN: Indiana University Press, pp. 229–41.*

Notes

1. Terencio Mamiani (1799–1885), Italian writer, philosopher, political theorist and professor; noted for the series of letters exchanged with Mancini in 1841. Mamiani argued, in opposition to Mancini, that the objectives of law and morality were identical and that punishment must reward evil with evil.
2. The reference is apparently to Zebulon Reed Brockway. However, Brockway was not a physician. Similarly, only a very liberal use of the term psychologist would warrant this label today.

8. Crime and criminals

Clarence Darrow

Preface

This address is a stenographic report of a talk made to the prisoners in the Chicago jail. Some of my good friends have insisted that while my theories are true, I should not have given them to the inmates of a jail.

Realizing the force of the suggestion that the truth should not be spoken to all people, I have caused these remarks to be printed on rather good paper and in a somewhat expensive form. In this way the truth does not become cheap and vulgar, and is only placed before those whose intelligence and affluence will prevent their being influenced by it.

Crime and Criminals

If I looked at jails and crimes and prisoners in the way the ordinary person does, I should not speak on this subject to you. The reason I talk to you on the question of crime, its cause and cure, is because I really do not in the least believe in crime. There is no such thing as a crime as the word is generally understood. I do not believe there is any sort of distinction between the real moral condition of the people in and out of jail. One is just as good as the other. The people here can no more help being here than the people outside can avoid being outside. I do not believe that people are in jail because they deserve to be. They are in jail simply because they cannot avoid it on account of circumstances which are entirely beyond their control and for which they are in no way responsible.

I suppose a great many people on the outside would say I was doing you harm if they should hear what I say to you this afternoon, but you cannot be hurt a great deal anyway, so it will not matter. Good people outside would say that I was really teaching you things that were calculated to injure society, but it's worth while now and then to hear something different from what you ordinarily get from preachers and the like. These will tell you that you should be good and then you will get rich and be happy. Of course we know that people do not get rich by being good, and that is the reason why so many of you people try to get rich some other way, only you do not understand how to do it quite as well as the fellow outside.

There are people who think that everything in this world is an accident. But really there is no such thing as an accident. A great many folks admit that many of the people in jail ought not to be there, and many who are outside ought to be in. I think none of them ought to be here. There ought to be no jails, and if it were not for the fact that the people on the outside are so grasping and heartless in their dealings with the people on the inside, there would be no such institution as jails.

I do not want you to believe that I think all you people here are angels. I do not think that. You are people of all kinds, all of you doing the best you can, and that is evidently not very well – you are people of all kinds and conditions and under all circumstances. In one sense everybody is equally good and equally bad. We all do the best we can under the circumstances. But as to the exact things for which you are sent here, some of you are guilty and did the particular act because you needed the money. Some of you did it because you are in the habit of doing it, and some of you because you are born to it, and it comes to be as natural as it does, for instance, for me to be good.

Most of you probably have nothing against me, and most of you would treat me the same as any other person would; probably better than some of the people on the outside would treat me, because you think I believe in you and they know I do not believe in them. While you would not have the least thing against me in the world you might pick my pockets. I do not think all of you would, but I think some of you would. You would not have anything against me, but that's your profession, a few of you. Some of the rest of you, if my doors were unlocked, might come in if you saw anything you wanted – not out of malice to me, but because that is your trade. There is no doubt there are quite a number of people in this jail who would pick my pockets. And still I know this, that when I get outside pretty nearly everybody picks my pocket. There may be some of you who would hold up a man on the street, if you did not happen to have something else to do, and needed the money; but when I want to light my house or my office the gas company holds me up. They charge me one dollar for something that is worth twenty-five cents, and still all these people are good people; they are pillars of society and support the churches, and they are respectable.

When I ride on the street cars, I am held up – I pay five cents for a ride that is worth two and a half cents, simply because a body of men have bribed the city council and the legislature, so that all the rest of us have to pay tribute to them.

If I do not wish to fall into the clutches of the gas trust and choose to burn oil instead of gas, then good Mr. Rockefeller holds me up, and he uses a certain portion of his money to build universities and support churches which are engaged in telling us how to be good.

Some of you are here for obtaining property under false pretenses – yet I pick up a great Sunday paper and read the advertisements of a merchant prince – 'Shirt waists for 39 cents, marked down from $3.00.'

When I read the advertisements in the paper I see they are all lies. When I want to get out and find a place to stand anywhere on the face of the earth, I find that it has all been taken up long ago before I came here, and before you came here, and somebody says, 'Get off, swim into the lake, fly into the air; go anywhere, but get off.' That is because these people have the police and they have the jails and judges and the lawyers and the soldiers and all the rest of them to take care of the earth and drive everybody off that comes in their way.

A great many people will tell you that all this is true, but that it does not excuse you. These facts do not excuse some fellow who reaches into my pocket and takes out a five dollar bill; the fact that the gas company bribes the members of the legislature from year to year, and fixes the law, so that all you people are compelled to be 'fleeced' whenever you deal with them; the fact that the street car companies and the gas companies have control of the streets and the fact that the landlords own all the earth, they say, has nothing to do with you.

Let us see whether there is any connection between the crimes of the respectable classes and your presence in the jail. Many of you people are in jail because you have really committed burglary. Many of you, because you have stolen something; in the meaning of the law, you have taken some other person's property. Some of you have entered a store and carried off a pair of shoes because you did not have the price. Possibly some of you have committed murder. I cannot tell what all of you did. There are a great many people here who have done some of these things who really do not know themselves why they did them. I think I know why you did them – every one of you; you did these things because you were bound to do them. It looked to you at the time as if you had a chance to do them or not, as you saw fit, but still after all you had no choice. There may be people here who had some money in their pockets and who still went out and got some more money in a way society forbids. Now you may not yourselves see exactly why it was you did this thing, but if you look at the question deeply enough and carefully enough you would see that there were circumstances that drove you to do exactly the thing which you did. You could not help it any more than we outside can help taking the positions that we take. The reformers who tell you to be good and you will be happy, and the people on the outside who have property to protect – they think that the only way to do it is by building jails and locking you up in cells on week days and praying for you Sundays.

I think that all of this has nothing whatever to do with right conduct. I think it is very easily seen what has to do with right conduct. Some so-called criminals – and I will use this word because it is handy, it means nothing to me – I speak of the criminals who get caught as distinguished from the criminals who catch them – some of these so-called criminals are in jail for the first offenses, but nine-tenths of you are in jail because you did not have a good lawyer and of course you did not have a good lawyer because you did not have enough money to pay a good lawyer. There is no very great danger of a rich man going to jail.

Some of you may be here for the first time. If we would open the doors and let you out, and leave the laws as they are today, some of you would be back tomorrow. This is about as good a place as you can get anyway. There are many people here who are so in the habit of coming that they would not know where else to go. There are people who are born with the tendency to break into jail every chance they get, and they cannot avoid it. You cannot figure out your life and see why it was, but still there is a reason for it, and if we were all wise and knew all the facts we could figure it out

[...]

There are more people going to jail in hard times than in good times – few people comparatively go to jail except when they are hard up. They go to jail because they have no other place to go. They may not know why, but it is true all the same. People are not more wicked in hard times. That is not the reason. The fact is true all over the world that in hard times more people go to jail than in good times, and in winter more people go to jail than in summer. Of course it is pretty hard times for people who go to jail at any time. The people who go to jail are almost always poor people – people who have no other place to live first and last. When times are hard then you find large numbers of people who go to jail who would not otherwise be in jail

[...]

First and last, people are sent to jail because they are poor. Sometimes, as I say, you may not need money at the particular time, but you wish to have thrifty forehanded habits, and do not always wait until you are in absolute want. Some of you people are perhaps plying the trade, the profession, which is called burglary. No man in his right senses will go into a strange house in the dead of night and prowl around with a dark lantern through unfamiliar rooms and take chances of his life if he has plenty of the good things of the world in his own home. You would not take any such chances as that. If a man had clothes in his clothes-press and beefsteak in his pantry, and money in the bank, he would not navigate around nights in houses where he knows nothing about the premises whatever. It always requires experience and education for this profession, and people who fit themselves for it are no more to blame than I am for being a lawyer. A man would not hold up another man on the street if he had plenty of money in his own pocket. He might do it if he had one dollar or two dollars, but he wouldn't if he had as much money as Mr. Rockefeller has. Mr. Rockefeller has a great deal better hold-up game than that.

The more that is taken from the poor by the rich, who have the chance to take it, the more poor people there are who are compelled to resort to these means for a livelihood. They may not understand it, they may not think so at once, but after all they are driven into that line of employment.

This crime is born, not because people are bad; people don't kidnap other people's children because they want the children or because they are devilish, but because they see a chance to get some money out of it. You cannot cure this crime by passing a law punishing by death kidnappers of children. There is one way to cure it. There is one way to cure all these offenses, and that is to give the people a chance to live. There is no other way, and there never was any other way since the world began, and the world is so blind and stupid that it will not see. If every man and woman and child in the world had a chance to make a decent, fair, honest living, there would be no jails, and no lawyers and no courts. There might be some persons here or there with some peculiar formation of their brain, like Rockefeller, who would do these things simply to be doing them; but they would be very, very few, and those should be sent to a hospital and treated, and not sent to jail, and they would entirely disappear in the second generation, or at least in the third generation.

I am not talking pure theory. I will just give you [an example].

The English people once punished criminals by sending them away. They would load them on a ship and export them to Australia. England was owned by lords and nobles and rich people. They owned the whole earth over there, and the other people had to stay in the streets. They could not get a decent living. They used to take their criminals and send them to Australia – I mean the class of criminals who got caught. When these criminals got over there, and nobody else had come, they had the whole continent to run over, and so they could raise sheep and furnish their own meat, which is easier than stealing it; these criminals then became decent, respectable people because they had a chance to live. They did not commit any crimes. They were just like the English people who sent them there, only better. And in the second generation the descendants of those criminals were as good and respectable a class of people as there were on the face of the earth, and then they began building churches and jails themselves.

Again, people find all sorts of ways of getting rich. These are diseases like everything else. You look at people getting rich, organizing trusts, and making a million dollars, and somebody gets the disease and he starts out. He catches it just as a man catches the mumps or the measles; he is not to blame, it is in the air. You will find men speculating beyond their means, because the mania of money-getting is taking possession of them. It is simply a disease; nothing more, nothing less. You cannot avoid catching it; but the fellows who have control of the earth have the advantage of you. See what the law is; when these men get control of things, they make the laws. They do not make the laws to protect anybody; courts are not instruments of justice; when your case gets into court it will make little difference whether you are guilty or innocent; but it's better if you have a smart lawyer. And you cannot have a smart lawyer unless you have money. First and last it's a question of money. Those men who own the earth make the laws to protect what they have. They fix up a sort of fence or pen around what they have, and they fix the law so the fellow on the outside cannot get in. The laws are really organized for the protection of the men who rule the world. They were never organized or enforced to do justice. We have no system for doing justice, not the slightest in the world.

Let me illustrate: Take the poorest person in this room. If the community had provided a system of doing justice the poorest person in this room would have as good a lawyer as the richest, would he not? When you went into court you would have just as long a trial, and just as fair a trial as the richest person in Chicago. Your case would not be tried in fifteen or twenty minutes, whereas it would take fifteen days to get through with a rich man's case.

[...]

Most of our criminal code consists in offenses against property. People are sent to jail because they have committed a crime against property. It is of very little consequence whether one hundred people more or less go to jail who ought not to go – you must protect property, because in this world property is of more importance than anything else.

How is it done? These people who have property fix it so they can protect what they have. When somebody commits a crime it does not follow that he has done something that is morally wrong. The man on the outside who has committed no crime may have done something. For instance: to take all the coal in the United States and raise the price two dollars or three dollars when there is no need of it, and thus kill thousands of babies and send thousands of people to the poorhouse and tens of thousands to jail, as is done every year in the United States – this is a greater crime than all the people in our jails ever committed, but the law does not punish it. Why? Because the fellows who control the earth make the laws. If you and I had the making of the laws, the first thing we would do would be to punish the fellow who gets control of the earth. Nature put this coal in the ground for me as well as for them and nature made the prairies up here to raise wheat for me as well as for them, and then the great railroad companies came along and fenced it up.

[...]

I will guarantee to take from this jail, or any jail in the world, five hundred men who have been the worst criminals and law-breakers who ever got into jail, and I will go down to our lowest streets and take five hundred of the most hardened prostitutes, and go out somewhere where there is plenty of land, and will give them a chance to make a living, and they will be as good people as the average in the community.

There is a remedy for the sort of condition we see here. The world never finds it out, or when it does find it out it does not enforce it. You may pass a law punishing every person with death for burglary, and it will make no difference. Men will commit it just the same. In England there was a time when one hundred different offenses were punishable with death, and it made no difference. The English people strangely found out that so fast as they repealed the severe penalties and so fast as they did away with punishing men by death, crime decreased instead of increased; that the smaller the penalty the fewer the crimes.

Hanging men in our county jails does not prevent murder. It makes murderers.

And this has been the history of the world. It's easy to see how to do away with what we call crime. It is not so easy to do it. I will tell you how to do it. It can be done by giving the people a chance to live – by destroying special privileges. So long as big criminals can get the coal fields, so long as the big criminals have control of the city council and get the public streets for street cars and gas rights, this is bound to send thousands of poor people to jail. So long as men are allowed to monopolize all the earth, and compel others to live on such terms as these men see fit to make, then you are bound to get into jail.

The only way in the world to abolish crime and criminals is to abolish the big ones and the little ones together. Make fair conditions of life. Give men a chance to live. Abolish the right of private ownership of land, abolish monopoly, make the world partners in production, partners in the good things of life. Nobody would steal if he could get something of his own some easier way. Nobody will commit burglary when he has a house full. No girl will go out on the streets when she has a comfortable place at home. The man who owns a sweatshop or a department store may not be to blame himself for the condition of his girls, but when he pays them five dollars, three dollars, and two dollars a week, I wonder where he thinks they will get the rest of their money to live. The only way to cure these conditions is by equality. There should be no jails. They do not accomplish what they pretend to accomplish. If you would wipe them out, there would be no more criminals than now. They terrorize nobody. They are a blot upon civilization, and a jail is an evidence of the lack of charity of the people on the outside who make the jails and fill them with the victims of their greed.

From: C. Darrow (1919) Address to the Prisoners in the Chicago Jail. *Chicago: Charles Kerr, pp. 1–32.*

9. The positivism of Clarence Darrow

P. Jenkins

It is a very striking inconsistency that almost all left-wingers should have analyzed so many aspects of their society in terms of class conflict, and yet in penology they adopted the ideology of positivism, with its assumptions about underlying social consensus and scientific objectivity. The nature of this paradox will become apparent from a study of the ideas of Clarence Darrow. Darrow often described how class bias worked within the justice system, and how 'every advantage in the world goes with power' (Darrow 1932: 50). Wealth and the spirit of tyranny have 'battered down the ordinary safeguards that laws and institutions have made to protect individual rights' (Darrow 1932: 65). Darrow was a socialist, a libertarian, and a Jeffersonian individualist, so he had excellent reasons to distrust the growth of the arbitrary power of experts. Moreover, he knew that prisons were 'living tombs, inhabited by doomed men living in everlasting blank despair.' On their gates should be inscribed the phrase 'abandon hope, all ye who enter here' (a socialist commonplace for prisons, also found in George Bernard Shaw's *Crime of Imprisonment*) (Darrow 1932: 53, 85).

But Darrow was a positivist. There were criticisms – parole boards were not sufficiently willing to make politically courageous decisions to release reformed men – but the system of parole was 'a step in the right direction, and it should be upheld by all who believe that offenders would have a better chance' (Darrow 1972: 267–8). Ideally, sentences should be totally indeterminate, though in the meantime the lack of 'men of courage and capacity' on parole boards necessitated the establishment of maximum terms by juries (Darrow 1972: 268). 'All prisons should be in the hands of experts, physicians, criminologists, and above all, the humane' (Darrow 1972: 278). It was vital to remove the element of punishment and revenge from a judicial system, and it must be in a spirit of kindness and consideration that those with grave criminal defects in mind and body should be confined for life. Darrow was fully in accord with the ideas of *Erewhon* – a work he cited with respect and approval (Jenkins 1983; Darrow 1932: 335–58).

Darrow's work seems very inconsistent. In one chapter of his autobiography he sees progress and humanity as lying in indefinite confinement of criminals until the objective and sympathetic administrators judged them fit to be freed; in the next, he states explicitly that the justice system was an arm of a state dominated by 'the exploiting class,' which would use any means possible to fight radical challenges (Darrow 1932: 218). Darrow exactly fits Chesterton's characterization of humanitarians as 'the very reformers who admit that prison is bad for people [and] propose to reform them by a little more of it' (Chesterton 1922: 167). Darrow did not merely support current positivist reforms. He believed in a massively expanded role for medical experts to an extent that would attract for some writers in the 1960s the charge of psychiatric imperialism (Weinberg 1957: 16–88; Darrow 1932: 335–57).

For example, some argued in the 1920s that the insanity defense had been overused so that the guilty escaped punishment. Not at all, said Darrow, such criticisms were senseless, insanity was rapidly increasing throughout the world. His determinism led him to doubt whether anyone was ever really morally responsible for an act. Crime should be 'considered as a *manifestation* of life due to cause and effect, and not due to the wicked will of the offender' (Darrow 1932: 281–342). The criminal should be treated: 'If a cure is effected, either through treatment or some other process the unfortunate one should be released. If he is not safe to be at large, he should be kept confined with all the kindness and consideration that are given to other diseased and defective men and women' (Darrow 1932: 342–3). In an explicitly Erewhonian comparison, he wrote in 1932 that 'to subject every inmate of prisons to the same treatment is like giving every hospital patient the same doses of medicine, or the same surgical operation' (Darrow 1932: 355; 1972: 175–6). In an ideal future there would be no trials, judges or lawyers. Those who could not live up to social rules 'should be examined by experts to find out why it is and what can be done.' 'If need be, they should be kept under proper and sufficient inspection' (Darrow 1932: 355; 1902). It was such opinions that led to Harry Elmer Barnes dedicating to Darrow in 1930 his *Story of Punishment*, a book that contains a very strong attack on the jury system and most aspects of due process (Barnes 1972).

The questions that clearly arise here are: Why did Darrow fail to foresee the abuses that such massive discretionary powers would give rise to, and how could anyone exposed to the class conflict of this period possibly expect scientists and doctors to be neutral? G. K. Chesterton was writing in the same years from a perspective much further removed from Marxist Socialism, and he was able to prophesy exactly the problems that would become fully apparent only in the 1960s. But on the issue it was Darrow rather than Chesterton who was the norm in radical politics, and this collective credulity requires explanation.

From: P. Jenkins, (1982) 'The Radicals and the Rehabilitative Ideal 1890–1930', Criminology, 20.3 and 4: 347–72.

10. Work in the courts

Thomas Holmes

The first time I met him he was in this condition; he had been picked up in the snow about three o'clock one February morning, and was charged at North London Police Court. Without hat or boots, with matted hair and beard, blood-shot eyes and inflamed face, he sat shaking in the prisoners' room. He was described on the charge-sheet as 'A man; address not tendered.' Truth to tell, he was unable to give his own name or to say where he came from. When I spoke to him, he looked up and said, 'Water!' I got him a full quart and held it to his mouth, for he trembled too violently to do it for himself. At two draughts he swallowed the lot. I could not get a word from him, neither could the police, and when before the magistrate he was dumb and vacant. The magistrate kindly sent him in a cab to the work-house infirmary. I promised to go and see him in a few days' time.

I went, and found him in workhouse clothing; his mental faculties were coming back to him, but he was not fit for removal, being ill and weak. He could, however, tell me where he came from and where he was employed. So I called on his employers, who had seen nothing of him since Christmas Eve. They were pleased to hear of him, and put me in communication with his daughter, a very accomplished young lady who had left her position as governess in the country and had come up to London to seek for him, for nothing had been heard of him for some weeks; in fact, he had disappeared. The daughter went with me to the workhouse to visit her father, and found it a very unpleasant experience. As he was approaching us I said, 'Here is your father coming, miss.' In his corduroy trousers, his brown coat with brass buttons, and his brown Scotch cap, she did not recognise him at first; when she did, she nearly fainted, but ultimately had a good cry instead. I got fresh rooms for him, and his daughter consented to live with him, giving up her own prospects in order to do it. His employer paid his debts, advancing a sufficient sum of money to his daughter. In a few days he went back to the office, the same elderly, benevolent-looking gentleman as he had been before his debauch, with not a suspicion of drink upon him.

For three months he worked almost night and day, and then he was at it again. His daughter left him and went I know not whither, for I have never heard of her since. Again he was left lonely in London. I sought him, but could not find him, so I arranged with his landlady to let me know at once if he returned home in the day-time, for his lodgings were handy. At night I waited for him in his own room. He returned one morning about two, when I quickly took possession of him. About four o'clock he insisted on going out, but I had locked his door, so he had to remain. The next day I cut short his debauch, by taking him home with me, and putting him under lock and key. This he was most indignant about, and questioned my right to make a prisoner of him. I told him that might was right, and that he had got to remain. In a week's time he went to his lodging and his work. For six months this time he worked well and regularly. He was a Roman Catholic, so I insisted on his going to his priest, making a full confession, and signing the pledge. This he did, not that it had much effect, for again, after six months, he was in the mud. I could not find him for a long time, and when I did he was penniless, and had, moreover, pawned everything he possibly could. He lost his employment; his firm would have no more of him. His landlady, too, would have no more of him, and so the door was closed against him. Penniless, homeless, and friendless, I took him in.

He stayed two years with us, regaining his situation and doing so well that the firm substantially increased his salary. He was saving money fast, but he became too grand and important for us, and left us for other lodgings. For a while he kept straight, coming to visit us every Saturday evening. His silvery hair, his deportment, and his irreproachable clothing conferred quite a lustre upon our establishment, and his visits were a pleasure to us; but his holiday-time came round. For this he made great preparations, for he loved to do things in style. He had not had a seaside holiday for years; his frequent lapses prevented the thought of such a thing. He wanted a cab to take him to the station, for his luggage was considerable – a trunk, two portmanteaus, a Gladstone bag, a hand-bag, two hat-boxes, all full. With a gold-mounted Malacca cane, a gold-mounted umbrella, a gold watch and chain, away he went.

From: T. Holmes (1902) Pictures and Problems from London Police Courts. *London: Edward Arnold, pp. 208–11.*

11. The individualization of punishment

Raymond Saleilles

A new epoch is approaching, marking a development or rather a disintegration of the older classic position. This disintegration is significant and is demanded by the logic of events. The older classic school rested upon a fiction which consisted in believing that in regard to the same act every man had a like freedom of action; the newer view replaces it by a truth. The older position was based on two assumptions: the first, the belief that every one who realized the nature of his acts was necessarily free, for every willed action was regarded as a free act; the second, the belief that freedom existed to a like extent for all men with reference to the same act. If such were really the case, if for all persons there were operative identical factors of equal value and degree, there would be no need to consider the individual. He might as well be eliminated from the penal equation – just as in an algebraic equation, equal quantities on the two sides may be cancelled.

But can the freedom of the will be so simply conceived? Let us consider the first assumption, that every willed act is a free act. The formula may be accepted in the sense in which the 'spiritualists' maintain that every voluntary act emanates from a being capable of exercising freedom. But this statement must not be confused with the classic formula of the French penal law which held that every voluntary act was a free act. Volition and freedom are not to be made identical. To posit these as the two terms of an equation is wholly false.

The fallacy enters because a possible state of affairs is confused with the situation that actually is realized. As a possibility the deed accomplished may be considered as on a par with the alternative of restraint. A man fires a gun at another; we know that to fire or not to fire are like possibilities. We conclude that the murderer was well able to realize the alternatives, to act or to refrain. If we believe thereby to have proven that he was as free to act in the one way as in the other, and thus to have established the freedom of his will, we are relying upon an argument that clearly is fallacious. The fallacy consists in substituting a general and abstract situation for a special and concrete one. It is true that man abstractly considered enjoys the potential power to realize an act or to refrain therefrom. But does this prove that a particular man at a particular juncture of his career enjoyed the moral freedom to determine his conduct? This we cannot know. It is as though one were to say that a horse when unrestrained may go forward or backward; he has the same control, the same possibility of either movement. If he goes forward, does it follow that he has chosen one alternative rather than the other? Does it follow that, as a free moral agent, he has made a free choice? [...] there can be no question of freedom when the idea of choice does not enter the mind. Freedom involves the power to anticipate one course or another, and the power to represent possible alternatives; but in particular it involves the consciousness of one's freedom. Now this is precisely the human prerogative; man foresees, mentally reflects upon his intention, has the consciousness of freedom, of the power to choose one course or another. The consciousness of self-determination involves the power to act, as is preferred, in one direction or in its opposite. Moreover, if in accord with the determinist position and the results of physiological experiment, the mechanical impulse to action depends upon the cerebral intensity of the thought, then the presence of the ability to realize the future, to have in mind appropriate images and ideas, is adequate to establish the presence of freedom. It becomes the power to distinguish between right and wrong.

In this argument there is at once a subtle confusion to disentangle and a distinction to be drawn. Is freedom as realized an intellectual process? If so, then the intensity of the thought determines the freedom. This would be a deterministic position, provided that it be established that the will is effective in the realm of ideas rather than in that of action. But it is just this that may be questioned. May it not be, on the contrary (approaching the thesis of M. Fouillée in his 'Determinism' and in his 'Insistent Ideas'), that the knowledge of our freedom makes us masters of our will, and free agents? But this, in turn, is but one aspect of a psychological determinism in that it makes freedom at once the cause and the effect of the idea of freedom. With this reservation we turn to the statement that freedom of the will consists in the idea of being free; it is man's consciousness of his own freedom. To have the consciousness of being a free agent is all that is necessary to realize one's freedom. This ideal aspect of freedom acts upon the will as an independent motive, and is summarized in the expression: It is my will because I wish it so. The thought of setting the will to act itself determines the will; and, likewise, the consciousness of possessing freedom exempts us from dependence upon merely instinctive impulses or physiological forces.

Approaching the question from this direction, and admitting the philosophical validity thereof and admitting likewise that the consciousness which we have of our own freedom is an effective force which in a measure makes real the freedom itself, does it follow, when the question is shifted to the practical field of penal law – which alone is here to be considered – that every one in relation to a given act has experienced such adequate consciousness of his freedom?

[...]

The conclusion that emerges from this discussion – that freedom is a potential quality of our nature – is a conviction capable of logical defense. The illusion, or better, the indefensible fiction, consists in supposing that such freedom is realized in each actual situation as a profound and intimate motive force that serves as an intermediary between the will and the external world.

It is undeniable, even for the most normal and well-regulated mind, that in regard to many actions, including crimes, this potential freedom (which is not questioned) does not exist as a real and available motive, acting independently and contributing the decisive impulse. This of itself demonstrates that the fundamental assumption of our classic penal law that every willed act is a free act, or, at least, an act committed in a state of freedom, is false, artificial, and fictitious.

Turning to the second assumption that serves as the foundation of the classic theory, we may examine the position that, inasmuch as freedom is a spontaneous force, unaffected by extraneous influences, every act involves the same measure of freedom. Under this view there is no question of greater or less – one is either free or not. The traditional conception of the freedom of the will inevitably reaches the surprising result that there is no partial freedom, no state of semi-liberty.

Considering freedom as something intelligible, and neglecting the metaphysical obscurity attaching to the concept, it can be nothing else than the inherent ability to resist. As applied to a criminal act, freedom is the power to resist the evil impulse; and this, in turn, is the strength of character that may be appealed to, to oppose the inherent instincts and passions. If this is true, how can it be maintained that the power to resist evil remains the same for every one, or for each individual at all times and for all situations? To put the question is to answer it. It is fact of consciousness, a common experience, that an act, above the purely automatic and instinctive stage, is often the issue of an apparent hesitation, of a choice implying antagonistic influences and at times fierce conflicts. And these occur precisely and particularly where the consciousness of freedom, and accordingly the sense of duty, is actively present. There come to consciousness the force of impulses and the push of instincts, and opposed thereto, rational considerations. The conflict grows, and the impulses succeed in obscuring the outlook, in suppressing the sense of duty and the sense of freedom; and in the end they overcome the surviving power of resistance, dissipate it into a vague and inert idea, and deprive it of value as a counteracting motive.

This cumulative power of the will depends upon many familiar conditions. It depends upon the state of health or the presence of a pathological factor, quite apart from the question of true mental disorder. To use the accredited expression, there may be a real disorder of the will involving an almost physical incapacity to will. Such aboulia is a common sign of neurasthenia. The status of the will depends upon habit, in short, upon character; and this varies for each individual and for each of the several possible aspects of his personality. It is unnecessary to enlarge upon what is established by common experience.

[...]

The view that seems likely to prevail substitutes a reality for a fiction; and inasmuch as it must deal with responsibility and hold to some belief in freedom, it builds upon a true responsibility in place of an assumed responsibility. It aims to substitute the realities of experience for pure judicial abstractions; to give fact a place above law, the spirit of observation a place above legal spirit.

[...]

The system of assumptions and fictions should long since have been recognized as untenable. It is time to replace by a concrete examination of the facts of the case.

[...]

The first application thereof was made by the jury. The latter naturally would not submit to the subtleties of legal assumptions. They might be informed that every man accused of the same crime had a like responsibility and consequently should be given a like punishment. But they were brought face to face with the defendant as he disclosed the details of his life, the impulses to which he was subject, the delusions that distorted his outlook; and the jury recognized that, quite apart from the question of insanity, there may be degrees of freedom, and consequently degrees of responsibility. But having no power to grade the responsibility, since the law made no such provision, they simply found for acquittal.

In 1824 with some limitations, and in 1832, in a more general provision, there was introduced a concession to this tendency of juries to recognize extenuating circumstances. The term indicates the purpose in mind. It was not to adjust the punishment to the degree of perversion of the individual, but to the degree of responsibility; that is, to the precise moral status of the act in question. It was an individualization based upon and measured by responsibility.

The penal code considered in the first instance the case of minors. It made the distinction as an individual one and not as the result of a presumption. The exemption of minors was not in deference to a period of presumed irresponsibility in regard to crime, but to a legal incapacity to commit crime, as the phrase goes. Any minor of whatever age, even a young child, may be liable to criminal prosecution. But the question of the presence of normal discretion must be raised, and thereby the question of responsibility becomes an individual one. Modern practice proposes to introduce and apply an analogous procedure in regard to adults.

[...]

But what other procedure is available? The question may be consistently answered. If responsibility is based upon freedom, it should necessarily end where freedom of the will ends. Every defendant should have the right to establish that the deed of which he is accused was not a free act. Unquestionably the absence of free will may be proven apart from the existence of true insanity. Hence a concession allowed by many modern legislatures is the admission that the establishment of irresponsibility is an evidence of a lack of free will, and that such evidence is possible apart from cases of true insanity. In dealing with this problem modern legislation was called upon to take a position upon the metaphysical question of free will.

[...]

The consequences of the new conception of responsibility are clear. If you start from the concrete question of the freedom of the will and determine to what degree a criminal act has been committed in full freedom, you necessarily reach two conclusions: the first, to exempt from punishment when it is established pathologically or psychologically that freedom of the will was absent; and the second, to reduce and lower the punishment when it is established that the defendant exercised only a partial freedom.

[...]

We thus reach an individualization of punishment, which, once and for all, replaces the entire punitive procedure prescribed by the law according to the outer character of the crime – an individualization adjusted not to the crime but to the organic, latent, or manifest criminality of the individual. This point alone persists; the conception of responsibility disappears, and individualization takes its place; and we reach the order of ideas and the sphere of action of the Italian school. Their definition of individualization becomes merely the utilization of repressive measures to attain the essential end, which is the elimination of criminality either by the moral reform of the criminal, or, if not amenable to reform, by his segregation; and in either case the adaptation of the punishment to the psychological character of the criminal.

From: R. Saleilles (1911) The Individualization of Punishment, trans. from the second French edition by Rachel Szold Jastrow. London: William Heineman, pp. 64– 67, 70–71, 72, 74, 75–76, 79, 83 and 134.

12. Reforming criminals

Thomas Holmes

To sum up what I conceive to be the reforms necessary to the abatement and cure of hooliganism:

1. Fair rents for the poor, and a fair chance of cleanliness and decency.
2. Municipal playgrounds and organized competitive games.
3. Extension of school-life till sixteen.
4. Prohibition to young people of alcoholic drinks for consumption on the premises.
5. Limitation by law of the alcoholic strength of malt liquor to 22 per cent and of spirits to 50 per cent under proof, with higher duty.

Give us reforms on these lines, and there will be no 'complaining in our streets.' The poorest of the poor, though lacking riches, will know something of the wealth of the mind, for chivalry and manhood, gentleness and true womanhood, will be their characteristics. The rounded limbs and happy hearts of 'glorious childhood' will be no longer a dream or a fiction. No longer will the bitter cry be raised of 'too old' when the fortieth birthday has passed, for men will be in their full manhood at sixty. Give us these reforms, and enable the poor to live in clean and sweet content, then their sons shall be strong in body and mind to fight our battles, to people our colonies, and to hand down to future ages a goodly heritage. But there is a content born of indifference, of apathy, of despair. There is the possibility that the wretched may become so perfect in their misery that a wish for better things and aspirations after a higher life may die a death from which there is no resurrection. From apathetic content may God deliver the poor! from such possibilities may wise laws protect them! 'Righteousness' – right doing – 'exalteth a nation;' and a nation whose poor are content because they can live in cleanliness, decency, and virtue, where brave boyhood and sweet girlhood can bud, blossom, and mature, is a nation that will dwell long in the land, and among whom the doings of the hooligans will be no longer remembered.

From: T. Holmes (1908) Known to the Police. *London: Edward Arnold, pp. 180–1.*

13. The probation system

Cecil Leeson

The attitude of the probation officer to the probationer is such as would be adopted by a sensible friend; for the essence of probation is constructive friendship. The officer will be neither a sentimentalist merely, on the one hand, nor a dictator or bully, on the other. At the same time, the officer is there to get things done. He must know what action to take, and with firmness as well as sympathy he must act up to his knowledge. And though he will not threaten without just cause, he will, when the occasion demands it, not hesitate to remind offenders refusing his suggestions of the court which is behind him [...] The following cases illustrate the value of home visitation:

> 'I visited a home some time ago, and among the complaints was that the husband came home in bad temper, and tried to get rid of the children. Then he would go to the saloon. He said to me, I get home at night, and the supper isn't ready; the lamps are not trimmed; the dishes, perhaps, are not cleared away: there is nothing to encourage me to stay at home. I visit the saloon, and So-and-so comes in and orders a glass of beer, sometimes two. The saloon-keeper told me the man spent most of his time in the saloon reading. About half-past-nine he gets up and goes home. We had a friendly visitor call on that lady (the man's wife), and after a while things were running along smoothly. The man didn't leave the house, and they got on very happily.'

Had this man been required merely to report himself at the probation office, the real cause of his home neglect could never have come to light at all. The reason for child delinquency is usually to be found in the home:

> 'Many parents will let their children go out in the evening, and then go to bed themselves. I found a boy on the street after twelve o'clock. I took him to his home, and rapped on the door till the father got up. He didn't seem to care whether the boy was out or in.'

[...]

In many places the probation office becomes something of an employment bureau; the probation officers have become well known to local employers, and thus have been able to do much in finding work for their probationers. Regular work has a special value to most probationers, a disciplinary and therapeutic value, and, of course, every effort should be made to keep them steadily employed. At the same time, it is a good rule to do nothing for the probationer that he can do for himself. And, in this instance, it may prove that the probation officer will benefit his charge more lastingly by explaining to him how to use the Labour Exchange, and by seeing that he perseveres with it, than he will by actually finding the work for him.

[...]

One of the principal things the probation officer has to do is to make use of existing social agencies. The officer knows that in the offender's life he is but a passing agent, not a permanent one. His endeavour, therefore, is to put his charges in touch with such permanent social and religious agencies as are appropriate to their individual need; his purpose, of course, being that these agencies shall continue to influence the offenders' lives long after the probationary period terminates.

From: C. Leeson (1914) The Probation System. *London: P. S. King & Son, pp. 114–24.*

14. Working with women

Mrs Cary

I think we are agreed that Probation work among women is more difficult and tedious than that among men [...] it is also more expensive. There are certain subtle sex differences – which, by the way, even the bestowal of the vote would not obliterate and these differences react upon the work: whether you want to or not, the women must be coddled more than the men. You fit a man out for work, give him a second pair of socks, and a second shirt in a parcel, or even the two simultaneously upon his hack, in the manner of a man of whom we heard the other day! – a secondhand suit of clothes, and a strong pair of boots, and, behold, he is more or less complete, and you may turn him out like a modern Don Quixote to tilt at Fortune! But you essay to place a woman or girl in decent domestic service, which is usually the best thing you can do for her, and you must fit her out from top to toe with the dozen and one odd things, including caps, collars, cuffs, ribbons, etc., which go to form a neat and attractive exterior. Then, to borrow the phrase of the defunct Free Trade parrot, even your food, or *her* food, will cost you more! With 6d. or 8d. in his hand, you may send your youth to get a good square meal at the nearest coffee shop, but send your girl – and, well, she *might* elope with the first carman or Carter Paterson's van boy who found time between the mouthfuls to steal a smile and a wink at her! Now for the figures of my actual experience of the Probation Act. During the last three years I have dealt with 108 cases on probation.

From: Mrs Cary (1913) *'The Value of the Probation System as Applied to Women'*, National Association of Probation Officers, 3: 14–15.

15. Social clubs for girls

Mrs Cary

Now to talk of the practical part of the work [...] Seventeen years have gone over my head since I first took up Police Court Missionary work, and for the last few years I have concentrated most upon the work among the girls. Those charged with theft, soliciting, drunkenness, and attempted suicide. Also some maternity cases, and some young preventives brought to the Court by friends or relatives. Working in the East End, I found that except for the girls having good or fairly decent homes, and being accustomed to business or factory work, and unwilling to take up any other line of labour, the wisest if not the only hopeful scheme was to remove them from their surroundings and get them into service in a good class neighbourhood. Where they are willing to enter Homes for a year or more the need of an evening club is not at first apparent. But many girls will not go into Homes, or, going, will not remain, or act in such a way as to be expelled [...] My method is to place such girls for a week or two, perhaps more, in a shelter, get them cleaned, give them such polish – alack! but little – as may be acquired in so short a time, fit them up with clothing, and then, by dint of much letter writing and many interviews, find a mistress who will take and train such a girl [...] Two years or more ago I found myself with half a score of girls in service near me, with nowhere – that is no good and wholesome place – to spend their evenings out. Streets and parks and picture palaces are hardly uplifting influences – at least, as these girls use them. Willy-nilly, therefore, I threw open my drawing room to them, and behold me returning, evening after evening, tired out and cross – yes, cross! [...] It was very bad for my nerves and furniture, and not amusing enough for the girls. So 15 months ago I rallied my friends to help me, and hired rooms at our local Church Institute in Chelsea. There we meet on one or two evenings a week. We gossip, play table games, partake of tea and cakes, skip, dance – how we do dance! [...] Singing and acting too is not beyond us, and a few months ago we gave what I was afterwards assured was one of the season's best concerts for our local Church of England Temperance [...]

Then in the club gatherings it is possible to get to know these girls in their relationship to others. To tone down the horseplay to which some are prone when excited, to try and lift conversation from silly innuendo and spiteful back-biting to a higher level. To teach them to play fairly and without loss of temper. Then, too, we never close without our little prayer gathering and hymn singing.

From: *Mrs Cary (1915) 'Social Clubs for Probationers; Their Needs and Objects'*, National Association of Probation Officers, *6: 102–3.*

16. Work with children

H. Chinn

The Probation Officer visits at the home of the offender, and introduces himself as the Probation Officer attached to the Court, and as discreetly as possible explains to the parents that he is making inquiries as to the character of the child, and it is his wish to help them in every possible way. I make it a point, if convenient, to interview the father, because you and I know that such a great deal is concealed from the knowledge of fathers by easy-going mothers, who fear his wrath in regard to the offending child. It may be assumed that this causes family discord, but I have never found this to be so; on the contrary, I generally find parents to be willing to give any information I may require. I find, too, that it is not wise when conducting this inquiry to question the child about the offence, or converse with parents in his presence. The Head Teacher at his school will often be a very useful source of information; and here I may say that in Birmingham we have a staff of Head Teachers who work with the Probation Officers splendidly, and do add considerably to their success. There are very few parents who really wish to see their children go wrong, and more than once it has struck me as marvellous how confiding the parents have been to me in this preliminary inquiry, and look to you as having a friend at court. In nearly every case you get these questions, 'Shall you be there?' 'How do you think he will get on?' This is where one's diplomacy steps in, and we must not, under any circumstances, raise false hopes, or we shall probably hear of it later on when the child is dealt with by the Court and placed on probation.

The report is impartial, and of such a nature that persons interested should be able to read it if required to do so, and is only handed to the Magistrates after they have heard all the evidence and decided to convict. Of course, this preliminary inquiry causes the Probation Officer considerable work, especially when he has about 100 cases on probation, but it is to the officer a great help, for you know from your observations of the home surroundings what kind of parents you have to deal with and the child's chances of making a useful citizen. You know a great deal more than you care to put on your report for the Magistrates' information, and as an experienced officer trusted by the Court you should know what kind of treatment is best for the influence that tells in the end. I have two brothers now on probation for larceny. Father and mother were living apart when brought before the Court; another member of the family in an Industrial School. Father allowed his wife 15s. weekly, and she lived in a furnished room with four children. After a few visits I found the mother was a secret drinker and neglected the children. Father was in regular work, and by pointing out to him the conditions under which the children were living and his own responsibility he consented to give his wife another trial. He provided a home in a better neighbourhood, and for the past two months they have gone on very well. The home is clean, the children are better cared for, and the mother has given up the drink. There was no chance at all for these children unless the home was put right. It is not advisable for Probation Officers to act the role of Relieving officers. Our duty is to try and teach self-reliance and thrift, but there are times when we have the power and know by what means we can get a little assistance for persons who, through no fault of their own, need a little lift. One of these instances occurred only last month. Father of boy on probation suddenly fell sick. He was employed as a labourer at a tube mill. He had five young children and only 10s. per week, panel pay, coming in. They managed all right for a fortnight, then things began to go out of the house. I suggested applying to our City Aid Society, and endorsed the application myself. They received sufficient relief to tide them over their misfortune and to escape the parish help. These people were honest folk, and too proud to ask for assistance. Perhaps it would be as well for me to mention that outside our ordinary Court work we are appealed to for advice by parents, and sometimes the police send on particulars of children who they think need a little friendly admonition, and I may say the police in Birmingham are very sympathetic in their treatment of juvenile offenders, and give Probation Officers much assistance.

From: H. Chinn (1916) 'Probation Work among Children', National Association of Probation Officers, *7: 123–5.*

17. Difficult cases

C. Rankin

Lawlessness, the lack of respect for law and authority, is today the greatest menace to our country and to its future. But when we see the home conditions of the children that are brought before the court, and the ignorance, the indifference, the incompetence of the parents, and that unskilled labour is not wanted anywhere, then we wonder that youth is as law-abiding as it is, and that our problems are not more difficult.

I know there is no universal panacea for these cases, but experience is the finest schoolmaster; an ounce is worth a ton of theory, and so I sought the co-operation of several Probation Officers in the country in the preparation of this Paper, inviting them to submit a problem from experience [...] I have selected a few, some very ordinary, others more complicated.

Problem No. 1

A child is charged with stealing and wilful damage. He is a truant from school. Parents are of dissolute habits, weak of character, anxious to get rid of the child until such time as he is old enough to become a wage-earning factor in the home. What shall the Probation Officer do? Endeavour to send the child *away* to an Institution, under the plea that it is in the interest of the child? In my humble opinion that is but pandering to the desires of the incompetent and unnatural parents, and should only be the 'die-hard' ditch of the Probation Officer, i.e., the last resort.

A suggested solution is: That the Probation Officer find out why he is beyond control, why he steals, or wanders abroad and commits damage. If the parents conduce to the offence and the Probation Officer is able to prove it, a special Bench of Magistrates might summon the parents under Section 99 of the Children Act, for conducing to the offence, and if found guilty bound over on probation to improve the home, etc.: thus the law becomes a redemptive power in the hands of the Magistracy and Probation becomes a success.

[...]

Problem No. 4

I remember having a very troublesome boy of 12 years, regarded by the Police as ringleader in offences. Home fairly good, control nil. Parents regarded his offences as not bad, and they allowed the boy to know what they thought. He was finally brought to Court for breaking and entering a shop and stealing. Placed under my supervision with a caution that he would be sent to a Reformatory if not careful, etc.

I began by emphasising my desire for his friendship, and my desire to help him. I found him mentally wrong; he had been examined by a doctor, but he refused to certify him; still I felt he was so and do now.

In a few weeks he was again in Court on a similar charge; the parents made an agonising appeal to me. This was my opportunity for dealing with them, and gained a pledge if I succeeded in getting a Probation Order again they would follow my instructions and control him and co-operate in my methods. I obtained a new Probation Order. Knowing the lad had some regard and affection I appealed to latter virtues and feigned illness, got him concerned, and then told him he was the cause of a big pain under my heart; thus he became interested in my welfare. I ventured to suggest that he could help me to get well, and he could give me the right medicine by letter. The idea took and I helped him to prescribe my remedies. If conduct good he sent me a bottle drawn on paper labelled 'This will do you good'; if conduct not so good bottle labelled 'A little nasty', and on my visits I was either better or worse. He became interested, and remained at home away from the company he had kept owing to parents becoming more anxious to help. After some time I asked him for a tonic to buck me up, as the medicine he had sent was doing me good. Then I was convalescent – this meant I visited less frequently. Later I changed from medicine and tonic to a few pills, pointing out the advertisement about Williams' Pink Pills, and so he finished his Probation satisfactorily to the wonder of Police, who were sure he never would go straight; but he has done to this day.

From: C. Rankin (1921) 'The Problem of the Difficult Case', National Association of Probation Officers, *16: 321–3.*

18. The failure of prison and the value of treatment

Mary Gordon

During my service I found nothing in the prison system to interest me, except as a gigantic irrelevance – a social curiosity. If the system had a good effect on any prisoner, I failed to mark it. I have no shadow of doubt of its power to demoralize, or of its cruelty. It appears to me not to belong to this time or civilization at all.

My main argument here is that we not only do not deter, but that we do actually make-over our criminal to crime. The fallacy of applying force to a being who is inherently insusceptible of being managed by force, lies in the fact that the proceeding ends, not in the alteration of the prisoner's point of view, but in his spiritually triumphing over us, and bringing the strong arm of the law to naught. We merely ill-treat a man or woman who still ignores and escapes us.

The time is ripe for us to convince ourselves of this. We should turn a fresh leaf in our treatment of the offender, fortified not by precedent, or by age-long prejudice, but by the findings of science which is, at last, in the act of discovering the mechanism of the whole man. We know enough already about how he 'works' to be able to consider when, under stress, he falls, what to be at in the matter of restoring him. We should act on what we know. When we have abandoned penal discipline we must not let ourselves be dismayed by the size of our scrap-heap, or the cost of our new road, but take up the problem anew, and get on with solving it. [...]

If it appears to us true that our system of penal discipline is a failure, and even something more; that ordinary short terms of imprisonment fail to impress, punish, or deter the vast majority of petty offenders; that the Borstal System owing to the preponderance of penal discipline punishes heavily, but shows no conspicuously good results; that penal servitude only sets a seal on our mistakes in dealing with the prisoner, what, to be practical, are we to substitute?

Certainly no ready-made System will serve our turn. We need, in the first place, the substitution of one principle of treatment for another.

Society has a right to define offences and to require its members not to commit them, and control must assuredly enter into the treatment of offenders. The only conceivable alternative to penal discipline is sufficient control to prevent offences, combined with scientific treatment of the prisoner's symptoms, that is, of his crime.

His symptoms are to be found rooted in the emotional and mental sphere, and must be met on that ground. Treatment must be founded on the psychology, attitude, and whole condition of the prisoner, and we must recognize that we cannot control his anti-social activities, unless we afford him as full opportunities as can possibly be arranged, for the exercise of those free choices which alone can preserve him as a sane, free man. Our control should provide that he is not shielded from natural consequences from which he can learn, nor prevented from acquiring anything lawful that is of value to him, nor punished under detention with petty punishments.

[...]

The deferred sentence appears to me to be one of the best methods by which offenders could be controlled. Under such a method the prisoner would understand, when it is the case that he is convicted, and that therefore whenever the community chooses it can take away his liberty. He should understand that he owes the community something which it intends to get from him, but that, if he pays something on account his bill will be allowed to run. In short, he should be convicted but not deprived of his liberty unless it is found absolutely necessary. The sentence should continue to be valid all his life or for a number of years, and meantime, whether it is executed or not, he should have to do something as a guarantee of good behaviour for a certain period.

[...]

Let us rather hand him over, not to the hangman, but to the doctor, to the man of science, to the student of the whole man, to the educator, to the man who knows himself in so far as human knowledge will allow of it, to the man who can bring the most of human knowledge, human resource, and human feeling to bear on the problem, which we – have utterly failed to solve.

The relationship has been called the soul of casework, while the processes of study, diagnosis, and treatment have been called the body. This analogy indicates a conceptual distinction and a real unity. Both are a species of human interaction. In both there is a back-and-forth movement of some form of human energy. In the relationship the interaction is primarily internal, and the energy consists of feelings and attitudes. In study, diagnosis, and treatment the interaction is primarily external, and the energy consists principally of words and actions. The unity of these interactions in actual casework is similar to the unity of living things. The external interactions may produce, manifest, and affect the internal interactions; the latter, in turn, may affect the former. They are inseparable in reality; without a good relationship the processes of interviewing, study, diagnosis, and treatment are lifeless services.

From: *Mary Gordon (1922)* Penal Discipline. *London: Routledge, pp. xi; 222–3; 225–6; 237–8.*

19. The spiritual factor

F. Poulton

It is here we come to the heart of our subject. The Probation Officer, viewing his probationers, will regard them not merely as so many cases but as individual human beings – spiritual as well as physical – and as such he will apply his efforts towards both parts of their nature. He will fully recognise the importance of such uplifting factors as education, good surroundings, employment and recreation – each having its part in the necessary discipline of body and mind and the production of the character which makes good citizens. But he will also see that along with, and perhaps above, them all goes the spiritual factor. These factors are not necessarily separate; it is not correct to divide them up into watertight compartments, e.g., social, religious, etc. In fact, they are all in a broad but real sense means employed by the divine spirit to bring about purposes in men and women. Probation, however, may be said to be essentially a spiritual principle and one clearly to be found in the teachings of Jesus Christ. He it was who made the Probation order in the Parable of the Fig Tree – 'Let it alone for this year also, and if it bear fruit – Well! – but if not, then punish.' I venture to say that no Probation Officer can have gone very far with his work without becoming deeply sensible of the tremendous part which spirit action occupies in the re-formation of a life.

From: F. Poulton (1925) 'The Spiritual Factor in Probation Work', National Association of Probation Officers, 23: 546–7.

20. Principles of a rational penal code

Sheldon Glueck

Underlying social-ethical principle of penal code

The basic social-ethical principle of any system of penal law should express the *raison d'être* of that system. Too often in the past has the basic principle of penal codes been implied, rather than expressed and defended, with the result that our penal statutes are full of confusions and inconsistencies, containing statutory and case-law accretions of many epochs and philosophies. We submit the following basic principle: *Society should utilize every scientific instrumentality for self-protection against destructive elements in its midst, with as little interference with the free life of its members as is consistent with such social self-protection.* This proposition is basic to any discussion of social problems. If one denies that a society should protect itself, he not only denies to it the fundamental right of self-preservation, but jeopardizes his own security. Only by repelling criminal attacks against itself or its members can organized society offer the peace, security, and traditional expectancy of orderliness which are indispensable to the pursuit of the affairs of life by itself and its members. One who denies this indirectly advocates his own destruction.

In this basic work of self-protection, society should utilize every available scientific instrumentality. This is dictated both by the principle of justice and that of economy. While society has a primary interest in maintaining the general security, it also has an interest in the welfare of the individual life, and a duty to use every reasonable instrumentality for the rehabilitation of its anti-social members. Even a socially harmful criminal has a right, in justice, to be treated with those instrumentalities that give him the greatest promise of self-improvement and rehabilitation.

Justice demands also that, in its work of self-protection, society interfere as little as possible with the free life of its members. If one conceives of society as a necessary instrument for the harmonious integration of the more or less conflicting desires of human beings with the demands of the general welfare, one must acknowledge that social interference should cease at the point where such integration cannot be brought about by interference. A law or procedure, which, in the general opinion, unnecessarily or arbitrarily overemphasizes the social interest in the general security to the undue interference with the social and individual interests in the life and well-being of each person, is unjust, for it unnecessarily enslaves human beings. Not only justice but economy dictates the employment of scientific devices in the work of social self-protection. It is wasteful for society to be satisfied with a continuance of the present judicial and peno-correctional regimes, because the large figures of recidivism are an indication that the present methods are not preventing criminals from repeating their anti-social behavior.

From: S. Glueck (1928) 'Principles of a Rational Penal Code', Harvard Law Review, *41: 453–82.*

21. The prison chaplain

Victor Serge

Only one visitor crosses the threshold of the cell: the almoner, priest, minister, or rabbi. He brings the alms of his presence, the alms of his words *and* gestures. His faith matters no more than the belief or disbelief of the man in the cell. Guards and officials blend into the walls themselves, the Judases, bars and bolts. You feel in the marrow of your bones that they are no more than cogs in the prison machine. And this is reciprocal: Human beings no longer exist for them. Only such and such a number occupying such and such a cell. The cell counts, not the crowd of inmates, not man. This chaplain is a man. And not an enemy. He is interested only in man. His profession is oddly anachronistic. He is concerned with that undefinable *je ne sais quoi*, the soul.

'The soul?' – laughed an eighteen-year old inmate, 'Catholic' and totally agnostic – 'I think it's a dumping ground for the old blues.'

[…]

This pastor, a man of great kindness, open and broadminded, had been carrying on his disconcerting mission as prisoners' chaplain and a prison official for perhaps a quarter of a century.

I remember his low voice, the heavy shaking of his head, his deep sigh when he said to me one gray afternoon:

'Many are those I have accompanied to the scaffold to hide it from them a few more seconds before the end, so that the last voice they would hear would be mine, crying: "May God help you!" Many …'

The whole ambiguous duplicity of the chaplain's calling was apparent to me here, as was the whole revolting sham of his function. Even more revolting because the man was sincere and kind, resigned to his sacerdotal calling with that inner toughness that a social conscience gives to the intelligent bourgeois. The guillotine, doubtless, is not Christian. But the guillotine is necessary to the Christians. The death of Pierre Durand, at a predetermined hour, 'by verdict of law,' on that seesaw plank, is a horrible thing. But the justice that commands that death is sacred. The pastor's duty is to sympathize with Pierre Durand's final anguish. His 'social' duty is to make sure the guillotine functions properly. Christian compassion plays its part, as does the oiling of the blade.

Once a week, the chaplain comes over to the prison. His stomach lined with a good lunch, his hands in the pockets of a well-tailored overcoat, appropriate to the season, his mind occupied by the ordinary things of life, our chaplain crosses the city. On the way over, he is perhaps distracted by the display in a bookstore window, an elegant silhouette, the morning's headlines, the stock-market quotations. In his mind he maps out his day:

Three to five o'clock, prison. Be at the editorial office of *Church Life* at 5:30 … 6:30 promised to call on such and such a lady …

He thinks, as he approaches the prison, that eighty men are waiting for him in their cells. Including: one condemned man who will not be pardoned; two or three who will probably be condemned; a dozen 'lifers'; that little D*** who is so ill; B*** who is always lying and begging for favors; H*** who prays and scoffs; Z*** who is becoming more and more unhinged. The thought of all these sufferings which he sees and cannot relieve saddens the chaplain. Eighty! And the prison is so big. Five minutes to get from the Fifth Division to the Fourteenth. The chaplain is out of breath.

At the gatehouse, the chaplain shakes some jailers' hands …

Whenever he hears the sudden clang of the doors being unlocked, the stoop-shouldered boy with the jaundiced face of a sick fox who occupies Cell Number 8–6 feels his heart beating anxiously. The chaplain has just read his card in the file: 'Nineteen years old, theft. Breaking and entering.' The name is unfamiliar. Sad. Let's go in. The hunted man, in his cage, gives an embarrassed greeting. Then he asserts that he is innocent. Innocent. That he is hungry: dying of hunger, the soup is nothing but water. That his father and mother no longer recognize him as their son. That he is without news of his wife, who has had a miscarriage. He is gentle. 'I can't go on,' he says, smiling, 'it's too much all at once.' It's true, all too true. Between the two men hangs an invisible balance, and with each little phrase the weights of suffering fall on the guilty man's side, keep on falling. The chaplain can do nothing. Theft with breaking and entering, he thinks: five years' confinement; with extenuating circumstances, two years of prison. And the disciplinary battalions in Africa, in all probability.

'Would you like a Bible, my son?'

Oh! Yes! the nineteen-year-old-theft-with-breaking-and-entering wants a Bible, a book, a fat book.

'Read the *Book of Job.* He, too, thought he was abandoned even by God …'

The nineteen-year-old-theft-with-breaking-and-entering will read the *Book of Job.* But the chaplain knows very well, deep down, that if the Almighty led Job out of captivity and blessed him until 'he had fourteen thousand sheep, and six thousand camels, and a thousand yoke of oxen, and a thousand she asses,' and 'he had also seven sons and three daughters,'

'… and after this lived Job an hundred and forty years,'

'… and died, being old and full of days,'

as is written in Chapter XLII, Verses 12, 13, 16, and 17 of the Holy Writ – this poor bastard here is poorer than Job, and no one will shorten his suffering by a day …

The next cell smells bad. The man *who coughs in it* never opens the window. Very clean, nonetheless, ageless, impassive, as if withdrawn from his own life. An undeniable murderer on his way to the scaffold. The matter is closed. His deepest concern is for his soul. Before this door had closed on him, he never even suspected he had a soul. He hardly ever thought. Gambling, the races, women, Mitzi (whose throat he neatly cut one night with a razor). Now he prays a great deal. His eyes have grown larger, round, shadowy, glassy.

'I go up in two weeks,' he says this time.

The chaplain understands the allusion to the next session of the criminal court. With his long experience, he is able to calculate fairly accurately the number of days this man has left to live: there are the three days allowed for filing an appeal, the examination of the appeal, the appeal for clemency to the President of the Republic, the time necessary to prepare the execution. It's now April; all of that will bring us up to July … This calculation is rapidly traced in the chaplain's brain. He rests his firm, ruddy hand on the shoulder of the man-who-will-be-guillotined:

'Would you like it if we prayed together for you, my friend?'

Eighty! The chaplain won't be able to see more than thirty today. In two hours, subtracting the time needed to get around the prison, that leaves three minutes and thirty seconds for each visit. At five o'clock the chaplain goes away.

[…]

Twice a month, on Sunday morning, the minister conducts a service. The prison has a rudimentary church, Protestant chapel, and synagogue: everything that is necessary to render unto God what is God's. The Protestant chapel is cellular in construction, and this invention simultaneously brings the science of prisons and the practice of religion to a remarkable degree of perfection.

There is a semicircle composed of several successive rows of cells. A man is placed in each of these compartments, divided from one another by oak partitions. They make you think of vertical coffins. All you can see in front of you are the pastor's pulpit and the two back windows. In one of these windows you can make out the corner of a window ledge. Birds come and perch there. Life! At the foot of the pulpit, looking bored, stands the guard on duty.

The pastor speaks of the Holy Writ and of terrestrial matters to his strange flock of pale men, each motionless in his cell. He sometimes quotes Saint Paul's words, quite appropriate in front of these starving sometime criminals ('Sloth is the mother of all the vices'): *He who does not work shall not eat!* His bass voice is deep; and what he says about the divine legend strikes deeply into these minds unhinged by a hellish existence; what he says about bourgeois morality touches the minds of these unlucky, defeated men to the very quick. Others go to chapel in order to pass a 'telegram' from hand to hand: 'to Number Seven in the row, look out – and don't get nabbed!' The latter keep their faces silent in respectful hypocrisy. Their hands joined, they bow their heads during the prayer.

'Our Father who art in heaven! Hallowed be thy name. Thy kingdom come. Thy will be done, on earth as it is in heaven …'

On the way out, someone murmurs: 'Go on, you windbag! You get plenty to eat!'

Back from the chapel [...] Obedient ciphers, we wait in front of our doors for the 'screw' to come along and lock us up. My neighbor bends over the bucket, looks up at me and says, mocking:

'"Our Father who art in heaven ..." He's a nice guy, the Father! Bastard!'

From: V. Serge (1967) Men in Prison. *London: Writers & Readers Publishing Co-operative (originally published 1930), pp. 73–79.*

22. Religion in the penitentiary

Philip Priestley

The story of religion in the penitentiary, then, is one of a 'glorious revolution'; one that succeeded beyond the imagining of its originators in capturing the minds of prison administrators all over the newly industrializing world. Its immediate appeal rested partly in the moral and intellectual splendour of the proposed edifice; partly in the pretty drawings of the prison buildings that accompanied it – symmetrical representations of order and purpose; and partly in the missionary fervour with which the apostles of separation preached their creed. But most fundamentally these proposals and these plans were of 'machines for the time': the moral equivalents of the engines that drove the wheels of industry and possible means of bringing under control some of the runaway social turbulence that factories and railways and burgeoning towns drew in their train. But if the mechanical analogy was part of the allure that sold the *idea* of the penitential prison, it also suggested the instrument by which its subsequent performance was to be measured. Machines serve no other purpose than ornament if they fail to produce finished goods; as pumps lift water, looms fabricate cloth and lathes turn out machined parts, so the penitentiary, by the terms of its prospectus, was to re-form the criminal into a morally improved and better behaved citizen. Previous forms of imprisonment had failed to produce the required results. Joseph Kingsmill 'heard the late Chaplain of Clerkenwell say, that out of 100,000 prisoners who had passed under him, he knew only of two cases of true repentance towards God. Subsequently he told me that he found himself disappointed in both. This is a melancholy picture of prisons as they were, even under respectable men such as he was.' Small returns indeed from such a mighty winnowing of souls. The penitentiary promised to do better than that, and for a moment – a very brief moment – it was a promise that seemed to tremble on the brink of fulfilment. Enough of the first few drafts who passed through Pentonville managed to acquire sufficient fluency in the rhetoric of reclamation to convince the chaplains and their supporters that success was almost assured. But it was not to be.

To many prisoners of the later Victorian period, the monstrous chapel buildings, and the empty rituals that filled them, must have appeared like the inexplicable relics of a lost civilization. To their inventors they made sense. The logic of their construction followed impeccably from their basic premises

– but the foundations of the great machine had been sunk into the soft sand of an unreal view concerning the human material that was to be fed into it. These men and women and children – a few of them wicked and dangerous by any standard, but most of them convicted of what can reasonably only be thought of as trivial and minimally damaging offences – taught their masters and the moral projectors of the new prison a salutary lesson. It was a lesson that was bought at a dear price, and as usual, it was paid by those least able to afford it, in a despairing currency of broken minds and ill-used bodies.

But the damage the penitentiary did went deeper than broken promises and hurt minds. The void left by its collapse was progressively filled by a disciplinary timetable from which all humanity and all hope were all but extinguished. The original vision foresaw a dark tunnel of suffering, at the end of which there shone – however distantly – the light of redemption and salvation. When the light went out, the darkness closed in around the Victorian prisoner. It was not to be lifted again for a generation.

From: P. Priestley (1998) Victorian Prison Lives: English Prison Biography 1830–1914. *Random House, pp. 118–19.*

23. Techniques of social work

H. Weiss

[...]

John M had been in court four times, once for larceny, twice for drunkenness and the fourth time on *two* complaints of larceny in two different courts at about the same time. The larceny case in the first court involved approximately $250 while the one in the second consisted of a number of thefts totalling nearly $1,000. The case in the first court was continued until a decision was reached in the second.

The investigation of the probation officer in Court B disclosed the following situation: John M was a mechanic of normal intelligence with a good working record and high pay for his trade. He came from a home with the usual standards of a laborer's family of the better type. At the age of twenty-five he married a girl of his nationality and faith, of whom he was extremely fond. Her family had been less harmonious and she was spoiled especially by her father who did not get along with her mother. At first, things went fairly well. During the second year of this marriage, the young wife began to make excessive demands on her husband for clothing and amusement. When she failed to get her way she would leave the house and spend the evening with friends. This continued even after children were born to the couple. The children were fonder of their father than they were of the mother. Frequent scenes about money, about neglecting the children and on many other subjects led things from bad to worse. John began to drink, neglected his family and paid a bill on his car with a forged check. He lost his job, failed to steady himself enough to keep another one, and, having been dishonest once before, he made a desperate attempt to avoid a complete crash by meeting pressing debts with forged checks. When things became too hot for him, he disappeared to a distant city with money he had taken from his last employer. He was brought back by the police and turned over to the court. His family had been supported by a social agency.

This information, with many more details, was collected by the probation officer from John himself, from his parents, from his wife and her father, from two previous employers and from three social agencies to whom the family was known. John's parents blamed the wife, and John's father-in-law blamed him for the whole situation. One employer spoke well of him, while the other one (not the one from whom he took the money) claimed that he was sulky, unreliable and inefficient as a worker. Two of the social agencies had nothing good to say for him; the third, which had made a rather careful analysis of John's background and which was supporting his family during his desertion, felt that the whole catastrophe would never have happened if John had been well adjusted with a wife who would have been more sensible and would have understood how to guide him. The probation officer had several long interviews with John, and went over the whole situation with him. His childhood and youth were discussed, and so were his marital life and his professional career. At first, John blamed his tough luck, his wife, his employers and even his parents for not having sent him through high school. He resented the fact that his probation officer, who was asking him so many questions, happened to be a woman. He then began to reason what might have happened if this thing or that thing had been different in his life. The probation officer led him on, and the next step of his analysis was that he began to ask himself what would have been the result if *he* had done a few things differently. He ended by feeling truly sorry over it all and by being greatly discouraged. At this point, the probation officer did her most intensive thinking. Had he the stuff in him to make good, or was his attitude of remorse merely a temporary mood? Was he essentially weak or did he have qualities in him on which one could build? Was it possible that these years of unhappiness could so completely cover up those qualities, or did they not exist in him at all? If they did exist, what were they? His children were fond of him; he had been a good worker at one time; he had tried to please his wife; he had been a good son to his parents. But this had been years ago; could these qualities revive under wise guidance? The probation officer remembered having seen in the back yard of John's house a skilfully constructed aquarium with a miniature amusement park around it; the oldest boy pointed at it with pride and said: 'Daddy done this for me.' The work of art was of fairly recent date. The probation officer weighed all this against the crushing mass of unfavorable facts. She decided to take the risk though she was fully aware of the grave responsibility involved. She claimed later that, very probably, the aquarium had given her the courage to try it.

From: H. Weiss (1933) 'The Social Worker's Technique', in S. Glueck (ed.), Probation and Criminal Justice. Essays in Honor of Herbert C. Parsons. *New York: Macmillan, pp. 190–1.*

24. Some pitfalls for probation

Sheldon Glueck

II. Some typical stigmata of crime-treatment agencies

All that can be claimed and expected of any device for coping with criminality by way of treatment is that it is of some assistance, in an appreciable number of cases, in putting certain offenders on the road toward rehabilitation. [...] Yet, however promising any crime-treatment device may be, it cannot successfully function *in vacuo*. It runs the danger of many of its efforts coming to naught, if it is not organically related to those institutions on which the community has already pinned its faith. Merely to add one more device to those already functioning, without carefully planning its relationship to existing institutions will not bring desirable results.

[...]

III. Pitfalls of probation

Propagandist methods borrowed from mercantile fields, instead of dignified educational programs, have too often been used 'to sell' probation to various judges and communities. Such a launching of the ship of probation on a sea of unbridled enthusiasm too often spells a wreck in the future. Every overstatement, unverified by reliable facts, will sooner or later prove a boomerang; and if the claims for probation are carried too far, the popular resentment over instances of its failure will be all the more unbridled, and the pessimism regarding the adequacy of *any* means tried thus far for keeping criminality in control will become more profound. There is but one sound argument in favor of probation, outside of the economic one frequently advanced, and that is that, *rightly administered, it substitutes intelligence and humanity for ignorance and brutality in the treatment of offenders*. These are values enough for any social institution, even though, judged by the incidence of success and failure in terms of subsequent criminality, probation may not today or ever give the absurdly high results frequently claimed. [...] In the beginning we must have trained and wholesome probation officers; let the elaborate office and the 'systems' and 'forms' and reports come later.

[...]

That probation is in large measure dependent for its success on the cooperation of other social institutions is evident to all but certain myopic probation officers. In the first place, the offender's attitude toward the law and its ministers has already been colored by his treatment at the hands of police, jail attendants, prosecutor and others by the time he passes under the supervision of the probation officer. If their actions have served only to strengthen the probationer's attitude of suspicion, cynicism, or other unwholesome reaction, the probation officer has so much more to undo before he can begin a constructive program of work with the offender. Secondly, the probation officer's efforts are contingent upon the good will of public and private social welfare agencies. In his use of the social service index, in his appeal to family welfare workers for constructive aid, in his utilization of employment and health services, the success or failure of his efforts must needs be dependent upon the intelligence, sympathy, and cooperation of workers in fields allied to his. Thirdly, the probation officer's work is to great extent conditioned by the intelligence and sympathetic attitude of the judges in his court. If judges cannot understand and effectively utilize thoroughgoing case histories embodying social, medical, psychiatric-psychologic, as well as legal, data, the work of the probation officer is in large measure futile. If courts exercise poor judgment in the selection of offenders to be placed on probation, the supervisory efforts of the probation officer are bedeviled by a clientele that is not suited to extra-mural oversight. If judges are either angrily repressive or sentimentally lenient – considerations that are beside the point if one truly believes in a scientific administration of criminal justice – then, again, the efforts of the probation officer too often come to naught. If, for example, a probationer again and again violates the conditions imposed by the court and probation officer, and yet goes unscathed, then the prestige of the probation officer suffers not only in the offender's eyes, but in his own.

[…]

These, and many more illustrations which might be given, indicate that effective probation work is intimately intertwined with, and in large measure dependent upon, an intelligent and cooperative attitude on the part of many of society's institutions and servants. But more, the effectiveness of probation (as well as parole) work is in a very real sense contingent upon the attitude of the public. If the press and large elements of the community are unsympathetic or uninterested, probation workers have a difficult task in enlisting the aid of useful persons on behalf of their clients. *In the final analysis, rehabilitation of criminals is a community responsibility.*

From: S. Glueck (1933) 'The Significance and Promise of Probation', in S. Glueck (ed.), Probation and Criminal Justice. Essays in Honor of Herbert. C. Parsons. *New York: Macmillan, pp. 7–12.*

25. Treatment plans and practice

L. Le Mesurier

Initial interview after making the Order

This first talk with the probationer is important, but there is danger in talking too much at such a time, when he is probably still suffering from the shock of the Court proceedings. It is not the moment for a moral discourse, nor is it wise to dwell on the alternatives if the conditions in the Probation Order are not observed. It is probable that much that is said at this initial interview will be forgotten. That does not matter; what is really important and what will unfailingly be remembered is the attitude of the probation officer. The probationer should leave the Court feeling that he can rely on help and guidance from an understanding friend, providing only that he himself pulls his weight in the boat.

The plan of treatment

At the outset a plan of treatment should be formed. This plan will be largely based on information obtained from the preliminary investigation, and should be carefully drawn up after weighing all the known facts. The plan must be subject to modification from time to time, and its success will depend partly on the ability of the probation officer to correlate the relevant facts and plan wisely, and partly on his power to win the genuine co-operation of his probationer. The plan must necessarily contain arrangements for employment, adjustments at home or in social relationships, and the enforcement of any conditions imposed by the Court.

Reporting by the probationer to the probation officer and visits to the home by the latter are complementary methods for maintaining contact, and the preferential use of either depends upon the needs of the individual case. It must be said, however, that only in peculiar circumstances, where, for example, the probationer is living alone in lodgings, or in those rare cases where there is no question of home or environmental influence, should reporting to the officer be regarded as a substitute for the home visit and allowed entirely to supplant it. The Probation Rules of 1926 state that the probationer should be seen at least once a week for the first month and, in the case of persons under the age of seventeen, the rule suggests subsequent fortnightly visits for the first six months of the Order. As a general guide and indication of the importance of constant and continuous oversight; this rule might be applied to adult probationers, but it should not be adhered to too rigidly. The frequency of contact should be determined by the individual requirements of each case, but for obvious reasons the probationer should be seen fairly often in the early stages of the period.

The second interview

Before making the first home visit it is advisable to see the probationer privately, and this interview should take place as soon as possible after the making of the Order. The probation officer should now repeat in more detail what he has already explained briefly at the Court. He should make clear at the outset that probation is not a 'let-off' or a casual giving of another chance, but a period of time prescribed by the Court during which, under sympathetic but firm supervision, the probationer has to make definite and continuous efforts to adjust his attitude to life, and so learn to conform to the ordinary standards of decent living. This is no easy task, and the probationer must be made to understand its seriousness. It means much more than the merely negative job of not getting into further trouble; it is a positive constructive task requiring constant effort from himself and needing, too, the guiding hand of a leader.

The personal problem

The probation officer should explain the nature of the problem, and encourage the probationer to face it. He must be shown that he has got to tackle the difficult job of rehabilitating himself in his own circle. He must be prepared to live down a bad name and create new confidence in those who, because of his previous misconduct, now look upon him with suspicion. In short, the probationer must realize that he has definite tasks to perform, not necessarily mentioned in the Probation Order, but additional to, and perhaps even more important than, those specified in the conditions of that Order.

After defining the problem the probation officer should find out what steps, if any, the probationer intends to take himself towards a solution; but to expect him to cope alone with a situation that has already proved too difficult for him would be, not only unwise, but unfair. The officer should outline the plan of treatment, showing how he proposes to co-operate with the probationer in the solution of his problem, but indicating clearly that the ultimate responsibility rests with the probationer himself.

At the end of this second interview the probationer should have caught something of the spirit of probation: a spirit of co-operative effort – not a shelving, but a sharing of responsibility.

Co-operation with family

When the probationer returns to his home he usually renews the old associations which probably played their part in the original cause of his offence, and co-operation between the probation officer and the family is essential in the interests of the probationer. When the family group feels, apparently, no interest in him, attempts must be made to foster it. In the case of a youth it must not, however, be assumed too readily that because the parents of a probationer do not appear sympathetic they have therefore, in reality, no interest in him. As soon as they realize that the probation officer is taking genuine interest and is capable of understanding and appreciating, not only *his* problems, but also the difficulties of the family, co-operation is usually assured.

It is often desirable to make the first home visit quite soon after the interview with the probationer, and at a time when he will not be at home. This visit provides opportunity for explaining the meaning of probation and discussing the plans made for him. Possibly one or other of the parents may have very decided views on the question of the future conduct of the probationer, which may be opposed to, or at least different from, those held by the probation officer. Such views must never be lightly or autocratically brushed aside, but listened to with courtesy and attention. If they are considered detrimental to the interests of the probationer, adequate reasons should be given for their rejection.

[...]

Liaison with social agencies

It is obviously impossible for him to possess specialized knowledge dealing with every aspect of human relationships, but it is necessary for him to be in a position to discuss all the needs of the family. In order to do this the probation officer must know the various social agencies, public bodies and religious organizations functioning in the district. It is sometimes difficult to decide which is the correct authority, and intimate knowledge of the various agencies is necessary if overlapping is to be avoided and time saved. The probation officer should not undertake services for probationers or their families which other agencies are better equipped to furnish, but he should be the mediating link between the probationer and the other social agencies. In any scheme of treatment, while co-operation with social and religious organizations is essential, the probation officer must never delegate his authority, but must remain always the executor of the plan, while the probationer whose welfare is the objective must be persuaded to exert himself and made to feel that all the steps taken are in his interest and intended to help him. When the probationer has developed confidence in and respect for the probation officer, care should be taken not to abuse his confidence or lose his respect. Any discussion with the family of his failings or shortcomings should not take place in his presence, and when admonition is necessary the probationer should be seen alone.

Probation reporting

The visits to the home of the probationer should be supplemented by direct personal contact at a time and place where private and intimate conversation is possible [...] If the right relationship has been built up it will be found that good use will be made of this informal opportunity for a friendly talk. The probation officer should take care to preserve the intimate nature of such personal talks; privacy is essential, and the interview should be arranged so that one probationer is not compelled to meet and wait with other probationers.

These informal talks may be more valuable than all the pre-arranged interviews. It is at these times that definite educational work is possible, such as discussion of books, topics of the day, or other interests of the probationer, and it is through these talks that interests can be stimulated and ideals formed. The probationer may come to look on his probation officer in a new light, respect ripen into friendship, and the foundations be laid for a lasting relationship, the nature and influence of which will be evident after personal contact is no longer possible.

From: L. Le Mesurier (1935) A Handbook of Probation. *London: National Association of Probation Officers, pp. 124–9.*

26. Social inquiry and treatment plans

R. R. W. Golding

Action [...]

I have stressed my belief that the only valuable knowledge I acquire is obtained from the probationer himself. There is one marked exception to this – the knowledge I gain from making pretrial or remand enquiries. When making these enquiries it is the factual knowledge which I seek, for what I want is as complete a social history as possible. For this purpose I get the information, as far as is practicable, from people who are not the subject of the report, i.e. parents, wives, close relatives. My interview with the subject of the report is comparatively short and superficial as I do not want to start any sort of a relationship at that stage, but only to confirm the opinion I have formed by the knowledge obtained from other sources. I consider this information not only necessary in enabling me (through my report) to carry out my function of helping the court as competently as possible, but also invaluable as a means of obtaining a background of the probationer's life and development which will cause him to stand out in some degree of helpful relief when and if he is placed on probation.

Usually immediately after the court appearance, or sometimes before, I tell the probationer's parents, wife or other intimately concerned persons, that I shall not visit his home and see them because I do not wish the probationer to feel that his relationship with me is shared. This fact almost always appears to be understood, though I realise that the readiness of these people's acceptance may be increased by their pleasure in the realisation that I shall not be bothering them. At the same time I assure them that should they wish to see me I shall always be anxious to see them and I impress on them that they must not hesitate to contact me if they wish to do so. In practice, this principle appears to work.

It may happen that after a time I realise that it is the mother rather than the child who most needs my help. In this case, it is the mother upon whom I concentrate and I usually see the child at far less frequent intervals and on a far more superficial level. If it seems apparent that both mother and child need considerable help – and for me to attempt to give this to both would be ineffectual – I ask a colleague to see one or other of them. Thus, they may come to realise that they are being treated as a person of worth in their own right and not merely as an appendage of the other.

To maintain this principle of individual confidentiality and because I believe the aura is more conducive to therapy, I see almost all my probationers by appointment in my office. Of course, it is not possible for some of them to visit me and there may be other reasons which make home visiting necessary or desirable but, with a caseload of 70 in an area which is city and country, I only visit between five and ten of my probationers. It is, of course, necessary to be very selective. I think that the limitation imposed on me by my own capabilities, time and the material circumstances of the work, compels me to keep the number on whom I can practise psychotherapy at some depth to between twelve and fifteen, though this does not mean that there are only that number in my caseload who, during their probation, will receive such treatment or who have received it; but I do not think that, at any particular time, I shall attempt this treatment with more than fifteen people.

Planning

I try to achieve this selection in the following way: The first half dozen or so interviews I have at weekly intervals, each lasting about three-quarters of an hour. At the end of six or seven weeks I try to decide whether I think it necessary for me to continue to see the probationer with such regularity or whether I can relegate him to 'outpatient treatment', i.e. interviews every three or four weeks. I usually make this transition gradually so that it may take two or three months before someone whom I have been seeing every week reaches the position where I only see him once every four or five weeks. I suspect that many of those who become 'out-patients' may have needed 'in-patient treatment', but since I am compelled to be selective I can only hope that by making the transition from 'inpatient' to 'outpatient' gradually I shall do something towards obviating this error of judgment. I do not intend discussing my interviewing technique in any great detail but I do propose to outline the general principles which afford me a framework. My first few interviews, as well as being primarily concerned with obtaining some understanding of the probationer and his difficulties, are directed into preventing him from fitting and manoeuvering me into an expected category or type. I try to avoid this for two reasons. The first is to prevent him from slipping me into an accustomed reference frame within which he can behave in an unthinking, pre-conditioned way towards me. Thus the persona he presents to me is that which he shows in his daily life to people whom he considers I am like or am a stereotype, with the con-comitant use of his customary defence mechanisms towards such people. Thus I try not to appear authoritarian or (and I find this harder) an all-forgiving very friendly, father confessor. If I appear authoritarian and if this way of him regarding me is not removed (it may be very difficult to do so), he may never dare to show me hostility or weakness: if I am very friendly he may never like to do so for fear of hurting or disappointing me. In either case, his unconscious defences towards me would diminish the likelihood of my understanding him or, at least, decrease its extent. The second reason for my attempting to prevent him typifying me is to allow, at a later stage of our relationship, the possibility of transference arising in a way which is less rigidly motivated or initially determined. If this takes place from the inception of our interviews it may be so spontaneous and natural-seeming that I am likely to miss it altogether, so that it will be several months before I recognise it and become aware of its importance. Though I appreciate that, from the start, his relationship with me will depend on his earlier relationships with people whom he thinks I am like or who have held positions similar to mine, I do not want to augment his typing of me by playing a role into which I can be readily pigeon-holed. Therefore, from the beginning, I am as colourless as possible so that, if anything, he can see the reflection of himself or his transference in me undisguised, unaided and unenhanced by my own personality, i.e. I attempt to preserve the reflection of himself or part of himself rather than the opacity of myself to which his preconceived ideas of me can adhere easily and with almost immovable adhesiveness. For these reasons, I am very wary of discussing his offence until I feel reasonably sure that he regards me as more of a therapist than anything else – this is usually some time later than two months after he has been placed on probation. The only impression I seek to give is that I am an expert in dealing with people like him, that I am immensely interested in him and solely concerned with him, and that I do not consider that it is any part of my job to make moral judgment of him. I believe that the practice and principles which I have outlined, in the barest possible way, apply to all my clients. I think it unlikely that the category into which society places a person is any reason for me to alter my approach towards his troubles and the way in which I should try to help him deal with them.

From: R. R. W. Golding (1959) 'A Probation Technique', Probation, 9: 47–9.

27. The principles of casework

F. P. Biestek

The conviction of the social work profession, distilled from years of experience with many clients in many settings, is that every request for help from a social agency is psychosocial. That is, even in those instances where the client requests a concrete service or a material form of assistance, it can be presumed that some kind of uncomfortable feeling, even though not verbalized or overtly manifested in behavior, is present in the applicant. An emotional component, in other words, inevitably accompanies social needs and problems. This springs, at least in part, from the sense of dependency which applying at a social agency represents. Environmental problems can produce a variety of immobilizing emotional reactions.

The kind and degree of emotion will differ from client to client. The social problem and the meaning of the problem to the client will differ; the ability of clients to cope with life situations, their emotional maturity, their personality strengths and weaknesses, will be different. But within these differences there is a pattern of basic emotions and attitudes that are common, in varying degrees of intensity, to all people who need help, however temporarily, from others. The sources of these basic emotions and attitudes are seven basic human needs of people with psychosocial problems:

1. The need to be dealt with as an individual rather than as a case, a type, or a category.
2. The need to express their feelings, both negative and positive. The feelings may be of fear, insecurity, resentment, hatred, injustice, and so on, or of their opposites.
3. The need to be accepted as a person of worth, a person with innate dignity, regardless of the person's dependency, weaknesses, faults, or failures.
4. The need for a sympathetic understanding of and response to the feelings expressed.
5. The need to be neither judged nor condemned for the difficulty in which the client finds himself.
6. The need to make one's own choices and decisions concerning one's own life. The client does not want to be pushed around, 'bossed,' or told what to do. He wants to be helped, not commanded.

7. The need to keep confidential information about oneself as secret as possible. The client does not want his neighbors and the world at large to know about his problems. He does not want to exchange his reputation for the help he will receive from the social agency.

[...]

Seven principles in relationship

To understand a thing well it is necessary to understand its elements. Thus far the relationship as a whole has been discussed. How can the relationship be divided conceptually? The following table illustrates two possible methods of division: the three 'directions' of the interaction and the seven 'principles.'

First Direction The NEED of the client	Second Direction The RESPONSE of the caseworker	Third Direction The AWARENESS of the client	The name of the PRINCIPLE
1. To be treated as an individual			1. Individualization
2. To express feelings	The caseworker is *sensitive* to, *understands*, and appropriately *responds* to these needs.	The client is somehow *aware* of the caseworker's sensitivity, understanding, and response.	2. Purposeful expression of feelings
3. To get sympathetic response to problems			3. Controlled emotional involvement
4. To be recognized as a person of worth			4. Acceptance
5. Not to be judged			5. Nonjudgemental attitude
6. To make his own choice and decisions			6. Client self-determination
7. To keep secrets about self			7. Confidentiality

It would seem that the directions are divisions of the interaction, while the seven principles are the elements of the casework relationship as a whole. Each principle necessarily involves the three directions.

From: F. P. Biestek (1961) The Casework Relationship. London: Allen & Unwin. pp. 13–17.

28. Gang-groups

D. Bissell

Introduction

'Never settle down within the theory you have chosen, the course you have embraced; know that another theory, another course exists and seek that.' (Follett, 1934, p. 54)

Mary Follett's stimulating exhortation rings out in challenge at a most apposite period of development in the probation service. As though in response, and breaking through the traditional concept of the 'one-to-one' relationship between probation officer and probationer, is the widespread interest which is being manifested in the possibility of group work practice within the probation setting. There is no denying the fundamental value and the indispensable nature of the bond between the worker and the client as afforded through the framework of the individual interview. Nor is it suggested that group work is an invariable alternative to the personal relationships which are created through the medium of confidential discussions. The group process does, however, provide a provocative addition to the growing nucleus of method and knowledge becoming available to the service. More important, the group climate can provide the opportunity for the client to move forward to achieve a more realistic and responsible attitude to life in a way which is frequently denied to the participants in the individual interview.

[...]

The following account of the gang-group meeting for discussions may prove of interest in highlighting both the problems and the potential of such an undertaking.

Demonstration

Eight youths and four girls were involved in sexual orgies on the recreation ground of a small industrial town. All the eight youths were proceeded against. The eldest, a person of twenty-one years with previous convictions for indecency, was sent to prison for six months. Of the remainder, a youth of twenty was fined £20 and the six younger lads, ages fifteen to eighteen, pleaded guilty to indecent assault and were each placed on probation for twelve months. The Chairman of the Magistrates asked each of the fathers present whether they were prepared to give moral instruction to their sons and all of them admitted their inability to do so. The probation officer was therefore asked to undertake this task. (Here it could perhaps have been legitimately argued that the parents were in need of the support and instruction and not the lads.)

After the proceedings the P.O. discussed with each of the boys individually what his feelings would be towards meeting as a group to comply with the wishes of the court. Each of them said that he was in favour of such a course being taken. They therefore met regularly at varying intervals for the next few months. The following is a brief résumé of the progress of the group. No attempt is made to give an account of the more involved aspects of group interaction which were revealed.

First meeting

All very punctual. Attitudes of the six lads anxious, forced, facetious. The P.O. served each of them with a copy of his probation order and explained it to them. They then discussed its implications stage by stage. It was possible to see from the outset that they derived a great deal of mutual support from each other's company. The P.O. then brought up the question of the purpose for which the group had been formed and there were long embarrassing silences. No one, it seemed, was prepared to talk or make any contribution. The P.O. therefore suggested that they might like to think in terms of how frequently they should meet. It was decided to meet in fourteen days.

Second meeting

Again all very punctual. There was a tense air of expectancy. The P.O. led the way into the discussion by asking them what their feelings were on probation now that they had had a chance to consider their position. Their response was reasonably spontaneous. There were differing levels of intelligence. The Grammar School boy was the leader, he verbalised quite easily, the others tending to re-echo some of his phrases. The P.O. then provided the opportunity for the question of sex instruction to be brought up and asked the group if they had any ideas on how they could talk about sex. Again there followed the long tense silence, and it was suggested to them that they might like to consider the wisdom or otherwise of their conduct. This brought forth some open indication of feeling. One youth maintained that what had been done was not unnatural, another supported him and went on to say that all the boys did it. The third wanted to know why the girls had not been dealt with. He considered that they were as bad as anyone in encouraging them. They were asked why the oldest one amongst them had been sent to prison. Why was this so? This led ultimately to quite an open discussion about society and why there should be laws to control and prohibit activity of this kind. Half an hour passed very quickly and it was noticed that all the members of the group began to share in the discussion. The P.O. found that he could sit back and allow them to express their opinions. They handed their cigarettes around freely. Eventually silence fell again and the P.O. stepped in to suggest that they might like to discuss when they should next meet. It was decided that they should come together again in a fortnight.

Third meeting

Again all present a few minutes before time. An air of informality began to creep into the pre-group chatter as the early arrivals waited for the others to come. It was interesting to note that they always wanted to occupy the same chairs, and there was some argument about this. They therefore had a discussion about rearranging the chairs. Those seated in front were only too happy to allow a greater share of the limelight to 'back-benchers' and after much grumbling and reluctance and moving around we attempted to resume where we had left off. It was quite obvious that some of them had been considerably unsettled by the move. For a time there was some difficulty in getting going. They again took up the subject of the last meeting – why society deems it necessary to make laws regarding sexual behaviour. What would happen if there were no laws covering our sexual conduct? They began to warm up and argued between themselves quite vehemently and with feeling. Parental attitudes began to show through. They began to refer more to the P.O., seeking his point of view, offering their points of disagreement for arbitration. The P.O. deliberately refrained from pronouncing judgment, simply restating the facts and allowing them, from their own reconsiderations, to draw conclusions. When the issue concerning society seemed to have been exhausted, the officer felt it necessary to inject the group with a new subject – the physical side of sexual development. Many of them were extremely well informed about this and no obstacles were revealed. When they saw that physically they were mature, yet in the eyes of society they were still children, some element of perplexity and anxiety crept in. 'What can we do?' they asked. This led them as a natural sequence on to the problem of masturbation, and they needed a great deal of help in verbalising their feelings in this connection. The P.O. acknowledged their anxieties both by referring to the normality of this practice and showing them how natural it was also to have guilt feelings about it. The remainder of this session was characterised by a strong feeling of hostility over parental inadequacy. They were all loud in their protestations about their parents' inability to help them. 'Why have they not told us?' they complained, 'Why do they not understand our needs?' Quite prolonged discussions over their parents' shortcomings took place. Identification with the P.O. at this stage was excessively strong, and it was difficult to remain detached. They almost press-ganged him into an onward upsurging mission on behalf of modern youth. Their feelings were extremely intense. The P.O. eventually enabled them to see that their parents were in the main reacting in accordance with the standards that they themselves had known and that their attitude was as understandable to them as indeed were the reactions of the group members to themselves. He also helped them to see that there was a point of reconciliation between past and present standards. There was considerable reluctance to leave the office and they talked for an hour and a half. Eventually all went, but one youth, a Roman Catholic, returned. He wondered whether his beliefs made it possible for him to accept an uninhibited view of sex. He was given a great deal of reassurance and he quite willingly agreed to the P.O.'s suggestion that he should discuss points of difference with his priest where he felt them to exist.

Fourth meeting

The Roman Catholic youth arrived early. He told the officer quite happily that he had been to see his priest and all was well; he did not feel out of things. Again the group assembled well before time. They wanted further discussion on the subject of the previous week and they got off to another promising start with more thinking of the same kind. Their need for reassurance was still very strong. The P.O. felt that they found this from their frankness towards each other in revealing their own anxieties; they also began to express themselves more confidently. They wanted to know what was regarded as normal social sexual development, and examined the criteria for this. They emerged in their own eyes as essentially normal beings and their satisfaction at this self-discovery was very clearly marked. Their confidence was mirrored in their open presentation of their various queries. At no time did the P.O. attempt to interpret to the individual concerned the issues involved in the problem he had introduced. General statements were made and they appeared able to relate their own position in this indirect way. Assiduously discussed were problems of V.D., prostitution, homosexuality, all of which had been raised by individual members. Again there was considerable reluctance in their finishing; they wanted to go on.

Subsequent groups

The next few sessions saw them meeting regularly, keenly thinking about all the aspects of living which they wished to consider. Their textbook became the *News of the World* and, at their request, its reporting was examined for some weeks. The P.O. saw this as the 'window on the world' for most of them. They were particularly concerned about the problem of pre-marital intercourse. Was it sensible that they should do this? Always they were challenged to see themselves as adults. Many of them were earning men's wages; they had men's bodies; they asked that society treat them like men. How does a mature person behave? This was the main problem which they had to resolve. A great deal of recapitulation was done. At no time was the subject portrayed in any narrow or carping sense. The Roman Catholic youth brought in the Church's attitude and the group found it surprisingly acceptable to them. They saw it as good sound common sense. Eventually they began to discuss the worth of girls who had 'principle.' What should they look for in a marriage partner? What were the essentials of a stable marriage? There was a sense of frankness, good humour and a 'growing-up-togetherness'. After discussions lasting several hours, spread out over four months, the P.O. reported back to his Case Committee on the progress that the group had made and obtained permission to apply for the discharges of the probation orders at any time that it was felt opportune. This was therefore put to the members of the group, and exactly nineteen weeks after the orders were made the court discharged them.

From: D. Bissell (1962) 'Group Work in the Probation Setting', British Journal of Criminology, *2.3: 229–50.*

29. Hostel groups

M. K. McCullough

In the treatment of delinquents there is no easy answer to the question of how to make contact. A probation officer may ignore the whole difficulty and proceed to deal with them by such methods of reasoning as commonsense and training suggest, counting on getting through to some of the clients some of the time, or, concerned by the shortcomings of this method, step off the well trodden paths and experiment, even if this may mean floundering out of one's depth at times.

It was on one of these forays some years ago that I first tried my hand at group work. I had heard a psychiatrist talk about his use of this technique in prisons and later had some opportunity to discuss its application to my particular field. I had also been daunted but not completely discouraged by reading accounts of the very much deeper, long-term work done in psychoanalytic groups. It is one of my duties to act as liaison officer to a probation hostel and I decided to start there.

[...]

Anyone who is the subject of a probation order may be sent to such a hostel but in the nature of things probationers so dealt with are likely to have more than usually severe behaviour problems or less than usually supportive homes, or both, and the following histories, selected at random, give some idea of the problems likely to be met and in particular of the paucity of close, continuing, meaningful relationships which is typical of the life experience of most seriously delinquent people.

Marion was illegitimate and, as often happens, was brought up as the youngest child of her mother's parents, regarding her grandmother as her mother. Grandfather was dead. She stayed with grandmother, two aunts and mother – whom she regarded as sisters, until she was six, when grandmother also died.

Meanwhile, Marion's mother's immoral conduct had continued and soon after their mother's death her sisters quarrelled with her because of this way of life and she went away leaving the child in their care. The married sister moved to another district leaving Marion alone with one aunt, who worked to maintain them both, receiving a little money from the mother. She was not a very stable person and when Marion was 14 she had a mental breakdown. Some months later, she became an in-patient and the child, after a short period with her married aunt, went to live with her mother. By this time she understood the facts of her birth. Mother had never married and shortly after Marion's arrival she became pregnant again.

The girl left school and would not work regularly. Just before her 16th birthday she was charged with stealing shoes from shops or two occasions and placed on probation. This was not a success – she would not work and was a determined liar and after six months she was brought back before the court and a condition of residence in the hostel was inserted in the order.

[...]

There is a growing amount of literature on the subject of group work and considerable divergence of aim and method, but there are certain basic requirements which are more or less common ground. It is generally considered that the group should consist of about seven or eight people. As few as five does not allow enough interrelationship to be significant and if there are as many as ten or eleven it is difficult for the worker to hold each member constantly in her attention, and for the group members to relate continually with one another. Chairs are placed in a rough circle, preferably without a table, and people left free to choose where they sit, the worker's position alone remaining constant. This allows the members of the group to sit in whatever position they choose in relation to the leader and to one another and to adopt the posture which suits their mood and to change it as their reactions change. This non-verbal communication is significant, particularly so in my setting because delinquents for various reasons are not usually going to verbalize easily.

Selection of group members is considered of primary importance by some workers in this field: whether people should be similar, because then they will have more in common, or different because this simulates the real-life situation – or some particular combination of the two, like the Noah's Ark method by which two people are selected presenting each of several different problems, which allows each person to feel that they have something in common with at least one other in the group. For myself, I feel that human nature is so complex a thing that while I could match some characteristics – intelligence for example, or the offence committed – I have no way of knowing whether these aspects of the total situation are the vitally important ones, and prefer to take my group members in the order they arrive at the hostel, which in effect produces a mixed group.

Then there is the question of how the purpose of the group is explained. With my groups I find it better to say very little, just that I think it sometimes helps them to talk over the problems they have in common. I give each girl the chance to refuse to come, although I only ever remember one doing so. The meetings last from an hour to an hour and a half and I begin to close them after an hour. I set a period to the group deliberately because in the delinquent authority situation people seem to tend to try and prolong a meeting which is due to close, whereas faced with an indefinite period of time they are more likely to resist with silence.

The groups meet weekly or bi-weekly on about six to ten occasions. This means in practice that a girl joins a group one to twelve weeks after her arrival at the hostel and stays in it for about three months. It will be appreciated that this is one of the critical times – the honeymoon period is over and people have not yet settled down. Before, during and after the group sessions I see the girls individually on an average of once every two weeks. My aim in the group is to deepen my relationship with the girls and to encourage real communication. The sort of group work that I do bears the same relation to group analysis that case work does to analysis – my aims are more limited and immediate and my interpretations rare and simple. I rely a great deal on the relief of tensions in the group, on the self-understanding which is achieved when the girl herself puts into words, perhaps for the first time in her life, something that she feels deeply and finds that these feelings are understood, and often shared, by others and also on the 'reflected' relief and understanding they sometimes get from hearing a fellow member express something they feel themselves.

At first I tried to achieve these ends by being the passive, silent enigmatic leader of the classical group-analytic situation. This puzzled and in a way frightened the girls who are used to me in a much more active role. I abandoned this attitude with reluctance only to find that the more I was willing to talk the less I was required to do so. My groups are now more or less leader-centred. In view of the total situation this would seem inevitable – and in fact has its advantages, because one of the ways in which the girls use the group is to come to terms with me as an authority figure, through this with authority generally, and so with their feelings about their parents.

In starting a session I make it clear that anything can be talked about and quite often they begin with a question – sometimes a very loaded one like 'Why are some girls sent to approved schools?' If nothing comes spontaneously I attempt to stimulate, but not guide, discussion; that is, I aim to get them to talk about almost anything because, once started, they will reach with surprising speed something that is important to them – more often than not their troubles with their parents, however unconnected this may seem to be with the original subject.

From: M. K. McCullough (1963) 'Groupwork in Probation', New Society, 21: 9–11.

30. Girl groups

M. Freeguard

Discussion and encouragement both from outside and from within the Probation Service were not enough to overcome the anxieties that the idea of starting a group provoked in me. I had for a long time wanted to run a group of girls round about the age of leaving school: it seemed to me that at his particularly stressful period, they could gain a great deal from others of their own age, and that a group would provide relationships to carry them over the breaking up of school friendships and the formation of work friendships and would offer continuity in the middle of these upheavals. In spite of a great deal of reassurance, it was not until a spate of shoplifting by girls in their last year or two at school had alarmingly increased my caseload, that the first meeting was arranged.

Five selected girls were invited to attend; two had been co-defendants, two others were connected in the same series of offences. All were shoplifters, all between 13-plus and just 16 […] all average or above average in their secondary modern school, all with strong anti-authority feelings. Not all were equally accustomed to probation-casework: one had had seven interviews, another five, two had had three and one was put on probation the day of the first meeting and so never had any solo interviews at all.

All were free to join or not as they pleased, and are free to withdraw at any time. They were told when invited to join that the group would be anonymous, only first names would be used, and unless they said why they were coming to the Probation Office, none of the others need know; they were told that the meetings would be in lieu of their other interviews, although I should be available before and after for private talk. I told them that the purpose of the group was, as in ordinary probation interviews, to try to help by providing an opportunity of discussing anything that might annoy or worry or upset them: it would be up to them what subjects they talked about. All five accepted. One or two parents were first doubtful. They had doubts about contamination which were soon overcome by my reassurance about personal supervision of the group, and a fixed time to end as well as to begin. We were to meet for one hour a week, from 5.30 to 6.30.

So on the first day, the five girls arrived; after introducing them by their first names and reiterating the purpose of our meetings, I sat back, hoping to be able to maintain the passive role I had imagined, but fearing that long silences would ensue which I could find unbearable. There began, however, after a little groping, the most intense activity as they set about the business of getting acquainted. Questioning went round and round the group on all manner of subjects, on everything, it seemed, except crime. I was both delighted and chagrined to observe that difficulties I had been sure existed in some of the girls, but which I had never been able to help them to talk about, were in this very first meeting more than hinted.

The following week there was a lengthy silence but it was not un-companionable and there was already apparent a feeling of solidarity. And once they did start talking, they spent more time on each subject instead of going rapidly from one topic to another: they were beginning to relax. The anti-authority feelings, which had already come up the first week, were still stronger this time: anti-school, anti-rules, anti-parents, anti-me. Crime was mentioned for the first time, somebody else's it is true, and also the way the actions of one or two can affect a whole lot of people. By the fifth meeting, they were saying when they were put on probation; in the sixth there was a great outpouring of anti-authority feeling with a full and steady flow of talk. The seventh was really a 50-minute silence: but there was intense non-verbal activity and a very strong feeling of solidarity. And so it has gone on, with the members really using the meetings and not just having a chat.

What do they talk about? There is intense interest in clothes and makeup and hairstyles; they are very anxious to establish their identity as individuals and as women: how can they adapt school uniforms or work overalls which might make them into dowds and nonentities, so that they are unmistakeably themselves? Will a hair rinse alter them beyond recognition? Connected with this is talk about boyfriends and beaches and coffee bars and dance halls and clubs: they are anxious to be in the swim, not to be left out or different. They talk again and again about misfits: people who are crippled or hairless or odd in some way and how they adjust more or less successfully and are accepted by society; these girls' delinquency makes them potential misfits and will they be accepted and integrated too? Great interest is also shown in leaving school and getting jobs and those going through this anxious period seem to get support from the group.

All these subjects come up quite spontaneously and are never suggested by me; in the same way, the group arrives at certain answers without my intervention and in this I see its main usefulness.

The group often turns to me for an answer on some subject. Where I feel there is real ignorance and that an answer is necessary for proper communication, I give it […] But in other cases, I make no reply but look enquiringly at them […]. They had demonstrated that they had the right answer within their power.

[…]

Out of control

There are other instances too of the right decision being within themselves and only needing to be discovered. On occasions the group became very uncontrolled: screams of hysterical laughter, a great deal of horseplay. This provoked considerable anxiety in me as I wondered whether I ought to depart from my passive role and quieten them. What would the rest of the office think? However, I managed not to add my tensions to those of the group members on these occasions. The following week, the group would put the matter right [...]

This internalization of authority was one of my main aims in running this group of very anti-authority girls. Their expression of these feelings continued through many meetings and still does; I accept these feelings as all the others, without check or criticism [...] Spontaneously the girls began also to comment on good aspects of authority [...]

Another achievement is, I think, the way the group has modified individual behaviour [...] There is a feeling of solidarity which never fails to impress; absent members are enquired after anxiously and there has been a remarkably conscientious attitude about notifying absence, which I don't think the social background of these girls could account for; it is not just the probation officer that they have a duty to make their apologies to, but to each other.

But it *is* to the probation officer too; my role may be a very passive one, but there is never any doubt that I am there, even when I say nothing except hello and goodbye. This passive role provoked some antagonism at first; quite early on, the group asked what qualifications were needed to be a probation officer; the question was thrown back at them and they decided with a certain relish that none was necessary. Thereafter the group produced its own leader, mostly one of the more disturbed girls. It is nevertheless quite clear that I am not regarded as a nonentity: the girls are very aware of my presence and support. In moments of great, personal distress, it is usually first to me in the group that they look and then to the group as a whole.

I confine my activity to greeting them as warmly as I can and calling each girl by her name, and saying goodbye in the same way. Usually I say nothing more after greeting them and they start talking when they are ready; but if anyone is unable to come, I tell the group so. I always end with something on the line of 'We'll meet again at the same time next week' and on occasion, after a difficult meeting, I haven't felt so sure of the next meeting as the words imply. But there always has been a next meeting so far.

What, it may be asked, are the practical achievements of these meetings, if any? They are very difficult to judge. The girls are mostly so near school leaving age that there is not enough time to measure any improvement at school. Anyway, modifications in their attitudes might be due to growing up and not to the group. But I fancy that there has been some acceleration in the growing up process. The gap between themselves and adults seems greatly to have narrowed in these six months. The unkind and arbitrary parents and teachers are largely replaced by the not unreasonable employers or the fairly civil teachers: they seem to have come to terms with some of their ambivalences.

So far none of the girls has offended again; but I did not expect them to. These were angry girls who, by stealing and getting caught, had succeeded in proclaiming their resentment and defiance of their respectable families. I think they were also making an attempt to establish their separate identity;

probation tries to help them do this and to meet continuing needs of this sort. Perhaps this is one of the reasons why they seem to like coming to the meetings.

There have been practical advantages from the point of view of the caseworker too, particularly in the way that one's own deficiencies in skill seem to be made up in the group. I was unable to help some of these girls to talk to me personally about problems which have been raised in the group by them or by others. Besides this, there is the economy of it all. Each of the girls did, in my opinion, need a great deal of help from probation. It would have been impossible to have devoted very long to each girl individually. As it is, an hour a week for each group gives us time to get going without any hanging about in the waiting room for them or anxiety about the queue for me.

From: M. Freeguard (1964) 'Five Girls against Authority', New Society, *pp. 18–20.*

31. Enforcement and therapy

A. W. Hunt

Developments in social casework practice and training have been exceptionally pronounced in the last two decades, and of overriding importance in these developments has been the provision, mostly during professional training, of a rationale for casework practice. Emphasis has tended towards the insight-giving processes, acknowledgment of the individual's right to self-determination, and to the importance of a non-directive and accepting approach by the caseworker. Much contemporary literature and general teaching reflect experience in casework where need is overt or openly acknowledged by the subject, and in consequence a dilemma is presented to probation officers and others employed in the correctional field who are called upon to reconcile the concepts of generic casework teaching with the fact that they work in a clearly authoritarian setting in which many of their professional relationships contain the element of enforcement. The nature and implication of the dilemma are underlined in two recent contributions to our thinking on this subject made by Clare Winnicott (1962) in her article on 'Casework and Agency Function' and Alan Roberton (1961), Governor of Hewell Grange Borstal Institution, in his paper on 'Casework in Borstal'. Mrs Winnicott observes that 'When a child or an adult commits an offence of a certain degree and kind, he brings into action the machinery of the law. The probation officer who is then asked to do casework with the client feels he ought to apply techniques implying the casework principle of self-determination, but he loses everything if he forgets his relationship to his agency and the court, since symptoms of this kind of illness are unconsciously designed to bring authority into the picture. The probation officer can humanize the machinery of the law but he cannot side-step it without missing the whole point of the symptom and the needs of the client.' Alan Roberton also refers to the conflicting demands of the institutional setting, seen as a microcosm of society, and the needs of the boy. Attention is drawn to the desirability of maximum flexibility and adaptation to individual needs within the framework, but Mr Roberton concludes that 'to be casual or inconsistent about it or to take undue liberties with the framework would be unhelpful. Such inconsistency can only confuse the boy, may cause him to have some doubts about our general integrity and we may forfeit his respect.'

Denial of the reality of the probation situation is often aided by the superficial fact that the probationer acknowledges need by virtue of the voluntary acceptance of a period of supervision, but there are few who would fail to recognise the naivety of a suggestion that such an undertaking in itself implies recognition of need in any form. Moreover, there appears little doubt that, if the probation officer attempts to approach the probationer without careful reference to the fact that in many instances co-operation may be grudgingly given, he may not only fail to develop an approach which can honestly reconcile the fundamentals of casework with the approach necessary in many correctional settings, but he will also find his capacity to help a number of deprived and maladapted people seriously impaired.

A relationship which is enforced by the full sanction of the law is clearly open to abuse and it is recognised that the insights developed in relation to the motivation of the practitioner have been invaluable in pointing to the dangers of dominating and pontifical control. However, a cause for increasing concern over the years has been the frequency with which the probation officer's special position in relation to his probationers and others under supervision has been described in relatively negative terms. Experience shows that the negative aspects of enforcement have been referred to much more frequently than the positive elements, and many occasions have arisen when, because of uneasiness about the coercive factor in their relationships, probation officers have tried to deny the facts of the situation and have exaggerated the positive quality of their relationships to a highly unrealistic degree. It would seem that one of the most important reasons for such a situation rests on the fact that so much of our dynamic casework practice is based on psychotherapeutic techniques developed within clinical settings where voluntary co-operation is assured and where such co-operation is deemed to be indispensable. Probation officers share with others the common experience of cases where a seriously disturbed person is considered unsuitable for treatment merely because he is not prepared to undertake treatment of his own volition or because of aggressive elements in the personality which conflict with special institutional or agency requirements. The basis of case selection of this type can be understood, but it is of very little assistance to the probation officer, many of whose cases would fall into such a category, and it would be a very great pity indeed if he concluded from such experience that lack of initial co-operation eliminated therapeutic opportunity or that maturation could not be encouraged.

With such problems as emotional disorder, personality defect or severe neurosis the relevance of the psychotherapeutic approach may be perceived. To see the relevance of such an approach is not easy when one deals with the many under-achieved, egocentric and extroverted delinquents where the primary problem appears to be one of defective character development, or encounters professionally the range of spontaneous antisocial behaviour normally apparent in the growing child who has clearly not developed a pattern of delinquent behavior.

[...]

A rational development of a social or individual therapeutic approach in conditions of full enforcement has not yet matured, but there is convincing evidence to show that, contrary to the opinion of some clinicians, probationers and other offenders can make some adjustment even when compelled to relate to authority. In support of this view it is held that the most important and influential relationships in any person's life are those which are, in their very nature, enforced. A child is born into a family whether he or she likes it or not, and with very few exceptions there are no opportunities for the child to evade the necessity to make some adaptation to the demands made by the parents and vice versa. Similarly in school, adjustment between child and teacher is necessary, even though in the first instance adjustment is unwillingly made.

[...]

The second example is the following letter from an 18-year-old Borstal boy to a probation officer known to him before committal:

'I am writing this letter to thank you for helping me out in court. I am sorry I have not written before, as I could not remember your name. I am hoping that when I come out of here that I will be under your supervision. I'm sorry if I seemed to be rude to you when we were outside of the court, but as you may already know, no one could hardly expect me to be happy about going to court.

'Well, I am a grade two now and the board is tomorrow and I am hoping to get my threes with a bit of luck. If I do get them tomorrow I expect I shall be having my home leave somewhere around January, which means I will have to report to you or whoever is going to be my probation officer.

'Please tell Mr. S .... if you see him that I'm sorry I let him down so much because I always did like him visiting my mother's house. And those little talks we had used to knock a bit of sense into me. Really what I needed when I was little was a good hiding but I always knew I would not get one, but this is just as good as one although it has taken me a long time to bring me to my senses.'

[...]

Such examples are far from uncommon in work with delinquents, and from such incidents it may be concluded that lack of criticism or annoyance may be interpreted by the emotionally deprived as indicating a lack of basic concern and by the delinquent with a weak ego as emasculated control. It is of significance that on many occasions an entirely unexpected response is encountered in a probationer or client who has become involved in further trouble. In spite of the fact that the probation officer does not feel resentful or annoyed, letters are received showing quite clearly that it is assumed that he will experience such feelings, and that such feelings will arise from basic feelings of regard and concern for the probationer.

[...]

Probation casework is rich in examples showing how people may be helped in an enforced situation and how even the very dull are able to perceive the positive implications which may in the first instance appear to be against their interests. Simple examples can illustrate the point.

The first case is of a young man in his early twenties who had drifted away from what was a relatively settled home, but one in which control and guidance were limited. During his independent life he encountered difficulties over employment, found himself in financial trouble and committed what was a relatively simple offence to solve his immediate problem. The early phases of supervision were marked by a general air of discouragement which did not amount to seriously morbid depression, and the young man was becoming deterred from energetic pursuit of necessary employment because of very real difficulties due to some prevailing unemployment. The probation officer concerned took practical and active measures to secure employment for this young man and they spent many hours together in this search. At one stage shortly before it proved fruitful the probationer was seen in the absence of his officer by a colleague. This colleague was surprised to encounter very positive warmth after what was a short period of supervision, and after some difficulty in describing the quality of his relationship the probationer eventually said 'I wish my father had been like Mr. Blank because when I am with him he makes me feel that things are going to get better for me at last.' Although a simple example it shows how much reassurance can be given by the competent management of the situation by a caseworker, and obvious parallels can be seen between this type of situation and the type of encouragement and reassurance which is given to children by the untroubled action of parents […].

The examples given are quite ordinary ones but they are representative and valuable in providing a focus for some general conclusions.

1. Probation is inescapably identified with punishment as well as reform and reclamation. If emphasis is given to the deterrent and revengeful element then this must create difficulties for the caseworker who is motivated by reparative feeling. If, however, it is seen that there are directly positive features of punishment, notably an explicit expression of concern for the offender, it is possible to draw on experience of primary family and social situations to provide a conceptual basis for casework activity.
2. Some external control of the individual can assist in the process of maturation because it provides real and promised stability, and again by implication can contain the unconscious and sometimes near-conscious anxieties about aggressive and destructive impulses.
3. Enforcement goes some way to counter superficial evasion and avoidance behaviour which prevents appropriate social action on the part of the individual.
4. The enforced relationship and casework are not mutually exclusive. Indeed, in many respects the probation casework process is enriched by enforcement, and the explanation appears to centre on the fact that enforcement is an essential component of all early socialising processes.

If there is anything distinctive about casework in enforcement, it is that the caseworker needs more often to show himself as concerned through positive action, even although it is found that such activity does not prevent the coincidental use of interpretive techniques or the relatively inactive processes of casework in the clinical setting.

From: A. W. Hunt (1964) 'Enforcement in Probation casework', British Journal of Criminology, *43: 239–52.*

32. Psychotherapy and reality

Melitta Schmideberg

Learning from probation

To elicit and develop these forewarning emotions is an important part of the socialising process. Probation has developed empirically and intuitively a most interesting approach – it is much more than just 'social work in an authoritarian setting'. Persons who can be reached neither with kindness nor strictness often respond to the peculiar combination of both inherent in probation. Probation utilises the emotional turmoil evoked by the arrest and trial, and the overwhelming relief of not being sent to prison, to establish an emotional relation with an unwilling offender. When on probation, he is likely to have more crises and difficulties – because this is his mentality and his mode of life – and then he is likely to turn to his probation officer for help again and again. Many offenders eventually describe the probation officer as their only friend. The probation officer then utilises his relation to teach the probationer simple everyday things that are obvious to the ordinary person, but above all helps in many situations and tries to give him a social philosophy. That he so often succeeds against heavy odds is because he puts so much of himself into his work and really cares for his probationer but also because this unique elastic combination of authority and friendship has been worked out.

The aim of criminal therapy should not be to undermine social structures and values but to utilise and develop them. The rationale of criminal psychotherapy cannot be the same as that of general psychotherapy because the offender does not suffer, except as a consequence of his misbehaviour. If the psychiatrist limited himself to systematically alleviating the suffering deliberately meted out by society – the punishment – and this was practised on a large enough scale, it would undermine our judicial system.

The function of psychotherapy as that of all medical specialities is to mitigate suffering and malfunctioning. The function of law is to control behaviour, to check and correct antisociality. Since medicine and law have different functions they are bound to have different professional ethics. 'Different' does not mean 'superior'. Statements implying that psychiatrists are well meaning and sympathetic while judges are 'sadistic' are unjustifiable, as is the tendentious stressing of the archaic phylogenetic aspects of law or morality. A social-minded British court of today is as different from a medieval torture chamber or dungeon as is a surgeon from Barts or a psychiatrist from the Maudsley from an African witch doctor. Goodwill and social-mindedness are not the prerogative of a single profession.

Therapy of offenders is psychiatric new land. It must by clinical experimentation develop new techniques and clarify its goals. These should be primarily to change the asocial behaviour that causes the friction with society. Most offenders are 'unwilling patients', and even those who come for treatment do so only in order to avoid something worse. Probation officers handle unwilling probationers, many of whom are difficult, abnormal, rebellious. Yet in England they get 70 per cent results on follow-up. So why should psychiatrists not be able to handle unwilling patients? While it is usually taken for granted that psychiatry has much to teach probation, I for one believe that psychiatrists could learn from probation. To be successful with offenders we must feel that by giving social values we do something *for* and not against the patient. We should come down from our Olympic heights and learn more and concern ourselves more about the patients' trivial day-to-day problem of living, the realities of employment and unemployment, the functions and rules of the courts, and above all care about the patient as a person. The detachment which we may glorify in our own mind as scientific objectivity or 'symptom tolerance' is often felt by the patient as callous indifference or therapeutic inefficiency.

Concentrating on reality

In the USA for the last fifty years 'insight therapy' in its manifold forms or various analytic approaches have been practised on millions and possibly tens of millions of patients with poor and sometimes dismal results. 'Insight' is a slogan, each school having its own particular type of insight that has to be believed fervently. The only thing these insights have in common is that they are usually retrospective and irrational.

Yet actually most of our anxieties and problems are directly or indirectly conditioned by our reality, and this most certainly applies to the offender. Therapists who do not even try to find out about the patient's reality, are in no position to determine the irrational nature of his reactions. It does not normalise a person to bring out his irrational side, it does not socialise him to elaborate his antisociality, it does not make him happier to dwell on his unhappiness. People are at least as much influenced by the present and the anticipations of the future as by the distant past. Offenders need all their mental energy to deal with their severe immediate problems and should learn to forethink consequences, not fritter away their energies trying to remember irrelevant details of their childhood.

To get a patient to cope with a real situation all his emotional and intellectual resources must be mobilised. Concentrating on irrational aspects diverts his attention and gives him an excuse for not facing the issue. To discover irrational reasons or a childhood pattern may or may not help with neurotics. With delinquents it is rarely effective and often has serious ill effects.

The great majority of offenders are not psychiatric cases in the strict sense, and for a proportion of those who obviously are – the bad alcoholics, abnormal homosexuals, severe psychopaths, open pscyhotics, etc. – neither drug, nor aversion therapy, nor present-day psychotherapy has much to offer. Offenders are mostly (a) ordinary persons (perhaps a little below par) gone wrong, (b) weak-willed irresponsible drifters, (c) truly antisocial personalities. The second group can be labelled schizoid or 'inadequate', the third one psychopathic. But giving psychiatric labels is not the same as doing therapy. England is an empirical country. In the long run criminal psychiatry will stand or fall by the therapeutic results it achieves. Many offenders are successfully handled by their probation officers who soon will take over the aftercare of discharged prisoners as well. There are, however, certain types of offenders, or certain individuals, who are better handled by an experienced psychiatrist. But merely being a psychiatrist or analyst with private practice neurotic or hospital psychotic experience is no qualification. Experience with offenders and of co-operation with the courts is necessary. Many therapists are overimpressed with relatively mild manifestations that are everyday occurrences to probation or prison officers. In England psychiatrists have been given very generous opportunities for treating offenders of which they have hardly availed themselves yet.

Offenders need special techniques

There is much general psychiatrists can learn from criminal psychiatry. The offender is not the only unwilling patient. Many who are in dire need are reluctant to see a therapist, but may do so under pressure of their families or others. If the therapist then knows how to approach an unwilling patient he may find many of them treatable. Many psychiatrists are too inactive and passive, easily overimpressed by some minor peculiarity of the patient. Some non-psychiatrists, Quakers, medical practitioners, clergymen or just kind-hearted people handle quite successfully persons who, if seen by a psychiatrist, would be given a dire diagnosis and prognosis. Analysts are the most selective ones; they set such high standards of co-operation, regular attendance, fee paying, etc., etc., that hardly a fraction of one per cent of the population would qualify. But in psychiatry, as in every medical speciality, the method should be adjusted to the patient and not the patient to the method.

The Association for the Psychiatric Treatment of Offenders (APTO) has developed specialised techniques for treating offenders and co-operating with the courts. Therapeutic methods applicable to neurotics or psychotics fail with offenders. Diagnosis based on knowledge of the neurotic-psychotic group of patients becomes inaccurate and unreliable for offender patients. Guidance given to parents and probation officers on the handling of delinquents is apt to be wrong if it is based on knowledge gained from neurotics.

Many offenders can be successfully treated, their emotional problems accurately gauged and realistic advice given to their families or the court – but only by therapists who are trained and experienced in the treatment of this group.

Offenders do not respond to classic analysis because they do not have the neurotic's concern with inner suffering. In fact, they do not have the inner suffering. Nor is there time to use any psychotherapeutic method which does not view the patient's real-life situation as the primary problem. The ultimate task is to re-educate and socialise the patient rather than to relieve him of inner tensions. The immediate task is to keep him out of jail. The release from destructive tension and the building of constructive inhibitions is part of the process of socialisation; rapport is established as the therapist helps the patient to live successfully within the law. Thus, the treatment of the offender represents a real departure from the generally accepted treatment of the neurotic or psychotic. The doctor who is accustomed to spending long months, or even years, on the inner life of his patient and to viewing reality as a reflection of the patient's neurosis cannot treat a person who may be in jail tomorrow because he has committed an antisocial act between interviews. There simply isn't time, and the patient is not interested, anyway, in his unconscious and cannot even be reached by such techniques.

Over forty years ago Janet wrote 'Anarchy and dogmatism rule in psychiatry'. Since then things have become much worse. If we returned to the self-evident goal, that the aim of treatment is to help the patient, if we watched realistically how the patient lives and geared our treatment to his problem and possible solutions, re-evaluated our treatment methods and results, we might lose some of our over-sophistication and over-intellectualisation and lessen our confusion. Above all we should return to the accepted normal patient–doctor relationship and not cultivate an irrational and abnormal transference relationship that hurts the patient and in the long run also the therapist.

From: M. Schmideberg (1965) 'Psychotherapy of Offenders: Its Rationale and Implications for General Psychotherapy', Probation, *11.1: 4–9.*

33. The persistent offender

Geoffrey Parkinson

Aggression

The aggressive client, on the other hand, needs not only the right probation officer, but the right technique. I have elaborated elsewhere the need with some offenders to support rather than attack their character defences. (*New Society* – 'The Challenge of the Borstal Boy', 29th October 1964). In this method the probation officer assesses the means by which the client has structured his personality in defence against his 'inner' and 'outer' fears, and expresses admiration for these defences.

'If you decided to hit someone' I once said to a client who was warding off anxiety about his physical condition by taking up weightlifting, 'I'd hate to be around to pick up the pieces'. He was clearly pleased, but then immediately replied, 'Yeah, but I don't feel I am strong' – an admission that set in motion a new level of relationship between us.

This approach would be regarded by many caseworkers as unorthodox to the point of heresy, yet it is often, in my opinion, surprisingly successful with a large number of persistent offenders. The aggressive client, it perhaps hardly need be said, is intensely frightened of the world. He knows he must never relax his guard. Attack from any direction is always possible. In essence he sees his response to threatening situations as confined to either retreat or attack, and unlike the inadequate he tends to prefer attack. Retreat for him is feminine and therefore to be despised. Attack is masculine and so to be admired. He is usually terrified of anything that seems to him to be feminine. This dilemma of extremes was expressed clearly to me by one client who had assaulted a policeman. One day in the street a constable had stopped him and asked him a few questions in a manner he felt to be provocative. I asked, 'But why hit the policeman?' He said that he wasn't going to crawl to the officer and treat him as if he were God. When I put it to this client that these were not the only alternatives – he could have discussed the matter with the P.C. without either being too aggressive or too servile – he was surprised. This had never occurred to him, nor does it occur to many of my clients. (Extremity and inappropriateness of reaction show themselves in many other areas and are crude means of dealing with anxiety. Clients can often face, on a conscious level, the hazards of their crimes and court appearances, or the desertion or death of significant figures in their environment, with little show of concern or feeling. On the other hand, they often find minor problems intolerable to bear.) In my view one of the major roles of probation with the aggressive client – and I of course do not only mean the overtly aggressive – must be to show him how to use his aggression appropriately. Once he knows his personality is respected and not to be challenged directly, he is willing to accept a small amount of friendly conflict. This, however, I feel should be linked closely with a splitting process:

ME: George, I think of you as being two blokes.
CLIENT: What do you mean?
ME: Well there is one George that is going to steal what he likes and hit who he dislikes; this George is happy-go-lucky and couldn't care less. Then there is another George inside you who is a bit unhappy about getting into trouble and is worried about the way things are going, because he wants to settle down and lead a happy life without always worrying about being picked up by policemen.

At this point there is an apparent contradiction. I have assumed in my initial contact that the tough, couldn't-care-less side is the only side and now I separate it off by the discovery and support of a soft, sensitive side.
[...]

Two persons?

The idea of viewing themselves as two persons certainly has an appeal which many clients often find attractive. It permits one side of them to be attacked while the other remains intact and this is a new experience. In the past any criticism was taken as a criticism of the whole personality; with splitting, however, this is no longer the case. The probation officer can gradually, though often quite vigorously, challenge the attitudes of the delinquent side of the client and make the client attempt to alienate this side. The process cannot, of course, in itself be a success. The delinquent side wants to hit back, and in this there must be active encouragement within the casework setting.

'You think I am a stupid bastard' I said to one client 'who is trying to turn you into a cissy'. He agreed: 'If I was soft I'd live a hell of a life wouldn't I?' The alternative to sadistic 'masculinity' is frequently seen as masochistic femininity.

When the client begins to show aggression in an appropriate way the split begins to heal a little, though this is rarely pointed out and, in fact, the client is left with a sense of conflict between the two sides which will continue indefinitely. I am increasingly inclined to think that it is vital for the probation officer to reveal as much aggression as he can in his relationship with the aggressive client. Casework may usefully become in part a mock-war in which the client is offered as a substitute for the real war he has with society, and also a lesson in more appropriate ways of expressing his hostility. A naive example will reveal this point perhaps more clearly. An educationally subnormal youth was on probation to me because he had an unpleasant predisposition for attacking park keepers and bus conductors. In a series of initial interviews I expressed admiration for him and his physical powers – he was a strong lad, though he saw himself as physically feeble. One evening he reported to my office. As soon as he came into the room I gave him a push on the shoulder – hard enough to be forcibly felt but not hard enough to effect totally unthinking response. His fists clenched and he glared at me with a look of hostility and confusion.

'Well' I said, 'what are you going to do if I am a bus conductor and I tell you to get off my bloody bus and start pushing you'. The boy smiled 'I don't hit him!' I often followed this routine through on many similar occasions with this lad and with others who have been involved in assault charges, or who I feel are predisposed to aggressive responses. They may sometimes enjoy it as a game but it also has a deeper meaning for the assault is also seen as a statement of a warm relationship. (Incidentally it is more possible than many officers may think to play 'games' with older clients. As an example of this I remember making a comment to one man, using an American accent. He enjoyed this and responded by doing the same. Thereafter when we got to difficult areas in his emotional life I would ask him a question in an American accent and he would reply in this way. He told me at the end of probation that but for such a method he could never have revealed many aspects of his life.)

If the persistent offender is not a concealed psychotic or overpressed with anxiety, he often feels more at ease with an aggressive officer, that is to say, an officer who recognises and uses his aggression appropriately. The reason for this is quite simple. The client, anticipating attacks, fears that the officer who does not reveal aggression is holding back. In phantasy the client may see such an officer as playing at cat and mouse – the claws are there but all that is felt is the soft padding. Such a client may attack the officer in the hope of assessing him as an enemy. If the officer accepts the aggression, merely offering interpretations, the client's anxiety increases and whereas in an analytic setting with a middle-class neurotic this technique may be all for the good, with the persistent delinquent the situation is uselessly aggravated.

In probation circles there has been some important discussion on the necessity of the probation officer accepting his authoritarian role and a suggestion that in fact the client needs, whether he knows it or not, to have a person who can control his destructive and aggressive impulses. This, in my view, is not so much an issue of technique as one which concerns the personal characteristics of the probation officer. I have a tendency to be a controlling person and, therefore, may usefully relax with my clients. Permissive personalities may, on the other hand, find the need to be more authoritarian. It varies from probation officer to probation officer and client to client.

I suspect far too many clients find themselves in a casework situation in which they are unable to experience the appropriate use of aggression. Many of them, therefore, sit passively with their pleasant passive probation officers, and periodically explode into delinquency elsewhere. It may often be unwise, even dangerous, to wait for the client to reveal his aggression. The officer very frequently has to go in and get it.

From: G. Parkinson (1965) 'Casework and the Persistent Offender', Probation, *11.1: 11–17.*

Part Two

Modern trends and forms

Introduction

Rehabilitation is an idea and an ideal; it is a theory and it is a practice. At every level – idea, theory and practice – rehabilitation is best represented as a set of contested categories. At the macro level there is the clash of ideologies between punishment and reform, a debate which in the modern era has been fought, won and lost in the political arena. In the USA and in England and Wales it has been settled decisively in favour of punitive responses to crime. Within the rehabilitation camp itself, there remain disagreements about how best to further the ideal, and increasingly the arguments have been about evidence. The readings in this section illustrate some of these developments, some of these debates, and some of their consequences in the real world.

The 1960s and 1970s and parts of the 1980s were good times to be alive and progressive and working in the criminal justice systems of England and Wales. Punishment, the old adversary, appeared to be on the run. There was broad acceptance of the social and psychological causes of crime, and widespread adoption of policies and penological practices based on the idea of 'treatment' or rehabilitation. Probation was the epitome of these ideas and trends in practice. Onto its founding concern for individual wrongdoers probation had grafted a commitment to providing alternatives to custody – an essentially social goal. Some of the alternatives took the form of innovatory sentences such as community service (Harding 1973) and day training centres (Vanstone 1993). Probation officers in different areas were also experimenting with new forms of group work aimed at addressing and reducing reoffending in specific offence categories (Weaver and Fox 1984; Jones *et al.* 1993) There were also scattered attempts to establish empirical evidence for the effectiveness of traditional methods of service provision and casework attention (Berntsen and Christiansen 1965; Shaw 1974).

On the other hand, the use of imprisonment as a penal sanction was under attack from all sides for its philosophical incoherence, its inhumanity and its ineffectiveness (RAP 1971). Radical criminology added to the debate a fundamental critique of the politics of criminal justice (Taylor *et al.* 1973) and prisoners themselves, influenced by the example of civil rights movements in the wider society, began to organise and demonstrate, demanding negotiations about conditions and a sharing of power within prisons (Fitzgerald 1977). Ex-prisoners formed theatre groups and some entered New Careers projects to be trained as criminal justice professionals (Bahn and Davis 1998; Priestley 1975; Caddick. 1994) There were campaigns to decriminalise whole categories of hitherto imprisonable behaviour and to recast criminal proceedings against juveniles in a wholly welfare mould (Rutherford 1986). On the fringes of these events voices could even be heard advocating the abolition of prison altogether (Mathiesen 1974).

Not a golden age by any means: probation was an imperfect instrument for delivering anything we would now recognise as an effective service – either to individuals or to society at large – but it was a time of optimism, sustained by a wider intellectual and social climate. Outwith the ranks of criminal justice professionals, there was broad support for the liberal agenda in Parliament, in the press and among the public at large. Even transatlantic popular culture contributed to the mood music. 'In the Ghetto' was written by Mac (Scott) Davis, a country singer and song writer who worked his way through college as an employee of the Georgia State Probation Service (Davis 1968). When he recorded the song in the American Studios, Memphis (night of 20–21 January 1969), Elvis Presley added a coda of his own by repeating 'and his mama cries' at the end (Jorgensen 1998).

As a crowd gathers 'round an angry young man
face down on the street with a gun in his hand
In the ghetto
As her young man dies,
on a cold and gray Chicago mornin',
another little baby child is born
In the ghetto.

Knowing what we now know, we can see that in the blue skies of this period of rehabilitative goodwill, there had already begun to appear tiny clouds, separated in time and space and origin, but pointers to a change in the weather. C. S. Lewis was to become a best-selling children's author with his 'Narnia Chronicles', including *The Lion, the Witch, and the Wardrobe* (1950), but his academic output included a lively attack on the Humanitarian theory of punishment and its interference in the sentences of the criminal courts (Lewis 1949) His article, first published in a Melbourne University journal, *The Twentieth Century*, was not widely read at the time, but it foreshadowed later and more fatal expressions of similar opinions. His contention was 'that this doctrine, merciful though it appears, really means that each one of us, from the moment he breaks the law, is deprived of the rights of a human being.' What Lewis failed to remark, but others have not, was that the wider failure to deliver social justice also deprives modern states of their right to impose retributive punishments on erring citizens (Cavender 1984.)

In her book *Social Science and Social Pathology* (1959), Barbara Wootton took aim at a different part of the treatment influence on sentencing. Two targets in particular attracted her ire – psychoanalytic explanations of bad behaviour, and woolly social workers plying their poorly thought out trade in its shadows. 'Psychiatrists since Freud have been busy doing for man's morals what Darwin and Huxley did for his pedigree, and with not much less success,' was her summary of their endeavours. C. S. Lewis, a philosophy don, and Barbara Wootton, an economist, both swam, in their different ways, against the intellectual currents of their time and place, but in the United States a bigger storm was brewing.

It is ironic that a committee of the American Friends, in their 1971 publication *Struggle for Justice*, provided ammunition for the coming assault of punishment on its rival ideology – rehabilitation (American Friends Service Committee 1971). The conclusions of *Struggle for Justice* were radical – that the treatment approach to crime was a historic failure and a source of injustice in judicial sentencing: 'Like other conceptions that become so entrenched that they slip imperceptibly into dogma, the treatment model has been assumed rather than analysed, preached rather than evaluated.' 'The report called for its replacement by a 'justice' model of the criminal law – one that focuses on offences rather than on the individuals who have committed them. Such a system would feature due process safeguards for defendants and tariff-based sentences that reflect the seriousness of the offence rather than the difficulty of treatment. To get to their findings, the working party had first to renounce a long Quaker history of humanitarian involvement in prison and mental health reform. Elizabeth Fry's work with women prisoners is dismissed as 'paternalistic' and the committee members hung their several heads in shame at the thought of their ancestors' contribution to the irresistible rise and eventual world domination of the nineteenth-century penitentiary model of the prison. But here, a hundred and fifty years later, the Friends of America have helped open the door to an expansion of prison places in the USA and elsewhere that dwarfed its precursor.

Probation in England and Wales experienced large structural changes during the period 1966–86, changes which, for the most part, were seen by practitioners as positive. In 1966 Probation Areas had assumed responsibility for the Prison Welfare function in all penal establishments, and this fitted with a growing emphasis in official policy on voluntary after-care for shorter sentence prisoners. There were also expansions of statutory parole and the number of

> Prison officials are claiming 'rehabilitation' has failed, and there is a call to return to the days of punishment, pure and simple. Rehabilitation has not failed; social scientists have failed to specify the conditions under which it might have a chance to work and to carry their convictions to the public and legislature. (Zimbardo 1975)

probation hostels was increased (Whitehead and Statham 2006). Some of the changes fitted easily with the traditional tasks of the service – welfare functions in prisons and voluntary after-care focused on services to meet concrete needs such as housing, income support and job search. Others widened the scope of what probation stood for; community service embodied the notion of symbolic reparation to the community for the harm done by offending. But the establishment of statutory parole supervision as a central plank in the probation platform was the thin edge of a wedge inserted where Borstal Aftercare had gone before. It threatened not only the notion of 'befriending', a cornerstone value of the service, but more importantly the requirement for 'consent' before a probation order could be made. 'Parole', like the word 'probation' itself, has undergone a reversal of meaning: from choice to coercion, from giving your word to doing as you are told.

Through all of these changes, most probation work in England remained relatively conventional; probation officers 'supervised' individuals by seeing them with diminishing frequency over the currency of their orders, dealing with problems in their lives, keeping an eye on troublesome issues, and giving support and encouragement for leading law-abiding lives. In some cases casework might be attempted, seeking to relate offending to underlying patterns of parental deprivation, promoting insight by the 'client' into such connections and using the 'professional relationship' to help him or her 'grow' into being a more trusting person who has less need to signal personal distress by committing an offence (Halmos 1965). More specific forms of one-to-one work, e.g. task-centred casework (Reid and Epstein 1972) and the Heimler approach (Morley 1986), found favour with some practitioners but did not become mainstream. Evaluations of the traditional mix of methods were occasionally undertaken. Berntsen and Christiansen (1965) report work in a Danish prison setting, and Shaw (1974) does the same at two prison sites in England – an open prison and a long-term, high-security establishment. Both studies, and both prisons in the UK work, reported substantial and statistically significant reductions in reoffending for the experimentals who received the 'treatment' (mostly enhanced amounts of time with social workers addressing release planning) compared with controls who did not. Davies (1974) also showed results for individuals under community supervision who received different amounts of 'environmental treatment'. He found no evidence of improvement in specific problem areas, but the differences in reconviction rates are striking. Only the Shaw work in prisons was subsequently 'replicated' – repeated at a different site with different staff to see whether the results were generalisable. In this case the experiment was repeated in a completely different kind of establishment – a busy local prison – and found not to produce any reductions in reoffending, and that was that (Fowles 1978). Limited though they are in scope and scale and sophistication, these research projects represent a persistent strand in the practice of rehabilitation and probation. They speak to an emerging recognition that a body of evidential knowledge is required on which to base a claim to expertise or professionalism. The theme is repeated at intervals in the history, but it never ever reaches that stage of critical self-awareness that can systematically codify and learn from its own experience.

At this time, new thinking also emerged about the purpose and organisation of probation, partly in response to the 'anti-treatment' and 'due process' strictures of the justice model, partly because of uncertainties about the adoption of more controlling and surveillance functions and partly to accommodate claims made in the US and the UK that the effectiveness of penal interventions could not be verified (Bean 1976; Martinson 1974; Brody 1976). A 'social work' model was proposed by Bryant et al. (1978) which disconnected probation from offending behaviour altogether and proposed the provision of help to convicted individuals simply on the basis of need. Bottoms and McWilliams (1979) proposed a 'non-treatment' paradigm which harked back to an earlier era of service provision and downplayed the possibility of bringing about changes in offending behaviour. Neither of the models, which were thoughtful responses to the pressures of their time, helped to shape the actual future of probation which in England and Wales was headed in a totally different direction.

The idea of probation day training centres evolved from the results of a survey carried out by prison welfare officers on the problems faced by six hundred short-term prisoners released from four local prisons: unemployment, accommodation, physical and mental health, drink – a familiar litany (Vercoe 1970). The data also suggested a process of drift: the people with the most problems returned to prison more often. Day training centres were put forward as an alternative sentence with the aim of interrupting the cycles of decline identified by the research. The theory of the proposal located the problems faced by so-called 'petty' recidivists, not in their 'souls' or their 'personalities' or their early experiences, but in their performance of roles (Brim and Wheeler 1966). The day training centre was to provide a curriculum of activities designed to promote positive roles, to teach the skills required for their successful performance and to offer other services to help in this process. Part of the appeal of day centres to staff who worked in them was that they re-created, in a non-institutional environment, aspects of the therapeutic communities (TCs) that existed in psychiatric settings and some prisons (Fenton 1956; Farbring 2000). TCs had a long pedigree in North America and the UK and were notable for their introduction of self-governing principles in residential settings. Over time, however, the idea of the day centre escaped from the intentions of the Home Office funded pioneer projects and became a wide-ranging function that embraced drop-in facilities, cafes, further education and social support. In the process the possibility of developing a promising new approach to rehabilitation was lost (Vanstone 1993).

Working with groups also had a long history in the United States, particularly in community development and as group counselling in Californian prisons (Fenton 1956). Several probation areas experimented with group intake procedures (Stanley 1982), and general group work without specified offence targets (Brown and Caddick 1993). In other areas, specific types of offence were targeted; there were sex-offender groups in Bristol and in Nottinghamshire where they also had groups for homeless men and ex-prisoners (Weaver and Fox 1984; Eldridge and Gibbs 1987). In Greater Manchester, Hampshire and elsewhere, there were groups for 'drink' drivers, and dedicated groups for women on probation were also set up. Many groupwork sessions, whatever their specific targets, tended to include varied elements of education, information giving, group discussion and behavioural rehearsal (McGuire and Priestley 1985; Jones et al. 1993) In some of the initiatives, basic data was collected about participation rates, participant responses and outcomes in terms of reoffending rates.

Two other developments in probation practice tested mainstream theory and practice in dissimilar ways – the New Careers idea and victim–offender mediation. Following the assassination of John F. Kennedy, the Poverty Program channelled substantial resources towards the inner-city slums for the relief of deprivation. One strand of that programme and of that largesse was the recruitment and training of local residents to become staffers in the poverty programmes themselves (Priestley 1975). The principles were also adapted to work in prisons. Thousands of people graduated through New Careers programmes and some of them became professional workers in community and criminal justice agencies. A few projects took root in Britain. 'The Bristol New Careers Project', according to Brian Caddick (1994), 'held firmly to its aim of providing practical experiences which were humanitarian in kind and affirmative in purpose', sharply contrasting with community service that had drifted into work that was 'almost exclusively manual, menial and arduous' (Blagg and Smith 1989). A handful of graduates from the Bristol scheme and elsewhere completed the transition from prisoner status to that of fully trained probation officer – a small step towards proving the idea, but a massive message for society, for those who made the journey themselves and for all those who might want to follow them.

Victim–offender mediation has had a chequered history in the criminal justice system of England and Wales. Subsumed under the rubric of restorative justice, as theorised by Christie (1982) in Norway, by Wright (1991) in the UK and by many others elsewhere, it presents an ideological and practical challenge to both *punishment* which effectively pays no attention to the victims in whose interests it claims to act, and *treatment* which focuses wholly on changing the thinking and behaviour of the convicted individual. Restorative procedures seek to replace those of criminal justice almost in their entirety, seeing both punishment and treatment as missing the point – which is to repair the social and personal damage done by the commission of an offence. Christie asked: 'Why should the impossible cases hinder a decent solution when decency is possible? Why not restrict the area for punishment to the utmost by actively taking away all those cases that might be taken away?'

The new ways of working described here and in the selected extracts are important for a number of reasons. Firstly, many of them were practitioner led, attempts by front-line staff to do their work in new ways, combining the traditional values and orientations of the probation service with contemporary sociological and psychological theory and technique. Secondly, some of the methods redistributed power between the workers and those they supervised. They rewrote the rule book about the roles and statuses of workers and 'clients', establishing collaboration on equal terms as a pre-condition of the work and promoting probationers or ex-prisoners to be agents of their own change as well as that of others. And finally, efforts were made to record the work in an experimental way and to gather evidence about the effectiveness of interventions in terms of reconvictions. They became, in other words, empirical. In two senses, therefore, the new-style sessions acted as occasions for social accountability – of individuals for their own behaviour to a company of their peers, and of the agencies themselves for the discharge of their duty to the community that paid for them. They became, for all concerned, lessons in democratic participation and schools for citizenship. With care, encouragement and extra resources, they could have originated a process of organisational change from below. Wise managements in some places stood aside and let such things happen; in others they actively encouraged them.

It is salutary, in this history of professional discourse, to reflect on the fact, true then and true today, that most of the personal change that goes on in the world is self-willed and self-activated. John McVicar (1974) and Jimmy Boyle (1977) are very different people. Both ended up in prison serving very long sentences for serious violence offences – armed robbery and murder. Both were unruly prisoners, attacking staff and attempting to escape. By different routes – via sociology, writing and introspection for John McVicar: 'The critical influence was my son, I was deeply ashamed of the way my criminal activities had affected his life', through yoga, art and the Special Unit at Barlinnie Prison for Jimmy Boyle: 'Now that I had all this awareness, what could I do with it?' – they each came to decisions to *become* something else, to *be* someone else. And they did. It can be argued that they are exceptional individuals, which is the case, but in the matter of self-change everyone has that unique potential.

All this while, the spectre of punishment had not gone away. The Conservative Green Paper, *Punishment, Custody and the Community* (1988), was instrumental in changing the terms by which probation was henceforth to be defined. John Patten, then a minister at the Home Office, spelled out part of its message in an address to the Association of Chief Officers of Probation:

> The Green Paper recognises that in some cases the perception of punishment can be met only by a custodial sentence. It argues, however, that it would be adequately met in case of significant other categories of offenders, by … punishment in the community. The fact is that all probation based disposals are already in varying degrees forms of punishment. For example, the offender who has to report to a probation officer, or work specified hours on Community Service or spend 60 days at a day centre is clearly being punished. It is bizarre to scratch around to find polite euphemisms for what is going on. (Patten 1988, 1992)

As the end-game for rehabilitation and probation approached, a final innovation in theory and practice came over the horizon. Robert Ross was a psychologist whose intervention in the Oshawa and Pickering Probation Office in Ontario was to prove influential in the spread of cognitive behavioural methods in criminal justice systems throughout the English-speaking world and in Europe. Ross and his co-authors Elizabeth Fabiano and Crystal Ewles had reviewed the professional literature on effective penal treatments and had come to conclusions which contradicted those of Martinson (1966, 1974) and other pessimists (Ross *et al.* 1988). There had been, they said, a number of effective interventions which produced enduring changes in reconviction rates. Other commentators had reached similar conclusions (Palmer 1978; Blackburn 1980; McGuire and Priestley 1985) but Ross *et al.* identified what they saw as the common element in successful programmes, which was their derivation from the theory of cognitive-behavioural psychology. Their reading of the literature further suggested the existence of cognitive deficits – poor social skills and personal problem-solving, impulsiveness and lack of empathy – as major causes of serious and persistent offending and reoffending. The answer, devised by Ross *et al.* (1986) was an 80-hour cognitive-behavioural training package that taught social skills, problem-solving and values (empathy skills). In a randomly assigned study, reconviction rates for the experimentals who received this package were reduced from almost seventy per cent to less than twenty per cent when compared to those who received 'probation as usual'. The results were, in their own words, 'dramatic'. After a demonstration project in Mid-Glamorgan, staff were trained and 'Reasoning & Rehabilitation', as the package was now called, was installed in several probation areas and prisons in England and Wales (Raynor and Vanstone 1997).

Jerome Miller had radically – and sensationally – done away with juvenile custody when he was Youth Commissioner for Massachusetts in 1968, with no perceptible worsening of crime rates (Miller 1991). In 1989 he summarised the progress of the punitive philosophy in the United States, and contested its reliance on an assumed failure in 'treatment' methods. 'Paradoxically,' he says, 'the idea that nothing worked in rehabilitating offenders appealed to Left and Right alike.' His own diagnosis was that of a false dichotomy:

> Corrections is a system of extremes – debilitating prisons vs. ineffective probation/parole. To use a medical analogy, it would be like asking a doctor for relief from a headache and being told there are only two treatments – an aspirin or a lobotomy. (Miller 1989)

On the political front, punitive thinking had also begun to entrench itself in UK policy and practice during the 1980s. It received powerful endorsement from the accession of Michael Howard to the Home Office in 1993 declaring that for him 'prison works'. True to his word, Home Secretary Howard promised more prison places and at a stroke abolished the requirement for probation officers to undergo professional training. Ex-military personnel would, he claimed, be better

> Speech to Conservative Party Conference 6 October 1993: 'Prison works. It ensures that we are protected from murderers, muggers and rapists – and it makes many who are tempted to commit crime think twice … This may mean that more people will go to prison. I do not flinch from that. We shall no longer judge the success of our system of justice by a fall in our prison population.' (Michael Howard)

suited to the work (Aldridge 2002), but the seeds he planted were nurtured and brought to fruition by successive Labour Party office holders following the change in government in 1997. New Labour had ridden to power on a platform which proclaimed, among other things, the idea of 'tough on crime, tough on the causes of crime' (Garland 2000). They continued the prison building programmes set in train by their predecessors and then expanded them to ever higher levels. They continued to endorse and even reinforced the punitive rhetoric they inherited, and they set about systematically undermining the existence of the probation service as a separate, rehabilitatively minded service with a mind of its own, centralising control of its local areas under the National Probation Service. Finally, probation was injected into a new organisation, the National Offender Management Service (NOMS 2004), charged with managing sentences seamlessly from the community into captivity and back again, a task it was to achieve by commissioning services from probation and prison resources. NOMS was thus nominated as a purse-holder and power-broker for all the sentencing services funded by the Home Office. Within it, the functions of the former probation services were reaffirmed as 'punishment in the community' and the words 'probationers' and 'clients' and 'help' were expelled and replaced by a language of 'offenders', 'enforcement' and 'tough sentences'. 'Befriending', 'treatment' and 'support' became distant memories. Following catastrophic failures in the management of National Probation and the resolute refusal of the Prison Service to be subordinated to any other agency, the net result is that the Prison Service has been redesignated as NOMS and the former National Probation Service is now part of its expanded remit. The old prisons swallowed new probation whole and in the process the values and working methods developed since its statutory inception in 1907 were excreted and dumped by the wayside.

Alongside this demolition work, and without any hint of irony, the Labour Home Office also instituted the largest test of cognitive-behavioural programmes ever undertaken by any criminal justice system anywhere in the world (Vanstone 2002). The What Works initiative of the late 1990s and the first years of the twenty-first century cost hundreds of millions of pounds in training and delivery, but not one programme was ever made the subject of a random controlled trial. Despite the official expenditure and the professional effort, accredited programmes were eventually delivered only to small minorities of those eligible to receive them in prison and on probation (Priestley and Vanstone 2006). Large-scale evaluations of the programmes were conducted as quasi experiments, typically comparing actual outcomes with expected rates of reoffending or with those of large comparison populations. Because the results were inconclusive and not politically advantageous, penal policy struck camp, as it is wont to do, and moved on to pastures new. It is of a piece with the whole history of criminal justice theory and practice since the replacement of the unreformed prisons by 'modern' penitentiaries at the beginning of the nineteenth century. None of the great tidal movements in penal policy have been guided, or even for the most part *informed*, by evidence; it has all taken place in a virtually fact-free zone. The prison star has waxed and waned and been born again as the brightest object in the penal firmament. Rehabilitation, probation, treatment, education – all have had their day, but now is no longer their time.

Sir Edmund du Cane, eminent Victorian and autocratic creator of the National Prison System of England and Wales, described criminals as 'a class of fools whom even experience fails to teach' (du Cane 1885). The description is just as apt for those who administered criminal justice in the twentieth century; they perpetuated a system that failed to learn from its own history – only on an altogether more monumental and ultimately tragic scale.

34. Humanitarianism and punishment

C. S. Lewis

In England we have lately had a controversy about Capital Punishment. I do not know whether a murderer is more likely to repent and make a good end on the gallows a few weeks after his trial or in the prison infirmary thirty years later. I do not know whether the fear of death is an indispensable deterrent. I need not, for the purpose of this article, decide whether it is a morally permissible deterrent. Those are questions which I propose to leave untouched. My subject is not Capital Punishment in particular, but that theory of punishment in general which the controversy showed to be almost universal among my fellow-countrymen. It may be called the Humanitarian theory. Those who hold it think that it is mild and merciful. In this I believe that they are seriously mistaken. I believe that the 'Humanity' which it claims is a dangerous illusion and disguises the possibility of cruelty and injustice without end. I urge a return to the traditional or Retributive theory not solely, not even primarily, in the interests of society, but in the interests of the criminal.

According to the Humanitarian theory, to punish a man because he deserves it, and as much as he deserves, is mere revenge, and, therefore, barbarous and immoral. It is maintained that the only legitimate motives for punishing are the desire to deter others by example or to mend the criminal. When this theory is combined, as frequently happens, with the belief that all crime is more or less pathological, the idea of mending tails off into that of healing or curing and punishment becomes therapeutic. Thus it appears at first sight that we have passed from the harsh and self-righteous notion of giving the wicked their deserts to the charitable and enlightened one of tending the psychologically sick. What could be more amiable? One little point which is taken for granted in this theory needs, however, to be made explicit. The things done to the criminal, even if they are called cures, will be just as compulsory as they were in the old days when we called them punishments. If a tendency to steal can be cured by psychotherapy, the thief will no doubt be forced to undergo the treatment. Otherwise, society cannot continue.

My contention is that this doctrine, merciful though it appears, really means that each one of us, from the moment he breaks the law, is deprived of the rights of a human being.

The reason is this. The Humanitarian theory removes from Punishment the concept of Desert. But the concept of Desert is the only connecting link between punishment and justice. It is only as deserved or undeserved that a sentence can be just or unjust. I do not here contend that the question 'Is it deserved?' is the only one we can reasonably ask about a punishment. We may very properly ask whether it is likely to deter others and to reform the criminal. But neither of these two last questions is a question about justice. There is no sense in talking about a 'just deterrent' or a 'just cure'. We demand of a deterrent not whether it is just but whether it will deter. We demand of a cure not whether it is just but whether it succeeds. Thus when we cease to consider what the criminal deserves and consider only what will cure him or deter others, we have tacitly removed him from the sphere of justice altogether; instead of a person, a subject of rights, we now have a mere object, a patient, a 'case'.

The distinction will become clearer if we ask who will be qualified to determine sentences when sentences are no longer held to derive their propriety from the criminal's deservings. On the old view the problem of fixing the right sentence was a moral problem. Accordingly, the judge who did it was a person trained in jurisprudence; trained, that is, in a science which deals with rights and duties, and which, in origin at least, was consciously accepting guidance from the Law of Nature and from Scripture. We must admit that in the actual penal code of most countries at most times these high originals were so much modified by local custom, class interests, and utilitarian concessions, as to be very imperfectly recognizable. But the code was never in principle, and not always in fact, beyond the control of the conscience of the society. And when (say, in eighteenth-century England) actual punishments conflicted too violently with the moral sense of the community, juries refused to convict and reform was finally brought about. This was possible because, so long as we are thinking in terms of Desert, the propriety of the penal code, being a moral question, is a question on which every man has the right to an opinion, not because he follows this or that profession, but because he is simply a man, a rational animal enjoying the Natural Light. But all this is changed when we drop the concept of Desert. The only two questions we may now ask about a punishment are whether it deters and whether it cures. But these are not questions on which anyone is entitled to have an opinion simply because he is a man. He is not entitled to an opinion even if, in addition to being a man he should happen also to be a jurist, a Christian, and a moral theologian. For they are not questions about principle but about matter of fact; and for such 'cuiquam in sua ante credendum.' Only the expert 'penologist' (let barbarous things have barbarous names), in the light of previous experiment, can tell us what is likely to deter: only the psychotherapist can tell us what is likely to cure. It will be in vain for the rest of us, speaking simply as men, to say, 'but this punishment is hideously unjust, hideously disproportionate to the criminal's deserts'. The experts with perfect logic will reply, 'but nobody was talking about deserts. No one was talking about punishment in your archaic vindictive sense of the word. Here are the statistics proving that this treatment deters. Here are the statistics proving that this other treatment cures. What is your trouble?'

The Humanitarian theory, then, removes sentences from the hands of jurists whom the public conscience is entitled to criticize and places them in the hands of technical experts whose special sciences do not even employ such categories as rights or justice. It might be argued that since this transference results from an abandonment of the old idea of punishment, and, therefore, of all vindictive motives, it will be safe to leave our criminals in such hands. I will not pause to comment on the simple-minded view of fallen human nature which such a belief implies. Let us rather remember that the 'cure' of criminals is to be compulsory; and let us then watch how the theory actually works in the mind of the Humanitarian. The immediate starting point of this article was a letter I read in one of our Leftist weeklies. The author was pleading that a certain sin, now treated by our laws as a crime, should henceforward be treated as a disease. And he complained that under the present system the offender, after a term in gaol, was simply let out to return to his original environment where he would probably relapse. What he complained of was not the shutting up but the letting out. On his remedial view of punishment the offender should, of course, be detained until he was cured. And of course the official straighteners are the only people who can say when that is. The first result of the Humanitarian theory is, therefore, to substitute for a definite sentence (reflecting to some extent the community's moral judgment on the degree of ill-desert involved) an indefinite sentence terminable only by the word of those experts – and they are not experts in moral theology nor even in the Law of Nature – who inflict it. Which of us, if he stood in the dock, would not prefer to be tried by the old system?

It may be said that by the continued use of the word punishment and the use of the verb 'inflict' I am misrepresenting Humanitarians. They are not punishing, not inflicting, only healing. But do not let us be deceived by a name. To be taken without consent from my home and friends; to lose my liberty; to undergo all those assaults on my personality which modern psychotherapy knows how to deliver; to be re-made after some pattern of 'normality' hatched in a Viennese laboratory to which I never professed allegiance; to know that this process will never end until either my captors have succeeded or I grown wise enough to cheat them with apparent success – who cares whether this is called Punishment or not? That it includes most of the elements for which any punishment is feared – shame, exile, bondage, and years eaten by the locust – is obvious. Only enormous ill-desert could justify it; but ill-desert is the very conception which the Humanitarian theory has thrown overboard.

From: Lewis, C. S. (1949) 'The Humanitarian Theory of Punishment', 20th Century: An Australian Quarterly Review, 3.3: 5–12.

35. The frying-pan of charitable condescension

Barbara Wootton

Perhaps the main difference between the social work of today and that of yesterday lies less in the nature of its presumptions, than in the degree of their explicitness. Social workers of the unashamedly charitable period had clear enough ideas of the qualities which distinguished the deserving from the *un*deserving poor: they were out to encourage the self-reliant, industrious, thrifty working-man at the expense of his opposite, and they were not afraid to say so. By contrast, the modern caseworker, under obligation to maintain an attitude of 'neither tolerance nor intolerance', and conceiving her function as concerned with 'psychological maladjustment rather than material need', necessarily finds it harder to say clearly what she is driving at. The one explicit and consistent factor in her handling of every kind of social problem is her unwavering dependence upon psychiatric interpretation. Moral and economic problems alike are reduced to common psychiatric denominators and expressed in identical terms. The probation officer and the psychiatric social worker at the child guidance clinic alike 'diagnose' their cases and conduct 'therapeutic' interviews with them; and the family caseworker goes one step further still, by using the same terms to describe his dealings with those who come to his notice for no better reason than that they cannot make ends meet. Before we know where we are, in fact, poverty no less than crime will rank as a form of mental disorder.

This psychiatric approach to social work, in short, makes it possible simultaneously to disown and to retain the attitude of superior wisdom and insight traditionally adopted by the rich towards the poor: to retain, to quote Virginia Woolf [...], the 'easy mastery of the will over the poor', and to preserve class attitudes, while denouncing class consciousness. In an article from which I have already quoted, Howarth (1951) gets dangerously near to saying this in so many words. The movement 'away from the idea of social work as a function of the privileged to the under-privileged' has, she believes, been a source of 'anxieties and of apparent loss of confidence. It is, too, a reason for a turning towards psychiatry and psychology for added understanding, for as soon as the individual is identified apart from his social category, it is necessary to come to terms with much in his behaviour which is difficult to understand.' While playing down material dissatisfactions as 'pegs upon which a client hangs his dissatisfactions with himself and with his social relationships', the modern caseworker no longer needs to fear the loss of the position of privilege on which her prestige has been founded. Psychology and psychiatry provide a new kind of authority, and one which, if necessary, can be independent of a client's 'social category'. So we pass out of the frying-pan of charitable condescension into the no less condescending fire – or rather the cool detachment – of superior psychological insight.

Apart from its lamentable arrogance, the danger of this social-scientific naïveté is that, once again, it has offered a convenient excuse for some social workers to neglect social action. In the days of the classical economists the individual was poverty stricken through personal fault. In the heyday of Freudianism he got that way because of his early childhood. At neither time did social workers have to become agitated about simple environmental factors such as low wages, inadequate housing, and lack of protective labour legislation. Even though 'there have always been heroic characters associated with social work', it remains true that 'the old-time charity organization societies and the modern voluntary casework agencies have never been havens for them' (Miles 1954).

From: B. Wootton (1959) Social Science and Pathology. *London: George Allen & Unwin, pp. 292–93.*

36. Faith and counsellors

Paul Halmos

The counsellors have come to realise that their personal intervention is so much more effective when it is carried out with spontaneous warmth and affection, than when they just go through the motions of interest and concern. The insincerity of professionally pretending cannot be concealed for long, and even when the 'role-playing of love' is diligently sustained by experienced, well-practised counsellors, it is still insufficiently convincing. There are several irreconcilable precepts professed here: both spontaneous lovingness and scrupulously thought-out strategy of technique are necessary, yet it is hard to see how the two can be had by the same person devoted to both, and identified with the roles required by both. Then there is the difficulty of prescribing lovingness for the use of the counsellor: the act of 'prescribing' cancels out the requirement of spontaneity and sincerity. For a similar reason, nor can the gestures of spontaneous sympathy be the subject of a didactic imparting of skills to counsellors by trainers of counsellors. In his recent book H. Fingarette (1963) relates this to the context to which it belongs, 'Time and again in the literature of both East and West, we meet the ideal person as one who offers love and sympathy and selfless devotion while remaining in some sense "disinterested", "detached", "uninvolved", "ruthless". Compassionate objectivity, human-hearted but disinterested understanding: *the paradox in these phrases is evident*.'[1] (Italics mine.) Unexpectedly, the psychoanalytically-minded writer falls in line with an ancient discipline and he is followed by the rank and file of the counselling professions.

The counsellor believes in the all-pervasiveness of the impulsive, the emotional, and of the so-called *Id* forces of life yet he is a firm believer too in the supreme rationality and intelligence of life. We are initially ruled from 'below' yet the very stuff of this low instinctiveness has the inherent potential of generating from itself the rational and intelligent knower and controller of itself. In addition to this, the basic instinctiveness of life is both loving and hating, and the counsellor takes the fundamental ambivalence of life as a cornerstone of his psychology. And though with one assertion he tells us of ambivalence as an equilibrium – disturbed or not – of originally equal forces, in another assertion he takes it as no less fundamental that love is always to prevail: the fact of his profession, his dedication to healing of a certain kind proves that he believes in the eventual triumph of positive forces. In the race between love and hate, he backs love *as well as* the stoical acceptance of death.

It is strange that the modern doctrines of counselling, which have done so much to disillusion us of the eighteenth-century fiction that man is a fundamentally rational creature, should be the very doctrines which enunciate that rationality of insight into our own motives is the condition of our freedom from neurotic suffering. The counsellor seems to believe in the ultimate rationality and ultimate irrationality of those whom he helps, and of the helping process itself. This belief is shown by his attitude to the problem of the counsellor's personal involvement in the client. In applying himself to the task of helping he must, on no account, get himself involved in what he is doing. But this prescription of detachment and complete impersonal objectivity will not work.

Firstly, it will not work, because it sets an ideal which is impossible to achieve, and secondly, because were it achieved – the counsellors seem to believe – the healing enterprise would fail. With no involvement at all, the client would be 'frozen out' and total involvement the client would be 'burnt up'. Therefore the counsellor must do both, antinomially, contradictorily, *and* complementarily, in the manner of T. S. Eliot's 'Teach us to care not to care', with much the same sentiment of awe and humility which informed the poetic phrasing.

The paradox of incentives for doing counselling work remains unresolved in the face of all the critical reappraisals. Whatever personal motives we may allow the counsellor, with which to sustain his efforts and warm his concerns, he is expected to continue to maintain vigilance over his compassion for the patient, using as a source of energy – necessary for maintaining this vigilance – the very compassion he is supposed to keep in check. That this feeling for the patient involves the counsellor in a relationship of reciprocity and mutuality is obscured by the professional status and presumed superior strength of the healer over the other. In private practice the patient pays the counsellor; the oath of secrecy binds the counsellor but not the patient; in public service the counsellor retains vestiges of the 'official' in him; and there are other features in the relationship which help to conceal this mutuality. Yet in fact, the professional status of the counsellor tends to be used as a defence against admitting that he does enter into a personal and non-professional mutuality of relationship, whilst paradoxically trying to maintain side-by-side with this a non-personal and professional relationship. We regularly encounter frank disclosures to the effect that mutuality is vividly experienced by the counsellor, and that it is essential for therapeutic success, and equally that its detached viewing and control are also essential.

It is interesting to observe that even in the philosophical-psychological theory of this mutuality we have a paradoxical structure perpetuated: some counsellors describe mutuality as a regression (e.g. 'return to the womb') taking the term in the psychoanalytic sense; others will represent it as an 'emergent', a product of ascending progress, ascending that is from the primitive instinctive beginnings. What is paradoxical is this: the careful reading of the texts as well as the implications of these contradictions suggests that, in fact, the counsellors believe both these interpretations. Here too there is a quietistic fusion of incompatible theoretical models.

From: P. Halmos (1965) The Faith of the Counsellors. *London: Constable, pp. 160–63.*

37. Resocializing prisoners

K. Berntsen and K. Christiansen

The documents of the criminal case and the information they contained about the previous crimes and the personal background of the sentenced criminal formed the starting point of the investigation. This material was supplemented and amplified through interviews with one of the social workers; in many cases the same social worker also began the work of social rehabilitation. The prisoners were then sent on to the psychologist, who conducted the necessary tests (Raven Matrix, Rorschach, and occasionally the Thematic Apperception Test), and also attempted to form an impression of the prisoner's personality structure at one or several clinical interviews. The main aim of these interviews and tests was to chart the background of criminality and other forms of maladjustment.

A survey was then made of the prisoner's career and his present situation, supplemented by an evaluation of his chances of resocialization, and a plan of treatment was worked out which was submitted to the committee for the project.

The actual treatment was thus begun at an earlier stage of the prison sentence. The social work consisted in funding work (54 cases), a difficult and time-consuming task during the winter of 1952–53 with the high rate of unemployment, in finding accommodation (24 cases), clothing (30 cases), and in helping the prisoner with trade union and health insurance membership formalities (47 cases). Sometimes very modest financial help was given on the prisoner's release (31 cases), and sometimes it was necessary to help the prisoners in negotiations with tax authorities (15), with Public Assistance offices (22), and other public authorities and institutions as well as private creditors (60). Often assistance was needed to straighten out difficulties with wives or husbands, parents or other relatives (58). Twelve prisoners began an anti-alcoholic treatment during or after their imprisonment; in six of these cases this was a condition of their pardon. Through talks with particularly unbalanced prisoners the psychologist tried to cure depressions and to ward off conflicts.

The majority of the prisoners were released after having served their sentences. On the recommendation of the committee fifteen had their sentence commuted after having served half time. Most of these persons were placed under supervision for one to two years. The investigators strove to create such a relationship of trust between themselves and the prisoners during their imprisonment and to arouse in them so sincere a desire to leave off their life of crime that a form of voluntary supervision could be established. Since their release, about half the prisoners have contacted the investigators.

[...]

Some of the most important results of the investigation are given below.

The Criterion of Recidivism. For the purpose of the investigation the most severe sanction awarded during the observation period was emphasized. The material was divided into four groups, which were classified in such a way that, when taken in the right order, they were mutually exclusive. Prisoners sentenced to special measures, e.g. workhouse, preventive detention for criminal psychopaths,[1] etc. were registered in the group entitled 'special measures', even if they had also been sentenced to prison, simple detention, or a fine. Prisoners registered in the 'prison' group may also have been sentenced to simple detention or a fine, while the group 'fine/detention' is homogeneous.

Table 1 shows that there is a considerably larger number of recidivists in the control group (the C-group) than in the experimental group (the E-group). If the dividing line between the recidivists and the non-recidivists is taken to be some form of recidivism which led to prison sentences or special measures on the one hand and fines/simple detention or no registration on the other, then the percentage of recidivism in the E-group is about 41% as against 58% in the C-group. This difference is statistically significant, u = 2.76, whereby P < 0.01.

Table 1 Most severe sanction during observation period

		E	C	total
No subsequent	abs. fig.	52	40	92
convictions	per cent	41.3	31.7	36.5
Fine/simple	abs. fig.	22	13	35
detention	per cent	17.5	10.3	13.9
Prison sentence	abs. fig.	46	66	112
	per cent	36.5	52.4	44.4
Special measures	abs. fig.	6	7	13
	per cent	4.8	5.6	5.2
Total	abs. fig.	126	126	252
	per cent	100.0	100.0	100.0

From: K. Berntsen and K. Christiansen (1965) 'A Resocialization Experiment with Short-Term Offenders', Scandinavian Studies in Criminology, *1: 35–54.*

Note

1. SS. 17 and 70 of the *Danish Criminal Code*, with an introduction by Dr Knud Waaben, Professor A. I. in the University of Copenhagen. Copenhagen: G. E. C. Gad Publishers, pp. 12–14, 25–6 and 44–5.

38. The age of treatment

Robert Martinson

In describing the processual nature of some deviance, Lemert (1964) distinguished *primary* from *secondary* deviance. Briefly, primary deviance was the pristine deviant act while secondary deviance was the reaction of the deviant to the social reaction called forth by the deviant act. The custody–treatment dimension forces upon us the recognition of further steps in this process.

There has increasingly appeared a new, social reaction to the persistent failure of the traditional social reactions to deviance. The original deviant act has been partially contained, controlled, semi-organized. This process often gives birth to secondary deviance – 'rejecting the rejectors,' if you like. But this rejecting has become unacceptable to those agents of society rejected by the deviant. They are somewhat in the position of the fanatic who might be defined as a person who, faced with failure, redoubles his efforts. This is what treatment has become or is becoming – a redoubling of efforts in the face of persistent failure.

There is no compelling evidence that this redoubling of efforts has as yet had an important effect on the rate of recidivism. One powerful component of the newer 'treatment' reaction is the growing social recognition that this is so. To the daily frustrations of the correctional treatment staff member involved in the intimate game of 'shucking' the inmate who is 'shucking' him, there grows the pressure for results from central state legislature, and society, and all those who would narrow correctional ambitions to reducing recidivism. This new urgency within the correctional system is beginning to be called: 'the correctional therapeutic community.' In probation and parole a similar process *can be* involved in the halfway house, the parole outpatient clinic, gathering parolees together for Nalline tests or group counseling sessions, the movement towards smaller caseloads – situations in which the agent of society may tackle his slippery client jowl-to-jowl.

I am not suggesting that this process has run its course or is even a major component of all correctional or medical situations. It has gone further in some areas than others. It is not a fatal drift. It is, nevertheless, a reality. It has laid a powerful basis for even more severe redoublings of effort by those standing in the wings with some new nostrums to sell the despairing but ever-hopeful 'treatment teams.'

From: R. Martinson (1966) 'The Age of Treatment: Some Implications of the Custody–Treatment Dimension', Issues in Criminology, 2: 275–93.

39. In the Ghetto

Mac Davis

As the snow flies
On a cold and gray Chicago mornin'
A poor little baby child is born
In the ghetto
And his mama cries
'cause if there's one thing that she don't need
it's another hungry mouth to feed
In the ghetto
People, don't you understand
the child needs a helping hand
or he'll grow to be an angry young man some day
Take a look at you and me,
are we too blind to see,
do we simply turn our heads
and look the other way
Well the world turns
and a hungry little boy with a runny nose
plays in the street as the cold wind blows
In the ghetto
And his hunger burns
so he starts to roam the streets at night
and he learns how to steal
and he learns how to fight
In the ghetto
Then one night in desperation
a young man breaks away
He buys a gun, steals a car,
tries to run, but he don't get far
And his mama cries
As a crowd gathers 'round an angry young man
face down on the street with a gun in his hand
In the ghetto

As her young man dies,
on a cold and gray Chicago mornin',
another little baby child is born
In the ghetto

From: Davis, M. (1968) In the Ghetto (The Vicious Circle). *See 'The Best of Mac Davis' songbook,* © 1975 Screen Gems – Columbia Publications.

40. The justice model

American Friends Service Committee

In the latter part of the nineteenth century and increasingly in the twentieth century, the decline of the prison as a productive economic institution has vitiated most of the purported therapy of 'hard labor.' Idleness or meaningless made-work is today the characteristic regime of many, perhaps most, inmates. More important, the concept of reformation as something achieved through penitence or the acquisition of working skills and habits has been de-emphasized because of developments in social and behavioral science. Varying scientific or pseudoscientific approaches to crime, although in conflict with one another and unconfirmed by hard scientific data, view criminals as distinct biological, psychological, or social-cultural types.

Such theories all share a more or less deterministic premise, holding that man's behavior is caused by social or psychological forces located outside his consciousness and therefore beyond his control. Rehabilitation, therefore, is deemed to require expert help so as to provide the inmate with the understanding and guidance that it is assumed he cannot achieve on his own.

The individualized treatment model, the outcome of this historical process, has for nearly a century been the ideological spring from which almost all actual and proposed reform in criminal justice has been derived. It would be hard to exaggerate the power of this idea or the extent of its influence. In recent years it has been the conceptual foundation of such widely divergent approaches to criminal justice as the President's Crime Commission Report, the British *Why Prison? – A Quaker View of Imprisonment and Some Alternatives* and the American Law Institute's Model Penal Code. Like other conceptions that become so entrenched that they slip imperceptibly into dogma, the treatment model has been assumed rather than analyzed, preached rather than evaluated.

The underlying rationale of this treatment model is deceptively simple. It rejects inherited concepts of criminal punishment as the payment of a debt owed to society, a debt proportionate to the magnitude of the offender's wrong. Instead it would save the offender through constructive measures of reformation, protect society by keeping the offender locked up until that reformation is accomplished, and reduce the crime rate not only by using cure-or-detention to eliminate recidivism, but hopefully also by the identification of potential criminals in advance so that they can be rendered harmless by preventive treatment. Thus the dispassionate behavioral expert displaces judge and theologian. The particular criminal act becomes relevant except insofar as it has diagnostic significance in classifying and treating the actor's particular criminal typology. Carried to an extreme, the sentence for all crimes would be the same: an indeterminate commitment to imprisonment, probation, or parole, whichever was dictated at any particular time by the treatment program. Any sentence would be the time required to bring about rehabilitation, a period which might be a few weeks or a lifetime.

The treatment model's judicious blend of humanitarian, practical welfare, and scientific ancestry was nicely illustrated sixty years ago by the Elmira Reformatory's Zebulon R. Brockway (1912):

> The common notion of a moral responsibility based on freedom should no longer be made a foundation principle for criminal laws, court procedure, and prison treatment. The claim of such responsibility need neither be denied nor affirmed, but put aside as being out of place in a system of treatment of offenders for the purpose of public protection. Together with abrogation of this responsibility goes, too, any awesome regard for individual liberty of choice and action by imprisoned criminals. The habitual conduct and indeed their related character must needs be directed and really determined by their legalized custodians....
>
> The perfected reformatory will be the receptacle and refiner of antisocial humans who are held in custody under discretional indeterminateness for the purpose of the public protection. Legal and sentimental inhibitions of necessary coercion for the obdurate, intractable element of the institution population will be removed and freedom given for the wide use of unimpassioned useful, forceful measures. Frequent relapses to crime of prisoners discharged from these reformatories will be visited upon the management, as are penalties for official malfeasance. The change will be, in short, a change from the reign of sentiment swerved by the feelings to a passionless scientific procedure pursuing welfare.

As with any model, of course, its implementation has been uneven, often halting, and seldom complete. Perhaps the closest approximation to the ideal is in certain so-called sexual psychopath statutes under which an indeterminate and potentially) lifelong incarceration can be ordered as a civil commitment without conviction of any crime. Judicial power is yielded grudgingly, however, and legislators cling to the notion that maximum penalties should be graded according to their idea of relative blameworthiness, so that the result is a patchwork quilt of inconsistent rationales. Overall, however, the movement toward the individualized treatment model is unmistakable. Every state has some form of parole, which provides a core indeterminacy. Compared to the median time served, the maximum possible sentence for most crimes is so excessive that the disposition of almost any conviction utilizes the treatment process in some manner.

While opposition to 'mollycoddling' prisoners still exists, the basic thrust of the model has been accepted by almost all liberals, reformers of all persuasions, the scientific community, probably a majority of judges, and those of law-and-order persuasion who perceive the model's repressive potential.

How has the model united such a motley collection of supporters? Its conceptual simplicity and scientific aura appeal to the pragmatism of a society confident that American know-how can reduce any social problem to manageable proportions. Its professed repudiation of retribution adds moral uplift and an inspirational aura. At the same time, the treatment model is sufficiently vague in concept and flexible in practice to accommodate both the traditional and utilitarian objectives of criminal law administration. It claims to protect society by incapacitating the prisoner in an institution until pronounced sufficiently reformed. This prospect is unpalatable enough and sufficiently threatening in its uncertainty to provide at least as effective a deterrent to potential offenders as that of the traditional eye-for-an-eye model. Maximum flexibility is required to achieve the model's goal, that of treatment individualized to each offender's unique needs, so the system's administrators are granted broad discretionary powers. Whatever the effect on offenders, these powers have secured the support of a growing body of administrators, prosecutors, and judges, for it facilitates the discharge of their managerial duties and frees them from irksome legal controls. Even the proponents of retribution, although denied entry through the front door, soon discovered that harsh sentences could be accommodated within the treatment model as long as they were rationalized in terms of public protection or the necessity for prolonged regimes of re-education.

The treatment model tends to be all things to all people. This partially accounts for the paradox that while the model's ideological command has become ever more secure, its implementation has tended to form rather than substance. In fact, the model has never commanded more than lip service from most of its more powerful adherents. The authority given those who manage the system, a power more absolute than that found in any other sphere of law, has concealed the practices carried on in the name of the treatment model. At every level – from prosecutor to parole-board member – the concept of individualization has been used to justify secret procedures, unreviewable decision making, and an unwillingness to formulate anything other than the most general rules or policy. Whatever else may be credited to a century of individualized-treatment reform effort, there been a steady expansion of the scope of the criminal justice system and a consolidation of the state's absolute power over the lives of those caught in the net.

The irony of this outcome emphasizes the importance of searching examination of the assumptions underlying the individualized treatment model. Hopefully such an analysis illuminates efforts to delineate the proper role of criminal justice in a free and democratic society. It may also help us understand what factors have perpetuated our present criminal justice system decade after decade in the face of compelling evidence of its systematic malfunctioning.

[...]

We have sketched a number of problematic features of a correctional treatment model of criminal justice. Most of the problems and defects that have been posed are not very difficult to understand; one might even categorize a number of them as obvious. How is one to account, then, for the enthusiastic and uncritical acceptance by most of the liberal and progressive elements in our society of reformative, indeterminate, individualized treatment as the ideal goal of a criminal justice system?

There is something about this phenomenon akin to religious conversion, an acceptance of what appears to be true and valuable, what we want to be true, even though it cannot be reduced to anything more precise than vague generalities. It seems obvious that extremely complex forces lie behind liberal treatment ideology's mission to control not just the crimes but the way of life of others. Guilt about the gulf that separates our material well-being from poverty and oppression may account for some of the prejudice against and irrational fear of the poor and the oppressed; or it may help to account for our eagerness to hand over the problem to specialists as a way of relieving our anxiety. Once you have delegated a problem to an expert, you are off the hook.

If we could make some sense out of this extraordinary willingness to believe unreasonable things about criminal justice and corrections, we might begin to have some understanding of the forces that perpetuate so unjust a system. We explore this problem further below; it is hardly necessary to state here, however, that we cannot provide a satisfactory solution to this major puzzle. We do, however, hope to promote its analysis end encourage its study. Such an inquiry seems to us to be prerequisite to effectuating basic changes in our concepts and practices of criminal justice. The most stubborn obstacles to such change are not, in our opinion, the growing problem of violent crime or the hard-line advocates of punitive law-and-order repression or the rigidity and increasingly conservative polarization of our law enforcement and correctional bureaucracies or the perversity of adverse public opinion. Serious as they are, such forces can be contained if adequate options are developed and promoted. We suspect that much of the current strength of these conservative forces derives from the fact that there is no tenable alternative model of a criminal justice system that affords accommodation of such competing values as equality, respect for individual dignity and autonomy, encouragement of cultural diversity, and the need for a reasonably orderly society. The correctional treatment model does not begin to meet this need.

From: American Friends Service Committee (1971) Struggle for Justice: A Report on Crime and Punishment in America. *New York: Hill & Wang, pp. 36–47.*

41. Task-centred casework

W. J. Reid and L. Epstein

Problems perceived by the client are elicited, explored, and clarified by the caseworker in the initial interview. The problem which the client is most anxious to resolve is normally seen as the primary target of intervention, if it meets the criteria of the model. If the client does not acknowledge a problem that would provide an acceptable target of intervention, the practitioner attempts to determine if one is present through a systematic review with the client of possible problem areas. If a target problem is not located through this process within the first two interviews, or in some cases through a more extended problem-search carried out with the explicit agreement of the client, there is no further basis for work with the client within the framework of the model. Assuming a target problem can be located, the practitioner and client reach agreement on the problem(s) to which their work will be addressed.

Once agreement on the problem has been reached, tasks are formulated and selected in collaboration with the client, in the first interview if possible. A task defines what the client is to do to alleviate his problem. The task represents both an immediate goal the client is to pursue and the means of achieving the larger goal of problem alleviation. In its initial formulation, a task provides a general statement of the action the client is to undertake rather than a detailed blueprint. For example, Mrs. Brown is to develop a firmer, more consistent approach in handling her child's behavior; Mr. and Mrs. Clark are to develop a plan for the care of their mentally retarded daughter. More than one task may be developed and worked on in a given course of treatment.

In general, the client's task is based on the course of action he thinks would be most effective in alleviating his problem. The caseworker may then help the client modify the task to make it more focused and manageable. If the client is unable to propose an appropriate course of action, the caseworker helps the client develop a task through exploration and discussion of task possibilities which the caseworker may draw from the client or suggest himself. The task is so structured that chances of it being accomplished, in whole or in part, are high. Consequently the caseworker is able to convey realistic positive expectations that the client will be successful in carrying out the task.

Once the task has been explicitly formulated and agreed upon, the caseworker and client decide on the approximate amount and duration of service. In most cases eight to twelve interviews are planned to take place during a period of two to four months. Interviews generally occur at weekly intervals though the frequency may vary.

Once an agreement has been reached on the nature of the client's task and the limits of service, the caseworker's interventions are then directed almost exclusively toward helping the client accomplish the agreed-upon task. As treatment proceeds, the task may be revised, usually in the direction of greater specificity. In some cases the task may be completely reformulated or new tasks added.

The model contains no 'diagnostic phase.' The practitioner continually makes diagnostic judgments which both guide and are guided by his activities. These judgments are first concerned with classification, specification, and exploration of the clients' problems, then with assessment of possible client tasks and finally with evaluation of his efforts to achieve tasks agreed upon. In general, the practitioner attempts to be both systematic and responsive in his communications to the client. Thus he tries to focus communication in order to accomplish agreed upon goals but in a manner that conveys interest and empathic understanding and in a way that builds upon the client's own communications. Specific types of communication include: (1) exploration of the client's problem, task possibilities, and task-related behavior; (2) structuring the treatment relationship and communication within it; (3) enhancing the client's awareness in ways to help him overcome obstacles to, or otherwise facilitate, task achievement; (4) encouragement of task-directed behavior; and (5) suggesting means of task accomplishment. Comparable types of communication are used when family members are interviewed together or in work with individuals on the clients' behalf. The caseworker's operations, whether carried out with the clients or with others, are used in whatever combination will best help the client achieve the task in the most direct and economical way possible.

The process of terminating treatment is begun in the initial phase when the duration of treatment is set. In the last, or next-to-last interview, the client is helped to identify his achievements, apply what he has done to remaining problems, and define future tasks he might undertake on his own. Extensions beyond agreed-upon limits are made only in exceptional cases and then usually for brief, specified periods.

This treatment design is offered as an addition to the relatively small number of casework models, and to the relatively large number of models of interpersonal treatment. As we have seen, it contains few elements that are really new, and nothing that is revolutionary. Its *raison d'être* lies in the particular synthesis that we have tried to achieve.

As a brief, time-limited service aimed at specific problems, the present approach belongs to a general class of models of short-term, interpersonal treatment. It differs from most psychotherapeutic approaches in respect to both target problems and methods of intervention. While the target problems of task-centered casework and those of models of brief psychotherapy share a good deal of common ground, there are important differences in range. Our model excludes certain disorders, such as phobias and psychophysiological problems to which brief psychotherapy models may be addressed. On the other hand, we include certain psychosocial difficulties, such as problems of relations with formal organizations and of inadequate resources, that are generally not seen as targets of short-term psychotherapy. Our range of intervention is somewhat broader, covering practitioner activities in the client's social network. Quite possibly (though this remains to be demonstrated) there are also differences in emphasis given to various types of interventions. We would expect, for example, that in task-centered casework there would be relatively greater use of direction, encouragement, and techniques to help clients increase their understanding of others and their social situations; there would probably be less use of methods designed to promote the client's awareness of the dynamics of his own behavior. In these respects, we think, the present approach incorporates certain characteristics that differentiate casework from psychotherapy models generally.

From: W. J. Reid and L. Epstein (1972) Task-centred Casework. *New York: Columbia University Press, pp. 21–4.*

42. Serving the community

John Harding

Traditionally, community service has been developed by middle-class groupings where the volunteers are usually of a higher actual class than those being served. Informal helping, however, has always gone on at the neighbourhood level in which the helper is not specially labelled as a volunteer. Probation officers will not be short of examples where offenders have inconspicuously given service in their own community or neighbourhood. Indeed, over the last few years social work agencies have begun to recognise the potentiality of using the offender as a helper in the community. How has this movement begun and what lessons have we already learned which can be of relevance to the new community service provisions?

In America we know of the New Careers project and Anti-Poverty programmes where ex-offenders, ex-mental patients and neighbourhood residents have been employed in their hundreds. These organisations are aware that ex-offenders and similarly disadvantaged groups have special abilities to offer – an understanding of subcultures, an easier entreé to a group than a professional and a built-in resistance to the 'con' since the worker may have used the approach so many times in the past. Some of these ideas have begun to germinate in this country and various probation departments are experimenting with using selected ex-offenders and clients to assist in groups and work with families. Similarly, Borstal boys have been used in work with the handicapped and elderly in several community projects, surprising staff and public alike with their tenderness and good humour.

What do these examples teach us, particularly when we are thinking about community service? Firstly, the desire to be wanted is basic to human nature. Many who feel rejected by their families or society can under the right circumstances find fulfilment in discovering that they are needed by others. In a sense community service is beginning to reverse the coin – instead of making people, in the old social work model, recipients of help, we are asking them to be dispensers of help and thereby gain status and approval for their actions.

I am also convinced that if community service is to be a genuinely rehabilitative alternative to a custodial sentence then the offender has much to learn by performing an act of service alongside volunteer groups already operating in the community. Naturally some tasks will be administered by probation ancillaries but in the main in Nottinghamshire we are looking for a creative mix of volunteers and offenders whereby the offender can come into contact with some of the values and attitudes of the volunteers themselves. A too heavy reliance on probation-administered tasks, even though attractive to the community service coordinator since it makes his job a little simpler to organise, overlooks the wide range and scope of voluntary organisations and the potential learning experience of offenders in the variety of tasks they seek to carry out.

From: J. Harding (1973) 'Community Service – a Beginning', Probation Journal, *1.19: 13–17.*

43. Extended contact with prisoners

Margaret Shaw

The experimental treatment

It was decided to focus treatment on the last 6 months of a man's sentence. This is one of the crucial periods of imprisonment, and one in which welfare officers might hope to act as a bridge between prison and the after-care officer outside. The experimental treatment was planned to take the form of weekly sessions with the welfare officer, lasting about 1 hour. All men selected for the experimental group were called up 6 months prior to their date of release, and asked whether or not they were willing to attend for weekly sessions. After some discussion it was decided to leave the method of approach to the individual officer. Some officers felt that certain men would feel uneasy about interviews if told that they were part of a Home Office experiment, and that other men would be suspicious or anxious if they were not given a clear reason for the proposed interviews.

Extended contact

Within the weekly sessions, the treatment given was not specified or defined. The aim was to provide social casework, but whether this should involve insight-giving, support, or the manipulation of the environment was not prescribed. To some extent, therefore, the treatment was of a 'Black-Box' variety, although case-records were examined, and it was agreed that diagnosis and planning of treatment should form an important part. Since the content of the case-records was not examined in detail, it was preferred to refer to the treatment plan as 'extended contact' rather than 'intensive casework', and to standardise as far as possible the length and frequency of this contact.

In keeping with the attempt to strengthen contact between the prison and the after-care officer, and to develop treatment in the prison which would be relevant to the problems to be faced on release, a special letter was devised by the senior welfare officers. They sent this to the after-care officer appointed to work with each of the experimental cases. The letter explained the purpose of the experiment, and invited a special interest in the case and collaboration in planning treatment to bring about a better transfer at the time of discharge.

The control group

Only the men in the experimental groups at the two prisons were offered this extended contact with the welfare staff. It was not intended, however, that other men in the prisons should be denied access to the welfare officer as a result of the experiment. Men in the control group, and the rest of the inmates, were able to make applications to be seen in the normal manner.

Selection of the sample

A total of 176 men were selected for the study, 80 from Ashwell and 96 from Gartree. They were drawn at random from lists of men on each wing or billet due for release from the two prisons during 1969. Allocation to the experimental and control groups was also random and the men were not matched in terms of their ages or other factors. The total population of men eligible for release was too small for any matching to take place.

[...]

Information about subsequent convictions, obtained from the Criminal Record Office in October 1970 and February 1971, yielded significant results: so a further check was carried out on 28 February 1972. Table 1 shows that fewer of the 'experimentals' were reconvicted.

Under half the 'experimentals' (43 per cent) had not been reconvicted compared with over a fifth of the 'controls' (21 per cent), and the difference was significant (P <0.01). This trend was observable at both prisons, although more marked at Gartree where only 6 (14 per cent) of the 'controls' had not been reconvicted compared with 16 (37 per cent) of the 'experimentals.'

Table 1 Numbers of men reconvicted within 2 years after release from prison (Ashwell and Gartree)

	Experimental group		Control group		Total
	No.	%	No.	%	No.
Reconvicted	43	57.3	57	76.0	100
Not reconvicted	32	42.7	16	21.3	48
Died	–	–	2	2.7	2
Total	75	100.0	75	100.0	150

$(2 \times 2 x^2 = 7.268,$ P <0.001)

From: M. Shaw (1974) Social Work in Prison. An Experiment in the Use of Extended Contact with Offenders, *Home Office Research Studies No. 22. London: HMSO, pp. 13–14 and 74.*

44. McVicar

John McVicar

The critical influence was my son. I was deeply ashamed of the way my criminal activities had affected his life, and might do so again, depriving him of a father as completely as I had been deprived. I was re-creating in his life many of the conditions which led to my own indoctrination into crime. I knew that my own relationship with my son could never be anything like that between my father and me; but I started thinking about my father for the first time since he died. I started to read books on child psychology; at first, I suppose, to try and understand the development of my own son, but it quickly grew into a passion to try to relive and understand my own childhood.

My effort left me with some understanding of, and insight into, my upbringing, but with very little grasp of how and why my criminality had emerged and developed. Remember that I had lived by crime and had known hundreds of professional criminals.

I knew that by and large they were not actuated by the simple motivations of lust, greed and hate; those that are, are often ostracized by the criminal community as ruthlessly as the criminal is by society. I also knew that all the penal measures adopted in this country are, as a means of reformation, a joke (e.g. remissions of sentence are fortuitous and unpredictable). But this was all knowledge which had been learned intuitively from my own experience and I could not articulate it for myself. One element in this store of acquired knowledge was the criminological fatuity of my prison dossier, which was an added stimulus to me to try and achieve the means of understanding which I needed. For myself, I found them in the sociology of roles and values, and tried to explain my criminality by the concepts it provided.

I have tried to summarize this explanation in this document. I said at the beginning that I wanted it most of all to be the truth. I could have failed to achieve this in two ways. I might have failed to communicate properly and/or I could have misinterpreted my own experience. I have been very conscious of both these dangers. I have been trying to communicate something which is at the very limit of my own understanding, and I have only a smattering of psychology, criminology and sociology to work with. But however much I may have failed in both respects, this account remains true for me. It describes what was a genuine advance in self-awareness, and its validity is that it has changed me.

From: J. McVicar (1974) McVicar by Himself. *London: Hutchinson, pp. 195–6.*

45. Social work in the environment

Martin Davies

The research method used precludes a rigorous assessment of the efficacy of environmental treatment; it may be, for example, that any or all of the groups would have improved even less than they did if they had not been given the treatment that they actually received. Nevertheless, while acknowledging the methodological shortcomings of the study, it is legitimate to record that there is here no hint that environmental treatment had an appreciable effect on the problems confronting the probationers when they first appeared before the courts, and that in particular it did not appear to make much impact within the group most in need of help. Table 1, which compares the same two variables not with improvement rates but with 12-month reconviction rates, is rather more complex.

Table 1   Reconviction rates and environmental treatment

Number of negative factors in the client's environment	The amount of environmental treatment given				
	Very great	Great	Moderate	Little/None	Probability levels
0	27%	24%	11%	10%	ns
1	30%	30%	8%	55%	p <.001
2	48%	36%	24%	76%	p <.001
3	33%	31%	45%	77%	p <.001
Probability	ns	ns	p <.02	p <.001	

Figures in each cell show the 12-month reconviction rates. N = 463.

If the differences in reconviction rates in each of the four horizontal rows are examined separately, it will be seen that:

(i)   Where there were no negative factors in the environment, there was no significant difference between the reconviction rates in groups given different amounts of environmental treatment.

(ii) Within the two middle-risk groups (1 and 2 negative factors) the lowest reconviction rates were obtained where a moderate amount of environmental treatment was given and the highest rates where little or no treatment was given. It seems probable that this significant but complex relationship between treatment and outcome masks a number of, so far as this study is concerned, unascertainable variables. For example it may be that the officer's active response to a moderate need for help actually did influence the likelihood of reconviction (but if that were so, then one might have expected those groups receiving 'great' or 'very great' amounts of environmental treatment to have lower reconviction rates than was the case); alternatively 'moderate treatment might have been given within the middle risk groups to those with the best prognoses, so that the lower reconviction rates observed in the study were merely a reflection of the officer's selection policy for treatment.

(iii) In the worst risk group (3 negative factors) the best results were obtained where the greatest amounts of environmental treatment were given, and it is tempting to draw firm conclusions about a causal relationship from these data.

Caution, however, forbids such a step, and not only because such conclusions would contradict much of the evidence presented earlier in this report. It should be noted that in the two left-hand columns (where the amount of environmental treatment given was 'very great' or 'great'), there was no significant difference between the reconviction rates in the four negative factor groups. This suggests that probationers given the most environmental treatment may have had more in common with each other than was apparent from their environmental assessment; in this analysis there is no way of knowing whether the reconviction rates obtained were determined more by initial personality and social circumstances than by the quality or quantity of the environmental treatment given. If maximum treatment were postulated as having a beneficial effect, the 0 negative factor group would provide contrary evidence, and the two middle-risk groups would seem to be inconclusive. Only the 3 negative factor group would support the notion.

Nevertheless, although it must be concluded that Table 1 fails to provide clear evidence of a statistical association between the amount of environmental treatment given and the reduction of reconviction rates during the first twelve months of the probation order, the significant relationship observed in the 3 negative factor group is sufficiently interesting to encourage further study, especially among bad-risk cases.

From: M. Davies (1974) Social Work in the Environment. A Study of One Aspect of Probation Practice. Home Office Research Study No. 21. London: HMSO, pp. 91–2.

46. New Careers

Philip Priestley

Declaring a bad past is one way of trying to ensure a better present – what New Careers adds to that is exactly what its title says – the notion of a future 'career'. Ex-prisoners and recovering alcoholics can spend a lot of time helping each other and helping themselves in the process, but they must normally earn their bread and butter in a work-world which is totally divorced from those activities. And even when they have managed to find full-time jobs in a related field these have tended to be low-order, low-pay positions which lead precisely nowhere. Hospital porters or assistant wardens in alcoholic or ex-prisoner hostels are often employed to do the dirty work so as to free the 'professional' staff to pursue more glamorous 'treatment' activities.

New Careers, on the other hand, starts by analysing the tasks which are performed by doctors, teachers and social workers. Critically assessed, many of their specific functions appear to require neither the lengthy training and supposed skill of the professional, nor the rate of reward which their practice presently commands. Some of these activities can clearly be hived off and reconstructed to form aide or sub-professional roles. These roles in turn can be filled and competently performed by quite ordinary people, given brief but adequate training and relevant supervision. And *extraordinary* people like ex-prisoners and chronic unemployees can bring to their performance of such roles a unique dimension of personal experience and understanding from the inside of the problems they have to deal with.

Classroom aides, for example, can organise and manage teaching materials, keep records and administer a whole range of other non-teaching activities. Health aides can encourage service take-up by target group members, engage in public education projects and carry out routine medical testing. Probation aides can help parolees and probationers to find accommodation, get work and negotiate initial payments from income maintenance agencies. The fact that the aides are black, live in ghettoes or have themselves been prisoners is necessary to the New Careers scheme of things, but not in itself sufficient to constitute the full programme. For that, there must also be opportunities for further training, access to progressively more skilled posts with higher statuses and salaries and eventual entry into the full professional grades of the service on equal terms with more conventionally recruited members) Pearl and Riessman 1965). The general promise of New Careers can therefore be summed up under the following six heads, which will also form the basis of a consideration of its prospects for implementation in this country:

1. Income for the poor.
2. Work for the 'unemployable'.
3. Status escalation for the stigmatised.
4. Manpower for the 'human' services.
5. Qualitative transformation of social work.
6. A revolution in training design and method.

It is an ambitious list to say the least – in fact a precis programme for the redistribution of status, power and wealth. The first question that should be asked is why the idea has taken so long to cross the Atlantic. In the ten years since its inception, an enormous and diversified movement has grown up in the USA. The first small-scale projects, based on its principles, are only now being set up here.

Funding is probably the most crucial element in the successful implementation of New Careers. It was the violence of the 'urban crisis' which struck loud responsive chords on the American public purse-strings. Similar conditions do exist here, but not of the scale and degree which preceded the explosion there. The British way with ghettoes has been the bulldozer and the partial dispersement of problem families on to new housing estates distantly sited beyond suburbia. The advent of large immigrant communities, a rapidly obsolescent housing stock and an intensified sense of relative poverty, as general standards of living reach ever higher levels, may lead in time to equivalent disorders on British city streets; but if and until they do, any widespread local adoption of the idea seems improbable. And in the absence of an official political constituency, driven forward by a fuel of high-octane fear, from where else should one expect the demand to provide the resources for New Careers to take root and grow? Obviously not from mainstream social work where the vested interests of 'professionalism' and 'conservative' local control converge in solid resistance to the role of prime mover in such a matter. Nor from the radical forces inside social work. Few in number, poorly organised, ideologically incoherent and lacking experience of changing anything, they are an unlikely source of irresistible pressure on the establishment.

[…]

Marcuse (1964) has identified the black, the poor and the stigmatised, i.e. the non-working classes, as the last islands of disorganisation in our over-organised consumer civilisation, and the only likely source of future resistance to the total triumph of technology over the free spirit of man. New Careers in its present nascent state offers both a promise and a threat to these groups. Within it can be discerned the seeds of a social and political transformation by peaceful means. Or as it develops, it may seduce and co-opt the potential leadership of the outsiders and institutionalise their critical functions into an impotent form of loyal opposition. However it turns out, the odds could be equalised at the outset by injecting the whole debate, together with its principal actors, directly into the political arena. New Careerists would make fine political activists, keen lobby correspondents for community newspapers, adventurous investigators for the Ombudsman, able research assistants for busy MPs, or even Liberal MPs. If, in the process, New Careers was consumed like a meteor striking the atmosphere, it would still leave as its lasting memorial an illumination of the indivisibility of social work and politics.

From: P. Priestley (1975) 'New Careers: Power Sharing in Social Work', in H. Jones (ed.), Towards a New Social Work. *London: Routledge & Kegan Paul, pp. 126–7 and 135–6.*

47. The effectiveness of sentencing: a review of the literature

S. R. Brody

Reviewers of research into the effectiveness of different sentences or ways of treating or training offenders have unanimously agreed that the results have so far offered little hope that a reliable and simple remedy for recidivism can be easily found. They have pointed out that studies which have produced positive results have been isolated, inconsistent in their evidence, and open to so much methodological criticism that they must remain unconvincing. The main criticisms, which are substantial ones, centre around questions as to the comparability of the samples (that is, whether influences other than the treatment are accounting for differences in outcome) and inconsistencies in standards of failure. It has seemed, therefore, that longer sentences are no more effective than short ones, that different types of institutions work about equally as well, that probationers on the whole do no better than if they were sent to prison, and that rehabilitative programmes – whether involving psychiatric treatment, counselling, casework or intensive contact and special attention, in custodial or non-custodial settings – have no predictably beneficial effects. The comparative advantages of other types of sentences remain, unfortunately, largely untested. Martinson's conclusions (1974), based upon a great number of investigations into a wide range of treatment and training, were so pessimistic that publication of his review was delayed for three years.

This apparent failure of research to demonstrate the corrective value of rehabilitation as a sentencing aim has nevertheless had one refreshing consequence. It has seen the rejection of reconviction as the sole criterion of success, and a growing concern for evaluation according to other standards. A noticeable trend has been a readiness to justify non-custodial or semi-custodial sentences in preference to imprisonment or incarceration, on the grounds that they cost very much less to implement, and decrease at the same time the risk of psychological and practical harm to the offender. As 'softer' sentences have apparently no worse effect on recidivism and still offer the chance of less tangible if as yet unknown advantages, they are seen as preferable by all schools of thought except perhaps the retributivist.

But is a pessimistic outlook entirely substantiated by the results of research? To the researcher, the subject is by no means closed. Just as methodological deficiencies and flaws in carrying out experiments make any results dubious, so they make unacceptable any assurances that corrective changes cannot be induced. Since the beginning of the present decade, and therefore not included in previous reviews, research has been continuing, and if it has not found any more positive results, at least there has been progress in understanding of the complexities to be faced. The climate of opinion in America seems lately to have become a little more optimistic. Adams, for example, writing in 1974, suggested that correctional research 'is doing as well as can be expected under the circumstances' and compared the productiveness of evaluation in correctional research favourably with that in industry or medicine. He has recently prepared a 'guide' (Adams 1975), in which he critically evaluates correctional research and indicates how it might be put to better use in the future. What has emerged more clearly is a recognition that simple comparisons between different sentences, no matter how carefully carried out, cannot be expected easily to find differences in effect.

From: S. R. Brody (1976) The Effectiveness of Sentencing: A Review of the Literature, *Home Office Research Study No. 35. London: HMSO. pp. 37–38.*

48. Rehabilitation and deviance

Philip Bean

The central concern of this book has been with rehabilitation. The discussion has operated at two levels, first to examine rehabilitation as a concept, and second to show that the implementation of that concept has led to some strange and curious results. I have tried to show that it is, if I might use Professor Flew's term, a shambles (1973). It means, as I understand it, that offenders require and need understanding, and as a result of this understanding they will receive insights which will substantially alter their attitudes. This will prevent them from committing further offences. The methods used are mainly psycho-therapeutic so that a relationship with a therapist provides the basis for treatment. All offenders are, by definition, thought to need treatment, and since offenders have different personalities, treatment must be individualized.

The conceptual shambles begins when we consider the social pathology perspective and the individualization of sentencing. In Chapter 2, I tried to show that social pathology was inappropriate to crime and deviancy and in the chapters concerned with individualized treatment I tried to show that there were numerous conceptual and theoretical difficulties which introduced some dilemmas, particularly for the experts. The net effect has been to produce in Matza's (1964) terms 'a system of rampant discretions'. What then needs to be changed? Or to put the question another way, is it possible to reduce the rampant discretions in a way which is both practical and feasible? In one sense yes, but the history of the penal system shows that change must of necessity be comparatively slow, and must at the same time preserve a system of balance between what Weber (1954) called 'vending machine' justice and individual discretions. The basis of my argument is that discretions are more in the hands of the experts than with the judiciary. The balance has shifted, and shifted in a way which has not always been in accordance with the offender's interests, nor in accordance with basic notions of fairness.

Now it is both understandable and acceptable that people involved in making important decisions should have their advisers. It is equally understandable that some discretions should be permitted in the decision-making process and no doubt the debate has been, and will always be, about the amount of discretion available. Where the rules are clearly formulated, and where sentences are determined by those rules, the system becomes inflexible. Conversely, where there are rules which permit discretion, the system produces powerful groups able to stamp their authority on that discretionary area. In the penal system as it currently operates there are wide discretionary powers. Davis (1969) made the point about discretion in a way which must be considered a definitive statement on this issue.

'Where law ends, discretion begins, and the exercise of discretion may mean either beneficence or tyranny, either justice or injustice, either reasonableness or arbitrariness.'

From: P. Bean (1976) Rehabilitation and Deviance. *London: Routledge & Kegan Paul, pp. 144–5.*

49. A sense of freedom

Jimmy Boyle

I now began a six-month period of solitary never leaving the cell once during this period. It began quite well with me very proud of our achievement in knocking down the walls of the solitary confinement block. The cops came and charged me with attacking the prison Governor and destroying the solitary block along with the others. All of us now had a long list of charges against us and knew that it would be another High Court appearance.

I took up yoga again during this period and became very involved in it, to the extent that it took over my whole existence. At first I dabbled in it and then went into the meditative side and became quite confident in my involvement in it. I restricted my diet and tried to eat as little as possible. Food was the only thing that I had to look forward to so I would test my willpower and self-discipline by eating less. This was a period in my life when I reflected on my whole being. Self-analysis became a daily habit as I was trying to find out more about myself and to come to some understanding of where I had come from and where I was going. I looked at myself critically and thoroughly till the pain was at times unbearable, and shook my very soul. What was I doing in this place? Was this my life? What was my life all about? The pain from the realisation of my position and its futility was so powerful that I would just curl up in a corner and try to endure it. I went through a period of deep shame about the life I had led. All of this I was finding very difficult to cope with and I sat in this cell suffering as I had never done before. I would think of the kids who were doing the same things as I had done and who would follow my pattern to eventually reach this point of torment only to realise the futility of it, and these thoughts would make me feel sick. Is this what it was all about? I had suffered every year since I was a child but hadn't a clue about anything as I was so dumb and inarticulate and here I was, now an adult feeling pain like I had never done before.

But now I was beginning to put it all together, probably for the first time in my life. Day after day I lay in this cell thinking, thinking, thinking. I didn't speak to the screws and never saw anyone else. At night I could see the moon when it was out and I would long to see it without having to look through bars and heavy metal frames. I could hear the occasional noises outside my window as the short-term prisoners walked past with the screws and I would have given anything to be in their shoes. During this period of self-analysis,

I heard the sound of civilian workers erecting a new security system on the wire fence that was inside the wall and the sounds of their voices travelled across to me and I would listen to them in great pain. I would hear them checking the alarm system and would latch onto their every word. I would look at the differences in our ways of life and feel the futility of mine. At night they would pack up their tools and I would feel envy running through my whole body as they left, chatting together, oblivious to the fact that a guy was lying on a floor, sick at their parting sounds. If only they knew what misery was going on around them. It was very difficult for me to cope with the fact that I had this big blank in my life with nothing to look forward to. The only alternative was to be an arse-licker to the screws, losing my own personality and individuality, and being their pet lion. The one they had tamed. The rewards being the occasional pat on the head.

The only change would be a modification in my behaviour, but the future outlook for me could never change. The one thing that I could hold onto was the fact that I was me. I felt that I mustn't give this up or all would be lost. I tried to look at myself and see what was happening to me at that moment. Was I cracking? Was my spirit breaking? Was this me just in a pathetic state and feeling sorry for myself? No, for the first time in my life I was looking at myself and seeing clearly what was happening to me. Seeing just what I was doing to myself. The important thing was that I had journeyed inside myself, got right under the skin and into the soul. The pain of finding out more about myself was terrible for I had been living a life of self-delusion ever since I was a kid. I now realised that some of the things I had done were very bad and was probably paying for it now, not by being sentenced, but by the real payment which comes with the realisation of what it's all about. Now that I had all this awareness, what could I do with it? As I said, by this time I was fully into yoga – in fact it had dominated me and purified me, having a calming effect. With all this clarity of thought came a realistic appraisal of the present and the future. I had come through this painful period and was now aware of all that had gone wrong in the past, but having reached that point I also realised that I would have to live in the jungle-like existences that reigned supreme within the walls of prison. In other words I had to pull myself together and prepare myself for the future. I had come out of this experience stronger and felt the power surging through my body.

From: J. Boyle (1977) A Sense of Freedom. *London: Canongate, pp. 190–2.*

50. Sentenced to social work

Malcolm Bryant, John Coker, Barry Estlea, Sheila Himmel and Ted Knapp

It is obvious that the reception area of the probation office would be very important, since it would act as a shop window for the service. It could be bright and colourful with a welcoming atmosphere and would offer a visual presentation of the various types of social work and welfare opportunities available. These would include such things as personal counselling, assistance with family problems, membership of groups, special education, assistance with welfare rights, development of work skills, information about employment and accommodation, day training centres, hostel placements, etc. The intention would be to encourage the motivation in clients to deal with problems, and ultimately external professional assistance in design of the reception area might be helpful. The receptionist would be in a key role, and would need to be both sensitive and skilled in dealing with clients who may find it difficult on occasions to articulate their requests for assistance, whilst allowing those who simply wanted to report to do so without difficulty.

The objective for the probation team would therefore be the creation of a wide range of opportunities for offenders and the effective development and management of its resources in order that a local service relevant to clients' needs would be provided. We believe that such a system would offer considerable advantages over current practice. The offender would be treated as a more responsible individual, and by allowing him to choose social work help, the dignity inherent in self-determination would be recognised. Courts would surely have more faith in an order where the level of supervision was defined in court, and where breach of this primary contract would lead to the offender's re-appearance unless the failure to report was unavoidable. The skills and time of probation officers as professional social workers would be given recognition as valuable resources and where subsidiary contracts were made these would be with motivated people who would thus be clients in the true sense.

As the system developed, a range of other people with relevant training and skills might be employed, such as accommodation and employment officers, psychotherapists, legal advisers, specialist teachers, welfare rights officers, etc. The services provided for clients could be monitored in terms of the successful resolution of personal and social problems, and if a positive impact should happen to be made in terms of reduced criminality this would be a welcome bonus. The redefined probation order would therefore be an expression of the community's s belief that some offenders may be dealt with appropriately through supervision in the community and that by virtue of the people they are and the problems they have, it is reasonable that social service resources should be made available to them.

From: M. Bryant, J. Coker, B. Estlea, S. Himmel and T. Knapp (1978) 'Sentenced to Social Work', Probation Journal, *25: 110–114.*

51. Compulsion and social work

Peter Raynor

Without labouring the point, I would suggest that the only situations in which we can fully control human behaviour are situations in which we exercise coercion, by removing another person's freedom of action through such means as superior physical force, hypnosis or incapacitating drugs. In doing this we also dehumanize him, by removing some essential components of our ordinary idea of a person as an interpreter of reality, a maker of choices and an initiator of actions. Such methods are not only impractical in social work, they are also likely to be counter-productive, as Jimmy Boyle (1977) has demonstrated in his moving account of his struggle to retain a sense of freedom and of personal identity in the more brutal and dehumanizing parts of the Scottish prison system.

Coercion is, in an important sense, an assault on identity, and any repressive, manipulative or exploitative social relations contain elements of such an assault. Pinker (1971) has suggested that stigma, or the subtle impu-tation of a spoiled or diminished personal identity, is 'the commonest form of violence used in democratic societies', and further argues that the more personalized a social service becomes, the greater is its potential stigmatizing effect. Perhaps the process of being helped always involves a risk of being humiliated, and this can only be avoided if social work retains scrupulously its traditional 'respect for persons'. However, in respecting persons we must also respect the reality of choice.

Choices made under constraint (like, for instance, choosing to be on probation or to apply for parole) are still real choices. As in all serious choices, the constraint arises from the fact that choices have consequences, and that the consequences of one alternative will be different from those of the other. In any situation short of total coercive control, the element of choice remains, and the influences on that choice are constraints rather than compulsions. We can try to influence people's choices by attaching constraints or sanctions to one alternative or rewards to another, but the attempt to influence does not negate or abolish the fact of choice. Of course, we can always pretend, and the sociology of knowledge teaches us that the social meaning of an action is influenced by the interpretation placed on it by actor, audience or both. In this way, both clients and social workers can pretend that influence, or constraints, are in fact coercive, and that choices are unreal. From the existential perspective, this is an act of 'bad faith', and we can in this way collude with or generate situations of mutual bad faith, in which people are relieved or deprived of a real sense of responsibility for their choices and actions. Constraints applied or received in this spirit can, like coercion, threaten identity. Perhaps all constraints which are imposed, rather than genuinely consented to or accepted, run this risk. Hence the need to explain and interpret them honestly to clients, rather than resorting to the ever-ready rationalization: 'It's for your own good'. We will never be fully reliable judges of someone else's good. Constraints or controls imposed for the benefit or protection of persons other than the subject of the constraint may well be necessary, but their nature and purpose should be explicit and not presented in a mystifying or mystified way. In this way choices and contracts, instead of being overlooked or obscured, can be made more informed and more real, confirming a sense of identity and responsibility rather than undermining it.

From: P. Raynor (1978) 'Compulsory persuasion: A problem for correctional social work', British Journal of Social Work, *8.4: 411–24.*

52. Non-treatment

Anthony Bottoms and Bill McWilliams

What exactly are the implications of adopting a 'help' rather than a 'treatment' model? The treatment model, in its pure form, begins with a diagnosis by the caseworker of the client's malfunctioning; then the treater decides upon the appropriate treatment with little or no advice from the client. The client is not offered choices about the form of the appropriate treatment; he is assumed to be dependent and in need of expert attention. In the 'help' model, all this is radically transformed. The caseworker does not begin with an assumption of client-malfunctioning; rather, he offers his unconditional help with client-defined tasks, this offer having certain definite and defined boundaries (we shall return to the 'boundaries' later). If the offer is accepted, this leads to a collaborative effort between worker and client to define the problem requiring help, and to work out jointly a set of possible alternative strategies; the worker is also absolutely explicit about what kinds of help his agency can and cannot offer. The client is then left to make the choices for himself. Hence, schematically:

Non-Treatment Paradigm for Probation Practice		
(a) Treatment	*becomes*	Help
(b) Diagnosis	*becomes*	Shared Assessment
(c) Client's Dependent Need as the basis for social work action	*becomes*	Collaboratively Defined Task as the basis for social work action

It is not appropriate for us here to spell out the full implications for day-to-day practice of this switch of approach; but three interim comments may be made. First, nothing that we have said should be interpreted to mean that 'help' means only material help. It is true that in past research studies clients have placed more stress than officers upon material assistance and the implications of this should be taken seriously; but clients should also be offered help with relationships and other areas of feeling as part of the agency's resources – which, of course, like all other types of help, clients are free to accept or reject.

Secondly, we are aware that many probation officers currently do offer 'help', in client-defined terms, in a range of situations. We have said earlier that officers do not always practise pure 'treatment', and some of the other things they do may certainly be defined as within the 'help' model. But at present they have no adequate conceptual apparatus with which to theorize these activities; so that the moment they begin to talk about them the language of treatment tends to be brought in and distorts what they are really offering to clients. We see it as a major task for social work theorists to provide an adequate conceptual understanding of 'help' for the benefit of social workers in their daily practice. Our experience suggests that once fieldworkers really grasp the notion of 'help', with its insistently client-centred emphasis, then this not only assists them to make better conceptual sense of many of their existing practices, it also enables them to revolutionize some of their practices which previously have not been adequately client-centred.

Thirdly, it is worth noting that various modern theoretical developments in social work may be interpreted as generally consistent with the switch from treatment to help – this would apply to 'task-centred casework' (Reid and Epstein (1972), welfare rights work, radical social work and community work, for example, and possibly also to 'systems theory' (Reid and Epstein 1972). Yet, as Tim Robinson (1978) has suggested, all these new techniques are potentially translatable still into the old officer-centred wisdoms of traditional social work. It is therefore of prime importance to emphasize that the ultimate test of the new model is that of client help – not 'task-centredness', or whatever.

There are all kinds of things which may seduce one away from this central test. Consider, for example, the following quotation:

> Students applying for courses leading to social work qualification often say that their aim is to be able to 'help people', thus implying that that is what social work is about. In recent years, however, more attention has been paid to the wide range of roles which every social worker finds himself fulfilling: from correction and even punishment to community direction and social reform. Many observers have found it difficult to reconcile what appear to be sometimes incompatible objectives, and one of the attractions of systems theory is that it allows for a recognition of conflicting elements in many situations. (Davies 1977)

Now of course it is not denied that social work has manifold functions; and the probation service certainly has other functions than to help clients. But to borrow a remark heard at a seminar discussion in another context, the danger with the approach implied in the quotation above is that it may turn 'the existing nonsense of day-to-day practice into systematised nonsense'. By stressing the manifold nature of social work functioning it is easy to forget about the client. But whatever else social work agencies may do, they must try to help clients, or they are not *social work* agencies. The centrality of this task among the others must not be abandoned.

The wider implications of defining client help as a central task are profound. As Meyer (1972) put it in the remark we have already quoted, 'we will be freer to attend to the improvement of services – to socialise *them* if you will':

in other words, the modern-day bureaucracies which probation services have become will be subject to 'bottom-up' monitoring from the client's eye-view, to see whether they are so organized as best to be able to deliver the services required by the clients. Thus there is a considerable re-thinking of the role of the agency *vis-à-vis* the client, as well as the role of the caseworker *vis-à-vis* the client, and the nature of what constitutes 'professional skill'. Other implications may follow: the decentralization of agency structures in order to be able to respond more closely to client requests for help, a greater use of voluntary associates, and so on. Above all, there is a need to develop specificity within the agency about exactly what kinds of help are available at the client's request, and to devote considerable care and thought to methods of ensuring that clients are informed of the range of services available.

As we have made clear, the 'help' model has been adopted in this paper because it is considered more likely than 'treatment' to facilitate a response to the expressed needs of clients. No expectation has been raised that the help model will be beneficial in the reduction of crime, and it is central to our argument to insist that this is not the purpose of shifting the focus from treatment to help. Nevertheless it must be pointed out that there is, ironically, at least a tiny shred of research evidence to suggest that, after all, help may be more crime-reducing than treatments.

The evidence comes from two sources – one indirect and one direct. The indirect source is a study of compulsory after-care in a group of young adults released from a closed borstal institution (Bottoms and McClintock 1973) The application of intensive casework methods was found to have no impact on reconviction rates, even when allowance was made (through a prediction instrument) for the previous history of the offender. On the other hand, and using the same statistical control for previous history, placement in certain sorts of post-institutional social situations did have a significant impact on reconviction rates – this included marriages, jobs, and so on. It is not suggested that probation officers become marriage brokers, but an implication of this study is that if offenders are genuinely seeking to 'settle down', and if probation officers are able to help them by collaborating in getting them into stable social situations, this will be more beneficial than intensive casework on the treatment model.

The more direct evidence comes from a Danish study of through-care work with short-term prisoners (Berntsen and Christiansen 1965). This is one of the very few studies to produce a significantly lower reconviction rate in an experimental 'treatment' group as against a control group (P <0.01); and, though its favourable result is not wholly unambiguous (Brody 1978), it is worth serious attention. This is particularly so in the present context, since we are told that 'normally help was only given when the prisoners themselves asked for it' (p. 53), and that the help given was overwhelmingly of a very practical kind.[1]

We repeat that we would not wish to build very much on these results. But for those who would be unwilling to adopt this part of our paradigm without at least some linked possibility of crime reduction, they are perhaps at least straws in the wind.[2]

From: A.E. Bottoms and W. McWilliams (1979) 'A Non-Treatment Paradigm for Probation Practice', British Journal of Social Work, *9: 159–202, at pp. 174–5.*

Notes

1. As Berntsen and Christiansen themselves describe it (N = 126): 'The social work consisted in finding work (54 cases), in finding accommodation (24 cases), clothing (30 cases), and in helping the prisoner with trade union and health insurance membership formalities (47 cases). Sometimes very modest financial help was given on the prisoner's release (31 cases), and sometimes it was necessary to help prisoners in negotiations with with tax authorities (15), with public assistance officers (22), and other public authorities and institutions as well as private creditors (60). Often assistance was needed to straighten out difficulties with wives or husbands, parents or other relatives (58). Twelve prisoners began an anti-alcoholic treatment during or after their imprisonment ... Through talks with particularly unbalanced prisoners the psychologist tried to cure depressions and to ward off conflicts' (p. 43).
2. The extension of this first aim to include the provision of appropriate help for *victims* would be entirely *congruent* with our theoretical framework and with recent developments in some probation areas. The subject is large, however, and space does not permit its inclusion here.

53. Still not working?

Ronald Blackburn

The recent studies reviewed, then, suggest that psychological treatment approaches can achieve some successes with offenders, but that the extent of their impact remains relatively slight. I would like to conclude by examining some possible reasons why success has so far been limited. These are that treatment interventions with offenders are being carried out in the wrong setting, that they are based on the wrong models of crime and psychological change, and that they are focusing on inappropriate targets.

To consider first the question of appropriate settings for therapeutic intervention, almost half of the programmes I have reviewed were carried out within penal institutions, and in Britain, at least, probably most psychologists working with offenders are employed in such institutions. But penal institutions are by their nature conservative and unsympathetic to therapeutic innovation. I have already noted my personal disenchantment with closed institutions as places for achieving relevant psychological change, and it has been argued by some that the social climate and organisational structure of prisons inevitably militate against the successful execution of behavioural programmes (e.g. Ross & Price, 1976). It has also been argued by Tittle (1974) that it is unreasonable to expect that prisons could serve both a deterrent and a rehabilitative function. It may be that treatment in the community permits more flexibility and control over factors conducive to further antisocial behaviour, such as peer reinforcement, work instability, or family conflict, as well as permitting more direct manipulation of relevant antecedents and consequences.

[...]

An alternative possibility is that *we* are operating within the wrong models of *crime and of therapeutic change*. Psychological approaches to crime typically reject a sickness model of antisocial behaviour, and this applies to both psychodynamic and behavioural models. In practice, however, the methods currently employed appear to involve, for the most part, some form of personal inadequacy model,[1] and as I noted earlier, the various methods currently in use are predominantly those originating in clinical settings. Implicit in most interventions appears to be the assumption that offenders are people who turn to crime because of deficits in their problem-solving abilities, or in their academic, occupational, or interpersonal skills. By correcting these deficits and increasing the offender's repertoire of constructive and socially appropriate behaviours, we are presumably enabling him to achieve his personal goals without resort to illegal means of achieving them. Literacy, effort, achievement, and good manners, it would appear, are incompatible with crime. (So much for the claim that the Protestant Ethic is dead!) But Martinson (1974), from the standpoint of a sociologist, proposes that criminals are merely responding to the facts and conditions of society. He suggests that we should abandon personal inadequacy models, and stop attempting to treat offenders.

The difficulty with this argument is that there is, in fact, clear evidence that offenders exhibit personal inadequacies. For example, when delinquents are considered as a group, they are found to be deficient in academic attainment (Prentice & Kelly, 1963), in social skills (Freedman, Rosenthal, Donahoe, Schlundt & McFall, 1978), have low self-esteem (Deitz, 1969), and are prone to anxiety and other emotional problems (Hoghughi & Forrest, 1970). The personal inadequacy assumption is not, therefore, totally unwarranted. On the other hand, however, offenders do not constitute a homogeneous population. Some may offend because personal deficits prevent them achieving their goals legitimately, but others may offend because of social barriers to their aspirations. Some may offend simply because they have learned behaviours appropriate for their particular social milieu, while still others may have personal attributes which make conflict with society inevitable.

If this is correct, then no single model, whether psychological or sociological, will account for all criminal behaviour, and similarly, no single method of change can be expected to influence all members of an offender population equally. In fact, from the studies reviewed, it can be concluded that, with the exception of the therapeutic community,[2] a variety of therapeutic methods can claim some success in resocialising the offender. Among the programmes identified as successful, procedures included personal counselling, casework, transactional analysis, modelling, and role-playing, and a behavioural approach to family therapy. Despite the frequent dismissal of verbal psychotherapies by behaviourists, behaviour modification does not emerge from the current survey as a conspicuously more promising approach to the rehabilitation of offenders. It may be the case that among the failures, some methods worked with some offenders. The problem is to identify which offenders. In one study (Sinclair, Shaw & Troop, 1974), a serendipitous finding was that introversion predicted successful response to casework. In another (Sarason, 1978), the anecdotal impression is reported that psychopathic delinquents responded less successfully to social skills training using modelling and role-playing than did neurotic delinquents.

[...]

It is of interest in this context that in a recent discussion of the current status of psychotherapy outcome in general, Frank (1979) notes that '... the results of outcome research strongly suggest that more of the determinants of therapeutic success lie in the personal qualities of the patient and the therapist and in their interaction than in the therapeutic method'. If, as I suspect, the same obtains when the 'patient' happens also to be an offender, then a pragmatic examination of how available methods can be matched to different clients and different therapists is a more meaningful question than which method is superior (see also Palmer, 1975).

The final issue I would like to consider is whether programmes fail because they focus on the *wrong psychological targets*. Very few interventions have attempted to reduce criminal behaviour by direct means, and given its nature and frequency, it may well be more realistic to attempt to influence such behaviour indirectly. However, in the present series, the most common targets seem to be institutional behaviours such as personal hygiene, housekeeping chores, compliance with the rules and participation in traditional occupational or educational activities. While this approach is sometimes defended on the grounds that behaviours incompatible with criminal activities are being strengthened, Emery & Marholin (1977) point out that whether such behaviours have anything to do with crime in the community has not been established. Moreover, such programmes primarily serve the custodial management goals of the institution. In fact, these programmes seem to be the least likely to be followed up, and for those that have been, success is not conspicuous [...]. According to preliminary data presented by Eitzen (1975), for example, the much publicised Achievement Place programme does not seem to have had any success in preventing subsequent delinquent behaviour on the part of its residents.

The same kind of criticism can be levelled at those treatments which focus on personal skills or on covert cognitive or emotional variables. In most cases, we have little firm knowledge as to which factors are most relevant to the commission of antisocial acts. Nevertheless the data [...] suggest that the strengthening of specific personal skills may be a promising strategy. Probably the most impressive project of those examined is that carried out at Cascadia (Sarason, 1978), where institutionalized delinquents were exposed to a comparatively brief social skills training programme using modelling and role-playing of problem situations commonly encountered by offenders following release. At a five-year follow-up, recidivism was found to be halved in experimental subjects when compared with untreated controls, although, incidentally, modelling and role-playing were no more successful that straightforward discussion of the same problems.

To sum up, although the recent outcome data provide little room for complacency, they offer at least modest encouragement for psychologists working with offenders. Martinson's pessimistic conclusion that nothing works in offender rehabilitation and his premature last rites on attempts to change offenders would therefore seem to invite the comment made by Mark Twain on reading his obituary in the New York *Sun*: 'The reports of my demise are grossly exaggerated!'

From: R. Blackburn (1980) Still Not Working? A Look at Recent Outcomes in Offender Rehabilitation. *University of Aberdeen. Paper presented at the Scottish Branch of the British Psychological Society Conference on 'Deviance', University of Stirling, pp. 9–14.*

Notes

1. It is sometimes argued that there is no difference between a medical or sickness model and one which emphasises personal inadequacy. I would maintain, however, that the essence of a sickness model lies not in its postulation of causes 'within' the person, but in its assumption that the causes of 'deviant' behaviour are discontinuous with those of 'normal' behaviour.
2. Five programmes were based on the principles of the therapeutic community (Angliker, Cormier, Boulanger and Malamud, 1973; Carson, 1973; Cornish and Clark, 1975; Feldman, 1977; Klein, Alexander and Parsons, 1977). Four examined subsequent recidivism but none found any significant effects.

54. Induction groups

A. R. Stanley

Four of the teams I visited were using 'induction groups' for assessment. Not all so-called induction groups in use in the South West Region were for purposes of assessment. Only three out of eight of their programmes sampled gave assessment as a primary aim. Only two of the four groups I visited were in the South West Region sample. In every case these groups were weekly and included from six to eight sessions, a number predetermined by each unit, and all were jointly supervised by two people, one at least being a probation officer with a third person as consultant; all of these groups were also followed by a three-way review interview involving each client participant separately. In the review interview the client met with his/her nominated probation officer (assigned for this purpose prior to the group) and one of the two people running the group. If the nominated officer happened to be one of the group supervisors the client met with them both. The review interview was used to draw up a written contract which then constituted part of the agency record. It indicated whether the client wished to enlist the assistance of the agency in bringing about change or preferred to fulfil his obligations (where an agency commitment existed) simply by reporting. Where help was sought an attempt was made to reach an agreed statement about the nature of the change, problem areas, priority objectives and preferred methods of work. Induction groups were so arranged that they could include new clients near the beginning of their involvement with the agency. Groups varied from unit to unit in criteria for membership. Some were only for probationers, others for voluntary clients; others included younger people who were the subject of Supervision Orders. The nature of such orders or their absence affected the sanctions which might be used to enforce attendance and some units (not all) considered it unhelpful to mix different categories in the same group. Each group normally opened with a session aimed at induction, the process of familiarising people with a new situation. Subsequent sessions were taken up in exploring reasons for offending, offence predispositions, whether people wanted to stop offending, what they might be prepared to do about it and what resources were now available to them through the agency. The following are taped extracts from SPOs talking with me about their induction groups:

Exclusion from these groups is only after the team agrees, officers cannot take this decision alone ... our induction groups are based on five questions. Why do people get into trouble? Why do people offend? What is the effect of offending on the offender? Do you want to stop? Is there anything you can do about that? Those five questions will be formally answered in the review meeting ... whether induction groups are about clients assessing us or us assessing them is sometimes not clear ... he was so inarticulate that he could hardly string the words together and had we operated on the basis of choosing who we put into induction we would have assumed it would have been much too difficult for him ... he very quickly blossomed ... he came out eventually with the fact he couldn't read ... he then chose to go into our feelings group ... he was discharged after six months ... our breach actions have soared ... well over 50% resulted in return to induction ... sanctions are often very necessary to hold people 'till we can capture their interests. Lack of sanctions for licencees is quite a difficulty ... it is often the clients in the group who are clearest about what someone needs and can get through to a particular person.

In at least two of the groups the leaders introduced information about recidivism which was calculated to heighten members' awareness of the likely consequences of criminal drift. Some were also using what SPOs described as 'hot seat' techniques whereby group members were questioned by their peers in an attempt to get at their motivation. In general, it seemed that these groups attempted to extend the process of assessment beyond what had been achieved by a social enquiry and to put greater emphasis upon client motivation and the selection of appropriate social work methods.

Three of these units claimed that induction groups had led to an increased use of probation orders by their courts, but also to an increased incidence of breach proceedings. These units had been using such groups from one to three years. The fourth unit had only been using them for just over two months. All four of the units using induction groups were also using allocation meetings; none was subjecting the contracts from review interviews to the team.

From: A. R. Stanley (1982) 'A New Structure for Intake and Allocation in a Field Probation Unit', British Journal of Social Work, *12.5: 487–506.*

55. Limits to pain

Nils Christie

Conflicts are not necessarily a 'bad thing'. They can also be seen as something of value, a commmodity not to be wasted. Conflicts are not in abundance in a modern society; they are a scarcity. They are in danger of being lost, or often stolen. The victim in a criminal case is a sort of double loser in our society. First vis-à-vis the offender, secondly vis-à-vis the state. He is excluded from any participation in his own conflict. His conflict is stolen by the state, a theft which in particular is carried out by professionals. I have applied this perspective in an article 'Conflicts as property' (Christie 1977), and will therefore not go into further details here, except for one quotation, which tries to illustrate the most important loss when conflicts are stolen (p. 8):

> This loss is first and foremost a loss in *opportunities for norm-clarification*. It is a loss of pedagogical possibilities. It is a loss of opportunities for a continuous discussion of what represents the law of the land. How wrong was the thief, how right was the victim? Lawyers are, as we say, trained into agreement on what is relevant in a case. But that means a trained incapacity in letting the parties decide what *they* think is relevant. It means that it is difficult to stage what we might call a political debate in the court. When the victim is small and the offender big in size or power – how blameworthy then is the crime? And what about the opposite case, the small thief and the big house-owner? If the offender is well educated, ought he then to suffer more, or maybe less, for his sins? Or if he is black, or if he is young, or if the other party is an insurance company, or if his wife has just left him, or if his factory will break down if he has to go to jail, or if his daughter will lose her fiancé, or if he was drunk, or if he was sad, or if he was mad? There is no end to it. And maybe there ought to be none. Maybe Barotse law as described by Max Gluckman (1967) is a better instrument for norm-clarification, allowing the conflicting parties to bring in the whole chain of old complaints and arguments each time.

[...]

Victim compensation is such an obvious solution and used by most people in the world in most situations. Why is it not used at the state level in highly industrialized countries? Or at least, why do we not immediately, with added insight, extend the system of victim compensation, and let the domain of penal law diminish? Three reasons often given are close to the obvious. Let us look at them in turn.

First it cannot be done in societies of our type. Ours are societies of specialization. We need experts to handle crime. I will soon go into this problem in greater detail. Here it suffices to mention that not all social arrangements are there because they are necessary. They might also be in existence because it once was a good thing for those with power that they should come into existence. Later, the arrangement continues by the very fact that it also serves other interests. The servants of the courts are well served by themselves. So are also their auxiliary personnel.

Secondly, compensatory justice presupposes that compensation can be given. The offender must be able to give something back. But criminals are most often poor people. They have nothing to give. The answers to this are many. It is correct that our prisons are by and large filled with poor people. We let the poor pay with the only commodity that is close to being equally distributed in society: time. Time is taken away to create pain. But time could be used for compensatory purposes if we so wished. It is an organizational problem, not an impossibility. Furthermore, it is not quite true that prisoners are *that* poor. Lots of young apprehended criminals have the usual range of youth-gadgets: bikes, stereo-equipment, etc. But the law and those running it are surprisingly hesitant to take any action to transfer any of these belongings from the youngsters to the use or benefit of the victim. Property rights are better protected than rights to freedom. It is simpler to take away a youngster's time than his bike. Property rights are important to us all. Imprisonment is highly improbable for the, ordinary citizen. In addition, those medieval sinners who were dealt with through systems of civil justice were not always all that rich. Herman Bianchi has in an article (1979), and also in lectures, described how sanctuaries functioned in those days. Churches and monasteries functioned as places where offenders could not be touched. Thus they became bases for discussions between representatives of the offenders and victims about guilt and compensation. A killer might be forgiven if he promised to pay 1000 guilders. He was then free to leave the monastery. But it might later become clear that he was not able to pay the 1000 guilders. In this case he was also a bad man, but less so. He was now converted from a killer to a debtor. New discussions might follow, and the parties might agree to reduce the debt to a size that could realistically be paid. A little to the victim was better than the life of the criminal to the state. Offenders completely unwilling to compensate were slowly and subtly pushed down in rank and comfort within the sanctuaries, and eventually out of them as refugees to other countries, or as crusaders in the combined fight for Christianity and trade privileges. Herman Bianchi is now engaged in attempts to re-establish sanctuaries in Amsterdam. That is one of the few original ideas within our field in the latter part of this century.

But here comes the third objection: this would lead to the most terrible abuses. The strong victim would squeeze the poor offender out of all proportion, or the strong offender would just laugh at the victim if compensation were mentioned. Or vendettas would threaten. Victims and their relatives or friends would take the law into their own hands, and the offender and his gang would do the same. Violence would not be limited to the mafia but spray its mischief all over the system. It is exactly to prevent this anarchy that we have, so to speak, invented the state. And again there are counter-arguments: Many crimes take place between equals. Abuses in the compensatory process are not all that probable. Furthermore, in a process of participatory justice, the offender and the victim are not left in limbo. Their discussion must be a public discussion. It would be a discussion where the situation of the victim was scrutinized, where every detail regarding what had happened – legally relevant or not – was brought to the court's attention. Particularly important here would be detailed consideration regarding what could be done for him first and foremost by the offender, secondly by the local neighbourhood, thirdly by the state. Could the harm be compensated, the window repaired, the lock replaced, the wall painted, the loss of time because the car was stolen given back through garden work or washing of the car ten Sundays in a row? Or maybe, once this discussion was started, the damage would not seem so important as it looked in documents written to impress insurance companies? Could physical suffering become slightly less painful through any action on the part of the offender, during days, months or years? And in addition: had the community exhausted all resources that might have offered help? Was it absolutely certain that the local hospital could not do anything? What about a helping hand from the janitor twice a day if the offender took over the cleaning of the basement every Saturday? The situation of the offender would have to be analyzed in the same way. This might expose needs for social, educational, medical or religious action. Not to prevent further crime, but because needs ought to be met.

And to all the objections: why should the impossible cases hinder a decent solution where decency is possible? Why not restrict the area for punishment to the utmost by actively taking away all those cases that might be taken away? Let us construct conciliatory bodies. Let variation blossom when it comes to the selection of personnel, rotation, training, etc. Let us just remember some of the basic lessons from their predecessors: Let us make them vulnerable. Let us not give them power. Let them not become experts. Let them not become distant.

From: Nils Christie (1982) Limits to Pain. *Oxford: Martin Robertson, pp 93–6.*

56. Sex offender groups

Christine Weaver and Charles Fox

The Berkeley Group for non-violent male sex offenders has been operating since February 1977. An account of the early period appeared in *Probation Journal* (September, 1978). The leaders of this highly consistent project now offer a review of its effectiveness and the response from members past and present.

Facts and figures

The group, run by two officers for up to ten men at any time, meets fortnightly. By July 1983, 38 men had attended more than three group sessions and were therefore included in the study. The legal definitions of their offences were indecent assault, indecent exposure, gross indecency and USI with children under 16 or 13 years old. The majority of men had committed offences of exposing (16) or indecent assault against children (17).
　　[...]

What happens?

Meetings start with about 15 minutes of informal socialising followed by discussion. Some of the topics are: how men feel about being labelled as a sex offender; how they can recognise when they are at risk of offending; whether they want to stop and how they can set about it. This includes building on other positive areas of their personalities and broadening their social activities and personal supports. Discussion therefore varies widely and may arise spontaneously. It may also be initiated by asking each man in turn to comment on how he is coping, or by the leaders introducing a previously agreed topic. Occasional use is made of other simple techniques – pairing, brainstorms, 'hot seat' and pencil and paper exercises. With the help of the members we have devised a short checklist covering five important areas which can be used to review progress or initiate discussion:

1. Acknowledgement of the problem.
2. Understanding of the build up to offences
3. Development of alternative strategies.
4. Implementation of these strategies.
5. Development of supports outside the group.

The presence of men with different offences involving different types of victim has encouraged rather than inhibited discussion. People don't automatically understand one another, they question and challenge and avoid the tendency to sink into a cosy exchange of anecdotes about similar offences. Although most of the group see the child molesters as perhaps the most serious offenders (reflecting views in the wider community) they are aware of the similarities in needs and loss of control amongst them all.

In the seven years the group has been running it has become very apparent that most of the men we deal with require long-term support if they are to manage their sexual feelings without re-offending. This makes the development of other relationships crucial if we are to move them on safely. Some men cling to the group and pose a problem for the provision of places for new members.

[...]

However, there is also no doubt that many men can develop controls or alternative means of expression, and this has encouraged us to become less accepting of the compulsive 'I can't help it'. Group discussions have become more focused and positive as a result.

[...]

Results

CRO check: Of the 38 full members of the group 30 had not re-offended sexually when the check was made in July 1983. Eight men had further convictions and of these, two returned to the group, staying another 18 months without further trouble. Three re-offended after leaving and have not returned, and three continued to offend during the time they were attending.

Amongst these 8 men it was not possible to find any common factors which were related to attendance or time spent in the group. However, seven of the eight were indecent exposers rather than any of the other categories of sexual offender and all these had more than three convictions before starting the group. Three had very long lists indeed – one clocking up an impressive total of 127 convictions.

Although we do not have figures relating to a control group, the fact that 30 men have not re-offended at all is very encouraging indeed, particularly since the average number of pre-convictions for all group members was four and eight had six offences or more.

[...]

Conclusions

As the group does not cater for first sexual offenders at all, and most of the men could be described as recidivists, i.e. well established in the commission of sexual offences in certain circumstances, the results of the CRO check were very encouraging. A comparison with people supervised in different ways would be needed to confirm conclusively that the group experience is a safeguard against future offending, but it can certainly be claimed that the general public is not being put at risk by these people being supervised in the community rather than being sent to prison.

The responses to the questionnaire clearly reflect the value of discussion in a supportive group, and given the isolation of this type of offender and their inability to discuss their difficulties in other circumstances, it seems to provide a sufficient rationale for the group's existence.

From: C. Weaver and C. Fox (1984) 'The Berkeley Sex Offenders Group: A Seven Year Evaluation', Probation Journal, *31.4: 143–6.*

57. Justice, sanctioning, and the justice model

Gray Cavender

Kant and the justice model

Many advocates of the justice model credit their retributivism to Kant's statement that rational people deserve punishment when they violate the law. For Kant, criminal sanctions are deserved because the law bears a promise of punishment for crime, and offenders essentially call forth that punishment or bring it on themselves when they violate the law. Offenders are responsible for their actions so the fulfillment of the promise of punishment respects the dignity they are due as rational people. In a sense then, they enjoy a right to punishment. Moreover, crime is said to give offenders an unfair advantage over people who obey the law and disrupt the equilibrium between benefits and obligations that law maintains. Punishment negates this advantage and restores the social equilibrium (Murphy, 1970: 109–35).

As they posit retributivism as the primary basis of sanctioning policy, proponents of the justice model accept Kant's justification for why offenders deserve punishment (van den Haag, 1975: 26, 182; von Hirsch, 1976: 47–49). However, they neglect several interesting debates that surround the Kantian model on the issue of justice. Offenders do deserve punishment in the Kantian framework, but those who rely on this model fail to elaborate fully Kant's link between deserved punishment and his conceptualization of justice. In Kant's model, law is based on principles of justice, principles that rational people arrive at through reason. Given this derivation, law is just, people are obliged to obey it, and justice is served by punishment when they do not. His theory of political obligation thus guarantees by definition that law and other social institutions reflect justice within the reality of social life (Plant, 1980: 62–64; Clarke, 1982: 33–39).

Now of course this situation obtains only within the strict confines of Kant's model. A true dilemma appears when we step from the model into reality. Kant describes a just society as one that is maintained by fair laws that reflect principles of justice and that apply equally to all. Unfortunately Kant's view of society does not fit our social reality. Notwithstanding his model of political obligation, society is characterized by structural inequities that affect the distribution of a variety of social advantages and disadvantages. Given these inequities, law and justice simply do not coincide. Even if the law is administered fairly, it cannot deliver a just society when it is imposed on a situation previously characterized by injustice. Similarly, sanctions do not restore an equilibrium but instead exacerbate injustice because they tend to fall disproportionately on people who are already disadvantaged by the inequities.

The dilemma of justice in an unjust world becomes even more of a concern when the justice model is transformed from a philosophical ideal into penal policy. Because such a transformation is an inherently political matter, legal practice may vary considerably from the ideal. With respect to the severity of sanctions for example, legal practice reflects a tension between the aforementioned corollaries of justice. If we adhere strictly to the 'equal treatment for equals' corollary, we then violate the 'principle of proportion' in sanctioning because the disadvantageous conditions that offenders have experienced may have a bearing on the amount of punishment they deserve. In many states judges may enhance or reduce penalties based on criteria that are specific to the offender's situation. However, these criteria seldom address inequities. Instead they usually are oriented to aspects of the offense or to the presence or absence of a prior criminal record. At the most, and sometimes even this is doubtful, law and the criminal sanction provide a form of legal justice that is fair in a procedural sense but that treats unequals as equals while masking structural inequities behind a facade of justice.

From: G. Cavender (1984) 'Justice, Sanctioning, and the Justice Model', Criminology, *22.2: 203–13.*

58. Offending behaviour

James McGuire and Philip Priestley

Beliefs and values A great deal has been written about delinquent or criminal 'sub-cultures', and while some offenders do hold views quite distant from those of 'straight' society, a much more common experience is of confusion, bewilderment, and mixed-up emotions and beliefs. It is however possible to help individuals clarify their attitudes and beliefs and even change them ...

Self-image Although the notion of a 'criminal identity' is a rather simplistic one, there is some evidence which suggests that many offenders do have a picture of themselves which contributes to their law-breaking behaviour. Offenders have been reported to be lacking in self-confidence and self-respect, and often anxious and uneasy in their dealings with others. Another way of helping them, therefore, could be based on the enhancement of their self-esteem.

Social skills Some individuals end up breaking the law because they react to particular social encounters in an inappropriate or stereotyped way. In addition, many offences are *joint* offences: they are partly instigated by group interaction and by the inability of some individuals to resist peer-group pressure. In both these cases people are lacking in certain social skills; and it has been shown that training in these skills (e.g. to become more assertive, or more flexible in our reactions) can help offenders to cope with people in ways that are more acceptable both to others and to themselves.

Self-control The issue of control is relevant to offending in two principal respects. First, some evidence indicates that many offenders' views about the world around them is characterised by fatalism: by a feeling that they are victims of circumstances or pawns of fate; that there is little they can do to alter their own lives. Second, some kinds of offences, notably those connected with addictions or with violence, may be the result of losses of control by individuals over very strong feelings or impulses. In both of these areas it has been shown that people are capable of change: their beliefs, feelings and behavioural failures of self-control can all be overcome through specific kinds of training methods.

Risk-taking and decision-making   Most offences entail risks of some kind: of being caught, of things going wrong, of escalating into more serious incidents than planned, or of being in real physical danger. Many offenders on the other hand are very bad decision makers and are very poor at estimating the extent of such risks. A better appreciation of their chances of success or failure might genuinely deter some people from some kinds of criminal acts. Or improved decision-making skills might enable them to make a more realistic appraisal of the ramifications of 'trouble' in their lives.

Each chapter in this central section has a similar format. First, an opening statement explains the rationale for the inclusion of the topic; this is followed, where it proved possible and seemed potentially worthwhile, by a review of evidence concerning the relevance of the area to the problem of offence behaviour. The rest of the chapter then consists of methods and exercises for use by anyone working with offenders who would like to address offence behaviour directly.

From: J. McGuire and P. Priestley (1985) Offending Behaviour: Skills and Stratagems for Going Straight. *London: Batsford, pp. 20–1.*

59. Heimler's Human Social Functioning

Hugh Morley

The Probation Service is in a period of transition and challenge to the way in which it works with clients. There is pressure from government to be economic, efficient and effective; local authorities carefully scrutinise budgets, and the judiciary, magistracy and criminologist question our ability to provide genuine alternatives to custody for a difficult group in society. The social work methods taught are questioned as to whether they are appropriate in practice for probation officers. Probation officers are looking for methods of work which will help clients make best use of their inner resources in being able to cope with life. One such method is Human Social Functioning (HSF).

HSF was a method of self help devised by Dr Eugene Heimler. It is well documented in his book, *Survival in Society* (1975). HSF is an attempt to find an alternate method of casework that helped individuals who were not often articulate assess and make changes they wished for in their own lives. Central to the method is the Scale of Social Functioning which allows individuals to see and make priorities about the areas of their life they wish to develop or change. It also allows the counsellor to determine the amount of support and help likely to be needed in the case of any individual. This statement clearly indicates that HSF is a method which could be used extensively in the Probation Service.

The Scale. The Scale of Social Functioning measures, the relationship of satisfaction and frustrations as experienced by the individual at any given time. Probation officers frequently find themselves in situations where they have to assess the client at a particular time. This could be at the social inquiry report stage, assessing a client for hostel, day centre programme, membership of a group activity or to consider which problems in a client's life need attention. It is a means by which a trained probation officer can administer a series of 25 questions about the client's satisfactions in life, 25 questions about his frustrations and 5 questions about his overview of life. A skilled analysis can quite clearly show how the client is functioning. The client can also be engaged in its analysis as the answers are his own and this interaction with a worker can lead to clarification of issues upon which work has to be done. The net result is that action can be taken on priority issues.

The Interviews. The interview methods are outlined in *Survival in Society* but perhaps could best be summarised as the worker being in charge of the structure and the client the content. The worker accomplishes this by using a reflective interview technique with no interpretation of what the client says. From time-to-time the worker summarises what the client says, asks the client to record it either by writing or by tape recorder. After this is repeated several times the worker invites the client to read through or listen to what has been recorded and identify themes which appear to be emerging. These are also recorded and the client is asked to state what action he would like to take and record that.

From: H. Morley (1986) 'Heimler's Human Social Functioning', Probation Journal, 33.4: 140–2.

60. Reasoning and rehabilitation

Robert Ross, Elizabeth Fabiano and Crystal Ewles

Introduction

The Reasoning and Rehabilitation Project was an experimental project designed to assess the efficacy of an unorthodox training program for the rehabilitation of high-risk adult probationers. Unlike many other correctional programs, it was based not on mere conjecture as to what might constitute an effective program, but on a series of sequential research studies on the principles and practices of effective correctional intervention.

Program rationale and development

Stage 1 of the research consisted of an examination of studies of rehabilitation programs conducted in North America between 1973 and 1978. This research identified a substantial number of carefully evaluated studies which had found significant reductions in recidivism among a wide variety of offenders in institutional and community settings (Gendreau and Ross, 1979; Ross and Gendreau, 1980). Many well-controlled studies were identified which had found reductions in recidivism ranging from 30% to 74%. Numerous studies included large numbers of offenders; as many as 2,000. The results of these programs were not short-lived; substantial reductions in recidivism had been demonstrated in follow-up periods as long as 3 to 15 years after treatment.

Stage 2 of the research involved a comparison of programs which had 'worked' and programs which had failed. This analysis revealed that effective programs were not only exceptional in their results, they were atypical in the intervention techniques that they employed. Although each successful program included a different selection and combination of intervention techniques, all shared at least one in common: some technique which could be expected to have an impact on the offender's *thinking*. Effective programs included as a target of their intervention not only the offender's behaviour, his feelings, his vocational or interpersonal skills but his cognition, his self-evaluation, his expectations, his understanding and his appraisal of his world, and his values (Ross, 1980).

In Stage 3, a review of forty years of empirical research revealed a considerable body of evidence that many offenders have developmental delays in the acquisition of a number of cognitive skills which are essential to social adaptation (Ross and Fabiano, 1980). A considerable number of offenders have deficits in the ability to conceptualize the consequences of their behavior and are unable to use means-end reasoning to achieve their goals. Often the offender is concretistic, action oriented, non-reflective and impulsive. Many offenders have not progressed beyond an egocentric stage of cognitive development and are unable to understand the behavior, thoughts and feelings of other people. Consequently, many juvenile and adult offenders have major deficits in social skills and in interpersonal problem-solving. These deficits constitute a serious personal handicap which put the individual at risk for developing an anti-social lifestyle. The deficits are not in general intelligence – in I.Q., but deficits in social intelligence – in the ability to understand other people and in the ability to deal with interpersonal conflicts in an adaptive and pro-social manner. The research indicated that not all offenders have these deficits. Those who are most likely to evidence such deficits are adolescent offenders, chronic offenders, alcohol-abusing offenders, violent offenders and sex offenders. White collar criminals or those who engage in fraud, embezzlement or false pretences are less likely to have such cognitive deficits.

In Stage 4, a component analysis clearly demonstrated that effective programs included some intervention techniques which could influence these cognitive deficits, whereas ineffective programs did not. The study suggested that cognitive training is an *essential* ingredient of effective correctional programs.

Stage 5 identified and refined a large number of cognitive training procedures, practices and techniques which have been or could be used in effective correctional rehabilitation programs (Ross and Fabiano, 1983).

Reasoning and Rehabilitation Program

The Reasoning and Rehabilitation Project represented Stage 6 of the research series. It comprised an experimental test regarding the value of a cognitive program in reducing the recidivism of high-risk probationers under intensive supervision. For this purpose, a comprehensive cognitive program was developed by combining some of the techniques used in previous effective programs with some of the new techniques which were identified and modified for offenders in Stage 5 of our research.

A continuing assumption of our research was that in order to have a major impact an effective rehabilitation program must be found which can be delivered not only by highly specialized professionals but by line staff. There are simply not enough psychiatrists, psychologists or social workers (or enough funds to support them) to enable a program which requires such services to be Reasoning and Rehabilitation provided to enough offenders to have a major impact in reducing recidivism. Accordingly, one of the goals of the project was to determine how effective a cognitive program designed to be applied by line probation officers could be in reducing recidivism among high-risk probationers.

High-risk probationers were selected as targets for the project because of the long recognized need to develop for these offenders additional programs to regular probation services. It was our thesis that high-risk probationers would provide a demanding test of the cognitive program. This type of offender is the one most likely to persist in criminal behaviour and most likely to be unresponsive to other programs.

Accordingly, the specific cognitive techniques which comprised the program were carefully selected to ensure they could be applied by probation officers as an additional component of probation supervision. The majority of the techniques were extensively modified to maximize their applicability to a probation setting. The program included adaptations of the following techniques: Structured Learning Therapy (to teach social skills); Lateral Thinking (to teach creative problem-solving); Critical Thinking (to teach logical, rational thinking); Values Education (to teach values and concern for others); Assertiveness Training (to teach non-aggressive, socially appropriate ways to meet their needs); Negotiation Skills Training (to teach alternatives to belligerent or violent behaviors in interpersonal conflict situations); Interpersonal Cognitive Problem-Solving (to teach the thinking skills required to deal with interpersonal problems and conflicts); Social Perspective Training (to teach how to recognize and understand other people's views and feelings); Role-Playing and Modelling (demonstration and practice of socially acceptable and efficacious interpersonal behaviors). A host of audio-visual presentations, reasoning exercises, games, and group discussion techniques were used which were designed to combat the offenders' egocentricity and to foster their social-cognitive skill development. The techniques have been described in previous reports (Ross and Fabiano, 1983, 1985). The program focussed on modifying the impulsive, egocentric, illogical and rigid thinking of the offenders and teaching them to stop and think before acting, to consider the consequences of their behaviour, to conceptualize alternative ways of responding to interpersonal problems and to consider the impact of their behaviour on other people, particularly their victims. The program comprised 80 hours of intensive training involving demanding but highly enjoyable exercises conducted with groups of 4 to 6 probationers taught by their probation officers.

[...]

Evaluation

The evaluation consisted of a true experimental study entailing random assignment of high-risk male probationers to one of three groups:

1. Regular Probation
2. Regular Probation plus Life Skills Training
3. Regular Probation Plus Cognitive Training

The Regular Probation group provided a 'no treatment' control group against which to compare the outcome for the cognitive group. Other than obtaining pre-post measures for these offenders, there was no experimental interference with the regular probation service provided to this group. They were supervised by the same probation officers who served as trainers for the Cognitive and Life Skills group.

The Life Skills group was primarily designed to serve as an attention-control group; members of this group received the same number of hours of training as those in the Cognitive group and were provided with regular probation. Their training consisted of a life skills program with training in such areas as money management, leisure activities, family law, criminal law, employment-seeking skills, alcohol and drug education. The life-skills program was provided by the same probation officers who provided the cognitive training and regular probation.

Judges in the regional courts assigned offenders to the project. As part of their probation order, offenders were required to 'participate in the social skills program as required by the probation officers.' Offenders were accepted into the project provided they had a Level of Supervision Inventory (LSI) classification as a high-risk offender. The LSI is a well researched Inventory used in Ontario as an indicator of risk and as a measure of the level of supervision required for an offender.

It had been planned to include 75 offenders (25 in each group) in the study. In spite of the court order to attend, many offenders in the Life Skills group failed to attend training sessions or were jailed for new offences before they completed their program. The hours of employment of some offenders prevented them from being available. Consequently, the number of offenders in each group was: Regular Probation, 23; Life Skills, 17; Cognitive, 22.

[...]

Recidivism

The experiment was conducted over an eighteen-month period. Information on the illegal behaviour of each offender was obtained from computerized Canadian Police files. Data for the present report refers to the nine-month period for each offender following his admission to the project. Table 1 presents recidivism data for each group in terms of the number of offenders convicted for a new offence during the nine-month period.

Table 1 Recidivism within 9 months

	Number	Convicted	Recidivism
Regular probation	23	16	69.5%
Life skills	17	8	47.5%
Cognitive	22	4	18.1%

These data provide support for the view that cognitive training can lead to a major reduction in recidivism. Support for cognitive training as an effective method in reducing the recidivism of high-risk probationers is clearly observed. This type of training can be effectively conducted by well-trained and well-supervised probation officers. Cognitive training may have substantial benefits as an alternative to incarceration. Table 2 presents information on the number and percentage of offenders in each group whose subsequent convictions led to a prison sentence.

Table 2 Number and percentages of offenders in each group who subsequently receive a sentence of imprisonment

	Number	Incarcerated	%
Regular probation	23	7	30
Life skills	17	2	11
Cognitive	22	0	0

The foregoing initial but dramatic results contribute to a growing body of research literature which demonstrates the fallacy of the prevailing view that in correctional rehabilitation, 'almost nothing works.' On the contrary, *some* programs – when they are applied by well trained staff – can be remarkably effective in offender rehabilitation (Gendreau and Ross, 1987).

From: R. R. Ross, E. A. Fabiano and C. D. Ewles (1988) 'Reasoning and rehabilitation', International Journal of Offender Therapy and Comparative Criminology, *32: 29–35.*

61. Does nothing work?

Jerome Miller

Late one gloomy winter afternoon in 1980, New York sociologist Robert Martinson hurled himself through a ninth floor window of his Manhattan apartment while his teenaged son looked on from across the room. An articulate criminologist, Martinson had become the leading debunker of the idea we could 'rehabilitate' criminals. His melancholy suicide was to be a metaphor for what would follow in American corrections.

On January 18, 1989, the abandonment of rehabilitation in corrections was confirmed by the U.S. Supreme Court. In *Mistretta v. United States*, the Court upheld federal 'sentencing guidelines' which remove rehabilitation from serious consideration when sentencing offenders. Defendants will henceforth be sentenced strictly for the crime, with no recognition given to such factors as amenability to treatment, personal and family history, previous efforts to rehabilitate oneself, or possible alternatives to prison. The Court outlined the history of the debate: 'Rehabilitation as a sound penological theory came to be questioned and, in any event, was regarded by some as an unattainable goal for most cases.' The Court cited a Senate Report which 'referred to the "outmoded rehabilitation model" for federal criminal sentencing, and recognized that the efforts of the criminal justice system to achieve rehabilitation of offenders had failed.'

But had they?

Robert Martinson's skepticism derived from his role in a survey of 231 studies on offender rehabilitation. Entitled *The Effectiveness of Correctional Treatment: A Survey of Treatment Evaluation Studies*, it was to become the most politically important criminological study of the past half century. Ironically, though the survey came to be virtually identified with Martinson's name, he had joined the research team only after they were well into their work. Senior author Douglas Lipton and co-author Judith Wilks found themselves eclipsed by Martinson's flamboyant personality and flair for the pithy in capsulizing his version of the meaning of an otherwise rather dry tome (Lipton, Martinson and Wilks 1975). His views were enthusiastically embraced by the national press, with lengthy stories appearing in major newspapers, news magazines and journals, often under the headline, 'Nothing Works!'

Paradoxically, the idea that nothing worked in rehabilitating offenders appealed to Left and Right alike. In an unusual four-part series in the liberal

New Republic, Martinson (1972) wrote, 'the present array of correctional treatments has no appreciable effect – positive or negative – on rates of recidivism of convicted offenders.' In the conservative magazine, the *Public Interest* (1974), he wrote, '... rehabilitative efforts that have been reported so far have no appreciable effect on recidivism.'

This was good news to civil libertarians concerned with the injustices of indeterminate sentencing. (In California, for example, offenders were routinely given 'day-to-life' prison sentences with release dates tied to such vague rehabilitative criteria as 'attitude'). But, if the idea that 'nothing works' was well-received by liberals, it was even better news for conservatives who demanded tougher handling of offenders. But, to a nation emerging from the Vietnam War and an unruly youth and drug culture, 'nothing works' was a slogan for the times.

The decade from 1963 to 1973 saw reported murders double from 4.5 per 100,000 to 9.07. Assault rose from 91.4 to 193.6, Robbery from 61.5 to 177.9, and Theft from 1,128.5 to 2,431.6. The idea that this explosion of street crime must be due to an attitude of permissiveness was particularly appealing. Barry Goldwater tried unsuccessfully to make crime an issue in the 1964 campaign. But as the crime rates rose, Richard Nixon elevated the matter to a high art. The 1968 campaign made crime a major issue. Ironically, John Mitchell led the attack, successfully focusing on then Attorney General Ramsey Clark, much in the fashion of the recent Presidential campaign. The implication was that the criminal justice system, and in particular corrections, had grown soft by over-relying on such vague concepts as 'rehabilitation.' Curiously, if budgets were any measure, rehabilitation was a straw man. There has never been a rehabilitative era in American corrections. Most correctional systems had few if any trained psychiatrists, psychologists, or social workers. Virtually all correctional budgets went to staff that operated traditional prisons, jails and reform schools. What looked to outsiders like permissiveness was more often neglect and chaos in a system overcome with an explosion of 'baby-boomers.'

Martinson cut a near prophetic figure as he criss-crossed the country debating criminologists, cajoling prison wardens, and advising legislators and policymakers that rehabilitation had had its day. And as the issue got hotter, others took it up.

Neo-conservative Harvard management professor James Q. Wilson added man's nature to the equation. In his influential book, *Thinking About Crime* (1975), Wilson wrote,

> It requires not merely optimistic but heroic assumptions about the nature of man to lead one to suppose that a person, finally sentenced after (in most cases) many brushes with the law, and having devoted a good part of his youth and young adulthood to misbehavior of every sort, should, by either the solemnity of prison or the skillfulness of a counselor, come to see the error of his ways and to experience a transformation of his character.

And, as Wilson would later conclude, that character was often more 'wicked' than errant.

Martinson had a less Calvinistic view. Arrested as a civil rights 'freedom rider,' he had spent 40 days in the maximum security unit of Mississippi's Parchman State Penitentiary. He was reluctant to posit an offender's intransigence to fallen human nature, unduly heaped upon the poor and minorities who people our prisons. But others, particularly Wilson (1975) and conservative writer, Ernest van den Haag (1975), soon moved the debate beyond Martinson's control. Since 'nothing works' in rehabilitating offenders, we must deter and incapacitate them through harsher prison sentences and occasional use of the death penalty.

Because of the controversy in 1976, the National Academy of Sciences (NAS) appointed a Panel to re-evaluate the Lipton, Martinson, and Wilks survey. The Panel's findings (Blumstein *et al.* 1978) (were subject to wide interpretation, but central to its conclusion was the comment, 'When it is asserted that "nothing works," the Panel is uncertain as to just what has even been given a fair trial.'

Most rehabilitative programs chalked up as failures were heavy on rhetoric and slim on services. The classic 30-year 'Cambridge-Somerville Youth Study' (Powers and Witmer 1951) begun at Harvard in the late 1930s and used ever since by critics of rehabilitation as a premier example of the 'nothing works' position, was summarized by Wilson in this way, 'The differences in crime between those youth who were given special services (counseling, special educational programs, guidance, health assistance, camping trips) and a matched control group were insignificant: "the treatment had little effect" (Wilson 1975).' But Wilson ignored other realities.

Three hundred and twenty boys were assigned to ten counselors who were told to do 'whatever they thought best' for their clients. Counselors had no formal training in the mental health field, much less in psychotherapy. Each youth was seen an average of five times per year during the early years of the project in meetings directed at such things as arranging physical exams or interesting a boy in summer camp. Not surprisingly, the subjects showed no drop in criminal behavior at 10-, 20-, and 30-year follow-ups. It seems bizarre to have expected otherwise.

Some rehabilitative models have failed even in their own terms. Most research, for example, suggests it is difficult to successfully rehabilitate offenders in prisons and reform schools. 'Rehabilitation' in institutions is mostly a matter of mitigating the amount of debilitation. In a comprehensive 'cohort' study, Ohio State University researchers (Buckner and Chesney-Lund 1983) found that the 'velocity of recidivism' among young offenders actually increased with each institutionalization. 'Our most important single finding emerges from an analysis of the impact of the court's disposition on the intervals between future arrests ... the actual number of months during intervals between arrests when the offender was free to commit an offense, diminished dramatically after each commitment to an institution of the Ohio Youth Commission.'

This experience has been confirmed in recent research by the Rand Corporation on adult inmates of state prisons (Greenwood and Turner 1987). The implication is that the prisons are criminogenic – producing the very thing they claim to treat.

Approaches which give the offender a brief 'taste' of prison also have a poor record. The much hyped 'Scared Straight' model, wherein teenagers are brought to prison to be intimidated by inmates to scare them 'straight,' doesn't lower recidivism. Controlled studies show that teenagers subjected to the frightening experience tended to commit *more* crimes than a matched sample of non-participants. Likewise, 'shock' probation, whereby an offender is incarcerated for a short time (often led to think it will be for longer), and is then suddenly released back to the community, doesn't work (Vito 1981, 1984). 'Shock' probationers fared worse than matched samples not sent to prison. The debilitating aspects of prison life apparently outweighed their aversive effect.

There is also the matter of how one assesses 'success' or 'failure.' Rather than making simple re-arrest or reconviction the measure of failure, recent research has taken account of the *winding down* of an offender's criminal activity. This is a profoundly important issue.

In most fields, limited progress is seen as productive. A person with viral pneumonia who has been treated in a hospital is not labeled a 'failure' and re-hospitalized at the first sign of a cough. But a rehabilitative program which *lowers the number* or *de-escalates the seriousness* of repeat crimes is usually seen as unacceptable.

As a result, one can have a 'successful' program with high rates of recidivism. In one study of a family therapy program geared to hard-core delinquents, 30 adolescents (each with 20 previous adjudicated offenses) were matched with a control group of 44 delinquents with similar offense histories (Barton *et al.* 1985). At the end of a 15-month follow-up, 60 percent of the family therapy group had committed a new offense. This looked like failure. But then, we see that 93 percent of the control group which didn't get the therapy had been so charged.

If this were not a political arena, rehabilitation would be judged against the alternatives proposed by those who reject it. And to quote Canadian researchers, Paul Gendreau and Robert Ross (1987), '… the (substantiated) claims for effective rehabilitation of offenders far outdistanced those of the major competing ideology, applied deterrence or punishment.'

Measuring recidivism is further complicated by other contemporary events. Simply residing in some communities increases the likelihood of contact with the criminal justice system and being labeled a recidivist. Nearly half (46 percent) of boys in some areas will appear in juvenile court during their teen years. Among young black men in certain parts of the country, seven out of ten can anticipate being arrested at least once. Though this may suggest failure, it is not necessarily a true measure of individual criminal behavior. But the NAS Panel identified the elements it saw as crucial to successful programs. '(The) critical fact seems to be the *conditions* under which the program is delivered.' Rehabilitation is less a matter of identifying specific treatment methods, than it is one of creating conditions which support a variety of intensive options. Where there is a wide diversity of strong alternatives, recidivism can be lowered. Where there is little choice, recidivism remains the same or increases.

This was what University of Southern California sociologist Lamar Empey found in the famous 'Provo Project' (1972) which showed that recidivism rates fell significantly for youthful offenders placed in community-based programs, when compared with youth in state institutions. It was reiterated a decade later by Harvard's Center for Criminal Justice (Krisberg *et al.* 1989), when researchers studied recidivism among youthful delinquents placed in community treatment as opposed to state reform schools. Serious delinquents placed in the community with no treatment showed no lower rates of recidivism than reform school youth, and in many cases did worse. Better performance wasn't simply a matter of maturation, but seemed related to the number and quality of treatment options. It was also what John Jay University sociologist, Jeffrey Fagan discovered with violent offenders (1986). The *intensity* and *integrity* of the treatment was crucial to lowering recidivism rates.

Though this may seem self-evident, it's foreign to corrections. The corrections establishment, made up, for the most part, of administrators, former guards, or political appointees with little background in such arcane subjects as social deviance and recidivism, has never been more than faintly interested in rehabilitation. Even programs ballyhooed as rehabilitative, such as the much maligned 'furlough,' are tolerated not so much for their rehabilitative effect, as for the fact that they provide incentives which lead to smoother prison management.

Corrections is a system of extremes – debilitating prisons vs. ineffective probation/parole. To use a medical analogy, it would be like asking a doctor for relief from a headache, and being told there are only two treatments – an aspirin or a lobotomy. More often, it's like going to the same doctor with a broken arm or an acute appendicitis and being told the same two treatments, an aspirin or a lobotomy, are all that's available. Criminal behavior is no more unitary than any other individual or social malady. If the treatment options are so narrow as to be irrelevant, the likelihood of success is diminished. The simple mathematics alone suggest that the chances of fitting the treatment to the individual offender are enhanced when there are more choices.

In Massachusetts, for example, recidivism fell among former reform school youth in those regions of the state where a wide range of community-based alternatives were created, … from group homes, to on-the-street advocates and monitors, specialized foster homes, family therapy, supervised independent living, individual therapy, in-home family support services, 'wilderness survival' programs with strong community follow-up services, arts and vocational programs, job finding, and an intensive one-to-one contact and support (Coates *et al.* 1978). Where there was no such array of services, recidivism remained the same or increased. It was not a matter of identifying any single regimen which worked for all offenders. Rather, success was in the *mix* of models. The common thread which wound its way through the most effective programs of whatever type was whether or not they had close ties to the community. Interestingly, such services, alone or in combination, were no more expensive than state reform schools.

In 1988, Gendreau and Ross published a survey of over 200 studies on rehabilitation from 1981–1987, many of which used mathematical methodology not available to earlier researchers. They concluded with no equivocation:

> Our reviews of the research literature demonstrated that successful rehabilitation of offenders had been accomplished, and continued to be accomplished quite well … reductions in recidivism, sometimes as substantial as 80 percent, had been achieved in a considerable number of well-controlled studies. Effective programs were conducted in a variety of community and (to a lesser degree) institutional settings, involving pre-delinquents, hard-core adolescent offenders, and recidivistic adult offenders, including criminal heroin addicts. The results of these programs were not short-lived; follow-up periods of at least two years were not uncommon, and several studies reported even longer follow-ups.

What specific techniques worked best? They run the gamut from family therapy, cognitive problems solving, and supported independent living, to on-the-street 'tracking' and monitoring, negotiation skills, modeling, training in interpersonal skills, behavior contracting, individual and group therapy, reading, job training, and intensive residential treatment for violent offenders. Though many of these models were toward classic rehabilitation, others concentrated on teaching skills for survival in an increasingly hostile economic environment. In short, many things worked. A year before his death, Martinson anticipated this in an article in the *Hofstra Law Review* (1979), pointing to a plethora of rehabilitative models which had proven effective with offenders, he wrote, '… such startling results are found again and again … for treatment programs as diverse as individual psychotherapy, group counseling, intensive supervision, and what we have called individual help.' As one observer commented, this was 'probably the most infrequently read article in the criminal justice debate on rehabilitation.' In the course of debate, the man who started it all had come full circle. But by now, no one was listening. He had served his purpose and his own issue was wrested from his grasp.

The final irony was that Martinson thought his well-publicized skepticism about rehabilitation would *empty* most prisons. 'The long history of "prison reform" is over,' he wrote. 'On the whole, the prisons have played out their allotted role. They cannot be reformed and must be gradually torn down.' But he misjudged the politics of the rehabilitation debate. Rehabilitation is, for the most part, now absent from contemporary American corrections. Harsher sentences, warehouse prisons, and corrections establishment which militantly rejects the idea of salvaging offenders has become the rule of the land. We must now wait for the swing of the pendulum. I fear it will be a long wait.

From: J. G. Miller (1989) 'The Debate on Rehabilitating Criminals: Is It True that Nothing Works?' Printed in the Washington Post, *23 April.*

62. Punishment in modern society

David Garland

From the mid-nineteenth century onwards, many of the official ways in which punishment was discussed and represented came to reflect the 'rational' and 'scientific' conceptions of professional penal administrators and criminologists, who endeavoured to define penality in ways which were not emotionally or morally charged. The management of reformatories, penitentiaries, or even of probationers was redefined as a scientific task, demanding knowledge, skill, and expertise and a cast of mind which could only be disrupted by considerations of an emotional or sentimental kind. These 'managerial' concerns gradually came to dominate penological discourse, turning it into a 'penitentiary science' rather than a moral philosophy. Issues such as reformatory method and institutional regime which would once have been seen as side issues, subordinate to the main task of punishing, came to be vaunted as leading issues which were often pitted against punitive considerations rather than allied to them. By the end of the nineteenth century, a scientific criminology and penology had emerged in Europe and North America which amounted to a kind of 'rationalization' of penal discourse. As Raymond Saleilles (1913) put it, this new criminology attempted to replace the value rationality of traditional penal morality with a new purposive-rationality, which would adopt whatever technical methods were best suited for the control of crime. Criminology was, in effect, an expression of the Enlightenment ambition to cure social ills by the application of Reason, and its emergence both expressed and reinforced the developing administrative logic of nineteenth-century penal systems.

Within these new ways of conceiving punishment, the problem of punishment was reformulated in technical terms as a question of social engineering and adjustment, and of course the role of the expert was deemed central to its solution. Not surprisingly, this new 'scientific' approach was enthusiastically adopted by prison administrators, wardens, medical officers, and probation officers who saw themselves as the new criminological technicians – just as it was vigorously rejected by others (including many magistrates, politicians, judges, police officers, and members of the public) who felt that this vocabulary failed to convey the social condemnation that crimes should properly receive. From the turn of the century onwards this 'progressive' vision of a scientific penology based upon therapy and risk-management – rather than moral censure and punishment – has formed the working ideology of significant sections of the penal professions. To the extent that this ideology influenced penal legislation and penal policy – and it did so to a considerable extent – these professional groups succeeded in transforming the culture of punishment. They introduced the rationality of value-neutral science, a technical 'non-judgmental' vocabulary, a 'passion for classification', and a horror of emotional forces, into a sphere which was previously dominated by candid morality and openly expressed sentiment. Of course one might argue, as many did, that this new technical discourse merely suppressed its affects and moral commitments, disguising them behind the bloodless language of social science. 'Rehabilitation', 'treatment', and 'correctionalism' all involve characteristic values and emotional attitudes (such as care, compassion, forgiveness, mercy) but the idiom which these policies preferred was one which talked not of moral values but of technical values, so that correctionalist policies tended to be argued for as expedient or effective rather than morally correct. Thus penality came more and more to be conceived, and talked about, and practised, in these rational, passionless terms wherein moral evaluation is displaced by scientific understanding. As Foucault (1975) says at one point, penality's fate was 'to be redefined by knowledge'.

An ironic consequence of this avoidance of explicit moral argument (and thus of moral education) has been that the values and attitudes which underpinned the rehabilitative ethos have been undermined by the technical failures of correctionalism. When, in the 1970s and 1980s, it became common wisdom that rehabilitation did not 'work' – or at least worked no better than traditional punishment – it became apparent in the back-to-punishment movement that the values of compassion and welfarism had not, after all, become solidly entrenched in public attitudes or in penal policy. It is also significant, as Stanley Cohen (1985) has shown, that the eclipse of the rehabilitative ethos has done nothing to diminish the extensive network of investigative, classifying, and normalizing practices which were initially introduced under the rubric of 'helping the offender', but which now form an essential part of the power–knowledge network of penal control.

From: D. Garland (1990) Punishment and Modern Society: A Study in Social Theory. *Oxford: Clarendon Press, pp. 185–6.*

63. Restorative justice

Martin Wright

Ms Turner, an office worker, divorced, suffered a burglary in which a beer stein of sentimental value was broken, and a £700 video which she had borrowed was stolen and later dropped, damaging it beyond repair. It was not covered by insurance. Mark, aged 20, was charged with the offence. He had already served three years in custody as a juvenile for burglary, and was currently on probation for taking a motor cycle without consent, possession of a weapon, and two other offences. (Case summarized from Marshall and Merry 1990: 80; names have been changed.)

Traditional justice

Punishment   Mark, with his record, would have been likely to get a custodial sentence or at least a fine. This would give the victim nothing, and would be unlikely to give Mark insight into the effects of his behaviour on victims.

Rehabilitation   If, despite his record, the court decided that he needed help with personal problems, he could have been placed on probation. This could have helped, but there would have been a risk that it would have allowed him to blame his conduct on his problems. In terms of 'just deserts' it would have appeared 'lenient'. Again, the victim would receive nothing.

Restorative justice

Mixed traditional and reparative   What in fact happened in Mark's case was that Ms Turner, when approached by the reparation project, was keen to meet him. Her own son had been involved in petty crime, and she wanted to ask him why he intruded into people's homes, and to tell him the effect of this violation on her. A meeting was arranged, and she did so. Mark, who did not have a close relationship with his parents, responded to her willingness to talk to him, explained that he had been drinking on the night in question. The mediator suggested that he might make a payment to Ms Turner as reparation.

She and M agreed to this, although his earnings were small, and he regularly paid £5 a week. The case then came to court, whose sentencing options included disregarding the private arrangement and imposing punishment, which would have been disillusioning for Mark; or taking it into account, which could have been seen as unfair on other offenders whose victims were not willing to take part. In the event court did apparently take note of what had happened, and put Mark on probation.

From: M. Wright (1996) Justice for Victims and Offenders: A Restorative Response to Crime. *Winchester: Waterside Press, 2nd ed. www.watersidepress. co.uk. pp. 146–7.*

64. Good or evil?

John Patten

Dwindling belief in redemption and damnation has led to loss of fear of the eternal consequences of goodness and badness. It has had a profound effect on personal morality – especially on criminality. Loss of faith is hard to measure. The best gauge of secularisation available to us statistically is church attendance. This is falling steadily throughout the United Kingdom. In a few areas church attendance remains relatively high, such as in Northern Ireland and parts of Scotland. While peace and personal happiness are not necessarily evident in those places, there does seem some link with lower levels of crime and better education results. The few churches where attendance is rising seem to be those which have allowed much abused fundamentalism to creep in again. In such churches, redemption and damnation are preached as they have been for the thousand years of Christianity in this country.

[…]

It is, to me, self-evident that we are born with a sense of good and evil. It is also self-evident that as we grow up each individual chooses whether to be good or bad. Fear of eternal damnation was a message reinforced through attendance at church every week. The loss of that fear has meant a critical motive has been lost to young people when they decide whether to try to be good citizens or to be criminals.

[…]

Today a tiny minority of people are responsible each year for the great majority of crimes. And they start very young. Glib talk of 'grubbing up the roots of criminality' means searching for the green shoots in the 10-, 11- and 12-year-olds. While each of these children ultimately has to make his (it is rarely she) own choice between good and bad, he can be helped in that choice by family, school and Church – the forgotten norm of the pre-1950s.

Enough has been written about the decline in family authority and values, and the way in which some have debauched their own authority, being kind, ultimately to be cruel. Delinquent parents need to feel the contemporary lash if they won't persuade their children to behave, and that is what the Criminal Justice Act allows. Parents will have to be in court with their children, pay their fines, and may be bound over against a hefty sum to stop their delinquent children doing it again. The other side of the coin is to mobilise some schools to be surrogate parents. Who knows, religious teaching may even come back into fashion, too. Communities and voluntary organisations can help persuade those children identified as at risk to grow up straight rather than crooked.

From: J. Patten (1992) 'There is a choice: good or evil', The Spectator, 18 April, pp. 9–10.

65. The new penology

Malcolm Feeley and Jonathan Simon

A central feature of the new discourse is the replacement of a moral or clinical description of the individual with an actuarial language of probabilistic calculations and statistical distributions applied to populations. Although social utility analysis or actuarial thinking is commonplace enough in modern life – it frames policy considerations of all sorts – in recent years this mode of thinking has gained ascendancy in legal discourse, a system of reasoning that traditionally has employed the language of morality and been focused on individuals (Simon, 1988).[1] For instance, this new mode of reasoning is found increasingly in tort law, where traditional fault and negligence standards – which require a focus on the individual and are based upon notions of individual responsibility – have given way to strict liability and no-fault. These new doctrines rest upon actuarial ways of thinking about how to 'manage' accidents and public safety. They employ the language of social utility and management, not individual responsibility (Simon, 1987; Steiner, 1987).[2]

[...]

Scholars of both European and North American penal strategies have noted the recent and rising trend of the penal system to target categories and subpopulations rather than individuals (Bottoms, 1983; Cohen, 1985; Mathiesen, 1983; Reichman, 1986). This reflects, at least in part, the fact that actuarial forms of representation promote quantification as a way of visualizing populations.

Crime statistics have been a part of the discourse of the state for over 200 years, but the advance of statistical methods permits the formulation of concepts and strategies that allow direct relations between penal strategy and the population. Earlier generations used statistics to map the responses of normatively defined groups to punishment; today one talks of 'high-rate offenders,' 'career criminals,' and other categories defined by the distribution itself. Rather than simply extending the capacity of the system to rehabilitate or control crime, actuarial classification has come increasingly to define the correctional enterprise itself.

The importance of actuarial language in the system will come as no surprise to anyone who has spent time observing it. Its significance, however, is often lost in the more spectacular shift in emphasis from rehabilitation to crime control. No doubt, a new and more punitive attitude toward the proper role of punishment has emerged in recent years, and it is manifest in a shift in the language of statutes, internal procedures, and academic scholarship. Yet looking across the past several decades, it appears that the pendulum-like swings of penal attitude moved independently of the actuarial language that has steadily crept into the discourse.

The discourse of the new penology is not simply one of greater quantification; it is also characterized by an emphasis on the systemic and on formal rationality. While the history of systems theory and operations research has yet to be written, their progression from business administration to the military and, in the 1960s, to domestic public policy must be counted as among the most significant of current intellectual trends. In criminal justice the great reports of the late 1960s, like *The Challenge of Crime in a Free Society* (see note 3), helped make the phrase 'criminal justice system' a part of everyday reality for the operatives and students of criminal law and policy.

From: M. Feeley and J. Simon (1992) 'The New Penology: Notes on the Emerging Strategy of Corrections and Its Implications', Criminology, *30.4: 449–74.*

Notes

1. A number of influential scholars have commented on this process, often calling attention to what they regard as the shortcomings of traditional individual-based legal language when applied to the problems of the modern organization-based society. See, e.g., Dan-Cohen (1986), Stone (1975).

2. In contrasting the 'old' and the 'new' tort law, Steiner (1987: 8) observes: 'They [judges with the new tort law] visualize the parties before them less as individual persons or discrete organizations and more as representatives of groups with identifiable common characteristics. They understand accidents and the social losses that accidents entail less as unique events and more as statistically predictable events. Modern social vision tends then toward the systemic-group-statistical in contrast with the vision more characteristic of the fault system, the dyadic-individual-unique.'

3. A good example of this is the President's Commission on Law Enforcement and Administration of Justice, created in 1966. Its report, *The Challenge of Crime in a Free Society* (1967), combined a commitment to the rehabilitative ideal with a new enthusiasm for actuarial representation. Indeed, that document represents an important point of coalescence for many of the elements that make up the new penology.

66. Day training centres

Maurice Vanstone

The origins and early history of the idea

The history of day training centres has been fully documented by a number of people (Burney, 1980; Mair, 1988; Wright, 1984). There is no need to repeat it here, but there are aspects of the history and the development of the idea which are not only of interest, but also of relevance to the broad issues which I intend to address. Although the original four centres emerged as facilities for the category of offenders designated as 'high risk' or 'deep end', the original concept related to those people whom Philip Priestley described as the short-term prisoners who not only 'account for about one in six of the prison population at any given time', but also for far more than one in six prison sentences (Priestley, 1970). Indeed the stereotypical image of the potential recipient of centre programmes is given its most illuminative shape as Tony Parker's 'unknown citizen' (Parker, 1963), the person whom Paul Senior locates in the network of 'homeless and rootless who drift around the periphery of offending' (Senior, 1985).

It is arguable that the centres never catered for this kind of individual to any marked degree. Instead, they quickly became part of a policy aimed at diverting from custody an altogether more sophisticated and more serious offender who typically might have attracted prison sentences of six months and above. They were generally people who committed offences of burglary violence and theft and would be perceived as 'heavy end' within the context of the community but as 'light end' within the context of prison. Whilst the main focus of interest in Philip Priestley's paper is the community training centre ideal itself, it is interesting to note that the paper contains a seam of thinking which links with the reasoning and rehabilitation programme of Robert Ross today (Ross and Fabiano, 1985). The arguments outlined in the paper are based on the findings of a survey of 614 men discharged from Swansea, Cardiff, Gloucester and Bristol prisons (Vercoe, 1970). Within the total sample, a significant sub-group of prisoners who were homeless on release was identified, and it was as a response to the needs discerned within that group that the community training centre idea was conceived. Priestley, imbued with a strong scepticism about the relevance and viability of traditional casework, eschewed the idea of the inadequate personality and supplanted it with the concept of role performance deficits and the idea of trainable skills. Interestingly, in view of current developments in the probation service (Raynor and Vanstone, 1992) the community centre that he envisaged, with its possible staffing of psychologists, social workers and programme assistants, was to be based not on traditional social work methods or therapy but on a model closer to further education; and its curriculum was to hinge around personal development, vocational preparation and social skills training. Although, as I shall illustrate later, the centres focused on individuals and their offending, Priestley's ideas and the programmes of at least two of the centres mark the beginning of an attempted break from the dominant medical model and are a precursor to the 'non-treatment paradigm' (Bottoms and McWilliams, 1979).

The historical climate in which the day-training experiment was established is of particular interest. As I have already intimated, it was launched on a ripple if not a wave of rehabilitative optimism, but at almost the same point in history as Martinson and his colleagues were about to deliver their pessimistic conclusion on rehabilitation (Martinson, 1974). Moreover, its sister experiment, community service, was by design low on rehabilitative content although the early experimental projects were tinged by what seemed to be a covert rehabilitative purpose (Pease et al., 1975). The day training centres were also established at the demise of the rehabilitative purpose of custodial institutions. Approved schools had been abolished, the training element of Borstal training was all but defunct, and the rehabilitative ideal of prisons had been long lost in the overcrowded morass of three-up cells and squalid dehumanizing conditions. This is particularly interesting. It can be said that rehabilitation continued to live within the spirit of the probation order, but it had done so in some form or another since the police court missionaries were saving the souls of the inebriate. It had, if you like, become part of the furniture. So why introduce a new and substantial piece of rehabilitative furniture at this particular time? The answer to the question is partly to do with a continuing belief in the possibilities of changing people, partly with a growing recognition of the negative effects of prison, and partly with concerns about prison overcrowding. The effect, I suggest, was to rekindle the flame of institutionalized rehabilitation, but this time in a semi-institution in the community. There is an interesting comparison in the field of mental health in which, for economic and perhaps social reasons, people are being moved out of the large Victorian hospitals into the community. The problems inherent in that policy are well known, but Carol Williams in describing a Hammersmith advice project for the unemployed outlines an interesting and positive attempt to help people 'overcome social withdrawal and demoralization' (Williams, 1987).

The semi-institution and rehabilitation

The idea that the day training centres were an expurgated form of prison which encouraged the drift towards punishment in the community was certainly promulgated during the early stages of their development. It was reported that some workers felt like 'community prison officers' (James, 1985), although such charges were indignantly dismissed by others. They shared one of the features of prisons in that the amount of time was a fixed requirement which created space which had to be filled, but there were a number of very significant differences, not least their purpose; in particular, they did not isolate those who had to attend from the normal day-to-day responsibilities of living. It is nevertheless an unavoidable conclusion that some of the characteristics of prisons can be discerned in the day training centres and, I would argue, their very existence as semi-institutions can be linked to the format and history of prisons. Mathiesen outlines four characteristics of the traditional prison: work; education; discipline; and punishment. In his general arguments against what he describes as the prison fiasco he catalogues the failure of the rehabilitative purpose of prisons:

> The overall reply to the main question posed in this chapter – Does prison have a defence in rehabilitation? – may be put briefly, an overwhelming amount of material historical as well as sociological leads to a clear and unequivocal no to the question (Mathiesen, 1990, p. 47).

He argues that the ideology of rehabilitation which can be traced in the history of prisons from their inception was formed through work, school, moral influence and discipline, or as he puts it 'co-elements in a bourgeois Protestant ethic'. Although the programmes of the original day training centres varied in methodology and theoretical framework they each contained those four elements. I am not suggesting that they did so with the same rigid adherence as in prisons, but to a greater or lesser extent they can be discerned within the published programmes of the day centres at that time. They are manifested by practical activities like pottery, car maintenance, and woodwork; educational activities like literacy and numeracy classes; attempts to influence and change through group and/or individual counselling; and specified attendance times, breach action and house rules. The London Centre's aims were originally expressed thus:

> To provide, in a non-custodial setting, the opportunity for offenders who appear frequently before the courts, and who show difficulty in coping with the complexities and demands of modern life, to examine their behaviour in the community and to become aware of its effects on others. To help such offenders learn how to satisfy their needs in ways that will not bring them into such continued conflict with the law, thus providing a greater protection for society through their rehabilitation (Inner London Probation Service, 1972).

They can, therefore, in some senses be seen as positively assisting the transition of the ideology of rehabilitation from the closed institution to the semi-institution. They were also part of a policy design which was initially concerned with diverting petty recidivist offenders, but latterly high risk offenders, from custody. They had to be effective in this sense whilst at the same time having a characteristic of acceptability to the divergent interests of the public, the courts, the probation service and offenders themselves. Prisons, whatever their abject failure in rehabilitating people and in preventing crime, are a very tangible and observable sentence; indeed it is possible that the observability of prisons is one of the main factors in their survival. The new alternatives to custody, therefore, have to satisfy both the test of observability and the test of tangibility in a way that a weekly or fortnightly visit to probation officers cannot, or, to put it another way, they need to be somewhere that magistrates and judges can send offenders and visit themselves. This was essential in order for the theory of individual prevention through rehabilitation in prison to be directly transferred to the day training centres. The argument about the deleterious effect of prison was in itself simply not adequate.

[...]

Conclusion

In this paper I have acknowledged the danger of exaggerating the significance of the day training centre experiment. In the history of criminal justice during the twentieth century it will be ascribed a small paragraph, and in the history of probation, a chapter. Neither the paragraph nor the chapter should be ignored. Its influence, I have argued, is wider than the *ad hoc* day centre development within the probation service which ensued in the late 1970s and 1980s. It had an impact on probation policy and practice in a number of ways, many of them helpful but some unhelpful. Furthermore, it has been attributed partial responsibility for the drift towards increased state coercion. It might not escape that attribution altogether, but its overall impact has been a positive one. The experiment might yet be seen as an essential element in preserving the concept of rehabilitation during its wait for a more enlightened and progressive criminal justice policy.

From: M. Vanstone (1993) 'A "Missed Opportunity" Re-assessed: The Influence of the Day Training Centre Experiment on the Criminal Justice System and Probation Policy and Practice', British Journal of Social Work, 23: 213–29.

67. Groupwork with women

Marion Jones, Mary Mordecai, Frances Rutter and Linda Thomas

Underpinning and informing all aspects of our model is offending behaviour. As stated earlier, it is this behaviour alone which authorises probation officers to work with offenders who are the subject of probation orders.

The key aims are to:

1. enable women offenders to explore fully the reasons for their involvement in offending, by providing a forum for challenging and confronting their behaviour and its consequences for themselves and others;
2. widen and develop the options available for alternative behaviour;
3. encourage group members to consider strategies for dealing with perceived powerlessness in changing their behaviour.

Group ethos

'... when women are spoken for but do not speak for themselves ... dramas of liberation become only the opening scenes of the next drama of confinement' (Showalter, 1987, p. 250).

The workers aim to create an atmosphere of honesty, openness, sharing and respect for others, which is both challenging and enjoyable. Each member of the group has her part to play in creating an atmosphere requiring the taking of risks. The group is orientated towards achievement of the task, i.e. to fulfil the group contract which is determined during session one. The concept of individual responsibility is promoted at every opportunity. Language which conveys and reinforces helplessness is always challenged, e.g. terms such as 'I can't ...', 'I must ...', 'I need ...', are substituted with 'I won't ...', 'I choose to ...', 'I want ...'. Sue would always say: 'I can't stop shoplifting'. When she went shopping alone, she said she felt compelled to shoplift, and believed it was out of her control. The only controlling factor she had was to shop with a member of her family. Only then was she able to avoid her urge to steal. At the first group session she attended she was encouraged to substitute 'I won't ...' for 'I can't ...'. The effect of saying 'I won't stop shoplifting' was immediate. From that point on she began to take more responsibility for what did or did not happen to her.

Contract

All women offenders participating in the programme do so on a contractual basis with aims and objectives clearly agreed beforehand. The contract is a commitment to herself to work towards breaking unhelpful patterns of thinking and feeling which contribute to her offending behaviour. It provides a sound basis for entry into the group by promoting the offender's sense of individual responsibility and giving the workers permission to highlight those areas of behaviour requiring change.

At the pre-group stage, the supervising probation officer and the offender will agree that group attendance is appropriate. A referral is made to one of the groupworkers and a three-way interview is arranged. The aim of the interview is to negotiate the offender's contract of attendance at the group. During that interview, the following questions in relation to participation in the groupwork programme are discussed: Why?, When?, How?, What?. She and her probation officer will have an opportunity to share aspects of the work they have undertaken together to meet her perceived needs. On this basis, the woman determines her reasons for joining the group and makes a statement about what she would hope to achieve through group membership. She will be expected to share her contract with the other group members at the first group session. The contract is signed and agreed by the three parties and a copy is placed in her probation record.

From: M. Jones, M. Mordecai, F. Rutter, and L. Thomas (1993) 'A Miskin Model of Groupwork with Women Offenders', in A. Brown and B. Caddick, (eds), Groupwork with Offenders. *London: Whiting & Birch.*

68. Last messages from a fading star

Brian Caddick

The Bristol New Careers Project came into existence in April 1973 following the efforts of NACRO and its supporters and with funding provided by the Home Office. It offered what was then a radical disposal for young adult male offenders at serious risk of receiving a borstal sentence: probation supervision and hostel residency coupled with a programme of training in practical social work. This was, in effect, an early excursion into the realms of empowerment, the aim being to build marketable skills on top of relevant life experiences, and thereby help talented but disadvantaged young offenders move from being a focus of intervention to being active practitioners in the provision of social and community services.

Although novel in the UK, the ideas on which the Project was based had originated in America during the 1960s. In an effort to combat the effects of growing poverty the US federal government had at that time provided funding for a wide range of social and community projects, the dual intention of which was to improve services in depressed areas and to create training and job opportunities for disadvantaged, discriminated against, underskilled or unemployed people. Legislation was enacted (see Wicks, 1978) to ensure the participation of the poor as project workers and also to encourage the kind of on-the-job training which would produce non-professional practitioners whose abilities and potential would bear comparison with their professionally trained colleagues. Such programmes thus came to be known as 'new careers' programmes (Pearl and Riessman, 1965), and the touchstone of many of these was that the life experiences of the project workers had, in effect, equipped them with insights which went a long way towards compensation for their lack of conventional professional training. Indeed this was a key principle through which – in California – the new careers philosophy was extended to offenders. There, Douglas Grant (1968) and his colleagues had developed a programme whereby selected prisoners were trained to provide rehabilitative services to other prisoners while in custody. The intention, subsequently realized by many, was that these trainees would then use their experience and training to continue in correctional or other human services work on their release from prison (Hodgkin, 1973; Briggs, 1975).

In Britain the establishment of the Bristol Project was eased, not by governmental initiative or legislation, but by the circumstances and arguments supporting the more or less contemporaneous introduction of the community service order and by the training traditions of the borstal system (Lowson, 1975). However the idea of actively training offenders for work in the human services was unusual and attracted wide attention. There were welcoming articles in the social work press (Briggs, 1973; Hinton, 1973; Davies, 1974); there was even a cautiously positive editorial in *The Times* (1973) on the concept that in many of those who had experienced troubled lives there was an untapped capacity to understand and assist others who were also troubled. The BBC produced a documentary (with the rather bleak title *This Is Your Last Chance*) and the first years of the Project's operation came under research scrutiny (Millham *et al.*, 1978). Then, as happens, interest shifted elsewhere.

Even so, for nearly twenty years the Bristol New Careers Project kept faith with the notion that disadvantaged and disaffected offenders had something to give and something to gain from acting in a supportive and caring role with others. Unlike community service – which was seen by some to embody a similar view but which, as Pease (1983) and Blagg and Smith (1989) have noted, drifted into work which was 'almost exclusively manual, menial and arduous' – the New Careers Project held firmly to its aim of providing practical experiences which were humanitarian in kind and affirmative in purpose. But in 1992 this rather singular experiment came to an end, restructured by the probation service (which in 1981 had taken over management responsibility) to make way for other priorities under the new Criminal Justice Act. Once a bright star, to which over 300 offenders were sent by the courts and where, as a further feature of its provision, nearly 40 ex-offenders gained social work experience in a staff role, the New Careers Project has faded from view.

From: B. Caddick (1994) 'The "New Careers" Experiment in Rehabilitating Offenders: Last Messages from a Fading Star', British Journal of Social Work, 24.4: 449–60.

69. Probation practice, effectiveness and the non-treatment paradigm

Peter Raynor and Maurice Vanstone

Reviewing the non-treatment paradigm

The context of the non-treatment paradigm stretches back to the history of the professionalization of social work, and in particular probation, between the First and Second World Wars. Status gained through training and qualifications required theoretically informed practice; uncomplicated help in itself was not enough. Psychoanalysis, handily placed in current vogue as it was, neatly fitted an approach to criminal behaviour premised on the notion of curing a disease. Offenders, even if they didn't know it (and invariably they didn't), were suffering from a pathological condition.

By 1979 the edge had been taken off the excesses of the medical model, although offenders were still suffering from authority problems and lack of insight (Foren and Bailey, 1968), and the IMPACT experiment with its assumption about the efficacy of increased doses of case-work was only a few years distant (Folkard *et al.*, 1976). However, it still permeated practice sufficiently for the authors of the paradigm to declare the need for:

> a new paradigm of probation practice which is theoretically rigorous; which takes very seriously the exposed limitations of the treatment model; but which seeks to redirect the probation service's traditional aims and values in the new penal and social context (Bottoms and McWilliams, 1979, p. 167).

Fourteen years on its main features make interesting and relevant reading, but its foundations, built as they were out of a mixture of doubt and scepticism about the crime-reducing potential of rehabilitation, have produced cracks in the structure. Before examining these cracks, and indeed what is still in sound condition, we shall summarize the authors' main arguments. In developing a critique of the treatment model which highlighted its theoretical fault lines, discriminatory processes and inequities, they argued that the model was theoretically incoherent and led to injustice. Inevitably, a summary will fail to do justice to the complexity of the arguments, but in essence they argued that crime is voluntary whereas disease is involuntary; that crime is not pathological but has social causes; and that enforced treatment is inherently unjust. These enduringly persuasive conclusions formed the basis of their conviction that a new framework for practice was needed, incorporating four basic aims.

The first, *the provision of appropriate help* for offenders, was described as something which the client rather than the worker defines. In other words, the appropriateness of the help is governed by the expressed needs of the client, and is separate from the crime reduction component of rehabilitation. Paradoxically, Bottoms and McWilliams suggested that the needs of the client were to be clarified within a process of joint assessment and collaboration; and furthermore, by a passing reference to successful work with offenders released from prison (Berntsen and Christiansen, 1965), that there might be evidence that help could reduce crime.

The second, *the statutory supervision of offenders*, was ensconced in acceptance of the reality that probation officers are law enforcement agents who must provide help which is consistent with agency function. Inevitably, this means that the transactions between officer and client occur within a context of authority and power imbalance. In order to resolve the problem created by that tension between client-defined needs and the statutory requirements of supervision, the paradigm draws on Raynor's exposition of the difference between coercion and 'choices made under constraint' (Raynor, 1978); within this conceptualization of the exercise of authority constrained choices are acceptable, but manipulative coercion is not.

The third, *diversion of appropriate offenders from custody*, required probation officers to abandon treatment, to eschew recommendations for custody or suspended sentences and to think creatively about alternatives to custody. These changes in turn would facilitate the use of community resources to hold offenders as effectively as prison but at less cost.

The fourth, *reduction of crime*, positioned uneasily as it is within an analysis which denies the reductive potential of rehabilitation, focused on crime prevention activity based on the expressed wishes of the community, and directed at increasing social cohesion. To help them in this, the authors draw on Abrams' (1978) notion of reciprocity (i.e. there is a mutual pay off for helper and helped alike), and Christie's (1977) ideas of structural change in criminal justice processes (such as a 'conflict-based, victim-orientated, non-professional neighbourhood court'). So, in the light of National Standards (Home Office, 1992), the Criminal Justice Act 1991, and the current social and economic context of crime, how do these four pillars of the paradigm stand up? Perhaps we should first clear the ground and state which of them remains firm. Statutory supervision of offenders premised on maximizing choice with due regard to the function of the agency, and the development of imaginative community sentences, both seem as relevant today as they were then. The problem lies in their relationship with activities which may both help offenders and reduce crime, which because of a priori assumptions were almost unavailable for consideration by the authors of the paradigm.

The non-treatment paradigm was written at a time when the received wisdom about work with offenders aimed at reducing their offending was that at best it was a waste of energy and commitment, and at worst it was counter-productive. It was also written before any published revision of the analysis of the causes of crime by the school of 'new criminology' (Taylor *et al.*, 1973). The more recent 'left realist' position (Young, 1988) takes account of *all* of the actors in the criminal justice process, including victims and potential victims. As a result Bottoms and McWilliams follow lines of reasoning which significantly affect the persuasiveness of some of their key arguments.

The acceptance that 'nothing works' confined them to consideration of crime prevention strategies which had a social focus, to the exclusion of any concern with influencing individuals. Such a connection between the reinforcement of social bonds and a reduction in individual offending could plausibly be made, as in Kevin Haines' recent application of Hirschi's control theories (Haines, 1990; Hirschi, 1969) to explain the possible greater success of after-care provision which achieves the social reintegration of offenders; however, such arguments play a minor role in the original non-treatment paradigm. By uncoupling 'helping offenders' from 'crime reduction', the paradigm is prevented from exploring whether work with individuals on their thinking, behaviour and attitudes has any relevance to crime reduction. Current knowledge of research into effectiveness necessitates, therefore, a redefining of the concept of appropriate help in a way which retains the principle of collaboration, and the stress on client needs, but which incorporates informed practice focused on influencing and helping individuals to stop offending (Raynor, 1988; Roberts, 1989; Lipsey, 1992). This should not detract from the need to address the social and economic context of crime. A further problem for Bottoms and McWilliams stemmed from the fact that their only alternative to attacking the social causes of crime is the treatment model, which they very effectively demolished. Not only, therefore, as we have argued above, were they unable to consider individual offence-focused work, they were also inclined to write about offenders as if they were a homogeneous group. Consequently their main argument fails either to address the degree to which crime harms victims and communities as well as offenders, or to attempt to explain why the majority of poor, disadvantaged people do not become persistent offenders. This requires some acknowledgement of individual differences, and of patterns of thinking or behaviour which increase the risk of some people becoming involved in crime.

From: P. Raynor and M. Vanstone (1994) 'Probation Practice, Effectiveness and the Non-Treatment Paradigm', British Journal of Social Work, 24.4: 387–404.

70. Drug treatment: a therapeutic community

Carl Åke Farbring

The Österåker Prison just outside of Stockholm has hosted a treatment programme on six wards for drug abusers during a twenty year period. It has been run within the frames of a therapeutic community (TC). Different aspects of therapeutic interventions have been emphasized over time and between the wards. The dominating approach to treatment has been behavior based although one ward has at least in part favored a psychodynamic approach.

[...]

Contents

Prior to being admitted to the programme every applicant had to write a letter explaining a little about his background and why he wanted to change. Prisoners could apply directly from remand prisons or other security prisons. Since the programme at the beginning was minimum 8 to 10 months they had to have more than a year left to serve which in reality meant that in the beginning the average sentence was about four years. Later on it was much longer. Applicants had to have a documented long and heavy dependence on drugs.

If accepted, every prisoner signed a contract according to which he had to conform to a few basic rules, i.e., no drugs, no violence, no threats, no conversations about crime if not as a part of treatment, etc. Breaking of these rules could lead to expulsion from the programme. Prisoners had to take active part in the programme eight hours a day: they had to act as chairman and secretary at many meetings: they had to act as hosts for study visits, etc. They were also responsible for cleaning the ward, took decisions on what to do during the physical exercise hours, etc. They also had to take active part in the treatment of their fellow inmates, state opinions about their attitudes and change, etc.

Every morning seven days a week prisoners had to leave urine samples. Prisoners produced these samples naked in front of members of the staff in a special room. On the experimental ward 1976–78, and in fact even up to 1982, we did not have the technique to test for cannabis so we relied confidently on social control. Later on prisoners told us that they had been using cannabis frequently during that period.

All activities were organized according to a timetable five days a week from 7 a.m. to 5 p.m. Even part of the leisure time was more or less obligatory for some individuals – for instance for those who had to take dance lessons. Conflicts, breaking of rules, etc., would break the timetable and were dealt with immediately during crisis meetings on the ward where everybody had to participate.

Every inmate had an individual treatment plan. In group counselling sessions prisoners were encouraged to make analyses of all kinds of problems and risk situations highly correlated to recidivism in drug use and crime. A very common undertaking was ending relationships with criminal friends, practicing withdrawal from situations where drugs were offered in real life, etc. Among the benefits of the programme were social visits on the ward from close family members 6½ hours during Saturdays and Sundays. This was probably one of the main reasons why prisoners applied to the programme since it was understood that motivation to change in the beginning was not always impressive or even sincere. (Most of our prisoners would be categorized as ambivalent to change, contemplating if change would be good for them; very few were determined or in the action stage according to the Prochaska & DiClemente model (1986). Sometimes it would take days or even weeks before prisoners could make themselves speak with members of the staff on friendly terms.) During visiting hours children would play on the open yard enclosed by the wards together with their parents. Although conjugal visits are allowed in Swedish prisons at least 50 percent of the visiting time had to be spent together with other families and the staff participating in games and other leisure activities organized by the staff. The demand from schools all over Stockholm for prisoners to inform and warn about drugs and crime was very high and often impossible to meet. Prisoners felt it was an important social undertaking and it was important for their self-confidence. Most of the criminogenic problem-oriented treatment was dealt with on the ward after lunchtime. In the mornings prisoners were studying or employed in workshops.

Theory

Even before the experimental ward was started almost everybody at the prison with formal academic training favored an approach based on learning psychology. A few of us had formal education and training in behavior therapy.

On the experimental ward especially in the beginning in 1976 we thought that group counseling, identifying and talking about solutions to problems was the most important element for change. A few test interviews changed that. We asked a small number of prisoners if they had remembered from our daily group counseling sessions how to deal with problem situations when they occurred in real life situations, for instance on furloughs. The unanimous answer was zero: no one had remembered anything at all!

From that moment on we put emphasis on actual training of behavior to deal with problems. We still used group counseling as a means to analyze individual problem situations and role playing according to Liberman's personal effectiveness model (1975) to correct behavioral deficits. We had to use an analogy with pilots to overcome resistance to the method. It was easier to persuade prisoners – and sometimes staff – that pilots would not learn how to handle difficult situations in the air just by talking about how to handle them or watching overheads but by practicing in a simulator; role playing was our simulator.

During one period we used extinction of arousal and anxiety triggered by visual contact with syringes, needles, and other utensils, until it was considered too radical to do so within the prison environment.

When the large-scale programme was started attempts were made to introduce a more psychodynamic model. Activities were still based on a weekly timetable and the approach to problems remained concrete. Later on, one ward developed a more psychodynamic touch to the group counseling and showed preference to deal with rule breaking individually and not in meetings, but the approach to many problem situations remained practical even there.

Multimodality in the sense that Arnold Lazarus (1976) used the word has also been a major theoretical underpinning. Change is not easy and if it is not correlated with whole sets of attitudes, family network and friends, feelings and social arrangements, it is likely to disappear once the 'campaign effect' is over.

What made Liberman and Lazarus influential in our work was the fact that they came to Stockholm and a few of us met them in person.

Family members were kept informed about the individual treatment plans during visiting hours and were sometimes invited to group counseling sessions. Sometimes even the victims of crime were invited to meet with their perpetrators.

Within the large-scale therapeutic community each ward had formed a minor therapeutic community of its own. Four of these wards were situated in one building (H-house) which belonged to the programme as a whole and two wards were situated in another house (G-house) – among them the 'psychodynamic' ward.

Workshops, school, library, school kitchen, gym, etc., were all situated in the H-house. Two wards especially took behavior therapy much longer and were the only ones to practice role playing up to the middle of the 1980s. These wards also used cognitive approaches – for instance, self-talk much as it was developed by Meichenbaum and Goodman (1971).

During all these years the specific ingredients of psychological 'therapy' have varied considerably over time and between the wards. However, the structure of the therapeutic community as such, the weekly timetable, and the attention on drug problems and crime have inevitably kept the focus on actual behavior.

From: C.A. Farbring (2000) 'The Drug Treatment Programme at Österåker Prison: Experience from a Therapeutic Community During the Years 1978–1998', American Jails, *March–April: 85–96.*

Part Three

The future – can rehabilitation be rehabilitated?

Introduction

In the modern world, criminal justice systems have two kinds of work to do – rhetorical and practical. At the rhetorical level they have to communicate a set of values about personal security, property rights and personal conduct, about right and wrong, good and evil, and in practical terms they have to act to protect the citizens of the state against those who do not observe these requirements in their daily lives – what sociologists might call their 'expressive' and 'instrumental' functions. In both areas there is controversy, and in both there is conflict about how best to deliver these public goods. Part One of this reader illustrated the rise of the rehabilitative ideal in criminal justice through the nineteenth and early parts of the twentieth centuries. In Part Two, the selected extracts told the story of its decline in the face of a punitive revolution that has transformed the way the state in the USA and the UK responds to crime and to those who commit it. In this the third part of the reader we address the future and attempt something that is dauntingly difficult – but necessary, and not so impossible as to be not attempted at all. We ask whether rehabilitation itself, as an idea and as a practice within probation and elsewhere, can be rehabilitated from the position it is now in, so that it plays a distinctive, effective and honourable role in twenty-first-century corrections. The materials we have assembled here are designed to further this debate in terms of the aims, values, structures and methods which might make this possible.

A restored rehabilitative ideal cannot simply turn the clock back as though the past fifty years have not happened. Any restatement of the aims of rehabilitation, and of probation, must take into account all that has taken place, and incorporate into its new vision of itself those elements of recent history which add to rather than detract from its historic mission. The new services should be above all about harm reduction: aiming to reduce the harm done to victims and communities by crime (de Haan 1990) and aiming to reduce the harm that individuals do to those close to them and to themselves when they commit offences. Harm reduction declares a behavioural goal, but it also makes a strong value statement. In pursuit of these aims, efforts must be made to reduce the harm done to social groups and individuals within them by the uneven, unfair and unjust processes of society itself, including the harmful effects of imprisonment and the operation of criminal justice – which is where probation came in. So their remit is not just to temper criminal justice with compassion, but to pursue a wider vision of justice for the communities it serves and for all those who live in them. 'Social work can invigorate its presence in corrections,' says Edward J. Gumz in an appeal to US social workers to re-engage in criminal justice work, 'by affirming its traditional commitment to social justice – one of the primary tenets of the profession' (Gumz 2004). In addition it needs to take its place as part of a plural response to crime which is a complex social phenomenon, lived out by complicated human beings. In doing this it does not need to take an imperialist or abolitionist position towards imprisonment, as punishment has done so successfully against welfare and treatment approaches to crime. Custody will remain as a protective function of last resort for difficult and dangerous people, but its methods can be transformed in ways that chosen extracts will spell out. Lawrence Kohlberg, who pioneered the study of moral reasoning as a developmental process in children, helped to set up a 'just community' experiment in the Connecticut Women's Correctional Center at Niantic. Inmates made and administered their own living unit rules. 'They said that for the first time they had lived in a setting where people treated each other fairly and with mutual concern' (Kohlberg *et al.* 1975). The results were also positive in terms of reconvictions following release, but Kelsey Kauffman, a prison official and co-researcher claims that 'Kohlberg never sought to justify the unit on such traditional grounds; that it served the ends of social justice was sufficient' (Kauffman 1990). The prisons that remain can be transformed in other ways as well – into 'residential colleges for example. Gilligan and Lee report on 'a college education program in which professors from Boston University volunteered their time in order to teach in the prisons, and more than 200 inmates earned a bachelor's degree. When we attempted to learn how many of them had been returned to prison for a new crime after leaving, we were unable to find any' (Gilligan and Lee 2004).

In order to reinvent itself probation-led rehabilitation needs to reassert its role as a social work service based in the courts. To do this it needs to go back to basics, to reaffirm its commitment to the individual who is caught up in the criminal justice system, and to do this with self-confidence – 'it is the moral thing to do,' is Francis Cullen's verdict (Cullen 2007). It needs to treat people as more than bundles of deficits or repositories of 'risk factors' that have to be 'managed' – as human beings, in fact, who add up to more than just digits in an aggregate or a population. And it needs to treat them with respect, as subjects with rights as well as obligations (Lewis 2005). One consequence of a 'rights' approach is a renewed emphasis on the quality of the service received rather than the results.

> Obsessive questioning of rehabilitation's effectiveness is understandable if it is merely a governmental interest. The rights perspective encourages a shift in the focus of concern. The effectiveness of rehabilitation would still be of interest, but would not be of overriding importance. Instead, one will ask how much it matters and in what ways. (Rotman 1986)

And it defines them, not as the passive recipients of welfare services delivered *de haut en bas* by charitably minded workers, but as active participants in a process that stimulates and supports self-change (Robinson and Raynor 2006). The goal of this change, and an organising concept for the services that surround it, is that of 'citizenship', helping people to become pro-social and contributing members of the society to which they belong. Finally, citizens are people who 'consent' to processes and programmes, community protection always entails constraint, and ordinary social pressures constitute modifications of autonomy, but the value base of the rehabilitative ideal favours consent, cooperation and willingly undertaken work towards agreed goals. While acknowledging the possible utility of compulsion in some cases, Fagan argues for 'getting these clients into therapy and treatment voluntarily by increasing their intrinsic motivations, making treatment options more attractive, and using the clients' own support networks' (Fagan 1999).

Two countervailing developments during the punitive revolution of the later twentieth century have major implications for the possible revival of rehabilitation and probation within criminal justice in the twenty-first. They are 'community justice' and 'restorative' justice, both sufficiently well articulated as to merit the use of the term 'paradigm', which the dictionary defines as 'a conceptual or methodological model underlying the theories and practices of a science or discipline at a particular time; (hence) a generally accepted world view' (OED 1993). These two models of justice overlap to some extent and there is continuing discussion about how to define their differences (McCold 2004; Arrigo 2004).

Community justice had its roots in community-oriented, problem-solving policing in the United States, a rival to the 'zero tolerance' approach, frequently and wrongly credited with bringing down crime rates – in fact crime went down at the same rates in problem-solving police areas (Young 1999). These initiatives stimulated the experimental establishment of problem-solving 'drugs courts' in which the goal was to use innovative, participative, consensual and collaborative proceedings to formulate action plans for individuals to deal with their addictions and lead more law-abiding lives – 'using a non-adversarial approach, prosecution and defense counsel promote public safety while protecting participants' due process rights' (Huddleston *et al.* 2005). Key elements in the model are the involvement of local communities in their own justice systems. They do not necessarily use the words, but they are about active citizenship at the local community level. Specialist drugs courts share some of these characteristics but not necessarily the community participation activities. Judges become more responsive to individuals in their sentencing and more closely involved in their supervision in the community.

> Problem-solving courts seek to move away from a one-size-fits-all approach to justice. Many court cases are not complicated in a legal sense, but they involve individuals with complicated lives. Problem-solving justice recognizes this and seeks to give judges the tools they need to respond appropriately. (Wolf 2007)

Community justice continues to retain control and surveillance functions but it does this in the community and within a context of joint problem-solving and multiple service provision:

Problem-solving initiatives have found that clear communication and rapid response is essential for holding offenders accountable: non-compliance must be communicated as soon as it is discovered and the court must make it clear that sanctions (e.g., letters of apology, curfews, increased frequency of reporting, even short-term jail) will be issued in response. By creating effective vehicles for communication between the court and probation and other service providers, problem-solving courts have helped improve service delivery and the accountability of treatment providers. (Wolf 2007)

In terms of the thesis represented in Part 3 of this reader, a critical characteristic of these community justice forms is their insistence on moral agency in those they process, and their aiding and seconding of the self-rehabilitation steps that individuals elect to pursue for themselves. There is a growing body of evidence that community justice and problem-solving courts satisfy key parts of the agendas of their contributing agencies and audiences (Huddleston *et al.* 2005). Consumer satisfaction, professional involvement, reduced costs and some indications of lowered risk compared to punitive disposals suggest that these approaches hold promise for a different kind of criminal justice on a wider scale (Finigan *et al.* 2007).

Restorative justice is a portmanteau term for a wide-ranging set of ideas, procedures and findings which stem from the rediscovery of the victim as a missing player in the modern drama of criminal justice (Rock 1990). Restitution, compensation, victim support services, victim offender mediation, family group conferencing – restorative justice is now a tradition that runs wide and deep and has its own extensive literature, schools of thought and published evidence. At the level of theory, de Haan (2002), believes that justice as 'redress' should 'continue to be directed at "decolonizing" parts of the life-world from domination by criminal law, through the system of "indirect rule". For example, conflicts might be re-appropriated by being absorbed or "stolen back" in order to use them as valuable aids to the social integration of the life-world and the prevention of social harm'. Restorative justice is thus both a critique of punitive justice, and a programme for replacing it. Grimsrud and Zehr (2006) define it as 'peacemaking', with biblical roots:

This peacemaking approach must take seriously (and vigorously critique) the philosophical and theological roots to retributive criminology. However, we are suggesting that the deepest roots of Western theology, found in the Bible, are indeed fully compatible with new, peacemaking approaches to criminal justice.

And they hypothesize literary approval from the past: 'Tolstoy would be pleased.'

At a practical level family group conferencing, which draws on Maori tribal precedents for dealing with miscreant youth, has been established system-wide in New Zealand and is one of the models that has been widely discussed and emulated in other parts of the world. Even in accounts of these concrete forms there is room to contest aspects of conventional justice.

Consistency and proportionality of outcomes are constructs which serve abstract notions of justice that stand in place of agreements that restore the social balance between victims and offenders within their communities. And while social control remains an integral part of restorative justice (and family group conferences), it must assume a new meaning as power and control are relocated within the social group. (Hudson *et al.* 1996)

And also for a 'critique of the critics' of restorative measures:

Restorative justice also emphasizes human rights and the need to recognize the impact of social or substantive injustice and in small ways address these rather than simply provide offenders with legal or formal justice and victims with no justice at all. (Morris 2002)

As in community justice, a critical characteristic of restorative justice is its emphasis on justice within a wider context and in particular the neglected needs of the victims of crime (Burnett and Maruna 2006). As with community justice, research evidence is accumulating to show that participants in restorative justice positively value its aims, its methods and its outcomes. There is also some empirical support for its ability to reduce reoffending (Sherman and Strang 2007; Shapland *et al.* 2008). If the best that can be said collectively of community justice, restorative justice and cognitive-behavioural methods is that they do no worse than conventional criminal justice that would still be an argument for considering them with an open mind. In fact on a number of measures they do better than no better – cost, consumer satisfaction and, in some categories of offending, lowered reconviction rates. In those terms they spell out a forward agenda for action by those who would revive the rehabilitative ideal.

Three developments of theory and method during the dark days of the punitive victory over plural corrections also show promise for re-establishing rehabilitation, both in the community and in prison.

What works

There have been a great many reviews and meta-analyses of 'what works' in the professional literature (McIvor 1990; Lösel 1995; Lipsey and Wilson 1998; Redondo *et al.* 1999). Overall they demonstrate the superiority of programmed over discursive methods and of cognitive-behavioural methods over others (Vennard *et al.* 1997). What they do not yet point to are detailed examples of independently replicated programmes that produce, when applied systematically, strong reductions in reoffending. But the legacy of 'what works' for a restored rehabilitation at the heart of criminal justice is important. Firstly, it has established the validity of certain ways of working to reduce reoffending – broadly speaking, but not exclusively, cognitive-behavioural methods. 'The best of the "What Works" developments', according to Robinson and Raynor (2006), can be seen as consistent with earlier social work modes of 'helping people to take responsibility by treating them as responsible'. They quote as examples 'the use of "Socratic questioning" to challenge people to think for themselves, and the development of skills and motivation to help people to overcome obstacles and take charge of their own lives'. Secondly, it has established empirical inquiry as an important tool for the justification and authorisation of public expenditure and provided a reflexive means of improving services to courts, communities and individuals.

Further scrutiny of this literature suggests that other, equally important factors are also at play in the situation. Small-scale, unreplicated studies in which the authors of programmes train the staff and remain involved in their delivery and evaluation do better than programmes that do not have these characteristics (MacKenzie 2000). The preferred modality of most programmes is to work with groups, partly to provide economies of scale and partly to acknowledge the presumed therapeutic benefits of group participation. Equally, what is not researched in these studies is the nature and quality of the professional relationships which individual programme participants have on a one-to-one basis with other agency staff members.

Desistance

Another strand in more recent thinking about issues of personal change has developed around the study of desistance from crime and narrative accounts of personal turning points. This work has a distinct and different intellectual pedigree to both the traditional view of rehabilitation and to much of the 'what works' literature, being more grounded in 'interactionist' theories and observations than in mainstream or cognitive psychology. In 1966, Orville Brim discussed 'socialisation after childhood' in terms of the knowledge, skill and motivation which individuals require in order to perform satisfactorily, i.e. pro-socially, within society, a 'role' theory of deviance rather than one rooted in 'personality' and requiring a plural response of education, training and re-motivation. To focus on only the motivational component of anti-social conduct was, thought Brim, a way for society to evade its own culpability.

> If a person confronts his society with a claim of ignorance or poor ability, it reflects on the adequacy of his prior socialization, which is society's responsibility. Motivational deviance, in contrast, is less easily attributable to defects in society's socialization process and is more easily viewed as being the individual's own fault. (Brim and Wheeler 1966)

Ideas about 'desistance' have developed from empirical studies of individuals who have 'desisted', i.e., given up crime and gone straight. At first sight the findings of this research are not encouraging for those employed in the rehabilitative services. For example:

> Most of the conditions for successful exiting are largely outside the control of correctional agencies and their programs. It well may be that the things that are conducive to change within criminal careers are primarily interpersonal, and thus are beyond the reach of the criminal corrections system. (Meisenhelder 1977)

In a more recent study, Maruna (1998) reviews theories about adult behaviour change in offending populations, that people 'grow out' of crime, or they form 'social bonds' by finding work or getting married, and concludes that the missing 'ingredient' is the 'subjective autobiography' that 'actually shapes our future choices and behaviour'. He quotes from Jerome Bruner (1987) about the importance of self-narratives in the making of the person:

> The heart of my argument is this: eventually the culturally shaped cognitive and linguistic processes that guide the self-telling of life narratives achieve the power to structure perceptual experience, to organise memory, to segment and purpose-build the very 'events' of a life. In the end, we become the autobiographical narratives by which we 'tell about' our lives.

Further research and a number of practical projects and proposals have flowed from this and similar conceptualisations. The 'Good Lives Model' of rehabilitation defines itself as 'a strengths based' approach which 'depends crucially on the possession of internal (skills and capabilities) and external conditions (opportunities and supports)' (Ward and Brown 2004). Burnett and Maruna (2006) describe a prison-based project, with echoes of the earlier New Careers experiments, where prisoners perform socially useful tasks for people in the outside world: 'In a strengths-based framework, prisoner work efforts would be voluntarily agreed upon, and would involve challenging, intrinsically interesting tasks that could utilize the talents of the offender in useful, visible roles.' In another study, interviews with almost two hundred UK probationers revealed the very small role that supervising probation staff had played in any successful 'desisting' from crime (Farrall 2002). Farrall's proposal in the light of these findings is for 'a research project which attempts to "fuse" together developments in individual cognitive abilities and changes in their social contexts. The current project has suggested that probation supervision "works" indirectly through allowing the probationer's life to develop positively' (Farrall 2002). Desistance approaches, therefore, insofar as they allow for professional involvement, recommend assisting individuals in the process of self-change, building on strengths and facilitating the construction of new personal 'narratives' or self-concepts, including that of volunteer, helper or 'citizen'.

Re-entry

When the prison population doubles, then doubles again, and then almost doubles again as it has done in the United States, from 338,000 in 1980 to 2,293,000 in 2007, and less spectacularly but still substantially in the UK over the same period, from 40,000 to 80,000, it follows that there will be large increases in the numbers of people being released from prison into the community. Given the greater attention being paid to re-conviction rates as an important measure of penal effectiveness, it also follows that prisoners re-entering society will be targeted as a very high-risk population. Petersilia (2004), however, seeks to widen the scope of these concerns:

> Evaluations should measure whether clients are working, whether that work is full or part time, and whether the income derived is supporting families. We should measure whether programs increase client sobriety

and attendance at treatment programs. We should track whether programs help convicts become involved in community activities, in a church, or in ex-convict support groups or victim sensitivity sessions.

The search for ways to reduce rates of reconviction and parole revocation after release from prison has led to a convergence of methods and experiments with those already being used in community corrections: a judicious mix of service supply, access to community resources, surveillance and supervision, and supported self-change. An earlier proposal for 'community centers' to broker services like these chimes with the model of probation centres which disappeared from the scene in England and Wales during the rush to accredited programmes during the 1990s (Vanstone 1993). They would, according to Kevin Wright

> serve two purposes in directing the offender towards opportunities for alternative behavior and in acting as an advocate-broker for the offender within the community. Serving in the latter role, centers would attempt to create better access to social and economic institutions as well as advocating greater community tolerance of deviancy through public relations and education. Not only out-client supervision but also in-client custody for individuals needing short-term constraint would be possible within the centers. (Wright 1980)

At the same time, models of reintegration stress the need for changes in both role and status for the released prisoner:

> Hence while the retributive model of accountability requires that harm be done to the offender in order to balance the harm caused to others (von Hirsch, 1976), the exchange theory concept of reciprocity (see Molm and Cook, 1995; Gouldner, 1960) suggests that only by taking responsibility for making things right with victims and victimized communities can offenders change either the community's image of them or their perceptions of themselves. This model views active involvement in meaningful civic roles as fundamental to both cognitive change in the service provider and change in community attitudes about such individuals. (Bazemore and Stinchcomb 2004)

The goal in other words, is for a restoration to working citizenship. A recent review of the possibilities for social work to help people 'staying straight' makes the case for a renewed rehabilitation/probation service of the kind we are proposing here:

> Positive re-construction of the ex-offender's story, enhancement of the possibilities for employment, establishing and improving family functioning, and focusing on management of the underlying feelings of depression and anxiety are all necessary components of a practice approach that is relevant to ex-offender clients. (Kenemore and Roldan 2006)

It is a description that would not look out of place in a nineteenth-century manual of probation practice.

At this point, we draw together some of the threads from Part Three of the reader in the form of a 'citizen model' of rehabilitation and probation. The model rests on four assertions: (1) crime has complex causes; (2) a plural response to crime is required; (3) individuals can assume responsibility for their own behaviour; and (4) agencies should be accountable for their activity.

Crime has complex causes

Individuals who break the law do so for a multiplicity of reasons: to seek advantage for themselves, to damage others or to finance addictions. Some do so knowingly, some recklessly without apparent thought for the consequences, some because it appears to them that they have no other choices, some because they **do** have no other choices, and some without thought of any kind (McCord 1959; Newburn 2007).

Most people break the law at some time in their lives – it is hard to live in the modern world without doing so. But most of the time, most people do not break the law, and not because they would not like to get caught, but because they think it is a good idea to respect other people, their privacy and their personal possessions. They are citizens. Then there are the opportunists – people who will offend if the chances of their getting away with it are high enough to make the risk worth taking. Thirdly, there are those who appear to live outside the law and in opposition to it; these are the outlaws. Some of them are rational criminals who treat it as a business and make good money at it; their organised crime rings deal in drugs, prostitution and extortion. But the foot soldiers in this business, and the majority of those who persist in the most serious and damaging forms of crime, are disproportionately recruited from the ranks of the poor, the deprived, the disturbed, the dispossessed, the abused and the addicted. They have been subjected to poor, abusive and inconsistent parenting; they are mentally ill, have poor physical health, bad attendance at school and limited economic prospects. Many of these adverse conditions are especially prevalent in deprived immigrant communities.

A plural response to crime is required

Society's response to crime needs to reflect this diversity and complexity. Professional robbers, serial sex attackers and dangerous and disordered individuals may need to be held in secure conditions to ensure the safety of others (social protection). Others may be detained to mark the seriousness of their offending behaviour (expressive function). Some may be required to engage in restorative justice proceedings (responsibility), others assisted to undertake personal programmes of re-education and self-change (empowerment), and others may need updated versions of the 'advise, assist and befriend' function of the pioneer probation officers, including mediated access to multiple, and in some cases lifelong, services and support (services and support). These are 'social' responses to a 'social' problem – not a narrowly conceived 'treatment' model of intervention. Many of these services can best be delivered within a 'community justice' framework whose outputs can be characterised as public safety and reformed citizens. Safety may require elements of coercion; citizenship requires consent.

Individuals can assume responsibility for their own behaviour

At the root of all this provision is a fundamental belief in the possibility that people can acknowledge the nature of their behaviour and its harmful consequences for others and for themselves, and that they can take responsibility for putting some of it right and for changing themselves for the better. There is wide variation in the ability of individuals to do this, but the underlying ideals are deeply rooted in many human cultures and traditions – religious, ethical, philosophical and political. It is the role of a renewed rehabilitative service to help people make pro-social choices and to progress towards becoming active, contributing citizens.

Agencies should be accountable for their activity

Rehabilitation and probation provided by citizens as services to other citizens must also be accountable to those they serve. They can do this most effectively via consciously constituted 'learning organisations' (Argyris and Schön 1978), ones that continuously challenge their own assumptions, that constantly adjust their working practices to changing needs and that monitor their own performance in terms of outcomes that are then used to modify their activities.

> The key is collecting basic data – such as demographics about participants, length of participation, and compliance – and analyzing it. This kind of 'action research' is vital to ensuring that an initiative adapts to changing community conditions and priorities, and remains as effective as possible over the long haul. (Wolf 2007)

Another way of expressing this is that they should operate as 'what works' organisations. They need to be first and foremost 'professional' organisations, chartered by government with clear objectives, informed by the values embedded in many of our selected readings, and staffed by self-confident, well trained and experienced criminal justice practitioners (Nellis 2003). In addition they need to create for themselves an area of professional autonomy based on evidence and expertise codified from a vast extant literature and the great corpus of unanalysed experience that resides in countless records and in the collective memories of thousands of employees (Senior 2008). Recovering this resource from the contemporary generation of criminal justice professionals would require a very great effort of intellectual archaeology.

But will it ever happen? There is no simple way to read the history that has led to the dominance of the punitive prison in the USA and England and Wales. There were intellectual antecedents; there were political forces at work (Reiman 1988). At a certain point the use of imprisonment began to increase – and it never stopped. Its rise was not predicted then by commentators and students of criminal justice (Young 1999). Even now it shows few signs of slowing down. So there is no easy recipe for reversing the trend and for re-establishing rehabilitation at the heart of the penal enterprise. Two features of the current situation may, however, suggest ways out of the Chinese puzzle; 1. the re-emergence into society of large cohorts of long-term prisoners, many of them damaged, maybe beyond repair, by their carceral experiences, and 2. the economic downturn (Bazemore 2000; Bazemore and Stinchcombe 2004). On both counts political administrations may come to the conclusion that imprisonment is an expensive luxury they can no longer afford. It may be significant that during an earlier period of relative economic scarcity Governor Ronald Reagan of California backed the Probation Subsidy initiative – an alternative to custody scheme – on fiscal grounds (Lemert and Dill 1978). Re-settlement and the reintegration of ex-prisoners also have the makings of a political hot potato: putting away large numbers of people for long periods of time may be politically advantageous in the short term, but it is a policy with an inbuilt postdated debt that must be paid for at some distant time in the future. In the USA and the UK that future is beginning to be now.

71. Socialization through the life cycle

Orville G. Brim Jr.

Types of deviance

The first task in the analysis of resocialization as a solution to deviance is to make a conceptual analysis of the types of deviant behavior. The chart introduced earlier [...] presented six types of content of the socialization effort, namely knowledge, ability, and motivation, each in relation to behavior and values. This same chart, therefore, indicates the six basic types of deviance, corresponding to failures of the socialization process in the six areas of content.

	Behavior	Values
Knowledge	A	B
Ability	C	D
Motivation	E	F

Consideration of the chart shows that the sources of deviance are an individual's ignorance, his lack of ability, or his lack of motivation, and that deviance may occur in behavior or values – or both. The intersection of these three sources with the two possible areas generates the six basic types of deviance. Illustrations of each type can be drawn from a familiar family situation involving the son's academic achievement and the expectations of his parents.

In the first type (Cell A in the chart), the actor is ignorant of the behavior that is expected of him. Consider the son who knows that he is required to get good marks but does not yet fully understand the importance of studying hard and completing homework on time.

In the second type (Cell B), the actor is ignorant of the ends to be sought. The child may conform behaviorally to his parents' expectations to study hard but does so because he is afraid of their criticism, not yet understanding that the value he should be pursuing is to obtain outstanding grades.

In the third type (Cell C), the actor deviates in behavior because of inability to conform. A simple example is a son's inability to carry out the prescribed studying because of weak eyes or poor physical condition.

In the fourth type (Cell D), inability is the source of deviance in values. There are familiar instances of how possession of a value may be impossible because of the punishing conflict it produces. Here, the son may not pursue the value of going to college because it involves him in direct competition with his father's record at college and he cannot tolerate the anxiety this arouses in him. He may still study hard and do well, but does so to avoid criticism by his parents rather than to be admitted to college.

In the last two types (Cells E and F), motivation is the source of deviance. In respect to Cell E, where the deviance is in behavior, the son simply may find studying difficult and unpleasant, being insufficiently motivated to carry out the prescribed action. He may pursue the value of obtaining the grades but seek to achieve them through deviant means such as cheating.

In the final type (Cell F), where the lack of motivation refers to the pursuit of appropriate values, while conformity exists in behavior, there is the familiar case of a person behaving in the right way but for the wrong reason. Thus the son may study hard but reject the parentally prescribed end of continued academic education; he pursues instead the goal of getting a higher rating in the Navy when he graduates from high school.

Note that the types represented in Cells D and F are quite different even though they appear similar. In Cell D, where the person is unable to pursue a given value, it is not because he is unmotivated toward this end, as is true of Cell F. A person can want something he is unable to pursue. Thus the child may wish that he could be interested in college, even though he cannot.

These are the six simple cases of deviance. They are the pure types, which are the building blocks of more complex deviant actions. Two illustrations will show the construction of these complex cases. For example, deviance commonly occurs both in behavior and in values. Where this is true, and the source is ignorance, the obvious illustrations are those of any untutored person: the newborn infant, the hillbilly recruit, the child during his first day at school, the mother of a newborn child. Where the source is lack of motivation, an illustration is the pacifist faced with the expectations of the infantry combat role in which he neither pursues the end of killing nor wants to engage in combat.

Modes of control

The modes of attempted control over deviance which are characteristically used by an individual, a group or a society reflect its theories and assumptions about the causes of deviance and are rooted in its ideas about human nature, for example whether man is inherently a stupid animal, whether he is possessed by demons or controlled by other supernatural forces, whether he is innately depraved, or burdened with original sin.

In our own society it is deviance in motivation and values (Cell F) which is viewed as most serious. The concept of motivation plays an important role in our theories of why human beings behave as they do, and deviance in motivation is viewed as a serious threat to the social order. If a person does not share with others the values of his society and/or rejects the means used to achieve them, he is untrustworthy and unpredictable as a fellow member of an established social group. It seems that our society is more willing to tolerate deviance stemming from ignorance or lack of ability if only a person means well, has his heart in the right place, has good intentions.

Because of these beliefs about motivation and the concern with which this type of deviance is viewed, there is a tendency to examine instances of deviance for possible motivational components in order to appraise how serious the deviance is. In return, the deviant person, challenged to account for his behavior and faced with punishments for having the wrong motives – punishments customarily greater than those for deviance from the other two sources – will plead ignorance or lack of ability as the cause for his actions. The result is that considerable time is spent in both legal and informal social control procedures, searching for possible motivational deviance behind the facade of ignorance or lack of ability.

Sometimes it appears that the law, to avoid the difficult problem of appraising the motivational component in deviance, simply assumes that the cause of the deviant act is motivation. Before the law, ignorance or lack of ability rarely constitute a satisfactory excuse for nonconformity. Lack of knowledge that a stop sign has been put on a corner, or a sudden brake failure in the automobile, do not greatly mitigate the individual's responsibility to stop at the intersection. Sociological analyses of the conditions under which one is allowed to claim he is ill, that is, allowed to take the role of the sick person, show that illness is under the continuous appraisal of responsible persons such as an employer, a spouse, or a parent for possible malingering and illustrate in microcosm the operation of group control over possible false claims of disability when poor motivation is the real cause.

Perhaps another reason for the *a priori* assumption that deviance is motivational in nature is that it places the blame on the individual for his behavior, rather than on society. If a person confronts his society with a claim of ignorance or poor ability, it reflects on the adequacy of his prior socialization, which is society's responsibility. Motivational deviance, in contrast, is less easily attributable to defects in society's socialization process and is more easily viewed as being the individual's own fault.

The burden of proof thus is placed upon the actor to show that his motives are pure. The demand that he do so is from society's viewpoint legitimate, since it is difficult to distinguish ignorance or lack of ability from hypocritical claims either that one did not know what the rules really were, or that he was unable to live up to them.

This view of human behavior may benefit society, but there is a price for using this approach in the resocialization of deviant persons. The treatment of deviance would be more effective if it made use of techniques which accord with the reasons for behavior: where ignorance is the cause, education; where lack of ability is the difficulty, improved training; where motivation is the problem, a planned and deliberately executed program of manipulation of rewards and punishments to reorient the individual to appropriate goals and behavior.

If deviance comes from ignorance or lack of ability and yet punishment is administered in the mistaken idea that motivation is the cause, a frequent result is the individual's rejection of the values of society which he formerly accepted. The child who wants to get good marks in school but cannot do so because he needs glasses and is unable to study without them soon learns to hate school if he is punished for his failure to achieve good marks. Similarly, the child from a lower-class home who does not understand the ways of the school or his classroom and is ignorant of much of what is expected of him soon learns to dislike school if he is punished by the teacher for his non-conforming behavior. Treatment of a case of deviance arising from ignorance or lack of ability as if it springs from the wrong motives actually may produce the more serious situation of deviant motivation, the very problem that society is trying to eliminate.

From: O. G. Brim Jr and S. Wheeler (1966) Socialization After Childhood: Two Essays. *New York: Wiley, pp. 40–44.*

72. The just community approach to corrections: a theory

Lawrence Kohlberg, Kelsey Kauffman, Peter Scharf and Joseph Hickey

The moral development approach, then, implies establishing a democratic community in which rules and decisions are made by staff and inmates together, and in which inmates in small living units have a responsibility for upholding the rules and settling conflicts in a fair and democratic way. In a democratic or just community, even though staff relinquish authority, they can – in the long run – have much greater constructive influence on the inmates' moral decisions. We can see that democracy is central to moral development if we see that the heart of morality is a sense of fairness and justice. Morality means a decision of what is right where there is a conflict between the interests and claims of two or more people. Justice means fairness in deciding the conflict, giving each person his due and being impartial to all. Democracy is a form of government designed so that the decision-making process will be considered fair by all. Only in a democratic setting can inmates have any sense of living in a community which is fair. While most inmates do not care about society's morality, they do care about justice or fairness. Because they feel they are treated unjustly and live in an unjust world, they do not try to be fair to others. To be motivated to act fairly, inmates must feel they are part of a just community. Inmates will accept the standards and authority of a community if these standards can be understood as fair from their point of view.

[...]

What are the advantages of such a 'just community' approach to custody and rehabilitation? First, within the context of a prison, the seemingly inherent conflicts between rehabilitation and control can be adequately reconciled. Both can be seen as being based on principles of fairness to the inmate and fairness of the inmate to the group or community. Not only can line staff avoid embittering decisions through this approach, but they can more adequately integrate custody and rehabilitation roles.

Second, a fair environment and a sense of community are ends in themselves; they make the lives of both staff and inmates better. Once a democratic environment is created the staff member is free from the roles of detective, orderer, and punisher and can engage in more human interactions with inmates. Higher standards can be developed in regard to inmates' and staff members' behaviour towards each other and towards the community.

Third, a just community approach promotes moral character development and responsibility: (a) through participation in moral discussions and exposure to new and different points of view, (b) through living in an atmosphere of fairness and developing relations of loyalty and trust, and (c) by taking responsibility for making and enforcing rules on oneself and other members of the group.

Fourth, by promoting moral development rehabilitation, goals can be achieved. As inmates come to understand and accept the morality of their small 'just community' and to be concerned about its welfare, they come to better understand and accept the morality of the larger and not-so-just society to which they return, and to seek a different pattern of life in that society. In interviews with inmates two years after release, many who were functioning well outside expressed why they thought the programme had led to significant changes in their lives. They said that for the first time they had lived in a setting where people treated each other fairly and with mutual concern. On leaving the programme they had decided that they wanted to have lives in which they could continue to have such relationships and chose life patterns which could enable them to do that.

From: L. Kohlberg, K. Kauffman, P. Scharf and J. Hickey (1975) The Just Community Approach to Corrections: A Theory, Journal of Moral Education, 4.3: 43–260.

73. An exploratory study of exiting from criminal careers

Thomas Meisenhelder

Conclusion

These findings provide a descriptive typification of exiting as a stage in the criminal careers of twenty non-professional property offenders. This typification indicates that the most significant motive underlying the formulation of the intention to abandon criminal behavior is the threat of doing more time in prison. Exiting is planned and implemented in order to avoid future convictions and incarcerations.

Upon implementation of an exiting project, the ex-felon strives to construct a conventional life and a coherent non-criminal social identity. Typically, one factor emerges as extremely influential in the success of these exiting projects: the early acquisition of a bond to, or investment in, conventionality. If the individual's intentions and expectations remain pragmatic, if a good job is obtained, if he receives support for his project from family and other conventional associates, and if his status and social identity as non-criminal is formally certified to the wider community, success is a more probable result of the individual's attempt to abandon his criminal career.

Theoretical implications

Typifications and descriptions of social action should be in line with formal theoretical explanations of that action. Thus several general implications can be drawn from these findings.

First, most of the conditions for successful exiting are largely outside the control of correctional agencies and their programs. It well may be that the things that are conducive to change within criminal careers are primarily interpersonal, and thus are beyond the reach of the criminal corrections system. In short what is done to or with those whom society has determined to be criminal may have little real effect on their future behavior

Second, the findings presented here are in support of the earlier work of Glaser (1964), Irwin (1970), and Stebbins (1971). These data suggest that attempts at exiting are a common occurrence within criminal careers. Further, this study points to the importance of pragmatic, everyday social conditions in the abandonment of criminal careers.

More generally, the findings presented here tend to support rationalistic control theory (see Hirschi, 1969) as a theory of criminal behavior. The control perspective emphasizes the importance of the social bond in the creation and direction of social action. Like control theory, this paper suggests that exiting is a pragmatically constructed project of action created by the individual within a given social situation. Exits are normal and deliberative rather than the result of therapy or resocialization. Prison, labeling, and other crisis events may lead the individual into a social psychological context where exiting is seen as reasonable and rewarding. Nevertheless, the specific content and direction of individual action projects are founded in the intentional and conscious deliberations of the actor within these situations. Jobs, relationships, and other meaningful contingencies relevant to the individual's purposes influence his or her attempt to abandon criminal behavior. But it is the individual's purposes and interests that give these conditions their relevance and meaning. As the men themselves stated: 'You rehabilitate yourself.'

From: T. Meisenhelder (1977) 'An Exploratory Study of Exiting from Criminal Careers', Criminology, *15: 319–34.*

74. A re-examination of correctional alternatives

Kevin N. Wright

A correctional alternative

Based on research conducted in California, Robison and Smith (1971) reached the following conclusion: (1) institutional confinement is no more effective than community supervision; (2) longer sentences do not reduce recidivism and possibly increase it; (3) treatment has little effect on post-incarceration success or failure; (4) intensive parole supervision, if anything, increases recidivism; and (5) inmates discharged outright are as successful as those released on parole. These findings provide a basis for the proposal of substantial changes in correctional delivery systems. They suggest, from the standpoint of recidivism reduction, that correctional systems can probably do *less* to convicted offenders and be as successful as they have been in the past. That is, most offenders can be supervised in the community for shorter periods of time without being forced into treatment programs, and the offenders will be no more likely to commit new crimes than in the past.

The idea of 'doing less' does not necessarily imply any modification of the goal of reducing recidivism. O'Leary and Duffee (1971) have identified a third method of influence, correctional internalization, which is appropriate for a system attempting to reduce the probability of future criminal behavior but de-emphasizing individual change. Internalization is implemented in the correctional setting via the simultaneous influence of community standards and offender attitudes. An attempt is made within the community to open new alternatives for the offender, to provide the offender better access to various social institutions and to increase the general public's tolerance of deviancy. Within this environment the offender is encouraged to explore new alternatives based upon his/her own background and values. The individual accepts influences of this type because they have some intrinsic value to the person and they provide the individual with an alternative which was not previously perceived. The individual is, thus, able to accept and maintain a given behavior, because it is, in itself, useful to the person.

Based on the above discussions, an additional correctional alternative often labeled *reintegration* can now be characterized. The system relies primarily on community-based programs which utilize internalization as their predominant mode of influence. Community centers serve two purposes in directing the offender towards opportunities for alternative behavior and in acting as an advocate-broker for the offender within the community. Serving in the latter role, centers would attempt to create better access to social and economic institutions as well as advocating greater community tolerance of deviancy through public relations and education. Not only out-client supervision but also in-client custody for individuals needing short-term constraint would be possible within the centers. Any 'treatment' activities (counseling, education, training, etc.) could be obtained from non-correctional agencies within the community.

The advantages of the reintegration model have been summarized by O'Leary and Duffee (1971).

Breaks with the community are minimised, lines of communication are kept open. The community itself is the centre of treatment; the institution, when used, is located in the community of release.

Similarly Bennett (1973) drew upon the following analogy to reach the conclusion that most criminal offenders could be handled better in a community-based setting:

When resources for dealing with the mental health problem (now defined as a community-based concern) were shifted to the local community, it was found that most clients could be given adequate service on an outpatient basis and that the vast majority of those requiring inpatient psychiatric hospitalization required only brief stays. The result: mental hospitals that are archaic and expensive to operate have been closed. Patients are handled largely on an outpatient basis and in the community where they are expected to adjust, where they are closer to family members who can provide emotional support and where they can sometimes be economically self-supporting.

From: K. N. Wright (1980) 'A Re-Examination of Correctional Alternatives', International Journal of Offender Therapy and Comparative Criminology, 24.2: *179–92.*

75. Probation in St Pauls

Jim Lawson

Much has been said and written on the subjects of race and ethnicity, prejudice, discrimination and disadvantage, topics which, for the Probation Service, took on a special meaning following the riots and disturbances which occurred in a number of inner-city areas in England in the early eighties. Whilst acknowledging that simple remedies do not exist to overcome the massive political, social, economic and, arguably, moral problems which were fundamental to those disturbances, it was felt appropriate here in St Pauls, as doubtless it was elsewhere, for probation officers, individually and as team members, to take a long, hard look at themselves and their operations, with a view to seeing if steps might be taken to deliver a more relevant service for persons and groups, living in the community and, especially, in the vanguard of those troubles.

[...]

The team began to ask itself questions although it is perhaps only now, three years later, that some possible explanations can be postulated [...] A fatalistic acceptance of the status quo had developed and no strategies or plans to improve this state of affairs had ever been successfully devised.

[...]

[Probation] officers cannot expect to enter such communities and to be respected or accepted simply by virtue of their position and status: this can only be earned and cannot happen overnight.

[...]

A second theme is that, in our experience, many young black, male offenders do not, on the whole, welcome probation involvement in their lives, do not fit into traditional models of Probation or social work and require more a relevant and flexible style of intervention. This has resulted in an approach which can be loosely described as community-based and detached, involving, as it does, the vast majority of the work being undertaken on the streets, in cafés and in pursuit of recreational activities.

Two aspects of this style of work need particular emphasis. Firstly, the use of sport, and especially football, as a medium through which to engage many of the young black clients. Thus, continuously, for the last three years, John has run a five-a-side football league one evening a week, pulling in young men, promoting competitions, arranging tournaments.

[...] Secondly, the importance of working in and with the community on a variety of levels: from involvement with the more formal groups and organisations, such as the CRE and the Police Crime Prevention panels, through membership of management committees for local hostels, youth workers and community centres to informal contacts with cafés and 'important' individuals.

[...]

A third aspect is the importance of team support. There is a popular myth that unless a team is working in the same way or according to a universally accepted model, it is not operating as a team. I would argue that a team which, consciously and explicitly, frees members to take on particular responsibilities and ways of working, so long as it conducts itself on the basis of mutual respect and trust, is functioning very much as an integral unit.

From: J. Lawson (1984) 'Probation in St Pauls. Teamwork in a Multi-Racial, Inner-City Area', Probation Journal, 31.3: 93–5.

76. The rights model and the relevance of rehabilitative effectiveness

Edgardo Rotman

Recent criticisms of rehabilitative programs have focused on their alleged ineffectiveness. The claim of ineffectiveness has not only been used as an independent argument against rehabilitative policies but has reinforced criticisms of a different nature. Those responsible for rehabilitative policies responded hesitantly at first to these charges, but new empirical findings have now changed the direction of the intellectual tide. More sophisticated research revealed serious weaknesses in the data and methodology used by the detractors of rehabilitation, undercutting their conclusion that 'nothing works' (Martinson 1974) The result was a considerable improvement in evaluative disciplines with significant effects on the quality of the new rehabilitative programs (Ross and Gendreau 1980; Gendreau and Ross 1981). Although no longer seen as a universal panacea, rehabilitation has been proven effective under certain conditions for certain categories of offenders. Today rehabilitation implies a differential strategy with various levels of effectiveness.

The significance of rehabilitation, however, goes beyond this empirical dispute. Making support for rehabilitation contingent upon its effectiveness has rendered it more vulnerable to empirical absolutists and other opponents. If rehabilitation is recognized as a right, its value no longer hinges exclusively on its effectiveness.

A theoretical inquiry into the relevance of rehabilitative effectiveness should consider rehabilitation from two perspectives: as a right of the offender and as a governmental interest. The traditional one-sided view of rehabilitation as a governmental instrument to attain social goals led to an overemphasis on the question of its effectiveness. This view was associated with an authoritarian notion of rehabilitation in which society is the only acting force and individuals, lacking any initiative, are mere passive recipients of such action. Like deterrence or incapacitation, rehabilitation was regarded as a social policy dictated without consideration for the offender's personal life. The real difference between specific deterrence and rehabilitation lies in the means by which the ends are achieved. Enhancing the human potentialities of the offender is a specific feature of rehabilitation, whereas the punitive approach relies on fear or the aversion of pain.

The rights model, in contrast, views rehabilitation from the perspective of the offender without losing sight of the societal impact of rehabilitation.

Where rehabilitation is conceived as a right, effectiveness becomes a secondary consideration and no longer encroaches upon other priorities related to the needs of individual offenders and to the requirements of their actual sociopsychological improvement. According to the rights model, learning activities, dialogue, social interaction and psychotherapy are provided without calculating their likelihood of ultimate success or guaranteeing their effectiveness.

A right to rehabilitation, however, includes the right to minimum standards of seriousness and quality in the performed services. In this respect, a certain degree of efficacy is inherent in any serious rehabilitative undertaking. Such efforts should be likely to improve on offenders' ability to live a crime-free life, enrich their skills, or improve their psychological condition according to the state of the art in psychotherapy. But the existence and force of the right is not dependent on the cost-effectiveness of its exercise or on any particular outcome.

Viewed from the perspective of society, rehabilitation is part of governmental planning and social policy. At this level, evaluation plays an undeniably important role. It is a legitimate governmental concern to report tangible results to taxpayers, but the real value of accurate evaluation goes far beyond this rendering of accounts. Improved evaluation research will provide indispensable feedback to ongoing or future rehabilitative efforts. This guiding function is essential for critical policy decisions. Empirical research on sanctions, for example, may make it possible to adopt humane and less intrusive penal policies if they can be shown to be as effective as harsher ones.

When rehabilitation is seen as a right of the offender, its independence from its outcome becomes evident. Obsessive questioning of rehabilitation's effectiveness is understandable if it is merely a governmental interest. The rights perspective encourages a shift in the focus of concern. The effectiveness of rehabilitation would still be of interest, but would not be of overriding importance. Instead, one will ask how much it matters and in what ways.

From: E. Rotman (1986) 'Do Criminal Offenders Have a Constitutional Right to Rehabilitation?', The Journal of Criminal Law and Criminology, 77.4: 1023–68.

77. The politics of redress: crime, punishment and penal abolition

Willem de Haan

The penal complex is open to progressive intervention. For example, given the 'fragmented' protection offered by criminal law with regard to interests located within the life-world (Smaus, 1986, p. 16), needs for more adequate compensation, participation, or, at least, recognition could be taken up and articulated. Moreover, as Garland and Young have observed, 'there is space, even within a society dominated by a capitalist mode of production, to create more progressive and emancipatory forms of penality' (Garland and Young, 1983, p. 33). It should be recognized 'that the desired communal collective form is already an existing, if unacknowledged, underemphasized, and undervalued, component of the capitalist legal order' (Henry, 1985, pp. 324). If we fail to see this, we 'will miss the most promising ways of institutionalizing' these alternatives (ibid., p. 325). If there is, indeed, a potential for reinstitutionalizing forms of practical discourse that allow for rational argumentation about conflicting norms, values and behaviours, our alternatives need to make use of this degree of autonomy belonging to community justice institutions even within the existing and dominant social order. Moreover, rational conflict handling itself can engender social change and is, therefore, a means toward the end of its own realization. The aim of a politics of redress would, therefore, be to 'arrange it so that the conflict settling mechanisms themselves, through their organization reflect the type of society we should like to see reflected and help this type of society come into being' (Christie, 1982, p. 113). This means imagining forms of social regulation which are not located in or defined by the state but operate (semi-)autonomously as alternative, progressive, and emancipatory forms of dispute settlement and conflict resolution. Struggles could continue to be directed at 'decolonizing' parts of the life-world from domination by criminal law, through the system of 'indirect rule'. For example, conflicts might be re-appropriated by being absorbed or 'stolen back' in order to use them as valuable aids to the social integration of the life-world and the prevention of social harm.

Experiments with informal justice in Western countries have raised the question whether a mere change in form or procedure has any real significance without its being complemented by a substantive change in law. The complex relationship between form and substance in law accounts for much of the controversy concerning the politics of penal reform. I have shown how with a little sociological imagination human potential can be uncovered and, I hope, mobilized in order to deal with morally relevant conflicts in a more rational way. However, I have also shown that there are limitations for establishing forms of informal justice within various social, political, and legal structures. I have concluded that in order for informal justice to be feasible legal form and legal substance must go hand in hand.

From: W. de Haan (1990) The Politics of Redress: Crime, Punishment, and Penal Abolition. *London: Unwin Hyman, pp. 166–67.*

78. Desistance and development

Shadd Maruna

The desistance literature: theory and research

In one of the most thorough analyses of the topic, Rand (1987) suggests, '(T)he phenomenon of desistance has received no specific theoretical or empirical attention' (p. 134). Though this is overstated (see Shover, 1985, for instance), studies of desistance tend to exist in relative isolation from one another and most are not theoretically informed. Certainly, nothing like a consensus exists for understanding why young offenders desist from crime. Shover (1985) writes, 'Although it is conventional wisdom that most offenders eventually desist from criminal behaviour, criminology textbooks have little or nothing to say about this process' (p. 15). Mulvey and LaRosa (1986) conclude, 'In short, we know that many youth "grow out" of delinquent activity, but we know very little about why' (p. 213). This gap in the literature is a result of both methodological and theoretical weaknesses in existing research. Critically, most of the leading desistance explanations continue to fall into the dichotomy of *ontogenetic* and *sociogenic* paradigms (Sullivan, 1996). While Lewin's (1935) assertion that behaviour is a product of an interaction between persons and environments has virtually been accepted as a truism in criminology, this acceptance has not led to a wealth of interactionist theories and research on the topic of desistance. As a result, a polarised debate has emerged regarding whether or not the phenomenon of desistance can even be explained at all (e.g. Gottfredson and Hirschi, 1990).

[...]

The ontogenetic paradigm ('They will grow out of it')

One of the first social scientists to address the question of personal reform was Adolphe Quetelet. Quetelet (1833) argues that the penchant for crime diminishes with age 'due to the enfeeblement of physical vitality and the passions' (cited in Brown and Miller, 1988, p. 13). Sheldon and Eleanor Glueck (1940) develop this into their theory of 'maturational reform', in which they argue that intrinsic criminality naturally declines after the age of 25. The Gluecks (1940) suggest that with the 'sheer passage of time' juvenile delinquents 'grow out' of this transitory phase and 'burn out' physiologically. Significantly, they conclude, 'Ageing is the only factor which emerges as significant in the reformative process' (p. 105). Although the Gluecks (1940, p. 270) explicitly urge future researchers to 'dissect maturation into its components', Shover (1985) points out that criminology's 'explanatory efforts have not progressed appreciably beyond [the Gluecks'] work' (p. 77). *Maturational reform continues to be the most influential theory of desistance in criminology.*

The sociogenic paradigm ('A steady job and the love of a good woman')

Beyond 'maturational reform', the next most influential explanation of desistance is the theory of social bonds or 'informal social control' (Farrington, 1992). Social bond theory suggests that varying informal ties to family, employment or educational programs in early adulthood explain changes in criminality during the life course. Therefore, unlike maturational or developmental theories, social theories posit that the experiences that lead to desistance from crime are not necessarily universal, and can often be partially under the control of the individual (as in the case of entering employment or finding a partner). Matza (1964) was among the first to address this issue with his notion of a 'drift'. To Matza, most delinquents are caught somewhere in between the social bonds of adulthood and deviant peer subcultures without a deep attachment to either. Once adolescence has ended, and adult roles become available, therefore, the majority of young people easily move away from their weak affiliation with crime. Trasler (1979, 1980) and Sampson and Laub (1993) also describe turning points that can redirect a person's life path away from delinquency. Trasler (1980, p. 10) writes, '(A)s they grow older, most young men gain access to other sources of achievement and social satisfaction – a job, a girlfriend, a wife, a home and eventually children – and in doing so become gradually less dependent upon peer-group support' (cited in Gottfredson and Hirschi, 1990, p. 135). Those who lack these bonds are the most likely to stay involved in criminal and delinquent behaviour because they have the least to lose from social sanctions and ostracism. Moreover, the stronger the ties to society (i.e. the higher one's legal income), the more likely a person is to desist from criminal behaviour (e.g. Pezzin, 1995). Substantial research confirms that desistance from crime is correlated with *finding employment* (Glaser, 1964; Mischkowitz, 1994; Sampson and Laub, 1993; Shover, 1985); *completing schooling* (Farrington *et al.*, 1986; Rand, 1987); *getting married* (Farrington and West, 1995; Gibbens, 1984; Irwin, 1970; Meisenhelder, 1977; Mischkowitz, 1994; Rand, 1987; Rutherford, 1992; Rutter *et al.*, 1990; Sampson and Laub, 1993; West, 1982; Zoccolillo et al., 1992); and *becoming a parent* (Leibrich, 1993).

[...]

Understanding change in adulthood

Essentially, what seems to be missing from both ontogenetic and sociogenic approaches is 'the person' – the wholeness and agentic subjectivity of the individual. Sartre (1958: 559) argues that trying to explain behaviour (and individual change in particular) by relying on 'the great idols of our epoch – heredity, education, environment, physiological constitution' allows us to 'understand nothing'. He writes:

> The transitions, the becomings, the transformations, have been carefully veiled from us, and we have been limited to putting order into the succession by invoking empirically established but literally unintelligible sequences.

Sartre makes the same point as an expanding group of researchers in cognitive and personality psychology: we need a literally *intelligible* sequence, or a coherent 'story' of the individual if we want to understand changes in behaviour such as desistance. This argument has considerable support from critiques of traditional criminology. Toch (1987) argues:

> Positivist approaches ... help us to 'understand crime.' These theories, however, do not permit us to 'understand criminals,' because they are segmental views rather than full-blooded portraits ... (T)hese must be supplemented with portraits of offender perspectives, and with a review of unique *personal histories* (162, italics mine).

The use of such personal autobiographies in social enquiry, occasionally referred to as 'narrative studies', has been called 'a viable alternative to the positivist paradigm' in social science (Sarbin, 1986, p. vii). According to narrative theory, in order to achieve a contingent, temporally structured and contextualised understanding of human behaviour (Toch's 'full-blooded portraits'), one needs to look at the self-narratives or storied self-concepts of individuals (Bruner, 1987; Giddens, 1991; McAdams, 1985). Essentially, understanding the person means understanding the person's 'story'. Narrative theories take many shapes (e.g. Gergen, 1991; Giddens, 1991; Ricoeur, 1984), but almost all of them take seriously Murray's (1938, p. 49) aphorism, 'The history of the organism is the organism,' by arguing that the 'self' is essentially a *storied construct*. In a seminal statement of the importance of narrative identity to understanding behaviour, Bruner (1987) writes:

> The heart of my argument is this: eventually the culturally shaped cognitive and linguistic processes that guide the self-telling of life narratives achieve the power to structure perceptual experience, to organise memory, to segment and purpose-build the very 'events' of a life. In the end, we *become* (emphasis added) the autobiographical narratives by which we 'tell about' our lives (p. 15).

The way each of us views our own history is interesting not only because of what it reveals about our personality and our background; *this subjective autobiography actually shapes our future choices and behaviour.* In this framework, life narratives reflect both aspects of Lewin's (1935) equation, providing useful information about the person *and* his or her environment, and also show how the two interact to form a person's personality. In one influential narrative theory, McAdams (1994) argues that human behaviour is guided by three internalised domains (often called personality): psychological traits, personal strategies, and identity narratives or self stories (see also Conley, 1985). Though traits are relatively stable over the life course, the second two, more contextualised domains of personality leave open the possibility of substantial change in adulthood. To understand the desistance process from this narrative framework, therefore, one needs to analyse each of these domains of the 'whole person'.

From: S. Maruna (1998) 'Desistance and Development: The Psychosocial Process of "going straight"', British Criminology Conferences: Selected Proceedings, Vol. 2. Papers from the British Criminology Conference, Queens University, Belfast, 15–19 July 1997, pp. 1–19.

79. Treatment for substance abusers

Ron Fagan

While the research does show that individuals who are required or encouraged to get treatment for their alcohol and other substance abuse problems can do well in treatment, the goal of most therapy, no matter what perspective or orientation, is the establishment of the person's sense of control over destructive or dysfunctional behavior and the elimination of inhibiting dependency and rigid social restraints. This goal is probably best realized where the client is voluntarily participating in intervention and treatment. Research shows that clients who perceive that others acted out of concern for them, treated them fairly, with respect and without deception, provided them with an opportunity to express their opinions, and took what they said seriously were much less likely to experience the coercion negatively (Winick 1997).

One of the fundamental principles of psychotherapy is that patients give their voluntary, informed consent to therapy or treatment (American Psychological Association 1992). Whether patients seek treatment voluntarily or treatment is required, what cannot be compromised is their right to be informed about the essential components of their treatment and care and to have some control over the conditions of their treatment. If involuntary commitments are made, they should be done with utmost care and consideration, guided by specific procedures and practices, balancing the needs of the client, the treatment personnel, and society.

While involuntary civil commitment and required treatment are controversial areas in the treatment of alcohol and other substance abuse, the evidence does show that their use can be effective with some types of clients. At the same time, increased efforts need to be directed at getting these clients into therapy and treatment voluntarily by increasing their intrinsic motivations, making treatment options more attractive, and using the clients' own support networks. If required or coerced treatment is utilized, guidelines need to be followed to protect the rights of the clients.

From: R. Fagan (1999) 'The Use of Required Treatment for Substance Abusers', Substance Abuse, 20.4: 249–61.

80. What works. What doesn't work. What's promising

Doris Layton MacKenzie

What works

Rehabilitation programs with particular characteristics. There is now substantial evidence that rehabilitation programs work (Andrews & Bonta, 1998; Andrews *et al.*, 1990; Gendreau, Little, & Goggin, 1995; Lipsey, 1992). A body of research supports the conclusion that some treatment programs work with at least some offenders in some situations. Several meta-analyses have supported the findings that effective programs are structured and focused, use multiple treatment components, focus on developing skills, and use behavioral (including cognitive-behavioral) methods (with reinforcements for clearly identified, overt behaviors as opposed to nondirective counseling focusing on insight, self-esteem, or disclosure). Effective programs also provide for substantial, meaningful contact between the treatment personnel and the participant, must be designed to address the characteristics of the offenders that are associated with criminal activities and can be changed, and must be of sufficient integrity to ensure that what is delivered is consistent with the planned design.

Incapacitating offenders who continue to commit crimes at high rates. Research on the effects of incapacitation does not lend itself to the scoring and decision rules described above because most of the studies use simulation-type models to estimate the crime reduction effect of incapacitating offenders. For this research, we reviewed the literature, and from this review, we concluded that there is evidence that locking up offenders who are not at the end of their criminal careers is effective in reducing crimes in the community. Studies investigating the effectiveness of this strategy show there are advantages in locking up the high-rate career criminals who commit serious crimes. The difficulty is in identifying who these high-rate offenders are and the diminishing return of invested dollars with the increased incarceration rates.

Prison-based therapeutic community treatment of drug-involved offenders and in-prison therapeutic communities with follow-up community treatment. Treatment of drug-involved offenders in prison-based therapeutic communities (TCs) is effective in reducing criminal activities. These programs are intensive, behavior-based programs that target offenders' drug use, a behavior that is clearly associated with criminal activities. Programs that combine the TCs with follow-up community treatment also appear to be effective. It is not possible to determine whether the combination of in-prison and community follow-up is effective because the drug-involved offenders spent a longer period of time in treatment or because the combination of in-prison and follow-up was a particularly effective combination.

Cognitive behavioral therapy. Two different types of cognitive behavior programs, Reasoning and Rehabilitation and Moral Reconation Therapy, were assessed. Both programs focus on changing participants' thoughts and attitudes, either through moral development (moral reconation) or problem solving (reasoning and rehabilitation). The research indicates that both of these types of cognitive behavior programs are effective in reducing recidivism. One disadvantage of this research is that much of it has been completed by the individuals who developed the programs. We do not know if their close oversight of the implementation and delivery of the program is an important aspect of the findings. Future studies will be particularly important to see if these results generalize to other settings with different researchers.

Non-prison-based sex offender treatment programs. Sex offender treatment provided outside of prison in a hospital or other residential setting using cognitive-behavioral methods was found to be effective in reducing the sexual offense recidivism of sex offenders (Polizzi, MacKenzie, & Hickman, 1999; Wilson, Gallagher, Coggleshall, & MacKenzie, 1999).

Vocational education programs provided in prison or residential settings. In general, the research on vocational education programs demonstrates that these programs are effective in reducing the recidivism of offenders. Several studies of relatively rigorous scientific merit found such programs reduced the recidivism of participants. Results were somewhat mixed in the less-rigorous studies. Thus, although there were some inconsistencies in the findings, the preponderance of evidence suggests that vocational education programs are effective.

Multicomponent correctional industry programs. The industry program evaluations examined multicomponent programs. Significant differences between industry participants and others were found in at least two studies. However, the differences between the recidivism rates of the groups were quite small (Wilson *et al.*, 1999). The differences were most likely significant due to the large sample sizes. An important consideration with this finding is whether the size of this difference is of practical significance. In most cases, the differences in recidivism rates were less than 5%. Because the research focused on programs with multicomponents, nothing can be said about the effectiveness of industry programs alone.

Community employment programs. Some types of programs are effective in reducing the recidivism of offenders. However, mixed results, particularly in a study by Milkman (1985), led us to be concerned about the effectiveness of different implementations of community employment programs.

What does not work?

Programs emphasizing specific deterrence, such as shock probation and Scared Straight, which attempt to scare offenders away from criminal activity, are not effective in reducing the criminal activities of offenders. Vague, nondirective, unstructured counseling programs are not effective in reducing recidivism.

Correctional programs that increase control and surveillance in the community (intensive supervised probation or parole, home confinement, community residential programs, urine testing) are not effective. There is now a large body of research examining the effect of increasing the control over offenders in the community. These sanctions called *alternative punishments* or *intermediate sanctions* have not been found to be effective in reducing recidivism. It is important to note that the research has focused on increased control over the offenders (e.g., more supervision, increased urine testing) and not the programming components sometimes used in conjunction with increased control. So, our conclusions that these programs are not effective are based on the research examining increased control, not on research examining combinations of treatment and control (see below under What's Promising). Programs emphasizing structure, discipline, and challenge (correctional boot camps using the old-style military model, juvenile wilderness programs) are not effective. There is no evidence that the correctional boot camps using the old-style military model of discipline, drill, and ceremony are effective methods of reducing recidivism (MacKenzie, 1997). Similarly, juvenile wilderness programs that focus on physical challenge activities are not effective. Increased referral, monitoring, and management in the community do not work. The well-designed studies of intensive supervision by Petersilia and Turner (1992), Treatment Alternatives to Street Crime (TASC) programs by Anglin et al. (1996), and TASC-like case management programs by Rhodes and Gross (1997) demonstrated that these methods were not effective in reducing recidivism.

What is promising?

Drug courts combining both rehabilitation and criminal justice control are rapidly spreading across the nation, yet to date, there is still little evidence that they are effective. However, Deschenes, Turner, Greenwood, and Chiesa (1996) did find that fewer drug court arrestees were sentenced to prison compared to probationer arrestees. Fines for criminal activities appear to be promising in reducing recidivism.

We do not know if this effect will be similar for the relatively new day fines. These day or unit fines are set by the judge to be proportional to the severity of the offense but are also equitable and fair, given the difference in the economic circumstances of the individual offenders. Overall, the results of studies of juvenile community supervision and aftercare are mixed (Altschuler, Armstrong, & MacKenzie, 1999). However, Sontheimer and Goodstein (1993) found juveniles in an intensive supervision program including intensive aftercare had fewer arrests than a control group, suggesting that this may be a promising avenue for reducing the recidivism of juvenile delinquents. Drug treatment combined with urine testing may also be a promising avenue for reducing recidivism. Taxman and Spinner (1996) found a reduction in recidivism for a group of participants who received a jail-based treatment program with follow-up treatment and urine testing. In contrast with sex offender treatment programs given in non-prison settings, there is less evidence that prison-based treatment is effective (Polizzi et al., 1999; Gallagher, Wilson, Hirschfield, Coggleshall, & MacKenzie, 1999). At this point in time, we conclude that prison-based sex offender treatment using cognitive-behavioral treatment methods is promising for reducing sex offense recidivism. The study with these promising results did not find any evidence that non-sex-offense recidivism was reduced. Considering the number of offenders who are offered or required to attend educational programs, it is disappointing that we located only one study (Adult Basic Education (ABE)) showing a significant difference between the treated group and the comparison. Few of the other studies conducted tests of significance, and the size and direction of the differences between the treatment and control groups varied among studies (Wilson et al., 1999). Therefore, at this point, we concluded that whereas ABE is a promising method for reducing recidivism, there is not enough evidence to conclude that the ABE is effective. Of transitional programs providing individualized employment preparation and services for high-risk offenders, some that begin employment reparation and job search assistance before the individual leaves prison and continue this help upon release hold promise for reducing recidivism. This may be particularly important for those who are at high-risk for recidivism.

From: D. L. MacKenzie (2000) 'Evidence-Based Corrections: Identifying What Works', Crime & Delinquency, 46.4: 457–71.

81. 'Punish and rehabilitate' – do they mean us?

Chris Hignett

The proposed 're-branding' of the Probation Service to become the 'Community Punishment and Rehabilitation Service' will effectively bring about its demise. The work of aiding offenders to achieve rehabilitation within society is not punishment (neither probation nor prison officers are recruited to 'punish' offenders). The skills and expertise gained in over a century are likely to be rapidly lost if this confusion is perpetuated. Probation staff work to assist offenders to become law-abiding stakeholders in society.

[...]

'Community punishers?'

To deal with punishment first, any normal language dictionary definition of this activity involves exacting retribution, imposing penalties and suffering, providing rough handling and abuse. I know there is a linguistic argument that says that the word is so value-based it is empty of meaning and therefore anything, including much current probation practice could comfortably scrape under the wire. This ignores the negative connotations associated with the term. Even in the case of imprisonment we are well aware that people are sent there as a punishment, not to receive punishment. Even the most rigorous of programmes provided by the Probation Service do not set out to 'punish' their participants, and we should never allow our activities to be so described.

If we allow such a shift, I believe the time will quickly come when people take the language at its face value and, confronted by the difficult client, begin to devise ways to hurt and damage them. Organisations that do not pay careful attention to this danger are soon into the process of systematic abuse and ultimately scandal, as the sad history of our institutional care of the dependent population, whether they be children, the elderly or the infirm, so amply demonstrates. We must do all in our power to prevent such a fate befalling us; at the end of the day, it is of course our clients who will really suffer, made up as they so disproportionately are of the least powerful and most bullied groups in society.

One of the most important reasons why probation officers succeed in changing behaviour is because they are able to form mutually respectful working relationships with offenders, which then provide a basis for constructive challenge. The philosophy of the Probation Service is premised on a belief in the possibility of change. Giving it an identity of punishment, and encouraging its staff to minimise the critical importance of relationship and human potential is counter-productive and ultimately nonsensical.

Community rehabilitators?

I also object to the word rehabilitation in this context where the implication is that probation officers will be doing the rehabilitating. This is equally wrong in a free society. It is the offender who has the task of seeking rehabilitation amongst his or her fellow human beings. To encourage any other belief is to take upon ourselves a task that is not ours to perform. To assist those who seek seriously to engage in the process of rehabilitation through skilled supervision, well-researched programmes and therapeutic and practical help, is a very different matter, and should not be confused with the task of rehabilitation itself.

Earlier generations understood this well enough. There has rarely been a more radical idea introduced to the Criminal Justice System than the notion of a trial period of law-abiding behaviour rather than punishment. The idea of probation is no more old fashioned or out of place today than it was when John Augustus, the Boston Cobbler, first approached the magistrates of that city in 1841 to argue that offenders should, under supervision, be allowed an opportunity to prove they could change. It opens up for them the possibility of reconciliation and reintegration, and for society a more creative outcome to the damage and destruction caused by crime.

From: Hignett, C. (2000) '"Punish And Rehabilitate" – Do They Mean Us?', Probation Journal, *47.1: 51–2.*

82. Rethinking God, justice, and treatment of offenders

Ted Grimsrud and Howard Zehr

The connection between religious belief, in particular how people in the West have viewed God, and retributive criminal justice practices runs deep. God has been understood to be the basis for the practices of human beings inflicting severe punitive pain upon other human beings judged guilty of violating community standards. God is understood, most of all, to be 'holy' (that is, unable to countenance sin of any kind). God's holiness 'forces' God to act punitively – and justifies God's agents (either in the church or in society) also acting punitively. This retributive theology dominated Western worldviews in the Middle Ages and formed the bases for criminal justice practices which began to be institutionalized during that time. However, a closer look at the founding document of the Christian tradition, the Bible, challenges such retributive theology. Biblical understandings of justice point more in the direction of restorative than retributive justice. Biblically, 'justice' has to do not so much with punishment as with healing, restoring relationships, and fostering the well-being of the entire community. Present-day alternatives to retributive criminal justice are emerging which reflect the general thrust of biblical justice. These include victim-offender reconciliation programs, sentencing circles, and family group conferences. The success of such programs provides encouragement for those who hope for criminal justice practices which effect healing more than simply punitive pain.

[...] 'Human beings cannot be handled without love,' Tolstoy wrote, and yet our concept and practice of criminal justice have been built upon the opposite. We have argued above that the Christian scriptures support Tolstoy's assumption that relationships are fundamental. However, misconstruction of God's nature, formed in part through an unfortunate symbiotic interaction between law and theology during a formative period of Western culture, has caused us not only to ignore but to pervert this understanding into a retributive concept of justice. It is this retributive understanding which underpins the unprecedented rate of punishment in today's world, providing conceptual justification for the 'corrections-industrial complex' or industry which is part of its driving force (Christie, 1994; Schlosser, 1998).

This concept of justice is not only morally questionable – it is counter-productive as well. James Gilligan, former head psychiatrist for Massachusetts Department of Corrections, notes that many offenders emerge out of injustice and victimization that offenders themselves have experienced or perceive themselves to have experienced: 'the attempt to achieve justice and maintain justice, or to undo or pervert justice, is the one and only universal cause of violence' (Gilligan, 1997, p. 12). Given that, Gilligan continues:

> What is conventionally called 'crime' is the kind of violence the legal system calls illegal, and 'punishment' is the kind that it calls legal. But the motives and the goals that underlie both are identical – they both aim to attain justice or revenge for past injuries and injustices. Crime and punishment are conventionally spoken of as if they were opposites, yet both are committed in the name of morality and justice, and both use violence as the means by which to attain those ends. So not only are their ends identical, so are their means. (pp. 18–19)

What would a concept of justice look like if it were based on love – that is, on respect and concern for the people involved, on a commitment to respond constructively (Claassen, 1990)? Could such a relational or restorative approach to justice not only be articulated but actually implemented?

During the past twenty-five years, a growing movement has sought to do just this. Eduardo Barajas, Jr., a program specialist for the National Institute of Corrections, has characterized it like this: 'A revolution is occurring in criminal justice. A quiet, grassroots, seemingly unobtrusive but truly revolutionary movement is changing the nature, the very face of our work.' He argues that it extends beyond most reforms in the history of criminal justice: 'What is occurring now is more than innovative, it is truly inventive, ... a "paradigm shift"' (Barajas, 1996).

[...] Critics point out that if restorative justice is to be taken seriously, it will need to expand its analysis of offender needs to encompass an understanding of rehabilitation. Drawing upon the 'What Works' tradition in rehabilitation (Levrant et al., 1999; Bazemore, 1998; Crowe, 1998), we suggest the following as essential building blocks of restorative or relational rehabilitation:

1. Restorative rehabilitation is victim-focused. Treatments and therapies are not conducted in isolation from understanding of impacts on, responsibilities to, and concern for, victims.

2. Treatment is not viewed as an entitlement – as may happen in the current model – but rather as part of accountability to victims and the community and as a form of social exchange.

3. Treatment is contextualized, focusing upon integration and the creation or strengthening of social bonds rather than isolation.

4. Interventions are tailored to the profiles and personal characteristics of individual offenders. For example, levels of service are matched to the level of risk; intensive services to low-risk offenders are often not only ineffective but often backfire. High anxiety offenders do not respond well to confrontation, and offenders with below-average intellectual abilities do not respond well to cognitive skills programs.

5. Interventions are designed to identify and change the criminogenic needs of offenders and, except for individuals not suited to it, are rooted in behavioral or cognitive-behavioral treatment models.

Tolstoy's assertion suggests that justice needs to be redefined in new terms, if not explicitly in the language of love, then in the language of peace and respect. Criminologists Richard Quinney and John Wildeman set the context like this:

> From its earliest beginnings ... the primary focus of criminology has been on retribution, punishment, and vengeance in the cause of an existing social order ... rather than a criminology of peace, justice and liberation. ... If crime is violent and wreaks violence on our fellows and our social relations, then the effort to understand and control crime must be violent and repressive. (Quinney and Wildeman, 1991, pp. 40–41)

However, such an approach only intensifies the spiral of violence leading to greater violence. What is needed is something which *breaks* the cycle of violence. Quinney and Wildeman suggest that finally a peacemaking school of criminology is beginning to emerge.

We have argued in this paper that such a peacemaking approach to criminal justice is indeed needed. This peacemaking approach must take seriously (and vigorously critique) the philosophical and theological roots to retributive criminology. However, we are suggesting that the *deepest* roots of Western theology, found in the Bible, are indeed fully compatible with new, peacemaking approaches to criminal justice.

Tolstoy would be pleased.

From: T. Grimsrud and T. Zehr (2002) 'Rethinking God, Justice, and Treatment of Offenders', Journal of Offender Rehabilitation, 35.3/4: 259–85.

83. Restorative justice values, processes and practices

Allison Morris

Although restorative justice values, processes and practices have been around for a long time, there was a resurgence of interest in them internationally in the 1990s (see, for example, Zehr 1990; Van Ness and Strong 1997), in part as a response to the perceived ineffectiveness and high cost (in both human and financial terms) of conventional justice processes and in part as a response to the failure of conventional systems to hold offenders accountable in meaningful ways or to respond adequately to victims' needs and interests. Conventional justice systems see offending primarily (and often even exclusively) as a violation of the interests of the state and decisions about how it should be responded to are made by professionals representing the state. In contrast, restorative justice returns decisions about how best to deal with the offence to those most affected – victims, offenders and their 'communities of care' – and gives primacy to their interests. Thus the state no longer has a monopoly over decision making; the principal decision makers are the parties themselves. In a sense, the state's role – or the role of its representatives – is redefined: for example, they give information, they deliver services and they provide resources. Restorative justice also emphasizes addressing the offending and its consequences (for victims, offenders and communities) in meaningful ways; attempting to reconcile victims, offenders and their communities through trying to reach agreements about how best to deal with the offending; and attempting to reintegrate or reconnect both victims and offenders at the local community level through trying to heal the harm and hurt caused by the offending and through trying to take steps to prevent its recurrence.

Restorative justice also emphasizes human rights and the need to recognize the impact of social or substantive injustice and in small ways address these rather than simply provide offenders with legal or formal justice and victims with no justice at all. Thus it seeks to restore the victim's security, self-respect, dignity and, most importantly, sense of control. And it seeks to restore responsibility to offenders for their offending and its consequences, to restore a sense of control to them to make amends for what they have done and to restore a belief in them that the process and outcomes were fair and just. And, finally, restorative justice encourages cultural relativity and sensitivity rather than cultural dominance.

Thus victims, offenders and communities of care come together and, with the aid of a facilitator, try to resolve how to deal with the offence, its consequences and its implications for the future. Generally, restorative justice offers a more informal and private process over which the parties most directly affected by the offence have more control. This does not mean that there are no 'rules'.[1] which must be adhered to or that there are no rights[2] which must be protected, but rather that, within a particular framework, there is the potential for greater flexibility, including cultural flexibility. Thus the procedures followed, those present and the venue are often chosen by the parties themselves.[3] Overall, the intention – or the hope – is to create a respectful and non-shaming environment in which participants can feel comfortable and able to speak for themselves.

The aims of restorative justice meetings are primarily to hold offenders accountable for their offending in meaningful ways and to make amends to victims certainly in a symbolic sense and, where possible, in a real sense too. Restorative outcomes are sometimes viewed as focusing on apologies, reparation or community work, as *ways* of restoring the property stolen or of compensating the victim for the injuries endured. But, in fact, *any* outcome – including a prison sentence – can be restorative if it is an outcome agreed to and considered appropriate by the key parties. For example, it might be agreed that a prison sentence is required in a particular situation to protect society, to signify the gravity of the offending or to make amends to victims. Neither protecting society nor signifying the gravity of the offending are excluded within a restorative justice system. The difference is that the offender, victim and their communities of care have had some input into the sentence, some increased understanding of the circumstances and consequences of the offence and, perhaps, some increased satisfaction in their dealings with the criminal justice system. Moreover, discussion of the consequences of the offences is seen as a more powerful way of communicating their gravity to offenders than simply imprisoning them.

One of the other hopes of restorative justice is that reconciliation between the offender and victim will occur. This is not always possible – victims may remain angry or bitter; offenders may remain unmoved and untouched. However, there is no doubt that reconciliation can on occasions take place between victims and offenders. Examples observed at family group conferences in New Zealand include invitations by a victim to the offender and his family to join the victim's family for a meal, hugs and handshakes all round at the end of the meeting, and victims deciding to attend the court hearing to speak on the offender's behalf. There is no 'right way' to deliver restorative justice and this paper does not seek to argue that, for example, the New Zealand youth justice system is the 'ideal' form of restorative justice. The essence of restorative justice is not the adoption of one form rather than another; it is the adoption of *any* form which reflects restorative values and which aims to achieve restorative processes, outcomes and objectives. Restorative processes and practices, therefore, should empower offenders and victims by giving them a sense of inclusion in and satisfaction with these processes and practices; they should enable victims to feel better as a result of participating in them; and they should hold offenders accountable in meaningful ways by encouraging them to make amends to their victims. If all these occur, we might then expect the restorative processes and practices to impact on re-offending and reintegration and to heal victims' hurt.

From: A. Morris (2002) 'Critiquing the Critics: A Brief Response to Critics of Restorative Justice', British Journal of Criminology, 42.3: 596–615.

Notes

1. In most jurisdictions, facilitators follow guidelines or practice manuals. In some, there are statutory guidelines or regulations to follow.
2. Again, these will be reflected in practice manuals or in statutory guidelines or regulations.
3. For example, in New Zealand, family group conferences may be held in a community hall, in the offender's home, on a *marae* (meeting house) or wherever the parties prefer. Conferences may be attended by a large number of people; they may last for many hours; they may begin with prayers; and they may end with the serving of food. They may be facilitated by a *kaawnuatna* (Maori elder) and they may follow Maori *kaawa* (protocol).

84. Rethinking what works with offenders

Stephen Farrall

Desistance, it is widely becoming accepted, is often the result of attachments to the labour force or to marriage partners or both (see, for example, Sampson and Laub 1993). The current research has found evidence to support these claims. The project also found that officers appeared to be reluctant to work with their probationers to address family and employment obstacles. Yet when officers did assist their probationers, their work appeared to supplement the efforts of the probationers and to be associated with greater rates of success […]. This reinforces the arguments put forward by Bottoms and McWilliams over twenty years ago (1979: 172–75) when they wrote that '… help may be more crime-reducing than treatment' (ibid.: 174). As such, more effort should be focused on how officers can support probationers to address either their existing family problems, or attempt to prepare them for events like parenthood. Similarly, more effort should be focused on getting probationers into employment (Bridges 1998). This might entail a shift in the orientation of probation work. One probationer […], when asked what would prevent him from reoffending, replied:

> Something to do with self-progression. Something to show people what they are capable of doing. I thought that that was what [my officer] should be about. It's finding people's abilities and nourishing and making them work for those things. Not very consistent with going back on what they have done wrong and trying to work out why – 'cause it's all going around on what's *happened* – what you've already been punished for – why not go forward into something … For instance, you might be good at writing – push that forward, progress that, rather than saying 'well look, why did you kick that bloke's head in? Do you think we should go back into anger management courses?' when all you want to be is a writer. Does that make any sense to you at all? *Yeah, yeah. To sum it up, you're saying you should look forwards not back.* Yeah. I know that you do have to look back to a certain extent to make sure that you don't end up like that [again]. The whole order seems to be about going back and back and back. There doesn't seem to be much 'forward'.

In other words, probation should assess what people require in their lives to ensure that they stop offending and then attempt to produce these features in their lives in such a way that they do actually stop offending. This might mean, for example, officers assessing whether a probationer's family offers him or her an avenue towards desistance. Of course, such efforts should be addressed in the contexts in which the probationer is living. Increasing individuals' social capital will probably ultimately mean providing them with legitimate employment, which will in turn help to foster the sorts of ties and social contacts which allow for the development of social capital. It is unclear exactly how well probation services will be able to influence local economic conditions. The suggestion made earlier, that probation services develop in some way employment schemes in which they are able to offer probationers work rather than referring them to other agencies, may be only one amongst a number of solutions. Other possible solutions would involve concerted efforts aimed at reinvesting in some of the most deprived and crime-ridden inner-city areas.

These suggestions entail a further point. Namely, a step back from the *exclusive* focus on cognitive behavioural work which has dominated the probation work and 'What Works?' agendas in recent years. As Rex (1999: 373) has correctly noted, even the original architects of such programmes saw them as *complementing* the social and economic problems faced by probationers. This is not to suggest that cognitive behavioural work is to be abandoned but, rather, that whilst it correctly focuses on increasing probationers' human capital, it is unable to address the wider social contexts in which these probationers live and as such is unable to address such social and economic needs. What is required is a research project which attempts to 'fuse' together developments in individual cognitive abilities and changes in their social contexts.

The current project has suggested that probation supervision 'works' indirectly through allowing the probationer's life to develop positively. Ensuring how best to enable those developments to occur and designing working practices which will enable probation officers to intervene more readily should form the next stage of research into probation effectiveness.

From: S. Farrall (2002) Rethinking What Works with Offenders: Probation, social context and desistance from crime. *Cullompton: Willan, pp. 227–8.*

85. A civic engagement model of reentry

Gordon Bazemore and Jeanne Stinchcomb

Civic service and identity transformation

A crucial element in successful reentry is the willingness of the community to accept the releasee's return, and a key determinant of such willingness may be a sense that the offender has acknowledged the harm of his actions to others and has made appropriate amends.

Lawbreakers returning to their home communities are perceived by most residents as having engaged in violations that would require significant compensatory effort to counterbalance. The norm of reciprocity dictates that they repair the damage caused and restore the community trust that has been violated. Despite the perception that serving a sentence 'pays a debt to society,' doing time does nothing to address the damage caused to others or the need to establish trustworthy relations. Hence, while the retributive model of accountability requires that harm be done to the offender in order to balance the harm caused to others (Von Hirsch, 1976), the exchange theory concept of reciprocity (see Molm and Cook, 1995; Gouldner, 1960) suggests that only by taking responsibility for making things right with victims and victimized communities can offenders change either the *community's image* of them or their perceptions of themselves.

According to the theory of 'earned redemption' (Maloney, 1998; Bazemore, 1998), community acceptance requires a concrete demonstration that the individual acknowledges the damage caused and is doing something to make things right. This positive affirmation of responsibility and the willingness to make amends to the community through visible, voluntary civic service can be a fundamental step in changing one's public image from liability to asset, thereby earning one's way back into the 'good graces' of the community.

Personal identity: changing self-image through civic service

Theories of reciprocity such as earned redemption may help to account for a change in the service participant's *public* image. But they do not address how persons currently or formerly under correctional supervision may undergo a change in *self-image*. In that regard, research indicates that it is constructing a new identity as a person with something to contribute that distinguishes those who 'go straight' from those who do not (Maruna, 2001). A key aspect of this new identity is a sense of oneself as someone who helps others through service, demonstrating an unselfish commitment to promoting the next generation – manifested through parenting, teaching, mentoring, and generating benefits for others (McAdams and de St Aubin, 1998, cited in Maruna, 2001, p. 99). Helping others becomes a vehicle for both ensuring one's own recovery and recasting one's identity as a person who 'makes good' by *doing good*. As one incarcerated person who later made a successful transition to community life described his experience helping the less fortunate: 'We took so much out of the community, [but] now we're putting something back in' (Maruna, 2001, p. 122).

Some inmates express skepticism or distaste for the idea of 'giving back' to the community that cast them out. But others find the service experience a meaningful avenue for personal growth (Uggen *et al.*, 2003). Because they also promote self-esteem and dignity in ways that are generally not feasible through either treatment or punishment, such civic service projects may also lead to a change in self-image and related behavior, regardless of the community response.

Like peer involvement in AA or NA, the general premise is that it is better to *give* help than to receive it (Pearl and Riessman, 1965; see Maruna *et al.*, 2004). This is especially true when such assistance enables the service provider to empathize with others in need or to understand how their actions contribute to public well-being (Batson, 1994; Schneider, 1990; Bazemore and Erbe, 2003). Research indicates (Uggen and Janikula, 1999) that voluntary service as a young person is negatively related to future crime, and is also *positively* related to employment, family formation, and other indicators of stability. In addition, service may create the opportunity for mentoring and apprenticeships, which provide social support and a bond to conventional groups. Thus, interactionist theory provides the basis for an experiential model of identity transformation.

This model views active involvement in meaningful civic roles as fundamental to both cognitive change in the service provider *and* change in community attitudes about such individuals. It is based on the logic that lawbreakers are more inclined to move away from criminal activity when they can practice new identities in productive roles (Uggen *et al.*, 2003), exhibiting both competency and trustworthiness during interaction with other community members – who, in turn, form a more favorable impression of them in their new pro-social role (Trice and Roman, 1970), thereby enhancing the likelihood of successful reintegration.

From: G. Bazemore and J. Stinchcomb (2004) 'A Civic Engagement Model of Reentry: Involving Community Through Service and Restorative Justice', Federal Probation, 68.2: 797–810.

86. American social work, corrections and restorative justice

Edward J. Gumz

Historically, American social work has contributed to the field of corrections through the practice of probation, participation in the founding of the juvenile court, and work with inmates in correctional institutions. Its role in corrections has been significantly shaped by philosophical and practice changes in the criminal justice system. As the ethic of rehabilitation in corrections lost ground, so did a social work presence in this field; however, its diminishment in corrections has also been shaped by changes in the social work profession itself. The profession of social work is increasingly devoting itself to psychotherapy and is moving away from a community focus. As social workers search for higher salaries and status, there has been a shift away from working with at-risk or disfranchised populations – such as those persons found in correctional settings. At the same time, students in schools of social work are specializing less in areas such as corrections, poverty and minority causes, and public social services.

Yet social workers continue to have contact with persons affected by crime. Young and Smith (2000) noted that of women who go to prison, 70% leave behind children younger than the age of 18 years. Frequently these children need child welfare services in the community, provided by social workers. Mumola (1999) indicated that more than 75% of prisoners are alcohol- or drug-related offenders. When these prisoners return to the community, they continue to need treatment, at times provided by social workers. In addition, in the United States more than three-fourths of mental health services are provided by social workers. Given this fact, many of the 16% male and 23% female jail inmates who have been identified as mentally ill will be seen for treatment by social workers (Ditton, 1999).

Thus, social workers in the United States continue to work with persons affected by correctional systems, in spite of the fact that their influence in corrections has diminished over the years. Social work can invigorate its presence in corrections by affirming its traditional commitment to social justice – one of the primary tenets of the profession. The concept of social justice in social work has usually stressed distributive justice, calling for a more equitable distribution of goods and services in society. In addition, social work as a profession needs to affirm the concept of restorative justice, which offers a holistic approach toward work in corrections in which justice for the victim, offender, and the community are all relevant. The increasing importance of restorative justice in criminal justice may attract more social workers to work in corrections and renew social work's presence in that field. While taking into account differences in culture, American social workers working in corrections can learn much about the application of principles of restorative justice from social workers in the United Kingdom. Studying the role of social workers in restorative justice in the United Kingdom holds promise for American social work's presence and contribution to corrections.

From: E. J. Gumz (2004) 'American Social Work, Corrections and Restorative Justice: An Appraisal', International Journal of Offender Therapy and Comparative Criminology, *48.4: 449–60.*

87. The good lives model

Tony Ward and Mark Brown

The GLM of offender rehabilitation is essentially a strength-based approach and as such, seeks to give offenders the capabilities to secure primary human goods in socially acceptable and personally meaningful ways (Kekes, 1989; Rapp, 1998; Ward and Stewart, 2003b). Primary goods are defined as actions, states of affairs, characteristics, experiences, and states of mind that are intrinsically beneficial to human beings and therefore sought for their own sake rather than as means to more fundamental ends (Emmons, 1999; Deci and Ryan, 2000; Schmuck and Sheldon, 2001). From the perspective of this model, humans are by nature active, goal-seeking beings who are consistently engaged in the process of constructing a sense of purpose and meaning in their lives. This is hypothesized to emerge from the pursuit and achievement of primary human goods (valued aspects of human functioning and living) which collectively allow individuals to flourish; that is, to achieve high levels of well-being. According to the GLM, the identification of risk factors simply alerts clinicians to problems (obstacles) in the way offenders are seeking to achieve valued or personally satisfying outcomes.

Thus the core idea is that all meaningful human actions reflect attempts to achieve primary human goods (Emmons, 1999; Ward, 2002). This applies to all individuals irrespective of their level of education, intelligence, or class. Primary goods are viewed as objective and are tied to certain ways of living that if pursued involve the actualization of potentialities that are distinctively human. Individuals can, therefore, be mistaken about what is really of value and what is in their best interests. Primary goods emerge out of basic needs while instrumental or secondary goods provide concrete ways of securing these goods; for example, certain types of work or relationships (e.g. excellence in work provides mastery experiences, while distinct types of work represent different ways of seeking this excellence). The primary good of excellence in work which provides mastery experiences can be achieved by working as a mechanic, psychologist or teacher. The primary goods of relationships can be achieved in heterosexual or homosexual relationships. Secondary goods are available to individuals by way of the numerous models and opportunities for attaining goods in everyday life (i.e. types of relationships, work) and dictate the form these goods take in specific contexts. The choice to seek a particular cluster of secondary goods will be determined by an offender's preferences, strengths, and opportunities. One individual might realize the primary good of work and mastery (mastery experiences are components of excellence at work) working as a mechanic, while another might train as a computer operator. Secondary goods put flesh on the bones of the more abstract primary goods; when the attainment of human goods is difficult the problem often resides in the type of secondary goods utilized. Thus a person might seek the primary good of intimacy in a relationship characterized by violence, controlling behaviour, and emotional distance. Such a relationship choice will clearly not realize the primary good of intimacy. What is the evidence that there are indeed primary human goods, that human beings seek them, and that their realization will result in higher levels of well-being? Concerning the first and second questions, there is converging evidence from distinct domains of research and knowledge that there is a finite list of basic human goods. These domains include psychological and social science research (Cummins, 1996; Emmons, 1999), evolutionary theory (Arnhart, 1998), practical ethics (Murphy, 2001), and philosophical anthropology (Rescher, 1990; Nussbaum, 2000). Support for the ubiquity of goal- or goods-seeking behaviour comes from the self-regulation literature (Austin and Vancouver, 1996). As Emmons (1996) states: 'Why are goals important for well-being? Simply, it is because that is how people are designed. Goal-directedness is a human enterprise' (p. 331). We propose that it is possible to identify at least nine classes of primary human goods from this literature. We argue that although other researchers might come up with a slightly longer or shorter list, the goods listed below will be present in some form. The list of nine primary human goods is:

(1) life (including healthy living and optimal physical functioning, sexual satisfaction), (2) knowledge, (3) excellence in play and work (including mastery experiences), (4) excellence in agency (i.e. autonomy and self-directedness), (5) inner peace (i.e. freedom from emotional turmoil and stress), (6) relatedness (including intimate, romantic and family relationships) and community, (7) spirituality (in the broad sense of finding meaning and purpose in life), (8) happiness, and (9) creativity. This list is comprehensive and is consistent with much recent work on human motivation, well-being, and social policy. Each of these primary goods can be broken down into sub-clusters or components; in other words the primary goods are complex and multi-faceted. To illustrate, the primary good of relatedness contains the sub-cluster goods of intimacy, friendship, support, caring, reliability, honesty, and so on.

The third question concerns whether primary goods are essential ingredients in good lives and as such result in higher levels of well-being. Research into personal strivings by Emmons has shown that there is a positive relationship between well-being and the achievement of goals that are important to individuals, that is, personal strivings (Emmons, 1999). For example, the goals of achievement, affiliation, intimacy, power, personal growth and health, self-presentation, independence, emotionality, generativity, and spirituality goals have all been associated with subjective well-being (note their resemblance to the list of primary goods noted above). Additionally, Cummins's (1996) research into well-being has identified important domains of life satisfaction and these echo the primary goods listed above (e.g. material well-being, health, productivity, intimacy, safety, community, and emotional well-being). Finally, Deci and Ryan have produced an important body of research on the three psychological needs of autonomy, mastery, and relatedness and their importance for happiness and well-being (Deci and Ryan, 2000). These needs cause individuals to seek a number of primary goods and therefore provide direct evidence for their critical role in promoting good lives.

The possibility of constructing and translating conceptions of good lives into actions and concrete ways of living depends crucially on the possession of internal (skills and capabilities) and *external conditions* (opportunities and supports). The specific form that a conception will take depends on the actual abilities, interests and opportunities of each individual and the weightings he or she gives to specific primary goods. The weightings or priorities allocated to specific primary goods is constitutive of an offender's personal identity and spells out the kind of life sought and, relatedly, the kind of person he or she would like to be (see Maruna, 2001). The assumption here is that personal identity is derived from our commitments and resultant ways of life. However, because human beings naturally seek a range of primary goods or desired states, it is important that all classes of primary goods are addressed in a conception of good lives; they should be ordered and coherently related to each other. Additionally, a conception of good lives is always context dependent; there is no such thing as the right kind of life for an individual across every conceivable setting. Therefore, all individuals are hypothesized to live their lives according to a GLM, either explicitly or implicitly. Thus, there is no such thing as the right kind of life for any specific person; there are always a number of feasible possibilities, although there are limits defined by circumstances, abilities, and preferences (Kekes, 1989; Ward and Stewart, 2003a).

Psychological, social, and lifestyle problems emerge when these GLMs are faulty in some way. When they do not achieve what they set out to, the well-being of individuals living according to such GLM is reduced. In the case of criminal behaviour, it is hypothesized that there are four major types of difficulties: (1) problems with the means used to secure goods, (2) a lack of scope within a good lives plan, (3) the presence of conflict among goals (goods sought) or incoherence, (4) or a lack of the necessary capacities to form and adjust a GLM to changing circumstances (e.g. impulsive decision making).

Taking into account the type of GLM problem an offender has, a treatment plan should be explicitly constructed in the form of a good lives conceptualization, that taking into account an offender's preferences, strengths, primary goods, and relevant environments, specifies exactly what competencies and resources are required to achieve these goods. This crucially involves identifying the internal and external conditions necessary to implement the plan and designing a rehabilitation strategy to equip the individual with these required skills, resources, and opportunities. Such an approach to offender rehabilitation is significantly contextualized, and promotes the importance of personal identity and its emergence from daily living (and actions). It is also clearly value laden in the sense that primary human goods represent outcomes that are beneficial to human beings and their absence harmful (to the individual and to others). Therefore, rehabilitation should be tailored to an individual offender's particular GLM and should only seek to install the internal and external conditions that will enable its realization.

From: T. Ward and M. Brown (2004) 'The Good Lives Model and Conceptual Issues in Offender Rehabilitation', Psychology, Crime and Law, *10.3:3, 243–57.*

88. What works in prisoner reentry?

Joan Petersilia

Questioning the 'evidence'

The author could end this article here, but is uncomfortable doing so. She sees three problems with using the above evidence to answer the important question, 'what works in reentry?' The first is that there are so few rigorous evaluations upon which to base any generalizable knowledge. Seiter and Kadela were able to identify just 19 reentry program evaluations that contained a comparison group (2003). Only two of these evaluations were randomized experiments. Without this methodology, virtually every finding of program impact is open to criticism. If we assume that each state operated a minimum of 10 reentry programs, using Seiter and Kadela's definition, each year during this 26-year period, then there were close to 10,000 programs nationwide that were implemented during this time period. The 10 per year estimate is actually low, if one considers the program data reported each year by Camp and Camp in *The Corrections Yearbook* (2002). Yet, just 19 evaluations (less than 1 percent of the total) were published from this experience and the majority of those use weak methodology and pertain to drug programs. Using this 'body' of research to conclude *anything* about which reentry programs 'work' or 'don't work' seems misguided.

Second, virtually all of these evaluations use recidivism as the sole outcome criteria. Programs that reduce the level of criminal behavior among program participants are said to work. Recidivism is an important, perhaps the most important, measure of correctional impact, but it is insufficient as a sole measure of the effectiveness of reentry programs. After all, the ultimate goal of reentry programs is reintegration, which clearly includes more than remaining arrest-free for a specified time period. The author has urged the expansion of outcome criteria for evaluating corrections programs previously (Petersilia 1993), and the argument seems even more germane to reentry programs.

If we wish to truly measure reintegration, we need to build into our evaluations measures of attachment to a variety of social institutions. Research shows that these factors are related to long-term criminal desistance. For example, evaluations should measure whether clients are working, whether that work is full or part time, and whether the income derived is supporting families. We should measure whether programs increase client sobriety and attendance at treatment programs. We should track whether programs help convicts become involved in community activities, in a church, or in ex-convict support groups or victim sensitivity sessions. There are many outcomes that reentry programs strive to improve upon, and these are virtually never measured in traditional recidivism-only outcome evaluations. Jeremy Travis (2003) makes this point powerfully when he writes of the far-reaching impacts of drug courts. He notes that one of the positive impacts of an offender's participation in a drug court is that the children born to drug court participants are much less likely to be born addicted to drugs. Drug courts reduce participants' drug use, and result in healthy children being born to sober mothers. When we use recidivism as the sole criterion for judging whether reentry programs 'work' or 'don't work,' we often miss the more powerful impacts of program participation.

Third, the author's experience suggests that the results from the academic 'what works' literature does not feel right to correctional practitioners. The results don't have much face validity. Of course, research has to go beyond face validity. We shouldn't implement specific programs because practitioners *believe* they are effective. This would be too vague and subjective. There has to be a corresponding body of scientific evidence proving that they are effective. But at the same time, the scientific or statistical results should make common sense, be persuasive, and have the appearance of truth and reality. In other words, they should be playing well in Peoria. This doesn't seem to be the case with the 'what works' literature in reentry programming.

From: J. Petersilia (2004) 'What Works in Prisoner Reentry? Reviewing and Questioning the Evidence', Federal Probation, *68.2: 4–8.*

89. Beyond the prison paradigm

James Gilligan and Bandy Lee

People often speak of the goal of prison reform as the 'rehabilitation' of criminals. Our only objection to that is that most criminals – especially youthful ones – were never 'habilitated' (or 'socialized') in the first place, which is why they became antisocial personalities, or criminals. Working with such individuals often requires beginning with the same kinds of issues with which one might begin the socialization of one's own children, or with a class of pre-school children. Many of them literally need to learn, for the first time, how to live with other people – which is, of course, the most complicated and difficult task human beings face, which is why it is a lifelong challenge for even the healthiest and most mature adults (and nations). With the violent, however, one needs to start this process from the beginning.

Another respect in which the anti-prison would differ from traditional prisons is that it would be reserved exclusively for those who have committed (or credibly threatened) a serious act of violence. We recommend that for several reasons. First, because only violent crimes create physical danger to others such that others are safe only if the perpetrator is physically segregated from the community. Property crimes, for example, can be dealt with by requiring the perpetrator to restore the value of the stolen or destroyed property (plus court costs, etc.); indeed, he can do that most efficiently only if he is *not* incarcerated.

Drug use, whether it is use of the most dangerous and addictive drugs, alcohol and tobacco, or of the less dangerous and addictive ones such as marijuana, heroin, or cocaine, should not even be treated as criminal, but rather as a potential public health problem most effectively dealt with by means of substance abuse treatment, not imprisonment, unless it has been followed by a violent or property crime, in which case *that* is the crime, not the drug use. For whenever the sale or use of a drug has been criminalized, be it alcohol or heroin, it is the criminalization itself that has increased the violence associated with its use, not intoxication by the drug. That is, most of the violence associated with illicit drugs is the violence engaged in by drug dealers competing with each other over access to this lucrative market, not violence by people intoxicated by the drugs, and the market would not be as lucrative as it is if the very act of criminalizing the drugs (Miczek *et al.*, 1994; Duke and Gross, 1993; Goldstein, 1985, 1989; Goldstein *et al.*, 1988) and thus reducing the supply of them had not made them more valuable (since like all other markets this one too follows the laws of supply and demand). Thus, if the purpose of the criminal law is to reduce the amount of violence in our society, the most effective policy we could adopt would be to decriminalize the drugs whose use we now prohibit, and treat them at worst, a public health problem rather than a criminal one, which could be responded to by making substance abuse treatment available to everyone who is addicted to one or another chemical, whether they are violent or not, and reserving incarceration exclusively for those whose behavior would warrant imprisonment even if they were not using drugs.

What leads us to conclude that replacing prisons with locked residential colleges would reduce the rate of violent crime? In the first place, the senior author's experience over twenty-five years participating in and directing mental health and violence prevention programs in the Massachusetts prisons and prison mental hospital, between 1967 and 1992. He and his colleagues found that by establishing mental health centers in every prison, with staff recruited from Harvard's teaching hospitals, that offered a full range of psychiatric services from emergency crisis intervention to ongoing long-term multi-modal treatments, it was possible to reduce the level of lethal and life-threatening violence in the prison system from war-zone levels (a murder a month and a suicide every six weeks, plus riots and hostage-taking incidents, in one 600-man prison alone) to a situation in which none of those forms of violence would occur throughout the entire state prison system for a full year at a time. And when he and his colleagues investigated which programs were most effective in reducing recidivism after inmates were released from prison and returned to the community, they found one program, and only one, that had been 100% successful over a twenty-five year period – namely, a college education program in which professors from Boston University volunteered their time in order to teach in the prisons, and more than 200 inmates earned a bachelor's degree. When we attempted to learn how many of them had been returned to prison for a new crime after leaving, we were unable to find any. At first we thought we must have made a mistake, and then we discovered that Indiana's prison system had reported the same result, as had Folsom State Prison in California – zero recidivism following acquisition of a bachelor's degree (Elikann, 1996). Even the best things in life are seldom 100% effective forever, of course, and not every state has had such good results. Nevertheless, many studies of this issue in many different states have documented that receiving a college degree while in prison is one of the most effective ways to reduce recidivism, even among men incarcerated for the most violent crimes. When we extended our own study to thirty years, we found that two inmates had been returned to prison – a recidivism rate of less than 1% over 30 years. (This does not mean that every inmate had been in the community for 30 years, only that a series of more than 200 men had been out of prison for staggered and variable periods of time, ranging from one year to as many as 30.) This can be compared with a national recidivism rate of approximately 65% during the first three years after leaving prison.

Now, it is true that the inmates who earned a college degree were exceptional inmates; they were better educated to begin with than most inmates, and it seems reasonable to speculate that they might also have been more motivated to find some alternative to a life of crime and violence than most of their fellow inmates were. But they were not exceptional in one respect: they had committed crimes just as violent as the others, including murder and rape, and the very fact that they were in prison long enough to earn a degree indicates that their crimes were serious enough to earn a longer-than-average sentence. Given how high the average recidivism rate is among men leaving state prisons, how few programs have been reliably reported to lower recidivism rates by more than 5 or 10% in any prison population, and the fact that this program was not even costing the taxpayers any money (the professors were donating their time), and that many of the men under discussion had committed some of the most violent crimes there are, one would naturally think that a program this successful. even among a small and self-selected portion of the prison population, would be enthusiastically supported by officials in the state government. Think again. When our new governor learned of the results of this study, after being given a copy of a series of public lectures the senior author had just given at Harvard, he promptly announced that he had not previously realized that prison inmates had access to a free college education, and that he was going to close down this program because otherwise people who could not afford to go to college might start committing crimes so that they could get sent to prison in order to get a free college education!

From: J. Gilligan and B. Lee (2004) 'Beyond the Prison Paradigm: From Provoking Violence to Preventing It by Creating "Anti-Prisons" (Residential Colleges and Therapeutic Communities)', Annals of the New York. Academy of Sciences, *1036: 300–24.*

90. Rehabilitation: headline or footnote in the new penal policy?

Sam Lewis

A rights-based model of rehabilitation

The central tenets of the model advanced in this article originate in the work of Cullen and Gilbert (1982) and Rotman (1990). These 'new rehabilitationists' (Hudson, 2003: 62), and others writing in a similar vein, accept the criticisms made of 1960s-style rehabilitative strategies but argue that 'we should give up the coercion rather than the rehabilitation' (Hudson, 1987: 184). They advocate a system of 'state obligated rehabilitation', whereby the state has a moral duty to offer (but no right to impose) rehabilitative measures. This approach 'takes seriously the betterment of inmates but legitimates neither coercion in the name of treatment nor neglect in the name of justice' (Cullen and Gilbert, 1982: 246). Rehabilitation should be provided within the context of a determinate sentence, the length of which is proportionate to the seriousness of the offence (see Hudson, 2003: 63).

First and foremost, under this model the state has a *duty* to provide and the offender has a *right* to receive rehabilitation. Such claims have been made before (see, for example, Rotman 1986, 1990). Of particular note is an influential paper by McWilliams and Pease, in which the thinking of moral philosopher Alan Gewirth is employed to argue that offenders have a right to receive the help needed to be 'a full member of society, with the status and obligations which that membership confers' (McWilliams and Pease, 1990: 15).

The second principle on which this model rests is proportionality, according to which 'the size of the sentencing "package"' (Raynor, 1993: xii), that is 'the amount of intervention by the criminal justice system in an offender's life' (p. xii), should be entirely separate from rehabilitative goals and should be based solely on offenders' culpability. This 'prohibit[s] the use of dubious rehabilitative arguments ... The options are not determined by rehabilitative prognosis but by explicit legal conditions, with relatively little discretion left to the sentencing authorities' (Rotman, 1990: 15). Thus offenders should not be given a longer sentence solely in order that they can be rehabilitated. This point has also been made by Raynor, on the grounds that 'even where beneficial effects can be shown to be probable, they cannot be guaranteed for a particular individual' (Raynor, 1997: 253).

Proportionality also requires us to distinguish between its ordinal and cardinal variants (Von Hirsch, 1993), and to recognize the centrality of both to a modern rehabilitative theory of punishment. The principle of ordinal proportionality requires that 'persons convicted of crimes of like gravity should receive punishments of like severity' (p. 18). Cardinal proportionality looks at the punishment system as a whole and asks whether punishments are generally too harsh or too lenient (p. 19). When overall punishment levels are too harsh, and relatively minor offences incur draconian penalties, 'the right of the offender to the least-restrictive sentence available' as established by virtue of the existence of rehabilitation as a right (Rotman, 1990: 15) is infringed.

The third principle concerns the contentious concepts of 'coercion' and 'voluntariness'. Winick suggests that the most effective rehabilitative strategies are voluntary – those 'who feel that they have no real choice but to [take part] may agree but resent it, and as a result, may simply go through the motions of performance without deriving real benefit' (Winick, 1991: 248). At first glance the 'new rehabilitationists' seem to agree, stating that rehabilitation programmes must be 'client centred and basically voluntary' (Rotman, 1990: 8). On close inspection, however, the relevant texts reveal that Cullen and Gilbert (1982, ch. 7) and Rotman (1990: 108–9) accept that 'voluntariness' might not always be possible or desirable in a penal context, and note the dangers of turning "voluntariness" into an absolute dogma' (p. 108). The finding that 'persons coerced into drug treatment programmes fare equally as well as those who enter voluntarily' (see Maruna and LeBel, 2003: 96) further complicates the debate (see also Hough, 1996).

A detailed discussion of the extent to which rehabilitative strategies undertaken as part of a court order can be truly voluntary is beyond the scope of this article. As Bazemore notes, however, 'the issue of coercion is a relative one which must be viewed along a continuum *and* in relation to current practice, not some abstract ideal' (Bazemore, 1999: 183, emphasis in original). What is clear is that offenders should have some choice about how to utilize rehabilitative opportunities in order to respect their right to autonomy and self-determination. The third principle, then, requires that the essential human attribute of moral agency be protected wherever possible. How this might be achieved in practice should be the subject of lengthy and earnest debate.

The fourth principle is that prison should be a sanction of last resort. Its negative and damaging effects mean that it should be reserved for the small minority of offenders whose potential to do serious harm necessitates their removal from society. Imprisonment, where necessary, should be humane and constructive. Prisons should not be overcrowded, as this 'not only defeats the basic purpose of fairness, but can make criminal punishment illegal and even unconstitutional when it exceeds the penalty prescribed by law' (Rotman, 1990: 15). Additional pains are caused by the loss of physical space and privacy, limited access to education and employment due to the high demand for both, reduced time spent out of the prison cell due to staff shortages, and so forth.

Finally, it should be remembered that the rehabilitative opportunities offered to offenders should be 'made in a social policy context which also guarantees opportunities to those who do not offend' (Raynor, 1997: 259). To offer such life chances to offenders alone contravenes principles of social justice. It also invites criticism from those who adhere to the principle of 'less eligibility', according to which a prisoner's standard of life should not exceed that of the poorest members of society (see Rotman, 1990: 111–12). A rehabilitative criminal justice strategy, then, must form part of a social policy agenda that recognizes everyone's right to have their basic needs met.

From: S. Lewis (2005) 'Rehabilitation: Headline or Footnote in the New Penal Policy?', Probation Journal, *52.2: 119–35.*

91. Problem solving courts

*C. West Huddleston III, Judge Karen Freeman-Wilson,
Douglas B. Marlowe and Aaron Roussell*

The publication *Defining Drug Courts: The Key Components* (NADCP, 1997) is
the point of origin for those who would understand what the Conference of
Chief Justices (CCJ) and the Conference of State Court Administrators (COSCA)
refers to as the 'principles and methods of well functioning [adult] drug
courts.' Although not all problem solving court models may adhere to each of
the ten Key Components, the parentage of most problem solving court models
can be traced to these principles and practices (Figure 1). As the literature

1. Drug courts integrate alcohol and other drug treatment services with
   justice system case processing.
2. Using a non-adversarial approach, prosecution and defense counsel
   promote public safety while protecting participants' due process
   rights.
3. Eligible participants are identified early and promptly placed in the
   drug court program.
4. Drug courts provide access to a continuum of alcohol, drug, and
   other related treatment and rehabilitation services.
5. Abstinence is monitored by frequent alcohol and other drug testing.
6. A coordinated strategy governs drug court responses to participants'
   compliance.
7. Ongoing judicial interaction with each drug court participant is
   essential.
8. Monitoring and evaluation measure the achievement of program
   goals and gauge effectiveness.
9. Continuing interdisciplinary education promotes effective drug court
   planning, implementation, and operations.
10. Forging partnerships among drug courts, public agencies, and
    community-based organizations generates local support and enhances
    drug court program effectiveness.

(NADCP, 1997)

Figure 1. Keeping the fidelity of the drug court model
Defining drug courts: the key components

on the drug court model continues to demonstrate its effectiveness on the offender and the justice system at large, many jurisdictions have implemented a number of problem solving courts designed to address other problems that emerge in the traditional court system. Often modeled after drug courts, problem solving courts seek to address social issues such as mental illness, homelessness, domestic violence, prostitution, parole violation, quality of life, and community reentry from custody. Recently, several new problem solving courts have emerged, expanding the model to new populations; two such permutations are truancy courts and gambling courts.

> *Adding the total number of operational drug courts and other problem solving courts, there are 3,204 problem-solving courts in the United States as of December 31, 2007.*
>
> National Drug Court Institute, May, 2008

From: C. W. Huddleston, III, Judge Karen Freeman-Wilson, D. B. Marlowe and A. Roussell (2005) 'Problem Solving Courts: Emerging Permutations', Painting the Current Picture: A National Report Card on Drug Courts and Other Problem Solving Court Programs in the United States. *National Drug Court Institute, Vol. 1, No. 2, pp. 9–10.*

92. Strengths-based resettlement

Ros Burnett and Shadd Maruna

Numerous observers have pointed out that the term 'restorative justice' has been misused and abused in criminal justice discussions, appearing to encompass almost any criminal justice intervention from public shaming to restitution, and meaning very different things to different audiences. As such, it is essential to define carefully what is meant by 'restorative' or 'strengths-based' approaches to resettlement. We will begin with one of the most fully articulated statements of purpose for restorative resettlement practices in the current literature, Bazemore and Stinchcomb's (2004) article 'Involving Community through Service and Restorative Justice'.

Bazemore and Stinchcomb argue that a crucial element in successful re-entry is the willingness of the community to accept the releasee's return and that a key determinant of such willingness is the sense that the offender has made appropriate amends:

> While the retributive model of accountability requires that harm be done to the offender in order to balance the harm caused to others (Von Hirsch, 1976), the exchange theory concept of reciprocity (see Molm and Cook, 1995; Gouldner, 1960) suggests that only by taking responsibility for making things right with victims and victimised communities can offenders change either the *community's image* of them or their perceptions of themselves. (2004: 17, emphasis in original)

In this and other formulations, restorative practices are based simultaneously on a normative theory of justice based around restitution, and an empirical theory of criminal recidivism based on labelling theory or the 'looking-glass' self-concept (Gecas and Schwalbe, 1983; Maruna *et al.*, 2004). That is, in order for justice to be done, offenders need to help repair some of the harm caused by an offence (Johnstone, 2001). Additionally, though, there is an assumption that this repair will lead to a change in public labelling. Johnson writes, 'released prisoners find themselves "in" but not "of" the larger society' and 'suffer from a presumption of moral contamination' (2002: 319). To combat this social exclusion, the strengths paradigm calls for opportunities for offenders to make amends, demonstrate their value and potential and make positive contributions to their communities.

In the language of the new careers movement, the goal is to 'devise ways of creating more helpers' (Pearl and Riessman, 1965: 88). Strengths-based practice, like the new careers movement before it, would seek 'to transform receivers of help (such as welfare recipients) into dispensers of help; to structure the situation so that receivers of help will be placed in roles requiring the giving of assistance' (Pearl and Riessman, 1965: 88–9). Such demonstrations send a message to the community that the offender is worthy of further support and investment in their reintegration (Bazemore, 1999). Ideally, these contributions can be recognized and publicly 'certified' in order to 'de-label' symbolically the stigmatized person (see Maruna, 2001). Although community reintegration of this sort (as opposed to simple relocation into a community) is always a challenge, it is far more likely to occur in a reciprocal situation: one needs 'to do something to get something' (Toch, 1994: 71). A participant in the US 'Rethinking Probation' conference discussed the intuitive appeal of such a narrative:

> Let me put it this way, if the public knew that when you commit some wrongdoing, you're held accountable in constructive ways and you've got to earn your way back through these kinds of good works, ... (probation) wouldn't be in the rut we're in right now with the public. (Dickey and Smith, 1998: 36)

It is crucial to distinguish such strengths-based efforts from traditional forms of prison labour and community service work, both of which can also involve prisoners 'giving something back' and can also be justified on reformative grounds ('learning a skill') in some circumstances. The scope of prisoner work is too diverse to cover in a short discussion (see, for example, van Zyl Smit and Dunkel, 1999), but most traditional forms of prisoner employment (e.g. factory labour, kitchen work, cleaning) would not be considered 'strengths-based' or restorative because they are not voluntary efforts that put offenders in visible, community-oriented 'helping' or leadership roles. Strengths-based approaches are intended 'to be focused on projects designed to meet community needs, build community capacity, and repair the harm caused by crime to affected communities' (Bazemore and Stinchcomb, 2004: 18). Dickey and Smith write:

> Probation and parole projects in which offenders visibly and directly produce things the larger community wants, such as gardens, graffiti-free neighbourhoods, less dangerous alleys, habitable housing for the homeless ... have also helped build stronger communities, and have carved channels into the labour market for the offenders engaged in them. (1998: 35)

Additionally, most forms of prison labour do little to utilize and develop prisoner strengths (see van Zyl Smit and Dunkel, 1999). Prison work is typically paid, yet the wages are so low that they allow almost no opportunity for prisoners to support their families or compensate victims in a meaningful way. The work tends to be viewed by prisoners as something to keep them occupied, preferable to doing nothing, but is far from being seen as a 'calling', let alone a career. In a strengths-based framework, prisoner work efforts would be voluntarily agreed upon, and would involve challenging, intrinsically interesting tasks that could utilize the talents of the offender in useful, visible roles.

Unlike traditional forms of prison labour, community service work does involve offenders doing visible work in support of their communities; however, many of these efforts would not qualify as 'strengths-based' either. The primary difference, according to Bazemore and Stinchcomb (2004), is that strengths-based work is voluntarily agreed upon, whereas traditional community service is judicially ordered as punishment. Rather than being designed to be punitive, strengths-based work is explicitly intended to be both enjoyable and rewarding. The idea is to 'turn participants on' to the satisfaction of this sort of work. Despite its origins as a rehabilitative panacea, dating back to the Wootton Committee (Advisory Council on the Penal System, 1970: 13), community service is no longer justified in this way. According to Bazemore and Maloney, 'Punishment now appears to have become the dominant objective of service sanctions in many jurisdictions' (1994: 28). This shift is made explicit in the UK context (see, for example, Halliday, 2001: 40) by the much criticized re-labelling of community service as a 'community *punishment* order'. Some critics have gone so far as to suggest that community service orders tended to be 'almost exclusively manual, menial and arduous' (Caddick, 1994: 450; see also Blagg and Smith, 1989), although this trend seems to be changing in more recent analyses (see Rex and Gelsthorpe, 2004).

There is some evidence that this is an important difference, as well. McIvor (1998), for instance, found that individuals who viewed their experience of community service as 'rewarding' had lower rates of recidivism than those who found it to be a punishment. This might suggest that when community service 'works', the impact is less about deterrence and more likely something to do with pro-social modelling or moral development (van Voorhis, 1985; Rex and Gelsthorpe, 2004). McIvor writes, 'In many instances, it seems, contact with the beneficiaries gave offenders an insight into other people, and an increased insight into themselves; ... greater confidence and self-esteem; ... [and] the confidence and appreciation of other people' (McIvor, 1998: 55–6). Likewise, longitudinal studies have tried to assess the long-term impact of volunteer work on life course trajectories. Uggen and Janikula (1999) investigated the question of whether involvement in volunteer work can induce a change in a person's likelihood of antisocial conduct. They found a robust negative relationship between volunteer work and arrest even after statistically controlling for the effects of antisocial propensities, pro-social attitudes and commitments to conventional behaviour. Uggen and Janikula conclude:

> What is it about the volunteer experience that inhibits antisocial behavior? We suggest that the informal social controls emphasized in social bond, social learning, and reintegrative theories are the mechanism linking volunteer work and antisocial behavior. Informal social controls are consonant with Tocquevillian conceptions of 'self-interest, rightly understood,' in which volunteers are gradually socialized or 'disciplined' by habit rather than will. (1999: 355)

Rather than coercing obedience, strengths-based practices are therefore thought to develop intrinsic motivations towards helping behaviours – what Michael Clark (2001) calls the difference between compliance and growth. Volunteers are supposedly 'turned on' to pro-social behaviour through involvement with activities that utilize their strengths and promote their individual dignity. In the words of de Tocqueville, 'By dint of working for one's fellow-citizens, the habit and the taste for serving them is at length acquired' (1956 [1835]: 197). In addition, as part of a helping collective, the 'wounded healer' or community volunteer is thought to obtain 'a sense of belonging and an esprit de corps' (Pearl and Riessman, 1965: 83).

From: R. Burnett and S. Maruna (2006) 'The Kindness of Prisoners: Strengths-based Resettlement in Theory and in Action', Criminology and Criminal Justice. 6.1: 83–106.

93. Staying straight: lessons from ex-offenders

Thomas K. Kenemore and Ida Roldan

Practice implications

Despite the serious difficulties and challenges ex-offenders face while adjusting to the free world, few access mental health services. This is partly due to a pervasive suspicion and distrust of mental health providers and their ability to help, and the stigma attached to mental health services. If talking to a counselor/therapist means you have "problems upstairs", ex-offenders will avoid reaching out to mental health providers. In addition, their need to fend off anxieties and feelings of vulnerability leads them to minimize or deny their problems. Consequently, they are very difficult to engage in treatment and present significant challenges to clinicians. The findings of this study suggest important implications for practice.

To overcome attitudinal barriers and to establish credibility and trust with ex-offender clients, the clinician must work actively to develop an authentic and empathic relationship. The findings suggest that an active style, emphasizing 'straight talk' and expressing the clinician's ability to 'hold their own,' enhances credibility. Positive re-construction of the ex-offender's story, enhancement of the possibilities for employment, establishing and improving family functioning, and focusing on management of the underlying feelings of depression and anxiety are all necessary components of a practice approach that is relevant to ex-offender clients. The clinician working with this population must include all these perspectives in his/her repertoire. An artful, individualized integration and application of these components should increase the chances that the practitioner can help the ex-offender in a successful transition into the free world.

First, the overriding need is to address the social realities of the ex-offender, who inevitably faces daunting social obstacles when transitioning into free society. With low educational achievement and few skills, the ex-offender faces overwhelming barriers to successful employment and affordable housing. Basic needs such as shelter, food and employment are often denied to them. In order to address the current complex needs of the ex-offender, the clinician must be willing to work flexibly with the individual, his/her family, and other institutions. Clinicians must be prepared to address the multiple case management needs of the ex-offender directly.

From: T. K. Kenemore and I. Roldan (2006) 'Staying Straight: Lessons from Ex-offenders', Clinical Social Work Journal, *34.1: 5–21.*

94. The future of rehabilitation

Gwen Robinson and Peter Raynor

One promising strategy is to involve sentencers themselves in the management and review of people under supervision (perhaps a better description than the constantly reiterated 'offenders', a recent usage which hardly contributes to reintegration and constructive relabelling). Such direct involvement of sentencers in following up people they have sentenced and helping to recognize progress or to resolve compliance problems is characteristic of some drug courts and American 're-entry' courts, and has recently been termed 'therapeutic jurisprudence' (McGuire, 2003); as a relational approach which also incorporates official recognition of success, it fits well with the approaches outlined in this article. This might also help to increase sensitivity to particular local needs, and might in principle lead to greater awareness of diversity. The removal of probation from 'ownership' by the courts in 2001 may come to be seen as one episode in the long cold war between the Home Office and the judiciary about who really controls criminal justice, but turning the probation service into what is virtually a branch of the Home Office renders it much more vulnerable to the twists and turns of government criminal justice policy than when its governance was more localized and more dispersed.

A related, more 'professional' aspect of the suggested way forward concerns the skills that would need to be developed in order to make it work. These should include the systematic learning, in initial and in-service training, of the motivational, pro-social and personal skills to build on the relational potential of the 'case management' role (social work skills in all but name, of course, and recognized as such in Scotland, Ireland and indeed most of Europe). The role of effective help in the rehabilitation of offenders needs to be re-emphasized and developed in its own right, together with rebuilding the research capacity to evaluate local initiatives locally (as envisaged in Merrington and Hine, 2001). The origins of 'What Works' in Britain were local projects built on alliances between enthusiastic practitioners, managers and chief officers who were prepared to take risks, and researchers who were prepared to depart from the 'nothing works' consensus. It would be difficult to do this now, when both career-minded managers and government researchers need to align themselves so carefully with Home Office expectations. It also seems likely that probation areas will become still larger, in the wake of mergers of police force areas: this will increase the need to rebuild local roots, links and dialogue, and the skills to develop them.

Finally, as we approach the centenary of probation in Britain, it makes sense to revisit some of the positive features of past practice and to consider what relevance they might have for the future. We are not arguing for a wholesale recreation of the past, even if such a thing were feasible; however, some almost forgotten concepts and traditions seem to us to have a clear contemporary application in pursuing the approaches to rehabilitation which we have tried to outline. For example, in a criminal justice system dominated by competitive political displays of 'toughness', the modern probation service 'manages offenders', who are seen as objects of assessment, 'intervention', control and enforcement. Not so long ago, within the memory of many still practising, probation was the outcome of the defendant's negotiated consent, and this model provided at least the basis for a collaborative and contractual style of work. Books about probation discussed negotiated agreements, the building of trust, and helping people to take responsibility by treating them as responsible – in short, respect for persons (see, for example, Raynor, 1985 and many others). The best of the 'What Works' developments are full of similar ideas: for example, the use of 'Socratic questioning' to challenge people to think for themselves, and the development of skills and motivation to help people to overcome obstacles and take charge of their own lives. These are in reality far more human and collaborative processes than are conjured up by the technocratic language of 'interventions' and 'offender management'.

Historically the probation service has been one of very few state institutions capable of listening both to respectable society and to people at the margins who cause and get into trouble. At its best, it has promoted some understanding between the two and brought them closer together. Until the mid-1990s it was quite possible to articulate a model of probation that faced in two directions, seeking to influence people under supervision to reduce their offending and to make better decisions about their own lives, while at the same time influencing sentencers and social policy makers to make better decisions about people who offended (Raynor et al., 1994). The Service, it was argued, should aim

> ... to engage offenders in a reintegrative dialogue and offer opportunities for them to participate in constructive responses to the harm caused by offending, including efforts to find alternatives to offending in their own lives. This also involves influencing criminal justice processes towards less coercive and more participatory outcomes. (Raynor and Vanstone, 1994: 401)

The more recent model of probation as a purely correctional service seems to face in one direction only, and sometimes behaves as if criminal justice has nothing to do with social justice. If the probation service survives on this basis, it does so at the price of becoming little more than a caricature of its former aspirations and potential. If, on the other hand, it returns to the task of developing and promoting its own distinctive vision of the place of rehabilitation in penal policy, there are obvious risks. The prevailing climate of populist punitiveness, rising prison numbers, criminal justice managerialism and political control-freakery may appear unfriendly to such developments: on the other hand, as we stated at the beginning of this article, these conditions are not inevitable but are the product of human choices. At the time of writing, all three major British political parties have or are about to have new leaders who will bring their own ideas and innovations to social policy thinking, and the Probation Boards Association and NAPO have just forced a significant delay and at least partial redesign of the legislation for the National Offender Management Service. There is everything to gain, or at least little to lose, by continuing to articulate a distinctive role and vision for a revitalized probation service. Such a Service would, we believe, gain much from an increased emphasis on renewing its engagement with communities and localities; from greater use of restorative approaches; and from a clearer focus on the relational and reintegrative components of rehabilitation.

From: G. Robinson and P. Raynor (2006) 'The Future of Rehabilitation: What Role for the Probation Service?' Probation Journal, 53.4: 334–46.

95. Designing and delivering programmes for minority ethnic offenders

Patrick Williams

There is little the probation service can do to change the social environments within which offenders live, but it can assist them through the exploration of self-identity and self-conceptualisation to change their views about the choices available within those environments. Maruna argues that what distinguishes *desisters* from *persisters* is not 'obvious external differences in the social environment ... but in the way people interpret their lives' (Maruna, 2001: 32). Crucially it is these variables that are found to be more influential in facilitating desistance from offending (Maruna, 2001; Rex, 2001). When thinking about desistance, control theories and empowerment models offer a framework within which interventions can be constructed, interventions that can help individuals re-evaluate their lives and the opportunities open to them within their communities.

Control theories provide an explanation as to why most people stay within the confines of the law, a central tenet being that an individual's needs are infinite and that they will tend to seek fulfilment by unlawful means if they can perceive no legitimate way of achieving satisfaction. They accept that poverty and deprivation are related to offending as they weaken an individual's bond with society (Hirschi, in Downes and Rock, 1988: 221; Chapman and Hough, 1998). However, deprivation does not inevitably lead to offending: many who live in poverty lead law abiding lives. Control theory therefore seeks to outline the controls which keep the behaviour of most individuals within the law, seeing these as the factors that mediate between poverty and offending. As a theory it acknowledges the existence of cognitive deficits, but does not regard them as central. Reckless and Dinitz (1967) itemised external controls such as the existence of reasonable limits, the availability of meaningful roles and relationships and 'several complementary variables such as reinforcement by groups and significant supportive relationships, acceptance, the creation of a sense of belonging and identity' (Reckless, 1967, quoted in Lilly *et al.*, 1989: 95). Internal controls, however, are thought to be particularly important as their impact endures independently of the environment. Reckless saw these as a strong self concept as a law abiding person; a goal orientation focused on legitimate, achievable goals; high frustration tolerance on the realisation that different opportunities are available to different groups; and an absence of norm erosion which may occur when previously accepted social rules come to appear less legitimate (Lilly *et al.*, 1989: 96–8). There could be a problem here, since if the society of which one is a member has criminogenic values then increasing social bonds could lead to an increase in offending. But this argument assumes that those who live within sections of society that tend to produce the highest levels of criminal activity necessarily hold values that favour offending, and this view has been challenged (Maruna, 2001; Sykes and Matza, 1996). As Sykes and Matza argue, the need to develop 'techniques of neutralization' to facilitate offending or minimise its seriousness presupposes a need to distance oneself from one's anti-social acts (Sykes and Matza, 1996: 206). Bowling and Phillips (2002) also argue that illegal acts sometimes result from situations where individuals feel they have no legitimate alternative rather than form a commitment to criminal values, a view endorsed by attendees at a Black self-development group in London (Durrance *et al.*, 2001). One strategy for assisting desistance then is through helping offenders identify positive roles within their communities through which they can achieve status without offending. Maruna's work wholeheartedly endorses this as a recognised route out of offending (Maruna, 2001).

Empowerment programmes, then, seek to reduce the propensity of individuals to offend through fostering the development of social controls. Whilst many Black and Asian people achieve a positive racial identity as family and community supports lead to the development of effective survival skills, it is likely that some people on probation may feel alienated from, or marginal to, wider society. Black Empowerment therefore involves the development and application of skills based on 'information sharing' whilst centralising the importance of 'we' rather than 'I'. Critically, the empowerment process requires that the individual look at their own situation from their own perspective to assist in the development of strategies to empower and improve their situation (Francis-Spence, 1994, in Mitchell-Clarke, 1998). Thus, an empowerment model.

> … must assist the individual in his/her understanding of the historical, social, economic and individual factors which have and will impact on the process of change, aid in the setting of realistic and achievable goals and assist in removing negative traits of behaviour. The individual must also be provided with an opportunity to identify strategies for coping with events that influence his/her lifestyle but for which he/she does not have ultimate control for change.

From: P. Williams (2006) 'Designing and Delivering Programmes for Minority Ethnic Offenders', in S. Lewis, P. Raynor, D. Smith and A. Wardak (eds), Race and Probation. Cullompton: Willan, pp. 149–51.

96. Rehabilitation is the moral thing to do

Francis T. Cullen

As part of a broader challenge to therapeutic thinking in modern society, rehabilitation is criticized for sending a corrosive message that offenders are not responsible for their actions. Punishment, it is claimed, reinforces moral boundaries and communicates that offenders are moral agents who deserve to be held accountable for their bad choices. This reasoning has surface appeal, but it also borders on the ridiculous – for three reasons.

First, it conveniently ignores the criminological fact that the choice of crime is not 'free' but bounded – often quite tightly – by the circumstances into which offenders are born. Advocates of the punishment model feel free to acquit society – us – of any complicity in the conditions that breed crime. They feel free to ignore the disquieting reality that the correctional system disproportionately supervises minorities and the poor – groups socially neglected in our society. This blindness might prove comforting, but it hardly comprises the moral high ground.

Second, rehabilitation does not excuse victimization but rather demands that offenders work to change those parts of themselves that lead them into crime – whether that is how they think or how they design their lives. However, in embarking on this reformation, offenders are not simply placed in a cell and told to make better decisions in the future – 'or else.' Rather, a recognition exists that change is challenging and that corrections should be a partner in enabling offenders to lead lives that do less harm and contribute more to the commonweal. Supporting others to live a better life hardly is morally bankrupt; indeed, it seems more akin to the Golden Rule.

Third, rehabilitation does not demean human dignity but emphasizes its value. It is the punishment crowd that depicts offenders as predators (if not 'scum'), embraces chain gangs and oppressive prison conditions, and wishes to turn prisons into warehouses. By contrast, advocates of treatment do not reduce offenders to a philosophical myth (rational actors fully free to make choices) or to the nature of the crime they committed (which might be minor or might be heinous). Rather, they confront offenders in the fullness of their humanity, not afraid to assess their level of pathology but also not afraid to recognize offenders' humanity and to inspire their personal growth.

In the end, the punishment and treatment paradigms offer different visions of offenders, intervention strategies of different scientific merit, and distinctly different moral choices. No correctional approach is a panacea, but neither are all approaches equal. And when we compare, as we must, these two correctional visions, their relative merits seem clear. What the punishment paradigm has wrought 'in the real world' over the past decades is disquieting; doing more of the same would be an unpardonable mistake. It is time to take a new pathway – one that draws on Americans' long-standing cultural belief in offender reformation and on the emergent 'what works' scientific literature. We should reaffirm rehabilitation as corrections' guiding paradigm.

From: F. T. Cullen (2007) 'Make Rehabilitation Corrections' Guiding Paradigm', Criminology and Public Policy, *6.4: 717–28.*

97. Principles of problem-solving justice

Robert V. Wolf

Collaboration. *Justice system leaders are uniquely positioned to engage a diverse range of people, government agencies, and community organizations in collaborative efforts to improve public safety. By bringing together justice partners (e.g., judges, prosecutors, attorneys, probation officers, court managers) and reaching out to potential stakeholders beyond the courthouse (e.g., social service providers, victims groups, schools), justice agencies can improve inter-agency communication, encourage greater trust between citizens and government, and foster new responses – including new diversion and sentencing options, when appropriate – to problems.*

Courts are at the hub of a complex system. They rely on law enforcement to conduct investigations and make arrests; they rely on prosecutors and defense attorneys to sort through the facts and help protect individual rights; and they rely on probation, corrections, and parole officials to deliver and oversee punishment.

Despite their interconnectedness, however, courts traditionally behave as if they are more or less self-contained, focusing on the specifics of cases and less on the circumstances that bring defendants through the door or what happens after they leave. Although they determine sentences, they often don't have a large voice in the types of punishments at their disposal, and rarely measure their results.

Problem-solving justice takes advantage of the centrality of courts within the justice system – and the prestige, visibility, and reputation for neutrality they have outside the system. The point is not for courts to dictate solutions but to facilitate planning and inter-agency partnerships, allowing all players in the criminal justice system – along with relevant stakeholders in the community – to work together toward a common goal. A typical community court, for example, is the result of a collaborative process. Bringing together justice agencies, community groups, and social service providers, community courts attempt to test new approaches to low- level crime. They create new options for punishment, like community service, which seeks to 'pay back' the community for the harm caused by offending, and mandated social services, such as drug treatment for addicts and health counseling for prostitutes – all options that require the expertise and resources of numerous partners. The Red Hook Community Justice Center in Brooklyn, New York, focuses on at-risk youth and low-level drug offending – priorities identified by local stakeholders during a two-year feasibility study. To address these problems, the justice center relies on dozens of partners, including local non-profits and government agencies that have agreed to place staff on-site to provide health care, youth counseling, job training, and other needed services.

Some problem-solving initiatives not only harness existing resources but use the synergy of collaboration to meet the needs of unique clients. In Clackamas County, Oregon, for example, the county's seven problem-solving courts worked with the local housing committee of the federal Department of Housing and Urban Development and two local non-profit agencies to create a staffed, permanent, six-unit housing facility for female court participants with children.

Individualized justice. *Using valid, evidence-based risk and needs assessment instruments, the justice system can link offenders to individually tailored community-based services (e.g., job training, drug treatment, safety planning, mental health counseling) where appropriate. In doing so (and by treating defendants with dignity and respect), the justice system can help reduce recidivism, improve community safety and enhance confidence in justice. Links to services can also aid victims, improving their safety and helping restore their lives.*

Problem-solving justice is dedicated to the notion that defendants should be treated as individuals not numbers on a docket. Indeed, one of the primary forces that has driven the expansion of problem-solving courts is the frustration of many front-line judges and attorneys, who have vowed not to practice 'assembly-line justice.' In contrast, problem-solving courts seek to move away from a one-size-fits-all approach to justice. Many court cases are not complicated in a legal sense, but they involve individuals with complicated lives. Problem-solving justice recognizes this and seeks to give judges the tools they need to respond appropriately.

By customizing punishment, problem-solving courts seek to address offenders' underlying problems, thereby reducing the likelihood of repeat offending and increasing the likelihood that the offender can become a productive member of society. The goal, in many cases, is to reduce the use of incarceration, which is both an expensive and arguably ineffective intervention, particularly for low-level and non-violent offenders.

To facilitate individualized justice, some problem-solving initiatives invite service providers to share space in the courthouse or at a centralized service center. Such 'one-stop shops' make it easier for offenders to get the help they need. The Seattle Community Court, for example, has an on-site clinic staffed by community-based organizations that address offenders' problems, including mental illness, substance abuse, and homelessness. Services are geared primarily to mandated offenders but are also available on a voluntary basis to walk-ins from the community.

Many initiatives, especially domestic violence courts, also provide services to victims, including links to shelter and safety planning as well as advocacy. The goal is to prevent 're-victimization' (the sense that victims are abused twice: once by the batterer and again by the system), to encourage involvement in the court case (including corroborating affidavits), and to reduce the likelihood of continued abuse.

Accountability. *The justice system can send the message that all criminal behavior, even low-level quality-of-life crime, has an impact on community safety and has consequences. By insisting on regular and rigorous compliance monitoring – and clear consequences for non-compliance – the justice system can improve the accountability of offenders. It can also improve the accountability of service providers by requiring regular reports on their work with participants.*

Problem-solving courts are not the first initiatives to attempt to link defendants to alternative sanctions. Unfortunately, past efforts to use community service, drug treatment, and other programs have often been undermined by significant no-show or drop-out rates. Clearly, it is not enough to hand someone a piece of paper and hope they will show up for an appointment with a drug counselor or a batterer intervention program.

An important goal of problem-solving justice is to demonstrate that criminal behavior – even minor, quality-of-life crime – has consequences. Thus problem-solving courts strive to enforce their sanctions and emphasize accountability. One of their primary tools for achieving this goal is compliance monitoring. By requiring offenders to check in regularly with the judge, clerk, or local partners, problem-solving courts can ensure that sanctions – even diversion programs and alternatives to incarceration – have real teeth. Dade County, Florida, for example, launched a judicial monitoring program that requires participants on probation to come back to court regularly to report on their progress in treatment.

Problem-solving initiatives have found that clear communication and rapid response is essential for holding offenders accountable: non-compliance must be communicated as soon as it is discovered and the court must make it clear that sanctions (e.g., letters of apology, curfews, increased frequency of reporting, even short-term jail) will be issued in response. By creating effective vehicles for communication between the court and probation and other service providers, problem-solving courts have helped improve service delivery and the accountability of treatment providers. The Brooklyn Domestic Violence Court, for example, stopped referring cases to a particular batterer intervention program when the program failed to report participants' absences swiftly and accurately.

Outcomes. *The active and ongoing collection and analysis of data – measuring outcomes and process, costs and benefits – are crucial tools for evaluating the effectiveness of operations and encouraging continuous improvement. Public dissemination of this information can be a valuable symbol of public accountability.*

Courts have customarily measured their effectiveness by studying process: How many cases are handled per day, week, and month? What is the average time between arrest and arraignment? How quickly do cases move through the system? What is the clearance rate? How long is the backlog?

Problem-solving initiatives take a different approach. They, too, are concerned about process, but they ask additional questions as well. Often these questions are rooted in research and the knowledge of experts outside the courtroom. Among other things, drug courts try to determine what participant demographics are associated with program success. The answers can help drug courts establish appropriate eligibility criteria and also hone their programs to better address participants' needs and thereby produce better outcomes.

Problem-solving initiatives also focus on the impact of courts on victims and communities. Domestic violence courts track compliance with orders of protection with an eye toward improving victim safety. Reentry courts monitor participants' success finding jobs and housing. Juvenile drug courts monitor participants' school attendance and grades. Mental health courts monitor success in treatment, and use that information to identify factors (such as client demographics, treatment modalities, and frequency of court appearances) that have a positive impact on clients' success in treatment. Community courts monitor neighborhood attitudes, including public confidence in justice. And virtually all problem-solving courts monitor recidivism, trying to determine if problem-solving justice can reduce the likelihood of a defendant's re-offending.

While some problem-solving programs have been able to partner with outside agencies, such as university researchers, to collect and analyze data about their performance, many initiatives make do with limited resources. Many use the data they collect to monitor operations, identify areas of success, and bring to light emerging problems. The key, they have found, is collecting basic data – such as demographics about participants, length of participation, and compliance – and analyzing it. This kind of 'action research' is vital to ensuring that an initiative adapts to changing community conditions and priorities, and remains as effective as possible over the long haul.

Conclusion. Problem-solving justice adapts to local conditions. That's why the principles described in this article emphasize collaboration, engagement with local stakeholders, and individualization of sanctions – strategies that avoid cookie-cutter approaches and encourage justice practitioners to embrace local priorities, resources, and circumstances.

Yet despite the emphasis on adapting to local conditions, the broad spectrum of problem-solving justice initiatives share a common outlook, an outlook that, at its heart, emphasizes outcomes over process.

In attempting to articulate the common underlying principles that define problem-solving justice, our goal is not simply to highlight what *is* but to help shape what will be. In the future, as courts explore how best to institutionalize problem-solving justice, it is our hope that these principles will serve as an important resource, ensuring that even as problem-solving finds more applications outside specialized courts, it remains true to its tenets, which have made it one of the justice system's most successful and resilient innovations of the past generation.

From: R. V. Wolf (2007) Best Practice: Principles of Problem-Solving. *Justice Center for Court Innovation, Bureau of Justice Assistance, New York State.*

98. 'A daft idea'

Rod Morgan

"I got bail even though I was initially charged with attempted murder. I think it was because I had a job, I was involved in the project and I was working as a volunteer at a legal advice centre. I'd had a series of jobs since I'd come out of Thorn Cross. I was on track. Ian [*his project co-ordinator*] spoke up for me and my Mum spoke up for me. I admitted I'd stabbed my Dad but I didn't plead guilty to attempted murder. He'd attacked me. If he hadn't attacked me nothing would have happened. He's bigger and stronger than me. He's built like a bulldozer. I said I'd acted in self-defence. But in the end I pleaded guilty to grievous bodily harm. And everyone said that because I'd been to prison before I was looking at five years. Everyone said that. And while I was on bail I couldn't live in or go to the house. I was banned from the whole area. I was waiting for a flat at the time, but it hadn't come through so I lived with my sister for a bit and then with Jessica.

'The dance project helped me enormously at the time. I didn't have a life coach. Everyone else did, but I worked with Ian and he came everywhere with me and helped me. I didn't talk about what was happening to me to people in the project and even though it was mentioned in the TV series most people in the project didn't know about it at the time. I was sentenced in May 2006 at Wolverhampton Crown Court, four months before the Hippodrome performance. Ian and my Mum spoke up for me again and, contrary to the sentence that everyone told me I was going to get, I got probation with various conditions that I go to groups and that sort of thing. I'd finished my licence at that stage, but now I had to start all over again. And I couldn't get jobs now. I've never had a proper job since. I used to be able to get them, but now I can't. I can only get casual, low paid stuff now.'

'The Ballet Hoo people were great. Though things have been a bit tough since the project finished it has helped me, though I've always been energetic and willing to have a go at things. [*Jessica comes in again* – she says 'It's definitely made him more confident in himself. He always used to say he would do things, but you could tell he wasn't that confident. Now he's really willing to do it and is confident he *can* about it.']

'I was going to be Lord Capulet in the final performance. But I had problems getting to some of the rehearsals towards the end because of other things that were going on at the time. I had to go to probation groups, for example. I think I was regarded as very important within the project because when I was at a rehearsal people didn't mess about as much. I motivated them. I got on with everyone and people said that the atmosphere was more positive when I was there. At the Hippodrome I played four different parts in the crowd scenes. They said I learned the steps really quickly. That evening was great. My Mum and Jessica were there. It was great. Afterwards people who saw me on the TV congratulated me and told me I had to do more of that.'

From: Rod Morgan (2009) Too Much to Ask? The Leaps and Bounds Story, *in reference to 'Ballet Hoo', a project designed by the charity Youth at Risk (UK). London: Arts Council England and Solomon White Publications.*

Conclusion

Although the purpose of this Reader has been to stimulate a debate about the most viable way forward for a constructive and effective criminal justice system, our position in compiling and editing it has been one that is unashamedly anti-punishment in so far as we believe it to be a counter-productive way of trying to protect communities from crime and rehabilitate those people who appear before our courts. Our approach to stimulating debate has been informed by two fundamental beliefs. Firstly, we believe that rehabilitation offers a much more realistic chance of protecting communities than a more restricted focus on reducing reoffending or reducing risk because it is concerned with the restoration of the individual to full citizenship; put another way it is concerned not simply with desistance from offending but also with fundamental change in the individual's self-awareness, self-perception and problem-solving abilities (Farrall and Calverly 2006). Moreover, that kind of change is dependent on attention not only to building on the personal resources of the individual through an emphasis on strengths as opposed to weaknesses (Burnett and Maruna 2006) but also to mobilising resources available to the individual in social and community networks, thus increasing realistic opportunities for change. Secondly, we share a view of rehabilitative work that is premised on collaborative relationships and offers of help relevant to the aspirations of the individual: in other words, work that gives due weight to the agenda of the person being offered help. In this sense, our vision of rehabilitative work incorporates the basic features of Raynor and Vanstone's (1994: 402) revised Non-Treatment Paradigm,[1] thus bringing the interests of the person who has offended and the community together within a commitment to community justice. (Community justice is the outcome of relevant, community-based agencies also sharing a commitment to problem-solving in all their processes and procedures.) Such work must incorporate a relationship between the practitioner and the individual in which belief and optimism about the latter's personal resources (to use the jargon, human capital) is not only communicated effectively but forms the foundation of that work (Farrall and Calverley 2006).

Many of the extracts in this reader lend weight to Ward and Maruna's (2007) argument that the starting point for rehabilitative work should be individuals' views of what helps them stop offending, but some also highlight the real danger,

297

in the current climate, of that important principle being lost. As those extracts have demonstrated, the general reason for this is the prevailing punitiveness of the political climate, but a more specific reason might be that the starting point for responding to people who have committed offences is invariably the notion of otherness. It is a notion entrenched in the processes of criminal justice and the representations of crime in the media and in much popular discourse. As the portrayal of car thieves as jackals in the 1990s television crime prevention campaign infamously emphasised, 'offenders' are another species, separate from the rest of society. (This is an ironic contrast, in these more enlightened times, to Darrow's insights expressed at the beginning of the twentieth century.) Little surprise then that for the most part they are targets of change rather than collaborators in change processes.

The 'citizen' model of rehabilitation and probation outlined in Part Three requires that Ward and Maruna's principle be endorsed, and perhaps one way of achieving that endorsement would be for policy-makers, practitioners and researchers alike to engage in a process of self-reflection that properly informs them about the keys to successful change. Self-directed questions might be – How have we changed in our lives? What has changed? What has remained obdurately the same? Who or what has helped us change? What were their qualities or what were the crucial elements in the circumstances in which we changed? What has motivated us to engage in the process of change? Honestly answering those questions might lead to important insights into the process of personal change, and in particular about such things as the difficulties of changing even from positions of relative advantage and privilege; the possible depth of resistance to change; and the loss that genuine change might entail. Perhaps more than anything else, the extracts in this reader have underlined the complexity and difficulty of personal change: change is rarely a dramatic epiphany, but instead it is slow, often imperceptible, and incremental. Engaging in that more realistic kind of process with those who offend is the great challenge confronting the criminal justice and penal systems as they progress into the twenty-first century.

This pursuit of citizenship is not an autonomous activity engaged in by solitary individuals, it is a profoundly social process. Citizens are products not only of their own self-imagined identities and self-willed change; they rely on and are incentivised by reciprocal relationships with significant others – partners, family members, friends and community groups; they are shaped by the influences of the work they do and the people they work with; and they use the services of social and educational agencies to achieve some of their goals. Rehabilitation fits into this social nexus as an expectation and as a service. As active citizens themselves, criminal justice professionals have an obligation to work with those who have broken the law to help bring them to those moments of self-realisation and motivation to change which are the precursors of 'going straight'. Beyond that the building of a new identity is an arduous process, and those who undertake it need all the help they can get. That is what newly professionalised rehabilitation and probation services can offer, building on the evidence base about cognitive and other skills that has begun to emerge from the 'what works' initiatives, celebrating the values of respect that inspired their founders, and striking that balance between the protection of the public and the needs of individuals which is the hallmark of rehabilitation in action.

That said, as the extracts in Part One illustrate, the field of rehabilitative practice and theory is a contested one: on the one hand, clear and unequivocal humanitarian instinct and on the other political and social inclinations towards social control and the continuation of centuries-old class divisions and powerful elites. Those extracts show also the danger of failing to challenge grand theories about criminal justice and penal processes and undervaluing the messages from practitioners like Augustus and Holmes. Attention to those messages at least exposes the intricacies of the story of rehabilitation and reminds us of the humanitarian motivations of some practitioners. In addition, the extracts demonstrate important lessons from history and warn against the reinvention of wheels.

Such things as respect for the individual, collaborative relationships, recognition of the importance of belief in the individual in the process of change, aversion to negative labelling, and the strength-based approach are not new, and Part Two illustrates the survival and continuation of those concepts (albeit in the fragile hands of the individual practitioner) against the backdrop of a burgeoning prison population and an increasingly vulnerable probation service. The extracts also provide evidence of the continuous development of practitioner-led innovation, the notion of sharing power with individuals, both one-to-one and in groups, the beginnings of recording work and gathering evidence in innovative ways (nascent empiricism), and processes of organisational changes from below.

The model shaped by the extracts in Part Three is clearly the offspring of these concepts, but it is important also because it sketches a possible means of reviving rehabilitation and dislodging prison from its central position in the criminal justice system. The extracts themselves throw glimmers of light on what kind of community justice might work and provide justifications for policy-makers and practitioners alike to embrace a rational and humanistic approach to responding to crime and the harm it does to the whole community. Effectiveness, of course, is important, and we all have a vested interest in successful rehabilitation because an individual who desists from crime becomes a citizen contributing positively to society. However, there are strong moral arguments for rehabilitation and community justice to replace imprisonment. The prison inflicts harm not only upon the imprisoned but also on members of their social and personal networks: it harms those innocent of crime such as partners and children. Moreover, prison inflicts harm on children and mentally disordered people who are imprisoned, and disproportionately targets people from minority ethnic groups. We also oppose punishment on aesthetic grounds; the punitive prison, like execution, and torture, disfigures the society that makes use of it. The 'civilisation' of civil society, according to Elias (1939), relies in part at least on distaste for the gruesome pageantry of popular justice in earlier periods. The spectacle has long since retreated behind closed doors, but our collective knowledge of its existence does damage to the view we have of ourselves as 'civilised' societies. It is surely reasonable, therefore, to question the moral integrity of a society that uses prison as its foremost response to crime and allows it to survive unchallenged in a kind of moral vacuum regardless of the absence of evidence of its effectiveness.

The unbridled proliferation of prison has occurred without empirical support, so positive change of the kind argued for in this reader is to some degree at least dependent on the triumph of progressive reformism over penal conservatism. That in turn is contingent on an effective counter, firstly to the influence of the neo-retributivist lobby in the United States and the kind of political opportunism in the United Kingdom epitomised by Conservative Home Secretary Michael Howard's assertion that 'prison works' (Conservative Party Conference 1993) which have done so much to entrench imprisonment as the favoured response to crime (Young 1999); and secondly to the reframing of one of the principal vehicles of rehabilitation, namely probation, as 'punishment in the community'. Such a counter-revolution will necessitate political courage and will entail revisiting the morality of the original vision of rehabilitation, the renewal of faith in, and respect towards counsellors, a broadening of our understanding of the technology of what works, and acceptance of the structural reforms necessary to guarantee the position of community and restorative justice in the processes of the administration of the law. That may be a tall order, but if successful it will go some way to reinstating rehabilitation in the community as the leitmotif of criminal justice in the rest of the twenty-first century. This is not 'woolly minded' liberalism, sentimental 'do-gooding' or 'expertological' treatment at the expense of the community. It has clear aims, a hard edge of evidence and a determination to serve whole communities and whole individuals within them – and its outputs will be measured in terms of the contributions they make to collective safety and general well-being, personal fulfilment and the creation of a just and caring society. In turn, that will depend on the nature of the stories we tell ourselves as a society because they shape the kind of society we become just as the stories we tell ourselves as individuals help to shape the kinds of people we can be. Personal narratives and social rhetorics perform the same functions at different levels. Punishment is the rhetoric of the powerful – it meets harm with harm; it is pessimistic about human nature; it is about hurt and exclusion. Rehabilitation is a powerful, alternative rhetoric that promotes inclusion, education and optimism about self-change towards active citizenship. It points to the kind of society we aspire to and its message is one of positive justice. We know which we prefer.

Note

1. '(a) Help becomes Help consistent with a commitment to the reduction of harm; (b) Shared assessment becomes Explicit dialogue and negotiation offering opportunities for informed consent to involvement in a process of change; (c) Collaboratively becomes Collaboratively defined task relevant to criminogenic needs, and potentially effective in meeting them.'

References

Abrams, P. (1978) 'Community care', in J. Barnes. and N. Connelly (eds) *Social Care Research*, London: Bedford Square Press.

Adams, S. (1974) 'Evaluative research in corrections: status and prospects', *Federal Probation*, XXXVIII.1: 14.

Adams, S. (1975) *Evaluative Research in Corrections: A Practical Guide*. Washington, DC: US Department of Justice.

Advisory Council on the Penal System (1970) *Non-Custodial and Semi-Custodial Penalties*. London: HMSO.

Aldridge, M. (2002) 'Probation Officer Training, Promotional Culture and the Public Sphere', *Public Administration*, 77.1: 73–90.

Altschuler, D. M., Armstrong, T. L. and MacKenzie, D. L. (1999). *Reintegration, Supervised Release, and Intensive Aftercare*. Juvenile Justice Bulletin. Washington, DC: Office of Juvenile Justice and Delinquency Prevention, U.S. Department of Justice.

American Friends Service Committee (1971) *Struggle for Justice: A Report on Crime and Punishment in America*. New York: Hill & Wang.

American Psychological Association (1992) 'Ethical principles of psychologists and code of conduct', *American Psychologist*, 47: 1597–611.

Andrews, D. A., and Bonta, J. (1998) *The Psychology of Criminal Conduct*. Cincinnati, OH: Anderson.

Andrews, D. A., Zingler, I., Hoge, R. D., Bonta, J., Gendreau, P. and Cullen, F. T. (1990) 'Does correctional treatment work? A clinically-relevant and psychologically-informed meta-analysis', *Criminology*, 28, 369–404.

Angliker, C. C., Cormier, B. M., Boulanger, P. and Malamud, D. (1973) 'A Therapeutic Community for Persistent Offenders – An Evaluation and Follow Up Study of the First Fifty Cases', *Canadian Psychiatric Association Journal*, 18: 289–95.

Anglin, M. D, Longshore, D., Turner, S., McBride, D., Inciardi, J. and Pendergast, M. (1996) *Studies of Functioning and Effectiveness of Treatment Alternatives to Street Crime (TASC) Programs: Final Report*. Washington, DC: National Institute on Drug Abuse.

Argyris, C. and Schon, D. (1978) *Organizational learning: A theory of action perspective*. Reading, Mass: Addison Wesley.

Arnhart, L. (1998) *Darwinian Natural Right: the Biological Ethics of Human Nature*. Albany, NY: State University of New York Press.

Arrigo, B. A. (2004) 'Rethinking Restorative and Community Justice: A Postmodern Inquiry', *Contemporary Justice Review*, 7.1: 91–100.

Augustus, J. (1852) *A Report of the Labors of John Augustus, for the Last Ten Years, in Aid of the Unfortunate: Containing a Description of his Method of Operation: Striking Incidents, and Observation upon the Improvement of some of Our City Institutions, with a View to the Benefit of the Prisoner and Society*. Boston: Wright and Hasty, Printers; Reprinted as *John Augustus, First Probation Officer* by the National Probation Association in 1939.

Austin, J. T. and Vancouver, J. B. (1996) 'Goal Constructs in Psychology: Structure, Process, and Content', *Psychological Bulletin*, 120: 338–75.

Bahn, C. and Davis, R. J. (1998) 'Day Reporting Centers as an Alternative to Incarceration', *Journal of Offender Rehabilitation*, 27.3/4: 139–50.

Barajas, E. (1996) 'Moving Toward Community Justice', in *Community Justice: Striving for Safe, Secure, and Just Communities*. Washington, DC: National Institute of Corrections.

Barnes, H. E. (1972) *The Story of Punishment*. Montclair, NJ: Patterson Smith.

Barton, C., Alexander, J.F., Waldron, H., Turner, C.W. and Warburton, J. (1985) 'Generalizing Treatment Effects of Functional Family Therapy: Three Replications', *American Journal of Family Therapy*, 13: 16–26.

Batson, C. D. (1994) 'Why Act for the Public Good? Four Answers', *Personality and Social Psychology Bulletin*, 20: 603–10.

Bazemore, G. (1998) 'Restorative Justice and Earned Redemption: Communities, Victims and Offender Reintegration', *American Behavioral Scientist*, 41.6: 768–813.

Bazemore, G. (1999) 'After Shaming, Whither Reintegration: Restorative Justice and Relational Rehabilitation', in G. Bazemore (ed.) *Restorative Juvenile Justice*. New York: Criminal Justice Press.

Bazemore, G. (2000) 'Evaluating Community Youth Sanctioning Models: Neighborhood Dimensions and Beyond'. pgs. 23–49, in *Crime and Place: Plenary Papers of the 1997 Conference on Criminal Justice Research and Evaluation*. Washington, D.C. National Institute of Justice Research Forum.

Bazemore, G. and Erbe, C. (2002) 'Reintegration and Restorative Justice: Toward a Theory and Practice of Informal Social Control and Support', *Youth Violence and Juvenile Justice*, 1.10: 246–75.

Bazemore, G. and D. Maloney (1994) 'Rehabilitating Community Service: Toward Restorative Service Sanctions in a Balanced Justice System', *Federal Probation* 58.1: 24–35.

Bazemore, G. and Stinchcomb, J. (2004) 'A Civic Engagement Model of Re-entry: Involving Community Through Service and Restorative Justice', *Federal Probation*, 68.2: 797–810.

Bean, P. (1976) *Rehabilitation and Deviance*. London: Routledge & Kegan Paul.

Beccaria, C. (1992) *An Essay on Crimes and Punishments* (2nd edn). Boston: International Pocket Library.

Bennett, L. A. (1973) 'Should We Change the Offender or the System?', *Crime and Delinquency*, 19: 332–42.

Bentham, J. (1823) 'Panopticon: or, The Inspection House', in P. Rock (ed.) (1994) *History of Criminology*. Aldershot: Dartmouth.

Berntsen, K. and Christiansen, K. (1965) 'A Resocialization Experiment with Short-term Offenders' *Scandinavian Studies in Criminology*, 1: 35–54.

Bianchi, H. (1979) 'Het assensusmodel – een studie over het binnenlands asylrecht', *Tijdschrift voor Criminologie*, 21: 167–79.

Biestek, F. P. (1961) *The Casework Relationship*. London: Allen & Unwin.

Bissell, D. (1962) 'Group Work in the Probation Setting', *British Journal of Criminology*, 2.3: 229–50.

Blackburn, R. (1980) *Still Not Working? A Look at Recent Outcomes in Offender Rehabilitation*. University of Aberdeen. Paper presented at the Scottish Branch of the British Psychological Society Conference on 'Deviance', University of Stirling.

Blagg, H. and Smith, D. (1989) *Crime, Penal Policy and Social Work*. Harlow: Longman.

Blumstein, A., Cohen, J., and Nagin, D. (1978) *Deterrence and Incapacitation: Estimating the Effects of Criminal Sanctions on Crime Rates*. Washington, DC: National Academy of Sciences.

Bochel, D. (1976) *Probation and After-care: Its Development in England and Wales*. Edinburgh: Scottish Academic Press.

Bottoms, A. E. and McClintock, F. H. (1973) *Criminals Coming of Age*. London: Heinemann.

Bottoms, A.E. and McWilliams, W. (1979) 'A Non-Treatment Paradigm for Probation Practice', *British Journal of Social Work*, 9: 159–202.

Bottoms, A.E. (1983) 'Neglected Features of Contemporary Penal Systems', in D. Garland and P. Young (eds), *The Power to Punish*. London: Heinemann.

Bowling, B. and Phillips, C. (2002) *Racism, Crime and Justice*. London: Longman Criminology Series.

Boyle, J. (1977) *A Sense of Freedom*. Basingstoke: Canongate.

Bridges, A. (1998) *Increasing the Employability of Offenders: An Inquiry into Probation Service Effectiveness*. Probation Studies Unit Report No. 5. Oxford: Centre for Criminological Research, University of Oxford.

Briggs. D. (1973) 'De-clienting social work', *Social Work Today*, 25 January.

Briggs. D. (1975) *In Place of Prison*. London: Temple Smith.

Brim Jr, O. G. and Wheeler, S. (1966) *Socialization After Childhood: Two Essays*. New York: Wiley.

Brockway, Z. R. (1912) *Fifty Years of Prison Service. An Autobiography*. New York: Charities Publication Committee.

Brody, S. R. (1976) *The Effectiveness of Sentencing*. London: HMSO.

Brody. S. R. (1978) 'Research into the Aims and Effectiveness of Sentencing', *Howard Journal*, 17.3: 133–48.

Brown, A. and Caddick, B. (1993) *Groupwork with Offenders*. London: Whiting & Birch.

Brown, W. K. and Miller, T. M. (1988) 'Following-up Previously Adjudicated Delinquents: A Method', in R. L. Jenkins and W. K. Brown (eds), *The Abandonment of Delinquent Behavior: Promoting the Turnaround*. New York: Praeger.

Bruner, J. S. (1987) 'Life as Narrative', *Social Research*, 54: 11–32.

Bruner, J. S. and Weinreich-Haste, H. (1987) *Making Sense: The Child's Construction of the World*. London: Methuen.

Buckner, J.C. and Chesney-Lund, M. (1983) 'Dramatic Cures for Juvenile Crime: An Evaluation of Prison-Run Delinquency Prevention Programs', *Criminal Justice and Behavior*, 10: 227–247.

Burnett, R. and Maruna, S. (2006) 'The Kindness of Prisoners: Strengths-Based Resettlement in Theory and in Action', *Criminology and Criminal Justice* 6.1: 83–106.

Burney, E. (1980) *A Chance to Change*. London: NACRO.

Bryant, M., Coker, J., Estlea, B., Himmel., S. and Knapp, T. (1978) 'Sentenced to Social Work', *Probation Journal*, 38: 123-6.

Caddick, B. (1994) 'The "New Careers" Experiment in Rehabilitating Offenders: Last Messages from a Fading Star', *British Journal of Social Work*, 24: 449–60.

Camp, G. M. and Camp, C. G. (2002) *Corrections Yearbook: Adult Corrections*. Middletown, CT: Criminal Justice Institute.

Carson, W. M. (1973) 'A Canadian Therapeutic Community for Disruptive Youths', *International Journal of Offender Therapy and Comparative Criminology*, 17: 268–84.

Cary, Mrs (1913) 'The Value of the Probation System as Applied to Women', *National Association of Probation Officers*, 3: 15–14.

Cary, Mrs. (1915) 'Social Clubs for Probationers; Their Needs and Objects', *National Association of Probation Officers*, 6: 102–3.

Cavender, G. (1984) 'Justice, Sanctioning, and the Justice Model', *Criminology*, 22.2: 203–13.

Celnick, A. and McWilliams, W. (1991) 'Helping, Treating and Doing Good', *Probation Journal*, 38.4: 164–70.

Chapman, T. and Hough, M. (1998) *Evidence Based Practice: A Guide to Effective Practice*. London: HM Inspectorate of Probation.

Chesterton, G. K. (1922) *Eugenics and Other Evils*. London: Cassell.

Chinn, H. (1916) 'Probation Work among Children', *National Association of Probation Officers*, 7: 123–5.

Christie, N. (1977) 'Conflicts as Property', *British Journal of Criminology*, 17: 1–19.

Christie, N. (1982) *Limits to Pain*. Oxford: Martin Robertson.

Christie, N. (1994) *Crime Control as Industry: Toward Gulags, Western Style*. New York: Routledge.

Claassen, Ron (1990) 'Prerequisites for Reconciliation', in *VORP Volunteer Handbook*. Akron, PA: Mennonite Central Committee.

Clark, M. D. (2001) 'Influencing Positive Behavior Change: Increasing the Therapeutic Approach of Juvenile Courts', *Federal Probation*, 65.1: 18–27.

Clarke, D. (1982) 'Justifications for Punishment', *Contemporary Crises*, 6: 33–9.

Coates, R., Miller, A. and Ohlin, L. (1978) *Diversity in a Youth Correctional System: Handling Delinquents in Massachusetts*. Cambridge, MA: Ballinger.

Cohen, S. (1985) *Visions of Social Control: Crime, Punishment and Classification*. Oxford: Polity Press.

Conley, J. J. (1985) 'A Personality Theory of Adulthood and Aging', in R. Hogan and W. H Jones (eds), *Perspectives in Personality*, Vol. 1. Greenwich, CT: JAI Press.

Cornish, D. B. and Clarke, G. (1975) *Residential Treatment and Its Effects on Delinquency*. London: HMSO.

Cox, E. W. (1877) *The Principles of Punishment as Applied in the Administration of the Criminal Law by Judges and Magistrates*. London: Law Times Office.

Crowe, A. H. (1998) 'Restorative Justice and Offender Rehabilitation: A Meeting of Minds', *Perspectives: A Journal of the American Probation and Parole Association*, 22.3: 28–40.

Cullen, F. T. (2007) 'Make Rehabilitation Corrections' Guiding Paradigm', *Criminology and Public Policy*, 6.4: 717–28.

Cullen, F. T. and K. E. Gilbert (1982) *Reaffirming Rehabilitation*. Cincinnati, OH: Anderson.

Cummins, R. A. (1996). 'The Domains of Life Satisfaction: An Attempt to Order Chaos', *Social Indicators Research*, 38: 303–28.

Dan-Cohen, M. (1986) *Persons, Rights and Organizations*. Berkeley, CA: University of California Press.

Darrow, C. (1902) *Resist Not Evil*. Chicago: C. H. Kerr.

Darrow, C. (1919) *Address to the Prisoners in the Chicago Jail*. Chicago: Charles Kerr.

Darrow, C. (1932) *The Story of My Life*. New York: Grossett & Dunlap.

Darrow, C. (1972) *Crime, Its Cause and Treatment*. Montclair, NJ : Patterson Smith.

Davies, M. (1974) *Social Work in the Environment. A Study of One Aspect of Probation Practice*, Home Office Research Study No. 21. London: HMSO.

Davies, M. (1977) *Support Systems in Social Work*. London: Routledge & Kegan Paul.

Davis, K.C. (1969) *Discretionary Justice: A Preliminary Inquiry*. Baton Rouge, LA: Louisiana University Press.

Davis, M. (1968) *In the Ghetto (The Vicious Circle)*. See 'The Best of Mac Davis' songbook, © 1975 Screen Gems – Columbia Publications.

de Haan, W. (1990) *The Politics of Redress: Crime, Punishment, and Penal Abolition*. London: Unwin Hyman.

de Tocqueville, A. (1956 [1835]) *Democracy in America*. New York: Knopf.

Deci, E. L. and Ryan, R. M. (2000) 'The "What" and "Why" of Goal Pursuits: Human Needs and the Self Determination of Behavior', *Psychological Inquiry*, 11: 227–68.

Deitz, G. E. (1969) 'A Comparison of Delinquents and Non-delinquents on Self-acceptance and Parental Identification', *Journal of Genetic Psychology*, 115: 285–95.

Deschenes, E. P., Turner, S., Greenwood, P. and Chiesa, J. (1996) *An Experimental Evaluation of Drug Testing and Treatment Interventions for Probationers in Maricopa County, Arizona*. Santa Monica, CA: Rand.

Dickey, W. J. and Smith, M. E. (1998) *Dangerous Opportunity: Five Futures for Community Corrections: The Report from the Focus Group*. Washington, DC: US Department of Justice, Office of Justice Programs.

Ditton, P. M. (1999) *Mental Health and Treatment of Inmates and Probationers*, NCJ 174463. Washington, DC: U.S. Government Printing Office.

Downes, D. and Rock, P. (eds) (1998) *Understanding Deviance: A Guide to the Sociology of Crime and Rule Breaking*. Oxford: Oxford University Press.

du Cane, E. (1885) *The Punishment and Prevention of Crime*. London: Macmillan.

Duke, S. B. and Gross, A. C. (1993) *America's Longest War: Rethinking Our Tragic Crusade Against Drugs*. New York: G. P. Putnam's Sons.

Durrance, P., Hignett, C., Merone, L. and Asamoah, A. (2001) *The Greenwich and Lewisham Self-Development and Educational Attainment Group: Evaluation Report*. London: London Probation Area.

Eitzen, D. S. (1975) 'The Effects of Behaviour Modification on the Attitudes of Delinquents', *Behaviour Research and Therapy*, 13: 295–9.

Eldridge, H. and Gibbs, P. (1987) 'Strategies for Preventing Reoffending: A Course for Sex Offenders', *Probation Journal*, 34.1: 7–9.

Elias, N. (1939) *The Civilizing Process, Vol. 2: State Formation and Civilization*, trans. Edmund Jephcott. Oxford: Basil Blackwell.

Elikann, P. (1996) *The Tough-On-Crime Myth: Real Solutions to Cut Crime*. New York: Insight Books.

Emery, R. E. and Marholin, U. (1977). 'An Applied Behavior Analysis of Delinquency: the Irrelevancy of Relevant Behavior', *American Psychologist*, 32: 860–73.

Emmons, R. A. (1996) 'Striving and Feeling: Personal Goals and Subjective Well-being', in P. M. Gollwitzer and J. A. Bargh (eds), *The Psychology of Action: Linking Cognition and Motivation to Behavior*. New York: Guilford.

Emmons, R. A. (1999) *The Psychology of Ultimate Concerns*. New York: Guilford.

Empey, L. and Erickson, M. (1972) *The Provo Experiment*. New York, NY: Lexington Books.

Fagan, R. (1999) 'The Use of Required Treatment for Substance Abusers', *Substance Abuse*, 20.4: 249–61.

Fagan, J. and Hartson, E. (1986) 'Innovation and Experimentation in Juvenile Corrections: Implementing a Community Reintegration Model for Violent Juveniles' (unpublished manuscript). URSA.

Farbring, C. A. (2000). 'The Drug Treatment Programme at Österåker Prison: Experience from a Therapeutic Community During the Years 1978–1998', *American Jails*, March–April, pp. 85–96.

Farrall, S. (2002) *Rethinking What Works with Offenders: Probation, Social Context and Desistance from Crime*. Cullompton: Willan.

Farrall, S. and Calverley, A. (2006) *Understanding Desistance from Crime: Theoretical Directions in Resettlement and Rehabilitation*. Maidenhead: Open University Press.

Farrington, D.P. (1986) 'Age and Crime', in N. Morris and M. Tonry (eds), *Crime and Justice: An Annual Review of Research, Vol. 7*. Chicago: Chicago University Press.

Farrington, D.P. (1992) 'Explaining the Beginning, Progress, and Ending of Antisocial Behaviour from Birth to Adulthood', in J. McCord (ed.), *Facts, Frameworks, and Forecasts: Advances in Criminological Theory, Vol. 3*. New Brunswick, NJ: Transaction Publishers.

Farrington, D. P. and West, D. J. (1995) 'Effects of Marriage, Separation and Children on Offending by Adult Males', in Z. S. Blau and J. Hagan (eds), *Current Perspectives on Aging and the Life Cycle, Vol 4: Delinquency and Disrepute in the Life Course*. Greenwich, CT: JAI Press.

Farrington, D. P., Gallagher, B., Morley, L., St Ledger, R. J. and West, D. J. (1986) 'Unemployment, School Leaving and Crime', *British Journal of Criminology*, 26: 335–56.

Feeley, M. and Simon, J. (1992) 'The New Penology: Notes on the Emerging Strategy of Corrections and Its Implications', *Criminology*, 30.4: 449–74.

Feldman, M. P. (1977) *Criminal Behaviour: A Psychological Analysis*. New York: Wiley.

Fenton, N. (1956) 'The Prison as a Therapeutic Community', *Federal Probation*: 26–29.

Ferri, E. (1972) 'The Positive School of Criminology', in Stanley. E. Grupp (ed.), *Theories of Punishment*. Bloomington, IN: Indiana University Press.

Finckenauer, J. (1982) *Scared Straight: The Panacea Phenomenon*. Rutgers University, Englewood Cliffs, NJ: Prentice Hall.

Fingarette, H. (1963) *The Self in Transformation*. New York and London: Harper & Row.

Finigan, M. W., Carey, S. M. and Cox, A. (2007) *The Impact of a Mature Drug Court Over 10 Years of Operation: Recidivism and Costs. Final Report*. Portland State University, Oregon.

Fitzgerald, M. (1977) *Prisoners in Revolt*. Harmondsworth: Penguin.

Flew, A. (1973) *Crime or Disease*. London: MacMillan.

Folkard, M. S., Fowles, A. J., McWilliams, B. C., Smith, D. D., Smith, D. E. and Walmsley, G. R. (1974) *IMPACT. Intensive Matched Probation and After-Care Treatment. Volume 1. The Design of the Probation Experiment and an Interim Evaluation*, Home Office Research Study No. 24. London: HMSO.

Folkard, M. S., Smith, D. E. and Smith, D. D. (1976) *IMPACT: Intensive Matched Probation and After-Care Treatment. Volume II. The Results of the Experiment*. Home Office Research Study No. 36, London: HMSO.

Follett, M. (1934 [1981]) *The New State, Group Organization and the Solution of Popular Government* (rev. ed). New York: Longmans, Green.

Foren, R. and Bailey, R. (1968) *Authority in Social Casework*. London: Pergamon Press.

Forsyth, W. J. (1987) *The Reform of Prisoners 1830–1900*. London: Croom Helm.

Foucault, M. (1977) *Discipline and Punish. The Birth of the Prison*. London: Allen Lane.

Fowles, A. J. (1978.) *Prison Welfare: An Account of an Experiment at Liverpool*. Home Office Research Study 45. Home Office research Unit. HMSO.

Frank, J. D. (1979) 'The present status of outcome studies', *Journal of Consulting and Clinical Psychology*, 47: 310–16.

Freedman, B. J., Rosenthal, L., Donahoe, C. P., Schlundt, D. G. and Mcfall, R. M. (1978) 'A Social-Behavioral Analysis of Skill Deficits in Delinquents and Non-Delinquent Adolescent Boys', *Journal of Consulting and Clinical Psychology*, 46: 1448–92.

Freeguard, M. (1964) 'Five Girls against Authority', *New Society*, 13th February pp. 18–20.

Gallagher, C. A., Wilson, D. B., Hirschfield, P., Coggleshall, M. B. and MacKenzie, D. L. (1999) 'The effects of sex offender treatment on sexual reoffending', *Corrections Management Quarterly*, 9.4: 19–29.

Garland, D. (1985) *Punishment and Welfare: A History of Penal Strategies*. Aldershot: Gower.

Garland, D. (1990) *Punishment and Modern Society: A Study in Social Theory*. Oxford: Clarendon Press.

Garland, D. (2000) 'The Culture of High Crime Societies', *British Journal of Criminology*, 40: 347–75.

Garland, D. and Young, P. (eds) (1983) *The Power to Punish – Contemporary Penality and Social Analysis*. New York: Humanities Press.

Gecas, V. and Schwalbe, M. L. (1983) 'Beyond the Looking-Glass Self: Social Structure and Efficacy-Based Self-Esteem', *Social Psychology Quarterly*, 46: 77–88.

Gendreau, P. and Ross, R. R. (1979) 'Effective Correctional Treatment: Bibliotherapy for Cynics', *Crime and Delinquency*, 25: 463–89.

Gendreau, P. and Ross, R. R. (1981) 'Offender Rehabilitation: The Appeal of Success', *Federal Probation*, 45: 45–8.

Gendreau, P. and Ross, R. R. (1987) 'Revivication of Rehabilitation', *Justice Quarterly*, 4.3: 349–407.

Gendreau, P., Little, T., and Goggin, C. (1995) *A Meta-analysis of the Predictors of Adult Offender Recidivism: What Works!* Unpublished manuscript, University of New Brunswick, St John, Canada.

Gergen, K. J. (1991) *The Saturated Self*. New York: Basic Books.

Gibbens, T. C. (1984) 'Borstal Boys After 25 Years', *British Journal of Criminology*, 24: 46–59.

Giddens, A. (1991) *Modernity and Self-Identity: Self and Society in the Late Modern Age*. Stanford, CA: Stanford University Press.

Gilligan, J. (1997) *Violence: Reflections on a National Epidemic*. New York: Vintage Books.

Gilligan, J. and Lee, B. (2004) 'Beyond the Prison Paradigm: From Provoking Violence to Preventing It by Creating "Anti-Prisons" (Residential Colleges and Therapeutic Communities)', *Annals of the New York Academy of Sciences*, 1036: 300–24.

Glaser, D. (1964) *The Effectiveness of a Prison and Parole System*. Indianapolis, IN: Bobbs-Merrill.

Gluckman, M. (1967) *The Judicial Process Among the Barotse of Northern Rhodesia*. Manchester: Manchester University Press.

Glueck, S. (1928) 'Principles of a Rational Penal Code', *Harvard Law Review*, 41: 453–82.

Glueck, S. (1933) 'The Significance and Promise of Probation', in S. Glueck (ed.), *Probation and Criminal Justice. Essays in Honor of Herbert. C. Parsons*. New York: Macmillan.

Glueck, S. and Glueck, E. (1940) *Juvenile Delinquents Grown Up*. New York: Commonwealth Fund.

Golding, R. R. W. (1959) 'A Probation Technique', *Probation*, 9: 47–9.

Goldstein, P. J. (1985) 'The drugs-violence nexus: a tripartite conceptual framework', *Journal of Drug Issues*, 15: 493–506.

Goldstein, P. J. (1989) 'Drugs and violent crime', in N.A. Weiner and M.E. Wolfgang (eds) *Pathways to Criminal Violence*. Newbury Park: CA. Sage Publications.

Goldstein, P. J., Brownstein, H. H., Ryan, P. J. and Bellucci, P. A. (1989) 'Crack and homicide in New York City, 1988: a conceptually based event analysis', *Contemporary Drug Problems*, 16: 651–687.

Gordon, M. (1922) *Penal Discipline*. London: Routledge.

Gottfredson, M. and Hirschi, T. (1990) *A General Theory of Crime*. Stanford, CA: Stanford University Press.

Gouldner, A. W. (1960) 'The Norm of Reciprocity: A Preliminary Statement', *American Sociological Review*, 25.2: 161–78.

Grant, J. D. (1968) 'The Offender as a Correctional Manpower Resource', in F. Riessmand and H. Popper, (eds), *Up From Poverty: New Career Ladder for Non-Professionals*. New York: Harper & Row, pp. 229–30.

Greenwood, P. and Turner, S. (1987) *Selective Incapacitation Revisited. Why the high-rate offenders are hard to predict*. Santa Monica, CA: RAND.

Grimsrud, T. and Zehr, T (2002) 'Rethinking God, Justice, and Treatment of Offenders', *Journal of Offender Rehabilitation*, 35.3/4: 259–85.

Gumz, E. J. (2004) 'American Social Work, Corrections and Restorative Justice: An Appraisal', *International Journal of Offender Therapy and Comparative Criminology*, 48.4: 449–60.

Haines, K. (1990) *After-Care for Released Prisoners: A Review of the Literature*. Cambridge: Institute of Criminology.

Halliday, J. (2001) *Making Punishments Work: Report of a Review of the Sentencing Framework for England and Wales*. London: Home Office.

Halmos, P.(1965) *The Faith of the Counsellors*. London: Constable.

Hamparian, D. M., Schuster, R., Dinitz, S. and Conrad, J. P. (1978) *The Violent Few*. D.C. Heath: Lexington Books.

Harding, J. (1973) 'Community Service – A Beginning', *Probation Journal*, 1.19: 13–17.

Heimler, E. (1975) *Survival in Society*. London: Weidenfield & Nicolson.

Henry, S. (1985) 'Community Justice, Capitalist Society, and Human Agency: The Dialectics of Collective Law in the Cooperative', *Law and Society Review*, 19.2: 301–25.

Hignett, C. (2000) '"Punish And Rehabilitate" – Do They Mean Us?', *Probation Journal*, 47.1: 51–2.

Hill, M. D. (1857) *Suggestions for the Repression of Crime Contained in Charges Delivered to the Grand Juries of Birmingham Supported by Additional Facts and Arguments: Together with Articles from Reviews and Newspapers Controverting or Advocating the Conclusions of the Author*. London: John W. Parker & Son.

Hinton, N. (1973) 'Offenders as Social Workers', *Social Work Today*, 25 January.

Hirschi, T. (1969) *Causes of Delinquency*, Berkeley and Los Angeles: University of California Press.

Hodgkin, N. (1973) *New Careers for the Disadvantaged*, London: NACRO.

Hoghughi, M. S. and Forrest, A. R. (1970) 'Eysenck's Theory of Criminality', *British Journal of Criminology*, 10: 240–54.

Holmes, T. (1902) *Pictures and Problems from London Police Courts*. London: Edward Arnold.

Holmes, T. (1908) *Known to the Police*. London: Edward Arnold.

Home Office (1988) *Punishment, Custody and the Community*, Cm 424. London: HMSO.

Hough, M. (1996) *Drugs Misuse and the Criminal Justice System*, Drugs Prevention Initiative Paper No. 15. London: Home Office.

Howard, M. (1993) Speech to Conservative Party Conference, 6 October.

Howarth, E. (1951) 'The present dilemma of social casework', *Social Work*, April.

Huddleston, III, C. W., Freeman-Wilson, Judge, K., Marlowe, D. B. and Roussell, A. (2005) 'Problem-Solving Courts: Emerging Permutations', *Painting the Current Picture: A National Report Card on Drug Courts and Other Problem Solving Court Programs in the United States*. National Drug Court Institute, Vol. 1, No. 1, pp. 9–10.

Hudson, B. (1987) *Justice through Punishment: A Critique of the 'Justice Model' of Corrections*. Basingstoke: Macmillan.

Hudson, B. (1996) *Understanding Justice: An Introduction to the Ideas, Perspectives and Controversies in Modern Penal Theory*. Buckingham: Open University Press.

Hudson, B. (2003) *Understanding Justice* (2nd edn). Buckingham: Open University Press.

Hudson, J., Morris, A., Maxwell, G. and Galaway, B. (eds) (1996) *Family Group Conferences: Perspectives on Policy and Practice*. Annandale: Federation Press.

Hunt, A. W. (1964) 'Enforcement in Probation Casework', *British Journal of Criminology*, 4.3: 239–52.

Ignatieff, M. (1978) *A Just Measure of Pain. The Penitentiary in the Industrial Revolution 1750-1850*. New York: Pantheon Books.

Inner London Probation Service (1972) *Proposal Paper for the Establishment of a Day Training Centre within the Area*. Unpublished paper.

Irwin, J. (1970) *The Felon*. Englewood Cliffs, NJ: Prentice-Hall.

James, P. (1985) 'Day Centres', in H. Walker and B. Beaumont (eds), *Working with Offenders*. London: Macmillan.

Jenkins, P. (1982) 'The Radicals and the Rehabilitative Ideal 1890–1930', *Criminology*, 20.3/4: 347–72.

Jenkins, P. (1983) 'Erewhon: A Manifesto of the Rehabilitative Ideal', *Journal of Criminal Justice*. 11.1: 35–46.

Johnson, R. (2002) *Hard Time* (3rd edn). Belmont, CA: Wadsworth.

Johnstone, G. (2001) *Restorative Justice: Ideas, Values, Debates*. Cullompton: Willan.

Jones, M., Mordecai, M., Rutter, F. and Thomas, L. (1993) 'A Miskin Model of Groupwork with Women Offenders', in A. Brown and B. Caddick (eds), *Groupwork with Offenders*. London: Whiting & Birch.

Jorgensen, E. (1998) *Elvis Presley: A Life in Music*. New York, St. Martins Press.

Kauffman. K. (1990.) 'The Prison as a Just Community', *New Directions for Child Development*, 47: 77–80.

Keith, C. R. (1984) 'Individual Psychotherapy and Psychoanalysis with the Aggressive Adolescent: A Historical Review' in C. R. Keith (ed) *The Aggressive Adolescent*, Glencoe, Free Press.

Kekes, J. (1989) *Moral Tradition and Individuality*. Princeton, NJ: Princeton University Press.

Kenemore, T. K. and Roldan, I. (2006) 'Staying Straight: Lessons from Ex-offenders', *Clinical Social Work Journal*, 34.1: 5–21.

King, J. (1969) *The Probation and After-Care Service* (3rd edn). London: Butterworth.

Klein, N. C., Alexander, J. F. and Parsons, B. V. (1977) 'Impact of Family Systems Intervention on Recidivism, and Sibling Delinquency; A Model of Primary Prevention and Program Evaluation', *Journal of Consulting and Clinical Psychology*, 45: 469–74.

Kohlberg, L., Kauffman, K., Scharf, P. and Hickey, J. (1975) 'The Just Community Approach to Corrections: A Theory', *Journal of Moral Education*, 4.3: 43–60.

Krisberg, B., Austin, J., Steele, P. (1989) *Unlocking Juvenile Corrections; Evaluating the Massachusetts Department of Youth Services*. San Francisco, California: National Council on Crime and Delinquency.

Lawson, J. (1984) 'Probation in St. Pauls. Teamwork in a Multi-Racial, Inner-City Area', *Probation Journal*, 31.3: 93–5.

Lazarus, A. A. (1976) *Multimodal Behavior Therapy*. New York: Springer.

Le Mesurier, L. (1935) *A Handbook of Probation*. London: National Association of Probation Officers.

Lee, J. in collaboration with Barnes, G., Bennett, S., Angle, C. M., Newbury-Birch, D., Woods, D. J. and Gill, C. E. (2007) *Program of Randomized Trials in Restorative Justice*. London: Smith Institute.

Leeson, C. (1914) *The Probation System*. London: P. S. King & Son.

Leibrich, J. (1993) *Straight to the Point: Angles on Giving Up Crime*. Otago, New Zealand: University of Otago Press.

Lemert, E.M. (1964) 'Social structure, social control, and deviant behavior', in Marshall B. Clinard (ed.), *Anomie and Deviant Behavior: A Discussion and Critique*. New York: Free Press of Glencoe.

Lemert, E. M. and Dill, F. (1978) *Offenders in the Community – The Probation Subsidy in California*. New York: Lexington Books.

Levrant, S., Cullen, F., Fulton, B. and Wozniak, J. (1999) 'Reconsidering Restorative Justice: The Corruption of Benevolence Revisited?', *Crime and Delinquency*, 45.1: 3–27.

Lewin, K. (1935) *A Dynamic Theory of Personality*. New York: McGraw-Hill.

Lewis, C. S. (1949) 'The Humanitarian Theory of Punishment', *20th Century: An Australian Quarterly Review*, 3.3: 5–12.

Lewis, C. S. (1950) *The Lion, The Witch, and the Wardrobe*. London: Geoffrey Bles.

Lewis, S. (2005) 'Rehabilitation: Headline or Footnote in the New Penal Policy?', *Probation Journal*, 52.2: 119–35.

Liberman, R. P., King, L. W., DeRisi, McCann, M. (1975) *Personal Effectiveness*. Champaign. IL: Research Press.

Lilly, J. R., Cullen, F. T. and Ball, R. A. (1989) *Criminological Theory: Context and Consequences*, London: Sage.

Lipsey, M.W. (1992). 'Juvenile Delinquency Treatment: A Meta-analytic Inquiry into the Variability of Effects, in T. D. Cook *et al.* (eds) *Meta-analysis for Explanation: A Casebook*. New York: Russell Sage.

Lipsey, M. W. and Wilson, D. B. (1998) 'Effective Intervention for Serious Juvenile Offenders: A Synthesis of Research' in R. Loeber and D. P. Farrington (eds), *Serious and Violent Juvenile Offenders: Risk Factors and Successful Interventions*. Thousand Oaks, CA: Sage.

Lipton, D., Martinson, R. and Wilks, J. (1975) *The Effectiveness of Correctional Treatment: A Survey of Treatment Valuation Studies*. New York: Praeger.

Lösel, F. (1995) 'The Efficacy of Correctional Treatment: A Review and Synthesis of Meta-evaluations', in J. McGuire (ed.), *What Works: Reducing Re-offending: Guidelines from Research and Practice*. Chichester: John Wiley & Sons.

Lowson, D. (1975) 'Borstal Training: Its History, Achievements and Prospects', in J. B. Mays (ed.), *The Social Treatment of Young Offenders*, London: Longman.

McAdams, D. P. (1985) *Power, Intimacy and the Life Story: Personological Inquiries into Identity*. New York: The Guilford Press.

McAdams, D. P. (1994) 'Can Personality Change? Levels of Stability and Growth in Personality Across the Life Span', in T. F. Heatherton and J. L. Weinberger (eds), *Can Personality Change?* Washington, DC: American Psychological Association.

McAdams, D. P. and de St Aubin, E. (1998) 'Introduction', in D. P. McAdams and E. de St. Aubin (eds), *Generativity and Adult Development: How and Why We Care for the Next Generation*. Washington, DC: American Psychological Association.

McCold, P. (2004) 'Paradigm Muddle: The Threat to Restorative Justice Posed by Its Merger with Community Justice', *Contemporary Justice Review*, 7.1: 13–35.

McConville, S. (1998) 'The Victorian Prison: England, 1865–1965', in N. Morris and D. J. Rothman, (eds), *The Oxford History of the Prison. The Practice of Punishment in Western Society*. Oxford University Press: Oxford.

McCord, J. (1959) *Origins of Crime: A New Evaluation of the Cambridge-Somerville Youth Study*. Columbia University Press .

McCullough, M. K. (1963) 'Groupwork in Probation', *New Society*, 21: 9–11.

McGowen, R. (1998) 'The Well-Ordered Prison: England, 1780–1865', in N. Morris and D. J. Rothman (eds), *The Oxford History of the Prison. The Practice of Punishment in Western Society*. Oxford University Press: Oxford.

McGuire, J. (2003) 'Maintaining Change: Converging Legal and Psychological Initiatives in a Therapeutic Jurisprudence Framework', *Western Criminology Review*, 4.2: 108–23.

McGuire, J. and Priestley, P. (1985) *Offending Behaviour: Skills and Stratagems for Going Straight*. London: Batsford.

McIvor, G. (1990) *Sanctions for Persistent or Serious Offenders: A Review of the Literature*. Social Work Research Centre, University of Stirling.

McIvor, G. (1998) 'Pro-Social Modelling and Legitimacy: Lessons from a Study of Community Service', in S. Rex and A. Matravers (eds), *Pro-Social Modelling and Legitimacy: The Clarke Hall Day Conference*. Cambridge: Institute of Criminology, University of Cambridge, pp. 53–62.

MacKenzie, D. L. (1997) 'Criminal Justice and Crime Prevention', in L. W. Sherman, D. Gottfredson, D. L. MacKenzie, J. Eck, P. Reuter and S. Bushway (eds), *Preventing Crime: What Works What Doesn't, What's Promising*. Washington, DC: National Institute of Justice, pp. 1–76.

MacKenzie, D. L. (2000) 'Evidence-Based Corrections: Identifying What Works', *Crime and Delinquency*, 46.4: 457–71.

McVicar, J. (1974) *McVicar by Himself*. London: Hutchinson.

McWilliams, W. (1983) 'The Mission to the English Police Courts 1876–1936,' *Howard Journal of Criminal Justice*, 22.3: 129–47.

McWilliams, W. and Pease, K. (1990) 'Probation Practice and an End to Punishment', *Howard Journal*, 29.1: 14–24.

Mair, G. (1988) *Probation Day Centres*. London: HMSO.

Maloney, D. (1998) *The Challenge of Restorative Community Justice*. Address at the Annual Meeting of the Juvenile Justice Coalition, Washington, DC, February.

Marcuse, H. (1964) *One Dimensional Man*. London: Routledge & Kegan Paul.

Marshall, T. and Merry, S. (1990) *Crime and Accountability: Victim/Offender Mediation in Practice*. London: Home Office, HMSO.

Martinson, R. (1966) 'The Age of Treatment: Some Implications of the Custody–Treatment Dimension', *Issues in Criminology*, 2: 275–93.

Martinson, R. (1972) 'Paradox of Prison Reform', *The New Republic*, 166, April 1, 6, 15 and 29.

Martinson, R. (1974), 'What Works? Questions and Answers About Prison Reform', *The Public Interest*, 35: 22–54.

Martinson, R. (1979) 'New Findings, New Views: A Note of Caution Regarding Sentence Reform', *Hofstra Law Review*, 7: 242–258.

Maruna, S. (1998) 'Desistance and Development: The Psychosocial Process of "Going Straight"', *British Criminology Conferences: Selected Proceedings. Volume 2. Papers from the British Criminology Conference*, Queens University, Belfast, 15–19 July 1997.

Maruna, S. (2001) *Making Good: How Ex-Convicts Reform and Rebuild Their Lives*. Washington, DC: American Psychological Association.

Maruna, S. and LeBel, P. T. (2003) 'Welcome Home? Examining the "Reentry Court" Concept from a Strengths-based Perspective', *Western Criminology Review*, 4.2: 91–107.

Maruna, S., LeBel, T.P., Mitchell, N. and Naples, M. (2004) 'Pygmalion in the Reintegration Process: Desistance from Crime through the Looking Glass', *Psychology, Crime and Law*, 10.3: 271–81.

Mathiesen, T. (1974) *The Politics of Abolition*. London: Martin Robertson.

Mathiesen, T. (1983) 'The Future of Control Systems – The Case of Norway', in D. Garland and P. Young (eds), *The Power to Punish*. London: Heinemann.

Mathiesen, T. (1990) *Prison on Trial: A Critical Assessment*. London: Sage.

Matza, D. (1964) *Delinquency and Drift*. New York: John Wiley and Sons.

May, P. (1991) *Probation: Politics, Policy and Practice*. Buckingham: Open University Press.

Meichenbaum, D. H. and Goodman, J. (1971) 'Training Impulsive Children to Talk to Themselves: A Means of Developing Self-Control', *Journal of Abnormal Psychology*, 77: 115–26.

Meisenhelder, T. (1977) 'An Exploratory Study of Exiting from Criminal Careers', *Criminology*, 15: 319–34.

Merrington, S. and Hine, J. (2001) *A Handbook for Evaluating Probation Work with Offenders*. London: Home Office.

Meyer, C. H. (1972) 'Practice on microsystem level.' in: E. J. Mullen, J. R. Dumpson and Associates (eds) *Evaluation of social intervention*. (1st ed.). San Francisco: Jossey-Bass.

Miczek, K. A., DeBold, J. F., Haney, M., Tidey, J., Vivian, J. and Weerts, E. M. (1994) 'Alcohol, drugs of abuse, aggression and violence', in A. J. Reiss, Jr. and J. A. Roth (eds), *Understanding and Preventing Violence, Vol. III*, Washington, DC: National Academy Press.

Miles. A. P. (1954) *American Social Work Theory*. New York: Harper.

Milkman, R. H. (1985) *Employment Services for Ex-offenders Field Test-Detailed Research Results*. McLean, VA: Lazar Institute.

Miller, J. G. (1989) 'The Debate on Rehabilitating Criminals: Is It True that Nothing Works?', *Washington Post*, April 23.

Miller, J. G. (1991) *Last One Over the Wall: The Massachusetts Experiment in Closing Reform Schools*. Columbus, OH: Ohio State University Press.

Millham, S,. Bullock, R. and Hosie, K. (1978) 'Another Try: An Account of a New Careers Project for Borstal Trainees', in N. Tutt (ed.), *Alternative Strategies for Coping with Crime*. Oxford: Basil Blackwell.

Mischkowitz, R. (1994) 'Desistance from a Delinquent Way of Life?', in E. G. M. Weitekamp and H. J. Kerner (eds), *Cross-National Longitudinal Research on Human Development and Criminal Behaviour*. London: Kluwer.

Mitchell-Clarke, V. (1998) *Groupwork with Black Offenders*, unpublished Masters Dissertation. Leicester: Scarman Centre.

Molm, L. and Cook, K. (1995) 'Social Exchange and Exchange Networks', in K. Cook, G. Fine, and J. House (eds), *Sociological Perspectives on Social Psychology*. Boston: Allyn & Bacon.

Morgan, R. (2009) *Too Much to Ask: The Leaps and Bounds Story*. London: Arts Council England and Solomon White Publications.

Morley, H. (1986) 'Heimler's Human Social Functioning', *Probation Journal*, 33.4: 140–2.

Morris, A. (2002) 'Critiquing the Critics: A Brief Response to Critics of Restorative Justice', *British Journal of Criminology*, 42.3: 596–615.

Mulvey, E. P. and LaRosa, J. F. (1986) 'Delinquency Cessation and Adolescent Development: Primary Data', *American Journal of Orthopsychiatry*, 56.2: 212–24.

Mumola, C. J. (1999) *Substance Abuse and Treatment, State and Federal Prisoners* NCJ 172871. Washington, DC: US Government Printing Office.

Murphy, J. (1970) *Kant: The Philosophy of Right*. New York: St. Martin's Press.

Murphy, M. C. (2001) *Natural Law and Practical Rationality*. New York: Cambridge University Press.

Murray, C. A. and Cox, L. A. (1979) *Beyond Probation: Juvenile Corrections and the Chronic Delinquent*. Beverly Hills, CA: Sage.

Murray, H. A. (1938) *Explorations in Personality*. Oxford: Oxford University Press.

National Offender Management Service. *HC Deb 20 July 2004 vol 424 cc17-8WS The Parliamentary Under-Secretary of State for the Home Department (Paul Goggins)*.

Nellis, M. (2003) 'Probation Training and the Community Justice Curriculum', *British Journal of Social Work*, 33: 943–59.

Nellis, M. (2007) 'Humanising Justice: The English Probation System up to 1972', in L. Gelsthorpe and R. Morgan (eds), *Handbook of Probation*. Cullompton: Willan.

Newburn, T. (2007) *Criminology*. Cullompton: Willan.

Newman, G. and Marongui, P. (1990) 'Penological Reform and the Myth of Beccaria', *Criminology*, 28.2: 325–46.

Nussbaum, M. C. (2000) *Women and Human Development: the Capabilities Approach*. New York: Cambridge University Press.

O'Leary, V. and Duffee, D. (1971) 'Correctional Policy; A Classification of Goals Designed for Change', *Crime and Delinquency*, 17: 373–86.

Palmer, T. (1975) 'Martinson revisited', *Journal of Research in Crime and Delinquency*, 12: 133–52.

Palmer, T. (1978) *Correctional Intervention and Research – Current Issues and Future Prospects*. New York, Lexington Books.

Parker, T. (1963) *The Unknown Citizen*. London: Hutchinson.

Parkinson, G. (1965) 'Casework and the Persistent Offender', *Probation*, 11.1: 11–17.

Patten, J. (1988) 'Punishment, the Probation Service and the Community'. Unpublished address to the Annual Conference of Chief Officers of Probation. Leeds: Home Office.

Patten, J. (1992) 'There Is a Choice: Good or Evil', *The Spectator*, 18 April.

Pearl A. and F. Riessman (1965) *New Careers for the Poor: The Professional in Human Service*. New York: The Free Press.

Pease. K. (1983) 'Penal Innovations', in J. Lishman (ed.), *Research Highlights 5: Social Work with Adult Offenders*. Aberdeen: University of Aberdeen.

Pease, K., Durkin, P., Earnshaw, I., Payne, D. and Thorpe, J. (1975) *Community Service Orders*, Home Office Research Study No. 29, London, HMSO.

Petersilia, J. (1993) 'Measuring the Performance of Community Corrections', in J. J. Dilulio Jr and J. Q. Wilson (eds), *Performance Measures for the Criminal Justice System*. Washington, DC: Bureau of Justice Statistics.

Petersilia, J. (2004) 'What Works in Prisoner Reentry? Reviewing and Questioning the Evidence', *Federal Probation*, 68.2: 4–8.

Petersilia, J. and Turner, S. (1992) 'Intensive Supervision Programs for Drug Offenders', in J. M. Byrne, A. J. Lurigio and J. Petersilia (eds), *Smart Sentencing: The Emergence of Intermediate Sanctions*. Newbury Park, CA: Sage, pp. 18–37.

Pezzin, L. E. (1995) 'Earnings Prospects, Matching Effects, and the Decision to Terminate a Criminal Career', *Journal of Quantitative Criminology*, 11, 29–50.

Pinker, R. (1971) 'Exchange and Stigma', in *Social Theory and Social Policy*. London: Heinemann Educational, ch. 9.

Plant, R. (1980) 'Justice, punishment and the state', in A. Bottoms and R. Preston (eds), *The Coming Penal Crisis: A Criminological and Theological Explanation*. Edinburgh: Scottish Academic.

Polizzi, D. M., MacKenzie, D. L. and Hickman, L. (1999) 'What Works in Adult Sex Offender Treatment?' A Review of Prison- and Non-Prison-Based Treatment Programs', *International Journal of Offender Therapy and Comparative Criminology*, 43: 357–74.

Poulton, F. (1925) 'The Spiritual Factor in Probation Work', *National Association of Probation Officers*, 23: 546–7.

Powers, E. and Witmer, H. (1951) 'An Experiment in the Prevention of Delinquency', *The Cambridge Somerville Youth Study Project*, Columbia University Press.

Pratt, J. (2002) *Punishment and Civilization*. London: Sage.

Prentice, N. M. and Kelly, F. J. (1963) 'Intelligence and delinquency: a reconsideration'. *Journal of Social Psychology*, 60: 327–37.

Priestley, P. (1970) *The Problem of the Short Term Prisoner*. Cheltenham, NACRO.

Priestley. P. (1975) 'New Careers: Power Sharing in Social Work', in H. Jones (ed.), *Towards a New Social Work*. London: Routledge & Kegan Paul.

Priestley, P. (1998) *Victorian Prison Lives: English Prison Biography 1830–1914*. Paperback edn. London: Random House.

Priestley, P. and Vanstone, M. (2006) 'Abolishing Probation – A Political Crime?', *Probation Journal*, 53.4: 408–16.

Prochaska. J. O. and DiClemente. C. C. (1984) *The Transtheoretical Approach: Crossing Traditional Boundaries of Therapy*. Homewood, IL: Dow Jones/Irwin.

Prochaska. J. O. and DiClemente. C. C. (1986) 'Toward a Comprehensive Model of Change', in W. R. Miller and N. Heather (eds), *Treating Addictive Behaviors: Processes of Change*. New York: Plenum Press.

Quetelet, A. (1833) *Recherches Sur le Penchant au Crime aux Différents Ages*. Belgium: Hayez.

Quinney, R. and Wildeman, J. (1991) *The Problem of Crime: A Peace and Social Justice Perspective*. Mountain View, CA: Mayfield.

Radical Alternatives to Prison (RAP) (1971) *The Case for Radical Alternatives to Prison*. London: Christian Action Publications.

Rand, A. (1987) 'Transitional Life Events and Desistance from Delinquency and Crime', in M.E. Wolfgang, T.P. Thornberry and R.M. Figlio (eds), *From Boy to Man, from Delinquency to Crime*. Chicago: University of Chicago Press.

Rankin, C. (1921) 'The Problem of the Difficult Case', *National Association of Probation Officers*, 16: 321–3.

Rapp, C. A. (1998) *The Strengths Model: Case Management with People Suffering from Severe and Persistent Mental Illness*. New York: Oxford University Press.

Raynor, P. (1978) 'Compulsory Persuasion: A Problem for Correctional Social Work', *British Journal of Social Work*, 8.4: 411–24.

Raynor, P. (1985) *Social Work, Justice and Control*. Oxford: Blackwell.

Raynor, P. (1988) *Probation as an Alternative to Custody*. Aldershot: Avebury.

Raynor, P. (1993) *Social Work, Justice and Control*. London: Whiting & Birch.

Raynor, P. (1997) 'Some Observations on Rehabilitation and Justice', *Howard Journal* 36.3: 248–62.

Raynor, P. and Robinson, G. (2005) *Rehabilitation, Crime and Justice*. London: Palgrave Macmillan.

Raynor, P. and Vanstone, M. (1992) 'Stop, Start', *Social Work Today*, 23,.21: 22–3.

Raynor, P. and Vanstone, M. (1994) 'Probation Practice, Effectiveness and the Non-Treatment Paradigm', *British Journal of Social Work*, 24.4: 387–404.

Raynor, P. and Vanstone, M. (1997) *Straight Thinking on Probation (STOP): The Mid Glamorgan Experiment*. Probation Studies Unit Report No. 4. Oxford: University of Oxford.

Raynor, P., Smith, D. and Vanstone, M. (1994) *Effective Probation Practice*. Basingstoke: Macmillan.

Reckless, W. and Dinitz, S. (1967) 'Pioneering with Self-concept as a Vulnerability Factor in Delinquency', *Journal of Criminal Law, Criminology and Police Science*, 58.4: 515–23.

Redondo, S., Sanchez-Meca, J. and Garrido, V. (1999) 'The Influence of Treatment Programmes on the Recidivism of Juvenile and Adult Offenders: A European Meta-analytic Review', *Psychology, Crime and Law*, 5.3: 251–78.

Reichman, N. (1986) 'Managing Crime Risks: Toward an Insurance-Based Model of Social Control', *Research in Law, Deviance and Social Control*, 8: 151–72.

Reid, W. J. and Epstein, L. (1972) *Task-Centred Casework*. New York: Columbia University Press.

Reiman.J. (1988) *The Rich Get Richer and the Poor Get Prison*. Boston: Allyn & Bacon.

Rescher, N. (1990) *Human Interests: Reflections on Philosophical Anthropology*. Stanford, CA: Stanford University Press.

Rex, S. (1999) 'Desistance from Offending: Experiences of Probation', *Howard Journal of Criminal Justice*, 38: 366–83.

Rex, S. (2001) 'Beyond Cognitive-Behaviouralism? Reflections on the Effectiveness Literature', in A. Bottoms, L. Gelsthorpe and S. Rex (eds), *Community Penalties: Change and Challenges*. Cullompton: Willan.

Rex, S. and J. Gelsthorpe (2004) 'Using Community Service to Encourage Inclusive Citizenship', in R. Burnett and C. Roberts (eds), *What Works in Probation and Youth Justice: Developing Evidence-Based Practice*, Cullompton: Willan.

Rhodes, W. and Gross, M. (1997) 'Case Management Reduces Drug Use and Criminality Among Drug-Involved Arrestees: An Experimental Study of an HIV Prevention Intervention'. Unpublished manuscript submitted to the National Institute of Justice and the National Institute on Drug Abuse, Washington, DC.

Ricoeur, P. (1984) *Time and Narrative, Vol. 1.* Chicago: University of Chicago.

Roberton, A. (1961) 'Casework in Borstal', *Prison Service Journal*, 1.2: 15–22.

Roberts, C. H. (1989) *Hereford and Worcester Probation Service Young Offender Project: First Evaluation Report.* Oxford: Department of Social and Administrative Studies, Oxford University.

Robinson, G. and Raynor, P. (2006), 'The Future of Rehabilitation: What Role for the Probation Service?', *Probation Journal*, 53.4: 334–46.

Robinson, T. (1978) *In Worlds Apart: Professionals and Their Clients in the Welfare State.* London: Bedford Square Press.

Robison, J. and Smith, G. (1971) 'The Effectiveness of Correctional Programs', *Crime and Delinquency*, 17: 67–80.

Rock, P. (1990) *Helping Victims of Crime: The Home Office and the Rise of Victim Support in England and Wales.* Oxford: Oxford University Press.

Rose, N. (1985) *The Psychological Complex. Psychology, Politics and Society in England, 1869–1939.* London: Routledge & Kegan Paul.

Rose, N. (1996) 'Psychiatry as a Political Science: Advanced Liberalism and the Administration of Risk', *History of the Human Sciences*, 9.2: 1–23.

Ross, R. R. (1980) *Socio-Cognitive Development in the Offender: An External Review of the UVIC Program at Matsqui Penitentiary.* Ottawa: Ministry of the Solicitor General.

Ross, R. R. and Fabiano, E. (1980) *Time to Think: Cognition and Crime: Link and Remediation.* Ottawa: Ministry of the Solicitor General.

Ross, R. R. and Fabiano, E. (1983) *The Cognitive Model of Crime and Delinquency Prevention and Rehabilitation: Assessment Procedures.* Toronto: Ministry of Correctional Services, Government of Ontario.

Ross, R. R. and Fabiano, E. (1985) *Time to Think: A Cognitive Model of Crime and Delinquency Prevention and Rehabilitation.* Johnson City, TN: Academy of Arts and Sciences.

Ross, R. R., Fabiano, E., and Ross, R.D. (1986) *Reasoning and Rehabilitation. A Handbook for Teaching Cognitive Skills.* Ottawa: University of Ottawa.

Ross, R. R. and Gendreau, P. (1980). *Effective Correctional Treatment.* Toronto: Butterworths.

Ross, R. R. and Mackay, H. B (1979) *Self-mutilation.* New York: Lexington Books.

Ross, R. R., Fabiano, E. A. and Ewles, C. D. (1988) 'Reasoning and Rehabilitation', *International Journal of Offender Therapy and Comparative Criminology*, 32: 29-35.

Rotman, E. (1986) 'Do Criminal Offenders Have a Constitutional Right to Rehabilitation?', *Journal of Criminal Law and Criminology*, 77.4: 1023–68.

Rotman, E. (1990) *Beyond Punishment: A New View of the Rehabilitation of Criminal Offenders.* Westport, CT: Greenwood Press.

Rutherford, A. (1986) *Growing Out of Crime.* Harmondsworth: Penguin.

Rutherford, A. (1992) *Growing Out of Crime: The New Era.* Winchester: Waterside Press.

Rutter, M., Quinton, D. and Hill, J. (1990) 'Adult Outcome of Institution-Reared Children: Males and Females Compared', in L. N. Robins and M. R. Rutter (eds), *Straight and Devious Pathways to Adulthood.* New York: Cambridge University Press.

Saleilles, R. (1911) *The Individualization of Punishment*, trans. from second French edition by Rachel Szold Jastrow. London: William Heinemann.

Sampson, R. J. and Laub, J. (1993) *Crime in the Making: Pathways and Turning Points Through Life.* Cambridge, MA: Harvard University Press.

Sampson, R. J. and Laub, J. H. (1990) 'Crime and Deviance over the Life-Course: The Salience of Adult Social Bonds', *American Sociological Review*, 55: 609–27.

Sarason, I. G. (1978) 'A Cognitive Social Learning Approach to Juvenile Delinquency', in R. D. Flare and D. Schalling (eds), *Psychopathic Behavior: Approaches to Research.* New York: Wiley.

Sarbin, T.R. (ed.) (1986) *Narrative Psychology: The Storied Nature of Human Conduct.* New York: Praeger.

Sartre, J. P. (1958) *Being and Nothingness*, trans. Hazel E. Barnes. London: Routledge.

Schlosser, E. (1998) 'The Prison-Industrial Complex', *Atlantic Monthly*, 282: 51–77.

Schmideberg, M. (1965) 'Psychotherapy of Offenders: Its Rationale and Implications for General Psychotherapy', *Probation*, 11.1: 4–9.

Schmuck, P. and Sheldon, K. M. (eds) (2001) *Life Goals and Well-being.* Toronto: Hogrefe & Huber.

Schneider, A. (1990) *Deterrence and Juvenile Crime: Results from a National Policy Experiment.* New York: Springer-Verlag.

Seiter, R. P. and Kadela, K. R. (2003) 'Prisoner Reentry: What Works, What Does Not, and What Is Promising', *Crime and Delinquency*, 49.3: 360–88.

Senior, P. (1985) 'Homely or Agent of Control?', *Social Work Today*, 26 August, p. 18.

Senior, P. (ed.) (2008) *Moments in Probation*. Crayford: Shaw and Sons.

Serge, V. (1967) *Men in Prison*. London: Writers and Readers Publishing Co-operative (originally published 1930).

Shapland, J., Atkinson, A., Atkinson, H., Dignan, J., Edwards, L., Hibbert, J., Howes, M., Johnstone, J., Robinson, G. and Sorsby, A. (2008.) *Does Restorative Justice Affect Reconviction?* The Fourth Report from the evaluation of three schemes. Ministry of Justice Research Series.

Shaw, M. (1974) *Social Work in Prison. An Experiment in the Use of Extended Contact with Offenders*, Home Office Research Studies 22. London. HMSO.

Sherman, L. and Strang, H. (2007) *Restorative Justice: The Evidence*. London: Smith Institute.

Shover, N. (1985) *Aging Criminals*. Beverly Hills, CA: Sage.

Showalter, E. (1987) *The Female Malady; Women, Madness and English Culture, 1839–1980*. New York: Penguin Books.

Simon, J. (1987) 'The Emergence of a Risk Society: Insurance Law and the State', *Socialist Review*, 95: 61–89.

Simon, J. (1988) 'The Ideological Effect of Actuarial Practices', *Law and Society Review*, 22: 771–800.

Sinclair, I. A. C., Shaw, M. J. and Troop, J. (1974) 'The Relationship Between Introversion and Response to Casework in a Prison Setting', *British Journal of Social and Clinical Psychology*, 13: 51–60.

Smaus, G. (1986) 'Gesellschaftsmodelle in der abolistischen Bewegung', *Kriminologisches Journal*, 18.1: 1–18.

Snyder, H. N. (1985) *Court Careers of Juvenile Offenders*, National Center for Juvenile Justice, U.S. Department of Justice Publication.

Sontheimer, H. and Goodstein, L. (1993) 'Evaluation of Juvenile Intensive Aftercare Probation: Aftercare Versus System Response Effects', *Justice Quarterly*, 10: 197–227.

Stanley, A. R. (1982), 'A New Structure for Intake and Allocation in a Field Probation Unit', *British Journal of Social Work*, 12.5: 487–506.

Stebbins, R. A. (1971) *Commitment to Deviance*. Westport, CT: Greenwood.

Steiner, H. J. (1987) *Moral Vision and Social Vision in the Court: A Study of Tort Accident Law*. Madison, WI: University of Wisconsin Press.

Stone, C. (1975) *Where the Law Ends*. New York: Harper & Row.

Sullivan, M. (1996) 'Developmental Transitions in Poor Youth: Delinquency and Crime', in J. A. Graber, J. Brooks-Gunn and A. C. Petersen (eds), *Transitions in Adolescence*, Mahwah, NJ: Lawrence Erlbaum.

Supreme Court of the United States (1989) *Mistretta v. United States*, No. 87-7028. Argued October 5, 1988; Decided January 18, 1989.

Sykes, G. M. and Matza, D. (1996) 'Techniques of Neutralization', in J. Muncie, E. McLaughlin and M. Langan (eds), *Criminological Perspectives: A Reader*. London: Sage.

Tallack, W. (1984) *Penological and Preventative Principles*. New York and London: Garland (originally published 1889 London: Wertheimer, Lea & Co.).

Taxman, F. S. and Spinner, D. L. (1996) 'The Jail Addiction Services (JAS) Project in Montgomery County, Maryland: Overview of Results from a 24 month Follow-up Study. Unpublished manuscript, University of Maryland, College Park.

Taylor, I., Walton, P. and Young, J. (1973) *The New Criminology: For a Social Theory of Deviance*. London: Routledge.

The Times (1973) 'Help from the Fellow Sufferer', 9 July.

Tittle, C. R. (1974) 'Prisons and Rehabilitation: The Inevitability of Disfavor', *Social Problems*, 21: 385–95.

Toch, H. (1987) 'Supplementing the Positivist Approach', in M. Gottfredson and T. Hirschi (eds), *Positive Criminology*. Beverly Hills, CA: Sage.

Toch, H. (1994) 'Democratising Prisons', *Prison Journal*, 73: 62–72.

Trasler, G. B. (1979) 'Delinquency, Recidivism and Desistance', *British Journal of Criminology*, 19: 314–22.

Trasler, G. B. (1980) *Aspects of Causality, Culture, and Crime*. Paper presented at the Fourth International Seminar at the International Centre of Sociological, Penal and Penitentiary Research and Studies, Messina, Italy.

Travis, J. (2003) *In Thinking About 'What Works', What Works Best?* Washington, DC: Urban Institute.

Trice, H. M. and Roman, P. M. (1970) 'Delabeling, Relabeling, and Alcoholics Anonymous', *Social Problems*, 17: 538–46.

Truax, C. B. and Carkhuff, R. R. (1967) *Towards Effective Counselling and Psychotherapy: Training and Practice*. Los Angeles: Aldine Books.

Uggen, C. and Janikula, J. (1999) 'Volunteerism and Arrest in the Transition to Adulthood', *Social Forces*, 78: 331–62.

Uggen, C., Manza, J. and Behrens, A. (2003) *Less than the Average Citizen': Stigma, Role Transition, and the Civic Reintegration of Convicted Felons*, Working Paper, University of Minnesota Department of Sociology.

Uggen, C., Manza, J. and Behrens, A. (2004) 'Less Than the Average Citizen: Stigma, Role Transition and the Civic Reintegration of Convicted Felons', in S. Maruna and R. Immarigeon (eds), *After Crime and Punishment: Pathways to Offender Reintegration*, Cullompton: Willan, pp. 261–93.

van den Haag, E. (1975) *Punishing Criminals: Concerning a Very Old and Painful Question*. New York: Basic Books.

Van Ness, D. and Strong K. H. (1997) *Restoring Justice*. Cincinatti, OH: Anderson.

Van Voorhis, P. (1985) 'Restitution Outcome and Probationers' Assessments of Restitution: The Effects of Moral Development', *Criminal Justice and Behavior*, 12: 259–87.

van Zyl Smit, D. and Dunkel, F. (eds) (1999) *Prison Labour: Salvation or Slavery? International Perspectives*. Aldershot: Dartmouth.

Vanstone, M. (1993) 'A "Missed Opportunity" Re-assessed: The Influence of the Day Training Centre Experiment on the Criminal Justice System and Probation Policy and Practice', *British Journal of Social Work*, 23: 213–29.

Vanstone, M. (2002) 'Cognitive-Behavioural Work with Offenders in the UK: A History of Influential Endeavour', *Howard Journal of Criminal Justice*, 39.2: 171–83.

Vanstone, M. (2007) *Supervising Offenders in the Community. A History of Probation Theory and Practice* (paperback edn). Aldershot: Ashgate.

Vennard, J., Sugg, D. and Hedderman, C. (1997) *Changing Offenders' Attitudes and Behaviour: What Works?* Home Office Research Study No. 171. London: Home Office.

Vercoe, K. (1970) *Men Leaving Local Prisons*. South Wales and Severn Valley Region and Information Paper. Cheltenham: NACRO.

Vito, G. F. (1984) 'Developments in Shock Probation: A Review of Research Findings and Policy Implications'. *Federal Probation*, 48: 22–27.

Vito, G. F. and Allen, H. E. (1981) 'Shock Probation in Ohio: A comparison of Outcomes'. *International Journal of Offender Therapy and Comparative Criminology*, 25: 70–76.

von Hirsch, A. (1976) *Doing Justice*. New York: Hill & Wang.

von Hirsch, A. (1993) *Censure and Sanctions*. Oxford: Oxford University Press.

Ward, T. (2002) 'Good Lives and the Rehabilitation of Offenders: Promises and Problems', *Aggression and Violent Behavior*, 7: 513–28.

Ward, T. and Brown, M. (2004) 'The Good Lives Model and Conceptual Issues in Offender Rehabilitation', *Psychology, Crime and Law*, 10.3: 243–57.

Ward, T. and Maruna, S. (2007) *Rehabilitation Beyond the Risk Paradigm*. London: Routledge.

Ward, T. and Stewart, C.A. (2003a) 'The Treatment of Sex Offenders: Risk Management and Good Lives', *Professional Psychology: Research and Practice*, 34: 353–60.

Ward, T. and Stewart, C. A. (2003b) 'Good Lives and the Rehabilitation of Sexual Offenders', in T. Ward, D. R. Laws and S. M. Hudson (eds), *Sexual Deviance: Issues and Controversies*. Thousand Oaks, CA: Sage, pp. 21–44.

Weaver, C. and Fox, C. (1984) 'The Berkeley Sex Offenders Group: A Seven Year Evaluation', *Probation Journal*, 31.4: 143–6.

Weber, M. (1954) Ed. and translated by Max Rheinstein. Translated by Edward A. Shils. *Max Weber on Law in Economy and Society*. Harvard University Press.

Weinberg, A. (1957) *Attorney for the Damned*. New York: Simon & Schuster.

Weiss, H. (1933) 'The Social Worker's Technique', in S. Glueck (ed.), *Probation and Criminal Justice. Essays in Honor of Herbert. C. Parsons*. New York: Macmillan.

West, D. (1982) *Delinquency: Its Roots, Careers, and Prospects*. London: Heinemann.

Whitehead, P. and Statham, R. (2006) *The History of Probation: Politics, Power and Cultural Change 1876–2005*. Crayford: Shaw & Sons.

Wicks, J. W. (1978) *Human Services: New Careers and Roles in the Helping Professions*. Springfield, IL: Charles C. Thomas.

Williams, C. (1987) 'Using Opportunities in the Community', in C. Patmore (ed.), *Living After Mental Illness: Innovations in Services*, London: Croom Helm.

Williams, P. (2006) 'Designing and Delivering Programmes for Minority Ethnic Offenders', in S. Lewis., P. Raynor., D. Smith and A. Wardak (eds), *Race and Probation*. Cullompton: Willan.

Wilson, D. B., Gallagher, C. A., Coggleshall, M. B. and MacKenzie, D. L. (1999). 'Corrections-Based Education, Vocation, and Work Programs', *Corrections Management Quarterly*, 3.4: 8–18.

Wilson, J. Q. (1975) *Thinking About Crime*. New York: Basic Books, p. 170.

Winick, B. J. (1991) 'Harnessing the Power of the Bet: Wagering with the Government as a Mechanism for Social and Individual Change', in D. B. Wexler and B. J. Winick (eds), *Essays in Therapeutic Jurisprudence*. Durham, NC: Carolina Academic Press.

Winick, B. J. (1997) *The Right to Refuse Mental Health Treatment*. Washington, DC: American Psychological Association.

Winnicott, C. (1962) 'Casework and Agency Function', *Case Conference*, 8: 178–84.

Wolf, R. V. (1978) *Human Services: New Careers and Roles in the Helping Professions*. Springfield, IL: Charles C. Thomas.

Wolf, R. V. (2007) *Best Practice: Principles of Problem-Solving*. Justice Center for Court Innovation, Bureau of Justice Assistance, New York State.

Wootton, B. (1959) *Social Science and Pathology*. London: George Allen & Unwin.

Wright, A. (1984) *The Day Centre in Probation Practice*, Social Work Monograph 22. Norwich: University of East Anglia.

Wright, K. N. (1980) 'A Re-Examination of Correctional Alternatives', *International Journal of Offender Therapy and Comparative Criminology*, 24.2: 179–92.

Wright, M. (1991) *Justice for Victims and Offenders: A Restorative Response to Crime*. Milton Keynes and Philadelphia: Open University Press.

Young, D. S. and Smith, C. J. (2000) 'When Moms Are Incarcerated: The Needs of Children, Mothers, and Caregivers', *Families in Society: Journal of Contemporary Human Services*, 81.2: 130–41.

Young, J. (1988) 'Radical Criminology in Britain: The Emergence of a Competing Paradigm', *British Journal of Criminology*, 28: 289–313.

Young, J. (1999) *The Exclusive Society*. London: Sage.

Zehr, H. (1990) *Changing Lenses: A New Focus for Crime and Justice*. Scottdale, PA: Herald Press.

Zimbardo, P. G. (1975) Letter to the Editor, *APA Monitor*, July, p. 3.

Zoccolillo, M., Pickles, A., Quinton, D. and Rutter, M. (1992) 'The Outcome of Childhood Conduct Disorder: Implications for Defining Adult Personality Disorder and Conduct Disorder', *Psychological Medicine*, 22: 971–86.

Index